CURRENT TRANSFORMATIONS
AND THEIR POTENTIAL ROLE IN REALIZING
CHANGE IN THE ARAB WORLD

CURRENT TRANSFORMATIONS
AND THEIR POTENTIAL ROLE IN REALIZING
CHANGE IN THE ARAB WORLD

**THE EMIRATES CENTER FOR STRATEGIC
STUDIES AND RESEARCH**

THE EMIRATES CENTER FOR STRATEGIC STUDIES AND RESEARCH

The Emirates Center for Strategic Studies and Research (ECSSR) is an independent research institution dedicated to the promotion of professional studies and educational excellence in the UAE, the Gulf and the Arab world. Since its establishment in Abu Dhabi in 1994, the ECSSR has served as a focal point for scholarship on political, economic and social matters. Indeed, the ECSSR is at the forefront of analysis and commentary on Arab affairs.

The Center seeks to provide a forum for the scholarly exchange of ideas by hosting conferences and symposia, organizing workshops, sponsoring a lecture series and publishing original and translated books and research papers. The ECSSR also has an active fellowship and grant program for the writing of scholarly books and for the translation into Arabic of work relevant to the Center's mission. Moreover, the ECSSR has a large library including rare and specialized holdings, and a state-of-the-art technology center, which has developed an award-winning website that is a unique and comprehensive source of information on the Gulf.

Through these and other activities, the ECSSR aspires to engage in mutually beneficial professional endeavors with comparable institutions worldwide, and to contribute to the general educational and academic development of the UAE.

The views expressed in this book do not necessarily reflect those of the ECSSR.

First published in 2007 by
The Emirates Center for Strategic Studies and Research
PO Box 4567, Abu Dhabi, United Arab Emirates

E-mail: pubdis@ecssr.ae
Website: http://www.ecssr.ae

ISBN: 978-9948-00-873-6 hardback edition
ISBN: 978-9948-00-874-3 paperback edition

CONTENTS

Figures and Tables   x

Abbreviations and Acronyms   xii

Foreword   xv
Jamal S. Al-Suwaidi

INTRODUCTION

The Dynamics of Change in the Arab World   3

KEYNOTE ADDRESS

Challenges to Development and Progress in the Arab World   13
  H.E. Abdulrahman bin Hamad Al-Attiyah

ARAB REFORM AND DEMOCRATIC TRANSFORMATION

1 The Dilemma of Reform in the Arab World   21
   Dr. Bourhan Ghalioun

2 Democratic Reform in Palestine and the Arab World:
   External Pressures or Internal Response?   41
   H.E. Yasser Abed Rabbo

3 Iraq as a Model for the Spread of Democracy
   in the Arab World   59
   Dr. Adnan Pachachi

4 The Imperatives and the Logic of Arab Economic Reform   65
   Dr. Atif Kubursi

POLITICAL ORIENTATIONS IN ARAB SOCIETIES

5 Moderate Islamists and Reform in the Arab World:
   Case of the Muslim Brotherhood in Egypt   93
   Dr. Amr Hamzawy

6 Causes of Terrorism in the Arab World and Ways to Counter it   121
   H.E. Dr. Mohammed Bin Ali Kouman

7 Structural Transformations in Arab Countries: Growing
   Legitimacy of the State and the Shrinking Role of Governments   143
   Dr. Ahmed Jameel 'Azm

COMPARATIVE EXPERIENCE OF POLITICAL REFORM

8 Modernity and Political Transformation: The Turkish Experience   173
   Dr. Metin Heper

9 The Principles of the American Republic
   in a Revolutionary Century   199
   Dr. Gary Hart

ROLE OF INSTITUTIONS IN THE PROCESS OF CHANGE

10 Managing Challenges to Sovereignty in an Era of Regionalism:
   Asia and the Arab World   227
   Dr. Amitav Acharya

11 The Role of Non-State Actors in Promoting Change   253
   Dr. Marina Ottaway

12 New and Future Leadership: Implications for Change   279
   The Hon. William S. Cohen

EDUCATION AS A BASIS FOR CHANGE IN THE ARAB WORLD

Keynote Address: The Role of Education in Development   287
H.E. Sheikh Nahyan Mabarak Al Nahyan

13 Education as a Catalyst for Social Change in the Arab World   295
   H.E. Dr. Faisal Al-Rufouh

14 One Goal, Different Agendas: Expanding the Scope
   of Education in the Arab World and Addressing
   the Requirements of the Labor Market   311
   Dr. Rafia Obaid Ghubash

15 Losing Expertise to Other Countries: Halting
   the Arab Brain Drain   349
   H.E. Dr. Ibrahim Guider

16 Boosting the Role of Women in Development:
A Case Study of Kuwaiti Women   367
H.E. Dr. Massouma Al-Mubarak

17 International Migration and the Demographic
Structure of the GCC States   391
Dr. Mattar Ahmed Abdullah

Contributors   423

Notes   437

Bibliography   467

Index   489

FIGURES AND TABLES

FIGURES

Figure 4.1 Number of Scientists and Engineers Working
in Research and Development by Region (1990–2000) 73

Figure 4.2 Ratio of Students Enrolled in Scientific Disciplines
in Higher Education in Selected Arab Countries
and S. Korea (1990–1995) 76

Figure 4.3 Mean Years of Schooling (Population 25 Years or
Older) by Gender for Arab Countries and Three
Asian Tigers 78

Figure 4.4 Number of Phone Lines per 1000 Persons* 84

Figure 4.5 Internet Penetration in Arab Countries: Users
as Percentage of Population (2001) 85

Figure 4.6 Personal Computers: Arab World and Other Regions 87

Figure 15.1 Number of Egyptian Scientists who have Migrated
Abroad (2003) 352

Figure 15.2 Percentage of Arab Scientists in the United States
by Nationality (2003) 353

Figure 15.3 Percentage Distribution of Egyptian Expertise
in Receiving Foreign States (2003) 354

Figure 17.1 Countries with the Largest Number of International
Migrants (2000) 396

Figure 17.2   Countries with the Highest Percentage
              of International Migrants   397

Figure 17.3   Population Development in the GCC States
              (1975–2015)   407

TABLES

Table 16.1   Development of Kuwaiti Population and Society
             by Gender (1995–2005)   386

Table 16.2   Development of the Kuwaiti Labor Force
             by Gender (1995–2005)   387

Table 16.3   Rates of Contribution to Economic Activity
             by Gender and Nationality (1995–2005)   388

Table 16.4   Women Workers in Government Sector by Major
             Professional Groups and Nationality (2004)   389

Table 16.5   Percentages of Kuwaiti Women in Leading
             Professions (2001–2005)   390

Table 17.1   Number and Growth of Migrants by Major Regions
             (1990–2000)   395

Table 17.2   Population Growth in the GCC States (1999–2002)   405

Table 17.3   Population Distribution (Nationals and Non-National)
             in the GCC States (2002)   409

Table 17.4   Scale of Remittances by Migrant Labor from
             GCC States and their Growth Rates (1975–2004)   420

ABBREVIATIONS AND ACRONYMS

ADCCI	Abu Dhabi Chamber of Commerce and Industry
AGM	annual general meeting
ALO	Arab Labor Organization
APEC	Asia Pacific Economic Cooperation
ARF	ASEAN Regional Forum
ASEAN	Association of South East Asian Nations
CAPMAS	Central Agency for Public Mobilization and Statistics (Egypt)
CEDAW	Convention on the Elimination of All Forms of Discrimination Against Women
CSCE	Commission on Security and Cooperation in Europe
BMEI	Broader Middle East Initiative
DP	Democratic Party (Turkey)
EMP	Euro-Mediterranean Partnership
EPC	Executive Privatization Commission (Jordan)
ESCWA	Economic and Social Commission for Western Asia
EU	European Union
FKWA	Federation of Kuwaiti Women's Associations
FP	Felicity Party (Turkey)
FTSE	Financial Times Stock Exchange
GATT	General Agreement on Tariffs and Trade
GCC	Gulf Cooperation Council
GDP	gross domestic product
GAFTA	Greater Arab Free Trade Area

GNP	gross national product
GNGO	governmental non-governmental organization
IAF	Islamic Action Front (Jordan)
ICBL	International Campaign to Ban Landmines
ICPD	International Conference on Population and Development
ILO	International Labor Organization
IMF	International Monetary Fund
IPO	initial public offering
IRA	Irish Republican Army
JDP	Justice and Development Party (Turkey)
KSPDC	Kuwaiti Small Project Development Company
ICT	information and communication technologies
LBC	Lebanese Broadcasting Corporation
LT	low tech (industries)
MB	Muslim Brotherhood (Egypt)
MHT	medium and high tech (industries)
MVA	manufacturing value added
NATO	North Atlantic Treaty Organization
NAM	Non-Aligned Movement
NDP	National Democratic Party (Egypt)
NGO	non-governmental organization
NIC	newly industrialized country
NOP	National Order Party (Turkey)
NRA	National Rifle Association (US)
NSC	National Security Council (Turkey)
NSP	National Salvation Party (Turkey)

NWP	New Wafd Party (Egypt)
NYSE	New York Stock Exchange
OAS	Organization of American States
OECD	Organization for Economic Cooperation and Development
OECS	Organization of Eastern Caribbean States
OSCE	Organization for Security and Cooperation in Europe
PAAET	Public Authority for Applied Education and Training (Kuwait)
PJD	Justice and Development Party (Morocco)
R&D	research and development
RB	resource based (industries)
S&T	science and technology
SEATO	South East Asia Treaty Organization
UDHR	Universal Declaration of Human Rights
UNDP	United Nations Development Program
UNESCO	United Nations Educational, Scientific and Cultural Organization
WCSS	Women's Cultural and Social Society (Kuwait)
WMD	weapons of mass destruction
WP	Welfare Party (Turkey)
WTO	World Trade Organization
ZOPFAN	Zone of Peace, Freedom and Neutrality

Since the beginning of the third millennium, the Arab world has witnessed extremely significant developments as characterized by the subjection of its states to the trans-border effects and repercussions of globalization and to the effects of the US-led war on terrorism in the wake of the events of 9/11; the pressures exerted by the US administration as part of its bid to combat global and regional terrorism by calling for political reforms and democratization; and the impact of the invasion of Iraq and the restructuring of its political regime under prevailing conditions of hostility, chaos and destabilization.

In addition, the Arab world has experienced other internal developments such as the strengthening of the so-called "political Islam" movements and the demands by popular and civil society groups in many Arab societies for bolstering democracy, basic freedoms and human rights.

Responses by Arab states to these transformations have taken the form of what has been described as political, social and economic "reforms." However, hopes for bringing about true, comprehensive and fundamental changes have soon faded away when these "reforms" turned out to be merely artificial and shallow, intended only for embellishing the performance of Arab regimes, providing these regimes with *raisons d'être*, and offering an outlet for venting suppressed feelings in Arab societies. Indeed, the Arab situation has not undergone real change, and these societies are still suffering from grave conditions of tension, frustration and fears of what the future may hold for the region.

Introducing genuine changes and reforms in Arab societies has become a vital issue closely connected to the fate of these societies and their strategic interests. Hence, Arab states have no option but to restructure their political and social systems towards expanding popular participation in power and decision-making; consolidating the values of transparency, accountability, rule of law, respect for basic freedoms and human rights; and offering their peoples greater choices for ensuring a decent way of life.

Recognizing the importance of the different transformations that the Arab world is currently undergoing, and the gravity of this historic moment for the region's future political and social development, the Emirates Center for Strategic Studies and Research (ECSSR) devoted its 11th Annual Conference held in Abu Dhabi from 12–14 March 2006 to explore the subject of *Current Transformations and their Potential Role in Realizing Change in the Arab World.*

The conference presentations compiled in this book assess the political developments taking place throughout the Arab world and their implications for the issue of change and reforms; examine the impact of emerging new leaderships on the process of political and social modernization in some Arab countries; and tackle the problems, the dynamics of change and the obstacles to the spread of democracy in the Arab world, while highlighting the Iraqi experience in this regard.

In addition, the book discusses the role of organizations and institutions in the Arab political system; the impact of non-state actors in promoting the process of change and development; the role played by the forces of political Islam in current transformations; and the Turkish experience in creating harmony between modernization, democracy and Islam.

In view of the accelerated economic growth in many areas of the Arab world, the book has sought to explore the relationship between economic growth, reforms and ongoing political transformations as well as the diverse, vital topics closely connected to the issue of progress and development in the Arab world. Emphasis is placed on the role of education as a basis for change in the Arab world and on the importance of expanding the educational systems and linking them to the needs of the Arab developmental process. The problem of the Arab "brain drain" and its effects on this process, and the impediments to the promotion of effective women's participation in the process, have also been assessed.

Issues of change, reform and modernization should claim the highest priorities on the agendas of Arab governments and institutions, political forces, civil society organizations and intellectual elites, and debates on these issues must be extended to include the "public sphere." It is my hope that this book will serve to enrich discussions about this fundamental issue for the future of Arab societies.

In conclusion, I would like to extend my thanks to the conference participants who have enlightened us with their contributions, which, in my opinion, serve to enhance the knowledge of the readers and enrich the debates focusing on the issue of change in the Arab world. I would also like to commend the efforts exerted by the team of editors, translators, proof-readers and typists who worked to produce this book in its present form.

Jamal S. Al-Suwaidi, Ph.D.
Director General
ECSSR

INTRODUCTION

The Dynamics of Change in the Arab World

In recent years the Arab world has witnessed crucial political events, starting with the second Palestinian *Intifada* (Al Aqsa uprising) in late September 2000, through the attacks of September 11, 2001 in New York and Washington and the subsequent US "war on terror" to the 2003 war in Iraq waged by the US-led coalition forces leading to the toppling of the regime in Baghdad.

During that period the Arab world witnessed unprecedented sociopolitical action, partly driven by those events. This was embodied in the escalation of popular protests such as demonstrations and sit-ins led by the Egyptian movement for change *"Kifaya"*; the quantitative and qualitative growth of human rights organizations[1]; more statements and petitions by intellectuals and political elites demanding political openness, popular participation and justice for marginalized groups, greater equality between citizens and control over public money.[2] Political action was also embodied in the wide participation by citizens in the elections and referendums conducted in several Arab countries, such as Palestine, Iraq and Egypt, despite Israeli obstructions in Palestine, the targeted killing of individuals and terrorist bombings in Iraq and security pressures and "thuggish" practices by supporters of the ruling party in Egypt.

Editorial Note: This volume contains several chapters translated from Arabic papers. Hence the quotations in these chapters represent a translated version rather than the exact wording of the original text.

Such political action coincided with a flood of foreign initiatives calling for reform, political participation and democratic transformation beginning with the US Broader Middle East Project, proposed at the end of 2003,[3] followed by the German–French initiative calling for a "Strategic Partnership for a Common Future with the Middle East" launched in February 2004 and finally the project announced by the G-8 in June 2004 entitled "Partnership for Progress and a Common Future" with the Broader Middle East and North Africa. This project led to the foundation of the Forum for the Future.

These foreign initiatives were followed by Arab moves, which included official initiatives represented by the "Declaration on the Process of Development and Modernization in the Arab World" issued by the 16th Summit of the Arab League Council held in Tunis in May 2004 and the initiatives of the civil society organizations embodied in the "Alexandria Declaration" issued by the Conference on "Issues of Reform in the Arab World: Vision and Implementation," hosted by the Alexandria Library, in March 2004.[4]

The above-mentioned developments indicate that the Arab political scene over the past few years has been tumultuous and marked by upheavals. It was expected that these events and such political action would lead to the birth of a new Arab order since the calls of domestic parties for change coincided with reform pressures exerted by external powers—though the two differ with respect to major goals and objectives. However, the existing Arab order managed to bypass the demands of the former and absorb the pressures of the latter. Nevertheless, it may be said that the Arab region has witnessed reform overtures in more than one sphere although the changes considered in their entirety do not amount to a transformation process.

New Political Leaderships

Since the last decade of the 20th century, the Arab world has seen new leaderships attaining power, succeeding historical leaders who had led their countries for decades, notably in Qatar, Jordan, Bahrain, Morocco, Syria, UAE and Palestine to some extent. The "generation of sons" differs from the generation of the founding fathers in many ways. Being younger and enjoying a higher level of education, they are more open to modern ideas and developments being witnessed by the world. Moreover, to a much greater degree, they are facing both internal situations and external challenges that are very different from those faced by their predecessors.

Some analysts envisaged that this transition in authority would help to relax the rigid political structure, provide for more popular participation and push towards politico-social liberation and economic reform on the basis that the new young leaderships, which have replaced the "inspired" leaderships, would need to boost their legitimacy by realizing such achievements.[5]

The new leaderships have brought in some "liberal" changes by expanding the margin of freedom, taking some steps on the road to political openness, adopting policies of economic liberalization and social modernization. However, these preliminary reforms have not led to a qualitative development in the basic political system and philosophy of governance in these countries.

The vital role of Arab political leaderships in driving change cannot be ignored in the light of the Arab-Islamic historical and cultural heritage, which emphasizes the stature of the individual leader and his role in national progress, and in the context of the contemporary experience of the Arab nation-state, in which institutions are overlooked. Hence these leaderships are called upon to spare their countries from the sharp contradictions between the realities of governance and public aspirations.

The Predicament of Change and Reform

At different local and international levels (whether governmental or non-governmental), terms such as change, reform, modernization, development, political transformation, democratic transition and others have reverberated.

Despite the absence of clear definitions and sometimes overlapping versions of these concepts, they are all aimed at achieving a common goal—improving the existing Arab situation by superimposing a better model.

Undoubtedly, the need for change or reform in Arab countries is not new. Rather, it is a requirement linked to the very progress of the Arab nation-state. Reform demands were never absent from the Arab scene in the past decades. However, they have assumed a new and different dimension at the beginning of the twenty-first century. The first *Arab Human Development Report*, published by the United Nations Development Program (UNDP) in 2002, provided the first methodological framework for these demands.

The new reformist wave arose amid unfavorable regional and international situations such as the ongoing Israeli occupation of the Palestinian territories, the emergence of yet another occupation (that of Iraq by the United States), in addition to the growing phenomenon of terrorism. Ruling Arab regimes used these issues as pretexts in dealing with their own nations and with external powers either to stop reforms in general or to postpone them by linking the settlement of the Palestinian–Israeli conflict and the achievement of regional stability as necessary preconditions to the initiation of the reform process.

Arab regimes continue to exhibit great reluctance in facing the forces of change and renewal. It is notable that most nations of the world live under democratic regimes of varying degrees. In the last decade the wave of democracy reached Latin America and Eastern Europe and even much of sub-Saharan Africa. However, the Arab world remains the only major region, besides China, where democracy has not yet dawned.

It is evident that the two principal pillars on which democracy is built – respect for various freedoms and the peaceful rotation of power – have not become rooted in Arab soil. Since their emergence, most Arab nations have not known a real, peaceful rotation of power. The painful paradox is that the two cases in the Arab world where semi-peaceful rotation of power was recently witnessed, took place in the shadow of occupation—the first, in Iraq under US occupation and the second, in the Palestinian territories under Israeli occupation.

The internal crisis of the Arab world is represented by the widening chasm between nations and governments and the growing external challenges imposed on Arab countries that are embarking on the path of change and democratic transformation and trying to emerge from the collective historical predicament enveloping the entire Arab world.

Non-Governmental Organizations and Good Governance

The pillars of good governance include the building of institutions and separation of powers. Institutions must work competently and with absolute transparency in accordance with rules of good public administration and be subject to effective accountability under a system involving the separation of powers with mutual checks and balances.[6] Now it is time for Arab countries to move from an oligarchic ruling system, which relies primarily on an elitist group, to a system that relies more on the rule of institutions open to popular participation.

It is impossible to achieve a pattern of good governance without a real and effective role for civil society organizations. Non-governmental organizations are an indispensable part of the civil society system, Moreover, the growing concern over the political and social roles played by such organizations reflects the vitality of a country's civil society.

Although there has been a huge rise in the number of civil society organizations in general and non-governmental organizations in particular, in recent years, this quantitative development in the region does not necessarily indicate the expansion of freedoms in the Arab world. Similarly, it does not reflect a qualitative development in terms of their efficacy, especially since many non-governmental organizations are restricted to the elites and are limited to a few members and their supporters.

In fact, the blurring of lines between "state" and "civil society" in the Arab world as a result of the intrusion of the state on society is the most significant obstacle that non-governmental organizations face in Arab countries. Many countries have sought to restrict the emergence of such organizations while besieging or tightening their grip on existing ones. A recent case in point is the attempt of the Egyptian authorities to close down the Cairo-based Ibn Khaldun Center for Development Studies. Moreover, most countries have taken the initiative since the 1990s to found so-called "non-governmental organizations" that actually revolve in the government orbit and are now known as Governmental Non-Governmental Organizations (GNGOs). On the one hand, their function is to support the political positions of these states, and on the other, to rob them of their essence and true function by nominally adopting the concept of non-governmental organizations.

In general, the effect of non-governmental and civil society organizations is still limited in the Arab world. In fact, the political authority is not solely responsible for their weakness since there are cultural and structural obstacles that have also left their mark on civic expression.[7] Certainly, cultural and political development will result in an enhanced role for Arab civil society but greater efforts must be exerted and new initiatives adopted so that this civil society with its non-governmental organizations becomes a major supporting pillar in a society that enjoys freedom and good governance.

Islamic Movements and Democracy

Democratic demands have escalated recently in the Arab world and have been voiced by societal and political forces with varying degrees of efficacy. While traditional religious thought condemns democracy and views it as western "secular" product, enlightened Islamic thought has engaged in a historical reconciliation with the mechanisms and values of democracy and attempted since the 1990s to reconcile democracy with the

Islamic principle of *Shoura* (consultation). This has reached the stage where most political Islam movements now urge the application of democracy on the basis that it is a vehicle to realize principles consistent with Islamic values such as the nation's right to appoint and oust the Ruler (as the nation is the source of all authority), guaranteeing fundamental rights and public freedoms, accountability in public affairs and finance and equality between citizens.

Nevertheless, suspicions are evoked as to whether these movements are merely using democracy as a ploy to attain power and then turn their backs upon it, or whether they are really convinced and committed, especially since Islamic experiences in approaching or attaining ruling power have reinforced the first view. This is evidenced by the case of Sudan, where the National Islamic Front immediately after seizing power through the National Salvation Revolution in 1989 excluded all political forces and exercised repression and authoritarianism against other parties. Hence the forces of political Islam should be urged to define their democratic choice unequivocally and thereby avoid confusion over their attitudes towards democracy, including respect for individual freedoms, unconstrained pluralism, the ultimate authority of the people and what this entails—recognizing that the elected legislative authority is the source of legitimacy.

On the other hand, Arab regimes should stop creating anxiety among their own public as well as external forces by highlighting the potential threat arising from Islamist groups and their attainment of power through free and just elections (as was the case in the last Palestinian legislative elections) and using this fear as a justification for impeding democratic transformation and freezing Arab political life.

Change and Development

On a humanitarian basis, people have a genuine right to live in dignity, both materially and morally. The "Declaration on the Right to

Development," issued by the UN General Assembly (Resolution 41/128 dated December 4, 1986) stated that finding favorable conditions for the development of nations and individuals is the first responsibility of all countries, and that the right to development is an inalienable human right.

Any project for democratic restructuring in the Arab world must be linked to achieving overall development, especially since modern development theories and contemporary experiences have confirmed a close, if not inevitable, link between freedom and development.

If education and women are two major subjects of development, they also simultaneously represent two important levers of change. Liberating the capabilities of Arab women and employing them without gender discrimination, and empowering them in a manner that reinforces their role in political, social and economic development will contribute to the process of necessary social change in the Arab world. The same is true of education and its links to the achievement of sustainable development.

In the past, Arab countries have been diverted from the mainstream of history as a result of lagging behind, failing to effect fundamental change and not carrying out real political, economic and social reforms. If this initiative is delayed again, it will isolate these countries from future developments. The Arab world now stands at the crossroads of history. It can choose to follow the path it has already taken for a long period and lag behind in the march of civilization and humanity. Alternatively, it can change direction and move towards a renaissance, thus reconciling itself with twenty-first century values and satisfying the aspirations of all Arab nations in terms of development and liberation.

KEYNOTE ADDRESS

Challenges to Development and Progress in the Arab World

H. E. Abdulrahman bin Hamad Al-Attiyah

In the context of this conference, which addresses the issue of current transformations and their potential role in realizing change in the Arab world, I would like first of all, to pinpoint some of the challenges facing the Arab nations. Internally, the process of modernization and development tops the list of important priorities that include political, economic and social progress, in order to enable the Arab nations as a whole to accomplish their goals in the fields of fundamental rights, social justice, economic self-sufficiency and scientific and cultural progress in keeping with the spirit of a changing era.

Political developments in the Arab world have led to major issues involving improved political and economic performance in seeking to adapt to global changes and one of the resulting imperatives is the building up of democratic processes. Such a process involves greater popular participation, creation of institutions based on the rule of law and constitutional principles, guarantees for the basic freedoms of citizens and their equality before the law in terms of duties and rights, without neglecting the cultural and other particular characteristics of Arab societies.

In this connection, one must keep in mind that the two processes of democracy-building and comprehensive development have to encompass all their vital elements, including education, health and social systems, with special focus on the family, which deserves the highest care and attention.

In order to tackle the problems that impede the development and modernization process, some observations may be made regarding the aforesaid challenges:

- Despite the growth of educational institutions and available international facilities, the percentage of illiteracy in the Arab world remains high because large numbers of Arab children are unable to attend school either due to poverty or the lack of schools in remote villages.

- The unemployment rate is also high as a result of population growth under conditions of limited resources and job opportunities. In this context, the process of comprehensive development is hampered by the widening gap between the output of the educational system and labor market requirements.

Any process of comprehensive development will require effective government and private organizations as they constitute the legal foundation, framework and principles governing diverse political, economic, social and judicial activities that could either advance or hinder the progress of any society.

The optimal utilization of human resources is a goal normally set by states in seeking to build up political, economic and social structures. Therefore, the success of the development process depends upon enlisting the contributions of both men and women in the fulfillment of plans and programs, instead of ignoring and thereby wasting their energies and potential, or at least failing to make the best use of them.

Despite the fact that women have achieved some success in the labor market, their contribution remains far behind those of men. Thus, enabling women to shoulder their social responsibilities is considered an essential element in the development and progress of society.

Against the current regional events and their repercussions on the security, stability and progress in the Arab world, the development process has become increasingly and fundamentally dependent on finding solutions to ongoing regional crises, notably the Palestinian question; restoring stability in Iraq; combating terrorism; and keeping the Middle East, including the Gulf region, free of weapons of mass destruction.

Unless all these crises and problems are confronted and resolved, it appears that the Arab world in general and the Middle East in particular, will remain susceptible to radical changes that are not necessarily positive. I am certain that such effective solutions will call for close regional and international cooperation. Within this framework, the following measures need to be considered:

- At the internal level, the adoption and effective implementation of realistic policies of reform and democratization; promoting respect for Arab human rights; and strengthening the role of civil society organizations in fostering modernization and political transformations, including popular participation.

- Introducing developmental programs and plans in all aspects of life, starting with education policies; guaranteeing equal rights for both men and women; combating unemployment, poverty, ignorance, disease and backwardness; providing health and social services for families, children and those with special needs; and facilitating access to sources of modern and advanced knowledge.

- Effective adherence to international legitimacy is necessary to resolve the current political crises in the Arab world, notably the Palestinian issue and tension in Iraq as well as to keep the Middle East – including the Gulf region – free of weapons of mass destruction. This would enhance the security and stability of the Arab world and strengthen the economies of its states. The ultimate outcome of such an approach would seem to be in the best interests of all states within the Arab world and beyond it, given the existing close links between international relations and interests.

[15]

On this occasion, I feel obliged to refer to the political, constitutional and legal achievements of the Gulf Cooperation Council (GCC) over the course of the past decade. The GCC states have embarked on a process of institutional development and conducted a serious review of their political, economic, social and cultural positions to mark the start of a period of active political and social mobility.

Moreover, the GCC has succeeded in maintaining a genuine and solid rapprochement among its member-states, including the coordination of policies in different fields, the deepening and expanding of the "economic citizenship" concept, and the implementation of promising, complementary projects. In this respect, I would recall the notion that taking one practical step based on consensus is better than dozens of decisions that are extensively detailed but yield little dividend.

This region is capable of consolidating the pillars of integration, relying on its nationalist identity and sense of belonging. With sound cooperation within the GCC framework, this cohesive regional Gulf gathering, through its achievements can have positive and favorable effects on the course of collective action through the entire Arab world.

To sum up, institutions in the wider sense, have codes and goals that differ from those of their administrators, whose energies must be devoted to developing and boosting these institutions to enable them to accomplish their stated goals. In this connection, there must be unanimous agreement among the Arab states on the need to create the proper environment for setting up and bolstering modern institutions. More importantly, all Arabs must be aware of the grave dangers that may threaten both state and society if these institutions are weakened or fail to accomplish their objectives. It has been recognized now that political, economic and social progress would prove to be an unattainable goal in the absence of political regimes based on the principles of accountability, transparency, effective popular participation, the rule of law and balanced constitutional institutions.

The hopes of a positive evolution of private and governmental institutions in the Arab world entails, *inter alia*, providing support for Arab intellectual elites and suggesting recommendations and proposals that would help to restructure key institutions that can nurture, protect and preserve the basic rights and freedoms of citizens. In this respect, it should be borne in mind that some Arab forebears played a significant part in shaping our contemporary history. Those pioneers have devoted all their energies and potential to serve national causes, experienced bitter political oppression, exile and imprisonment, in order to allow this generation the scope of freedom they currently enjoy, even though it may appear limited in the eyes of others. We must also remember those farsighted Arab leaders who recognized that the time is ripe for implementing genuine changes in the structure, concept and institutions of the ruling power.

ARAB REFORM AND DEMOCRATIC TRANSFORMATION

1

The Dilemma of Reform in the Arab World

Dr. Bourhan Ghalioun

The issue of reform in the Arab world has surfaced since the 1970s when several Arab authorities discovered the limited efficacy of the developmental models they had adopted. Apart from traditional programs of structural reform based on the recommendations of international financial institutions and the general concepts of economic openness that constituted the first Arab reformist experiment after years of economic isolationism and strong protectionist policies, there has been no clear vision in Arab countries of the scope of reform, its agendas and practical tasks. Notwithstanding the fact that policies of openness have not always led to successful outcomes, there have been no other theoretical alternatives. Therefore, the economic, political and moral state of Arab societies has continued to deteriorate.

Since the 1980s the signs of an escalating crisis have started to emerge owing to the failure of the initial policies of openness. This was highlighted in the bread revolutions, which included all relatively poor Arab countries where a small margin of collective initiatives was still allowed—notably Morocco, Egypt and Jordan. The victims of those popular upheavals included thousands of dead and injured people. However, the authorities succeeded in restoring security and stability by adopting limited changes in economic policies. Foremost among these was the institution of subsidies for the prices of basic goods like bread and offering a few political compromises, which had the effect of allowing the functioning of opposition groups that had been banned for a long time. Through these limited reforms the existing regimes ensured a period of deceptive stability for over a decade. Subsequently, the crisis erupted once again in a more violent way and on a very large scale. This is evidenced by the spread of Islamic movements of opposition and protest. In some countries, these movements turned into a widespread rebellion against the authorities, aimed at establishing alternative regimes that rely on an Islamic frame of reference and call for a new legitimacy.

These protest revolutions and internal conflicts awakened broad sectors of Arabic public opinion and stirred apprehensions in the industrialized countries, which rely heavily on oil exports from the Middle East region. However, the reactions of these countries tended to support an anti-reform direction for more than a decade. Fears about the spread of religious protest movements and the resulting threat to the hegemony of the industrialized countries over the region drove these countries to support the ruling Arab elites against the protest movements, and hence the industrialized countries obstructed these movements from attaining power. Thus the 1990s have witnessed destructive regional conflicts from Palestine to Iraq as well as civil conflicts—whether pronounced or potential.

New Reform Wave: Convergence of Internal and External Factors

The new reform project, which has begun to crystallize since the beginning of the twenty-first century, is built on two pillars: the growing influence of Arab civil society and its ongoing pressure, on the one hand, and the changing policies of influential western actors in the region, on the other. Parallel to both pillars is the regional quest to adapt to the requirements of pervasive globalization and respond to the challenges stemming from political upheavals and related violence.

[22]

The increasing erosion in the credibility and legitimacy of the existing regimes triggered a strong critical current of opinion among intellectuals and independent political personalities, which has been growing since the 1990s. It relates to the declining Arab situation in all fields, the exacerbation of corruption, the astounding accumulation of wealth, the extreme use of violence in controlling societies and the need to resolve their exploding crises, the recurring defeats and retreat in the international arena and the confrontation with external challenges and aggressions. On the basis of this critical current, repeated calls for reform became crystallized. Since 2002, the United Nations Development Program (UNDP) reports on human development in the Arab world, written by Arab intellectuals, embodied these calls for reform and widened the circle of forces demanding change. These reports expressed the maturity of Arab reform concepts, which explains the broad impact of the First Arab Human Development Report not only within Arab public opinion circles, but in international circles as well.

Arab societal developments have reinforced these reform demands and attracted support from greater segments of public opinion. These developments relate to the deteriorating strategic situation of the Arab countries and the slow pace of economic growth, if not its regression to a negative figure, over two successive decades. This economic regression has led to the exacerbation of poverty, higher rates of unemployment, deteriorating standards of administration, falling levels of education and rising social tensions. Economic and social studies conducted at the end of the 1990s confirmed the direct link between the nature of existing political systems and bad socio-economic performance. This link added an increasingly political dimension to the concept of reform, which was previously confined to the economic and administrative planes, thus making democracy the central slogan in the reform movement all across the Arab world. This is also true of the resource-rich Gulf region, where living conditions declined owing to continuous warfare, first, between

Iran and Iraq and second, between Iraq and its neighbor Kuwait. The high costs of these wars have been reflected generally in investment and growth levels. There is now a widespread belief among Arab intellectual and political circles that there is a close link between political and administrative reform on one hand and the impetus for progress and development. It is also closely linked to bridging the growing scientific and technological gap between Arab and international societies and other Third World societies.

Undoubtedly, these highly destructive wars and internal conflicts have set the Arab world back by several decades in terms of social, political and strategic relations, and also atrophied the existing Arab regimes politically and morally, thus driving more and more segments of the public to abandon them. This undermining of the credibility and legitimacy of Arab regimes converged with the rising wave of democracy since the 1990s, which has ushered the countries of Eastern Europe and the Republics of the former Soviet Union into the camp of democratic countries. International developments have revealed what Arab countries have experienced in terms of stagnant conditions and narrow horizons. These developments have also encouraged a review of the nature of existing political regimes and shattered the prevailing belief that the Arab world does not possess the constituents necessary for a successful transformation towards democracy.

The drive towards reform relates in no small measure to the continuous changes in the global geopolitical and geocultural environment. After a long period of western policies that have persistently supported existing regimes and reinforced the ruling elites under the pretext of maintaining stability and sparing internal eruptions in the region, the transformations of the post-Cold War era set a new agenda for the major industrialized countries. In the face of terrorism, which has broadened its global base, the intent of the industrialized countries to reinforce the chances of transformation and change in Arab countries has strengthened. The dramatic events witnessed in New York and Washington on 9/11 have driven the United States to adopt new Middle Eastern agendas. These new agendas link the mission of responding to the challenge represented by global terrorism to that of restructuring the Broader Middle East in the light of the concepts and ideas disseminated by the neo-conservatives. These concepts and ideas combine active, aggressive policies that ensure American global hegemony and transform democracy into one of its goals—as a means to confer legitimacy on such hegemony and claim that it is necessary for the stability, progress and happiness of humanity.

The Republican Administration of the United States has succeeded in imposing its ideas on reform and change in the Broader Middle East upon the European countries, which have been less enthusiastic about the US initiative. The European countries have linked the focus on opening up regimes and reinforcing democracy in the region to preserving their vital strategic interests. Prior to this, the European Union had developed the concept of the Euro-Mediterranean Partnership (EMP), in the context of organizing the relations between the shores of the Mediterranean in the light of globalization. The goal of the EMP is to qualify the Arab countries to engage and participate in the global market.

As the western bloc adopted reform, change in the Arab world has become a pressing objective for the first time. As the weakness of Arab civil societies and their inability to balance external pressures were revealed, reform has been transformed gradually into a foreign project. Thus it has posed a new and unprecedented dilemma. This dilemma relates to the relationship between the internal and external forces and their respective roles in achieving reform and guaranteeing its successful progress.

Thus the victory of the old alliance between the industrialized countries and oligarchic Arab regimes in their battle against Islamic protest movements, which were under siege during the past quarter century has yielded contradictory results. The great powers viewed the growth of such movements as a dangerous portent and considered that the increasing violence emanating from these movements could not be confronted in the long run without structural reforms that would affect the fabric of existing regimes. The objective of these reforms is to minimize social pressures, expand the circle of participation of elites, marginalized middle classes and those who are totally excluded from public life, which currently favors narrow and interconnected vested interest groups that form the core of all monopolies. Oligarchic Arab regimes saw in this triumph another chance to renew the contract of understanding with the major industrialized countries and revive the idea of security and stability as a leading concept in the region and build political and economic systems based upon it. These regimes hoped that the new terrorist threats would be an additional incentive for the industrialized countries to endorse their own positions as the only way to rein in uncontrollable political opposition and build dams to stop the flood of Islamic movements. These regimes expect the industrialized countries to reinforce their own position as agents for their countries in reward for their past services in offering to guarantee security, stability and preserve the existing regional situation. However, these past services have only deepened the dichotomy between the ruling Arab elites and society.

In reality, the position of the industrialized countries is not very different from that of the Arab regimes in viewing stability and preservation of the status quo as a strategic concern of all parties. Accordingly, the proposed democratic transformation is an adventure that is best avoided. Therefore, the Euro-Mediterranean Partnership agreements and the strategic cooperation between Washington and several Arab countries did not recognize, till the dawn of the third millennium, any necessity to change the prevailing rules and system of governance in the region. Washington sought to improve the political and administrative performance of the existing regimes and modernize them by tempting them materially and politically. Western countries believed till very recently, that expanding the base of economic openness and building a market economy would constitute the best guarantee for driving regimes gradually towards greater reform and openness. However, this moderate view was shattered by the massive political shock caused by Al Qaeda's attacks on the World Trade Center towers in New York and the Pentagon building in Washington and the inclination of the United States to restore its hegemony over the Middle East and place it under direct US supervision so as to control regional developments. This explains the mounting US pressures, in the context of the war on terrorism, to rehabilitate existing regimes or substitute new democratic regimes that may be more loyal or favorably inclined towards the United States. A case in point was in 2003 when the United States toppled the Baath regime in Iraq and dissolved its state authority.

Aborting the New Reformist Wave

In an unprecedented way, the Arab Human Development Report sparked the intellectual and political debate over the issue of reform in the Arab world. This debate became the axis of Arab intellectual and political life and gained priority on the agenda of popular movements. This internal Arab discussion responded to the requirements of change and reform as perceived by the western industrialized powers. For the first time, it seemed that the Arab will for reform had coincided with the Western will for change.

Yet this coming together of wills, which for a while seemed the strongest guarantee for achieving the reform sought for decades, did not realize all the promises it generated. The convergence of the internal reform demands and the external policies of qualification generated some confusion and contradiction, which the Arab reform forces could not overcome or find effective solutions for. The sudden external pressures, especially from the United States, scared the ruling elites, who saw any real political openness as a threat to their existence. At the same time, these pressures reinforced the anger of wide segments of Arab public opinion, whose traditional suspicions with regard to the intentions and designs of the great powers were enhanced by the American war in Iraq.

Arab regimes benefited from the historical negative stand of Arab public opinion toward US policies in the region and from the mistakes committed by the civil administration in Iraq, which robbed the American and European discourse of its credibility. They succeeded in mobilizing this segment of public opinion against what they called reform imposed from abroad. The deterioration in the security, political, economic and humanitarian situation in Iraq during the last three years gave them an invaluable negative model to showcase the risks stemming from foreign intervention and the adoption of western recommendations. Large segments of public opinion, which resent these regimes, have now become skeptical of the feasibility of intervention and of applying pressure for the sake of reform. These segments subscribe to the government's theory, which sets stability in opposition to reform and perceives reform, especially democratic reform, as the enemy of security.

Thus, Arab public opinion views the promised reform and political transformation as a foreign project aimed at camouflaging a new plan for the revival of western colonial hegemony over Arab countries or the manipulation of their destinies. The organized forces committed to reform within the context of democratic opposition and the organizations of civil society have been forced to take a defensive rather than an offensive position. They waste time and effort in denying charges that they are acting as agents for the West, or that they form part of an international strategy aimed at tightening its grip on Arab regimes in order to obtain essential strategic or political compromises.

In this context, the eight western countries, which adopted the modified Broader Middle East Initiative in 2004, were forced to reduce their pressures and confirm that they had no desire to spin the wheel of change at a speed which could jeopardize stability. Eventually, these countries practically abandoned their application of pressure for the sake of reform and started exaggerating the significance of the partial reforms achieved, such as the municipal elections in the Kingdom of Saudi Arabia, the competitive presidential elections in Egypt, the legislative elections in Iraq, or the formation of consultative councils in some Gulf states.

The ruling Arab elites did not hesitate to exploit this western withdrawal, which occurred in a public opinion climate that was hostile to foreign interventions, and its attendant apologies and semi-apologies issued by western officials denying any intention to impose foreign agendas on the Arab countries, and declaring their support for the notion of gradual reform as proposed by the governments of those countries. It is clear for those who monitor reform in Arab countries that regimes try to bypass reform projects either by discrediting the reform provisions that represent a danger to them, or by implementing some symbolic aspects of these reforms after devoiding them of any political content. Also, in the past two years, these regimes have embarked on an organized strategy of besieging civil society organizations—whilst declaring some nominal reforms and affirming abstract commitments to reform without any clear action program. This is evidenced by the document entitled the "March of Development and Modernization in the Arab World," adopted by the Arab Summit in Tunis in May 2004. This strategy includes limiting the activities of these organizations, periodically harassing and detaining their members, occasionally beating up civil activists and politicians and maintaining a stranglehold to prevent them from influencing public opinion.

It would be a truism to state that the division over reform issues fueled by the existing political regimes has plunged reformist Arab thought and politics into a state of deep confusion and aborted all the efforts that sought to drive Arab societies towards adopting the reform process and sacrificing everything for its sake. The reform process is now caught in a circle of secondary contradictions—between the internal and the external, between identity and otherness, between independence and imperialism, and between politics and economics. If the reform forces fail to rescue this process from these contradictions, it cannot emerge from the present impasse and state of inertia. The result will be the exacerbation of the deep crisis smoldering within Arab societies and perhaps resounding explosions whose effects surpass what has happened in the past decades owing to the neglect and neutralization of reforms.

The abortion of the reform process in the 1970s led to excesses on the part of elites and attempts by the hijacking states to turn them into instruments for supporting sole, absolutist authorities. This led, in turn, to the crisis situation of the 1980s, highlighted by the bread revolutions in which hundreds died and thousands were detained. Similarly, the destructive regional crises and civil conflicts of the 1990s exacted a high cost from Arab societies, with hundreds of thousands dead and it was followed by many decades of recession because of the bloody confrontation between the Islamic protest movements and the existing regimes. In the same vein, aborting the reform process at the beginning of the third millennium will prove immeasurably costly. It is quite possible that its outcome will be the explosion and disintegration of the societies themselves. This may well spill over into other societies—the foremost being those European societies close to the Arab world.

Responsibilities for Faltering Reform

The Western countries have erred, not in applying pressure on Arab regimes to reform but in the way it has linked these reform pressures to their own strategic agendas—whether to tighten control over sources of oil, or guarantee the full security and safety of Israel without consideration for the security and sovereignty of Arab countries and societies. This is the credibility gap which has allowed Arab governments to cast doubts on Western reform pressures and to show that the essential quest of the

Western bloc is not to enact political, economic and social changes in the interest of Arab nations but to use reform as a pretext for securing their colonial and semi-colonial interests. Thus Arab regimes have succeeded in neutralizing these pressures and in turning the table on Western governments, which have been accused by public opinion of planning to destroy the remnants of Arab sovereignty and independence.

However, this grave strategic error committed by the Western coalition – not to mention the use of democracy to camouflage schemes of international hegemony – does not negate the responsibility borne by the local forces of change. This responsibility lies in the failure of these forces to grasp the high stakes attaching to reform, a point that has not been missed by oligarchic Arab regimes. These forces believed that if the ruling elites were convinced about a peaceful reform program, which excludes any change in ruling regimes, such reform could take place under normal conditions at very little cost. In reality, the current call for Arab reform has been based from the very beginning on a grave misunderstanding, or perhaps on self-deception on the part of both the local reform forces and the Western coalition. These forces viewed reform as a prelude to change or an attempt to alter regimes from within—perhaps the kind of internal change based on an understanding with the regimes and an agreement on a transitional action program that allows an eclipse of the current situation and the creation of true pluralist regimes in the future.

Ruling elites have realized that the implementation of the necessary reform program means negating their own existence and recognizing the ascendance of new elites—in effect, a form of self-annihilation. Accordingly, they have employed all possible methods to block the reform agenda, which, in reality, amounts to a programmed coup against the ruling regimes and their replacement by pluralist systems. Truly, in the context of regimes that exclude society from any decision-making, any political change, regardless of its extent can constitute a dangerous step and remind the public of its situation and role, and rapidly convert

[31]

symbolic reforms into real reforms. Hence it was not surprising that the existing regimes imposed obstacles from the start, refused to engage in any reform process or commit themselves to any specific agendas of change. It was also not surprising that the reforms carried out by these regimes were a camouflage for reinforcing the existing exclusivist security system instead of modifying or abolishing it. These regimes refuse to shift from their originally designed framework, which is based on preserving total control of all material and non-material sources of authority and guaranteeing their monopoly of power without the participation of any other party. Moreover, the civil society movements have been transformed into distant and dispersed bubbles, lacking weight and efficacy, detached from their contextual situation. This explains the continuing failure of civil organizations, parties and associations to penetrate barriers and communicate with the communities in which they operate.

Thus the reformist forces wasted many years seeking reform via dialogue, understanding and positive interaction with oligarchic Arab regimes, without any concessions. Then they discovered that it was impossible to achieve any reform program, however limited, without altering the formulas of the existing rules and administration. In other words, they had to build resistance forces capable of effectively confronting the existing authorities as well as the elites and interests they represented. Reform succeeds only within generally sound systems, which are characterized by a minimal level of resilience, pluralism and competition and acknowledge the mechanism of social negotiation. In this case, the aim of reform is to liberate the regimes – suffering from the effects of senility, deterioration or bureaucracy – from the obstacles that prevent them from working at maximum capacity, or to partly modify the rules governing their performance to enable them to respond to new or emerging challenges. Thus reform is achieved by individuals and groups that are more faithful to the spirit of order and its principles. The outcome of this reform is to reinforce order and preserve it by improving its performance and deepening consistency in its movement. The legitimacy of reform stems from the natural inclination of social systems towards lack of dynamism and efficacy—the propensity towards stagnation and ossification. Reform comes about as a means of renewal to revamp systems that have lost their efficacy, but are still linked to fixed and acceptable values.

Conversely, change means finding a new system based on different rules of action, either because the existing regime is unable to respond to the new needs and societal challenges or because the regime itself has collapsed and come to a standstill. Change is based on substituting one system for another and it requires some force to effect this substitution; whether this comes from outside the regime, outside society and the country, or via coups and civil revolutions. Therefore, in the case of Arab reform, the inevitable question that arises is: Can Arab regimes be reformed, or do they have the capacity to reform?

Why has Reform Become a Predicament?

Regimes that are not based on popular choice, but on the exclusion of people and public opinion regardless of ideology or locale, cannot accept any reform that entails applying the rule of law, annulling privileges and preferences, widening the base of transparency, competence and responsibility, respecting the rights of individuals and propelling them towards shouldering responsibility. They cannot do so without jeopardizing the foundations they are built on—loyalty, clientship, widespread payoffs and arbitrariness, suppression of facts revealing responsibility, hiding truths from society, dealing irresponsibly with the rights and futures of individuals and imposing intellectual and political unilateralism. Any real transparency shown by the regime, even within limits – such as accepting pluralism and different viewpoints, reviving the rule of law, weakening the monopoly on sources and resources of power, and creating competitive dynamisms at any level – threatens to undermine the foundations of the existing regime. This kind of openness abolishes the main repression mechanisms, which maintain the balance of the regime and releases the deep currents of protest and opposition that have been bottled up for many decades and are just awaiting a simple signal or a small gap to give vent to long pent-up tensions. In other words, every step on the road to real reform—legal, administrative, economic and political, should lead at an unexpected pace to successive steps towards change. Change, for instance, will be the inexorable result of abolishing the deliberate and structural confusion between authorities, whether directly or via elevating the presidency to a sanctified rank by entrusting it with exceptional tasks and putting it above the law and accountability as is the case with most Arab regimes.

Change will also be the inexorable result of abolishing control over security apparatuses and political life. This control is usually achieved either by imposing a state of emergency and martial laws, or without them—yet putting all social, political and civil activities under the mandate of the security forces. This means exaggerating the security function in these regimes and making it the main axis of national life and the nerve center of the state at the expense of both politics and law.

Change will also result inexorably from the dynamics of accountability and transparency, not only in political affairs, but also in the economic spheres, both in the realm of the private sector and the state-run public sector. Transparency is the avowed enemy of the kind of speculative capitalism that relies on the nexus between the ownership of wealth and formal and informal political connections.

In reality, the main asset of these regimes, which constitutes the major source of the accumulation of wealth and capital, is not funds as such, but rather the totality of the political relations embodied in influential links or alliances with decision-makers at all formal and civic levels. Hence, the power of private commercial projects, even small, family-oriented ones, does not derive from their success in applying sound economic and administrative criteria as much as from the relations, understanding and sometimes partnership that their owners have with politicians or officials, who provide them with protection and cover up their violations of the law.

The continuity of these regimes or their reproduction does not tally with the actual separation of powers, the independence of the judiciary, the existence of a legislative power truly representative of various segments of public opinion, applying the rule of law, reinforcing the role of institutions, especially the institutions of control, respecting the rules of accountability and transparency, and acknowledging equal citizenship for all. The essence of these regimes is to manipulate law in pursuit of reproducing a parasitic class as an aristocratic class—which is simultaneously an heir and owner and by definition does not admit of change or modification. In this pursuit, it can only succeed by abolishing social movements, entrenching positions and ranks and reproducing the notion of the class–sect hierarchy, which has characterized all traditional systems in the past. Perpetuating the ruling class as an aristocratic class necessitates perpetuating society also within fixed hierarchies and hence abolishing the concept of citizenship with legal and moral equality and equal opportunities in favor of confirming the priority of one social group over the other and nourishing the belief in the natural supremacy of a cultural elite as two necessary conditions to preserve stability and guarantee social security and peace.

In short, it is not possible to change the current regimes into democratic, pluralist regimes, as reformists have dreamed of doing, because their very existence depends on excluding the people and thrusting them beyond the circle of political or civil efficacy and keeping them in a state of paralysis. This is done to impose a mandate on the people and exclude them from participation in sharing revenues which constitute the main source of wealth. Contrary to the needs of capitalist regimes, what is required and prevalent here is not the kind of investment which generates surplus value; but rather serfdom, unpaid and worthless labor. This is true of entire societies. Also, a rentier economy leads to a consumer economy that tends to squander money and carry out celebratory and massive symbolic expenditure. The capital formed through speculation, if not through economic spoils and plunder cannot be transformed into a means of investment, renewal and development. It increasingly pulls societies back into the Middle Ages and generates and generalizes values of nepotism, self-subordination and sycophancy so that modern society and public opinion are replaced increasingly by a society of subordinates and yes-men. In reality, in the societies where these anomalous formulas of rule prevail, there is only one feudal master and the rest of humankind are slaves, regardless of their political, responsibilities, social rank and their religious, cultural or civic positions.

This explains why all the reform plans failed and were aborted when they clashed with the issue of political reform. The prerequisite for the survival of these regimes of collective exclusionism and their continuity is a political game whose constituent elements are violation and suspension of law, abolition of the political identity of societies by dissolution of the national and citizenship structure and the perpetuation of positions, ranks and offices.

What is the Solution?

The above review has revealed that the failure of reform in the Arab world has resulted from a combination of material and moral, internal and external factors, all inextricably linked. To confront this integral, composite and interactive reality, concerted collective efforts are required at the regional level between active cultural, political and economic elites, and at the global level, in terms of the international system that plays a significant role in determining the existing balances in the Middle East. In my view, this means the following:

- Reform in the Arab region is not possible if the current political direction of the Atlantic powers (American and European) and their policy choices towards Middle Eastern politics do not change, at least in three spheres:

- *General Outlook on the Region*: According to the current outlook, the Middle East region is still a region of influence and disputes over interests. It does not take into consideration any interests of the major Arab countries, the foremost being their strategic and security interests. This has allowed the major powers to continually violate recognized international traditions, laws and principles and encouraged the use of political and economic pressure, coups and outrageous military interventions to defend vital or less vital private interests. This has devalued the concept of popular sovereignty and even erased it entirely and allowed the exclusion of public participation in favor of the supremacy of the ruling elites, who are supportive of the external powers.

- *Security of Israel*: Currently, this objective eclipses all others and provides justification for sacrificing those vital interests that need to be respected if any civil order or normal political life is to flourish in any Arab country, including that of regional strategic cooperation. This has helped to define Arab–Western relations in a manner that has humiliated the Arabs and the Levant to a greater extent than any likely damage to Western interests despite the problems faced by European countries as a result of the spread of terrorism. In this sphere, the problem lies not so much in the existence of Israel, as in the unconditional and unlimited support given to Israeli policies, which serves as a tool for exerting pressure and exercising external control over the Arab world.

- *Isolation and Marginalization of the Arab World*: The third sphere relates to the current strategy of countering the rise of any hostile Arab-Islamic power by isolation and marginalization and by imposing an economic, political and strategic embargo upon the Arab world. However, this policy creates a regional environment that produces tension, violence and sustained conflict. Such moves cannot encourage productive investment or reinforce the spirit of stability among nations and foster hope and optimism with respect to the future. The obvious result today is despair, frustration and resentment of the West as being primarily responsible for Arab misfortunes. This policy generates escape mechanisms and provides a justification for corrupt Arab elites or those who lack competence, expertise and leadership qualifications to exonerate themselves from responsibility.

- No reform is possible by following special regional strategies, racing to provide services to industrialized countries or offering compromises to them. All Arab countries will be losers in such a game. Reform requires cooperation between Arab countries as well as a collective strategy so that reform in each country constitutes part of a comprehensive reform plan for the entire region. This means there can be no hope for the progress of reform without cooperation and understanding between Arab countries.

- No reform is possible in any Arab country without an integral program which combines the tasks of economic transformation, social justice, scientific qualification and political participation. The essence of reform is to create a political, legal and social environment that encourages material and moral investment and creates new trends and values that drive people towards exerting greater efforts and sustains feelings of confidence in the self, society and its collective future.

- No reform can be effective if it does not involve the people or is aimed at misguiding the nation, bypassing it or using limited benefits to justify continuous national deprivation by banning political practice and participation in the government for formulating policies and decisions that control its fate and that of its sons. The essence of reform is to inject a spirit of responsibility into individuals and groups and reinforce the spirit of mutual understanding, communication and solidarity. This cannot be achieved without boosting social confidence, which can only grow in an atmosphere of honesty, fairness, equity in dealing with people and real participation, which convinces people that they are effective partners who are indispensable to the process of building public life. This means that the greatest challenge to any reform process is how to achieve success in engaging people in the political process. This is so, not because it is the primary condition for achieving the desired change but also because it is the only way to help individuals change themselves and reinforce their social feelings by reaching out, interacting and participating among themselves. Without these processes it is not possible to build a public life or civil societies.

In my view, the past few years have shown the failure of societies to reach an internal understanding that allows them to break out of the current stalemate and enter into the stage of democratic transformation and reform via a negotiated consensus. To move beyond the stalemate and create a fresher, more positive atmosphere, as well as avoid great upheavals and the disintegration of communities, it is necessary to form an international committee for good offices, which can act as a mediator to start a dialogue between opponents, remove impediments in the way of communications between parties and demonstrate the importance of having a stake in negotiated political solutions and their feasibility. In my view, such political and moral mediation by an international committee formed of global personalities who enjoy great credibility, such as Nelson Mandela and other famous Nobel laureates, constitutes the only alternative to military interventions or economic and financial sanctions, which have so far been employed in several countries with negative consequences.

2

Democratic Reform in Palestine and the Arab World: External Pressures or Internal Response?

H.E. Yasser Abed Rabbo

Arab countries suffer from a universal structural crisis in all spheres—political, economic, social and cultural. The Arab Human Development Report 2002, published by the United Nations Development Program (UNDP), revealed that the Arab world is lagging behind other regions in the developing world with respect to expanding political participation, applying representative democracy and respecting freedoms. In the economic sphere, the report demonstrated that the combined GDP of 22 Arab countries is less than that of a single European country, Spain, while 15 Arab countries fall below the poverty line with regard to sources of water (less than 1000 cubic meters per capita annually). Outright unemployment is estimated at 15 percent of the labor force and the number of unemployed persons is expected to reach 25 million by 2010. In the sphere of empowering women, the percentage of Arab women's politico-economic participation is the lowest in the world. The percentage of women in Arab parliaments is less than 5 percent and there are 65 million illiterates in the Arab world, two thirds of whom are women. In the sphere of knowledge, the amount of translation done in the Arab world per annum is one-fifth that of Greece alone.[1]

Since the report was issued, Arab countries in general have started to witness socio-political transformations. Recently, the State of Kuwait granted women the right to vote in, and nominate themselves for, municipal and parliamentary elections. The Kingdom of Saudi Arabia organized municipal elections in stages. In Jordan, there is an ongoing domestic discussion over the national agenda, the development and building of democratic institutions and approval of the law on political parties and elections in preparation for the parliamentary elections scheduled for 2007. At the same time, 20 percent of the seats of municipal councils have been allocated to women in the new bill of municipalities. As for Palestine, it witnessed presidential and legislative elections in 2005 and 2006, respectively, and municipal elections in stages (2004–2005). Lebanon witnessed the withdrawal of the Syrian troops followed by parliamentary elections in May 2005. For the first time, Egypt experienced a presidential election in 2005 with more than one nominee as well as parliamentary elections in which the Muslim Brotherhood achieved a prominent position. In Iraq, a constitutional referendum and parliamentary elections were organized in late 2005.

The above-mentioned UNDP report concluded that the Arab world was suffering from poverty, repression and marginalization. Hence the US proposal (the Broader Middle East Initiative)[2] viewed the dire situation described by the report as a wellspring of terrorism (of the kind that led to the attacks on New York and Washington on September 11, 2001). Therefore, the US initiative urged that it was imperative to develop democratic life in the Middle East region, expand the political participation of youth and women and enhance respect for human rights, especially freedom of opinion and expression. This would confer legitimacy on different governments in Arab countries, reinforce political stability and eradicate the motives for extremism and terrorism.

The US initiative declared its support for reform in the region and promised to intensify efforts via partnership and dialogue with governments, business sector and civil society in pursuit of deepening democracy and expanding political and public participation. The initiative supports efforts to guarantee the conduct of free, fair and transparent elections by cooperation with interested countries through the following measures:

- helping independent election commissions; conducting programs for registering voters; and programs for raising civic awareness with special emphasis on female voters
- reinforcing the capability of national parliaments by encouraging parliamentary exchange programs; training and conducting of legal and legislative reforms
- supporting women's participation in political, economic, social and cultural committees
- following up judicial reforms to ensure the independence of the judiciary
- enhancing the freedom of expression and encouraging independent media
- encouraging good governance and combating corruption.

Some believe that the initiative was timed against the backdrop of the US failures in both Iraq and Afghanistan, as well in Palestine, and as a result of the widening global opposition to the war in Iraq. Hence, Washington presented the initiative to the G-8 summit in Georgia in June 2004 in order to gain wider support.

The Broader Middle East Initiative received additional criticism from some Arab intellectuals who attacked the credibility of the originator, either on moral grounds (based on US policy in Palestine and Iraq) or on account of the questionable priority accorded to democracy on the originator's agenda and the continuing US support for authoritarian regimes in the Arab world.

Many Arab governments have dealt cautiously with the initiative for various reasons and pretexts: that the initiative is an act of intervention in their internal affairs; that initiatives must come from within; that there is a cultural particularity in the Arab world; that the solution of the Palestinian question is a prerequisite for reform; and that US-style reform is conducive to disorder and extremism.

However, Arab leaders pledged solidarity and cohesion in a statement issued by the 16th Arab Summit convened in Tunis in May 2004, committing themselves to the following:

> ...to continue the universal reform steps started by Arab countries in the political, economic, social, cultural and educational spheres in order to achieve the desired sustainable development...expanding the sphere of participating in public affairs, supporting methods of responsible freedom of expression, fostering human rights in accordance with the Arab Charter on Human Rights and the different international conventions and charters, and enhancing the role of Arab women in building society.[3]

Civil Society and Political Reform

Civil society institutions in the Arab world held a parallel summit meeting to the Arab Summit in Beirut in March 2002. They issued a statement entitled "Towards a Political Reform Initiative in the Arab Countries," observing that the rejection of international reform initiatives by some Arab governments really amounted to the rejection of reform irrespective of its source—whether internal or external.[4]

In the statement, these institutions rejected the citing of civilizational or religious specificity as a pretext for objecting to, or undermining the universality of human rights, or justifying the violation of these rights. They confirmed that respect for human rights represents a higher interest for every individual, group, nation and all humanity. They also condemned attempts to manipulate nationalist emotions and the principle of sovereignty to neutralize commitment to international human rights principles. They emphasized that the Palestinian issue and the war against terrorism should not be used to justify moves restricting freedoms, negating democratic transformation and undermining respect for human rights. They demanded guarantees for citizens' rights by allowing their participation in managing public affairs through fair and free elections and condemned the use of violence in the political sphere and all forms of instigating hatred.

Civil society institutions confirmed that real equality between men and women must go beyond equality before the law to changing concepts and challenging the stereotypical images of women. Hence women must be accorded equal opportunities for political participation through the allocation of posts in decision-making and other institutions. It is also important to allocate a proportion of seats in parliamentary and other representative institutions for women, as well as to abolish the effects of discrimination in national regulations. Furthermore, women who are married to foreigners must be guaranteed the right, on par with men, to have nationality conferred upon their children This measure is in accordance with Article 9(2) of the international Convention on the Elimination of All Forms of Discrimination Against Women (CEDAW).

On the eve of the Arab Summit in Tunis, anticipating the impact of international moves for reform, the Alexandria Library in collaboration with the Arab Academy for Science, Technology and Maritime Transport, the Arab Business Council, the Arab Women's Organization, the Economic Research Forum and the Arab Organization for Human Rights, convened the conference on *Issues of Arab Reform: Vision and Implementation* in March 2004. The document issued by the conference, which was entitled the "Alexandria Declaration on Reform in the Arab World," linked reform to the resolution of the Palestinian question and the liberation of the occupied Arab territories.[5]

The document confirmed that the notion of democracy is that people rule themselves through a pluralistic system that facilitates the rotation of power and is rooted in respect for all personal freedoms in the realms of thought, association, expression and opinion, as well as the existence of effective political institutions. At the highest level, these institutions have elected legislative institutions, an independent judiciary, a government subject to both constitutional and public accountability, and political parties with diverse intellectual and ideological orientations.

The document demanded the separation of legislative and executive powers, revival of forms of governance that would ensure peaceful, periodic rotation of power, the conduct of periodic, free elections that preserve democratic practices and a limited tenure of office.

The orientations and priorities of the document are clear and comply with the position of Egypt and a number of Arab countries with regard to reform in the Middle East. The document emphasizes that the driving force of reform must be "from within our own societies" and that "border problems" must not be a pretext for foreign intervention in the affairs of Arab countries, or for putting them under a new mandate," and that reform should not obscure other priorities, "heading which is the just solution of the Palestinian question…and the need to make the Middle East a WMD-free zone." Moreover, the need was stressed for preserving "cultural specificity," dealing separately with each country and ensuring that reform takes place within the parameters of the partnership between governments and civil society.

Representatives of civil society institutions in the Arab world issued the "Amman Declaration for Reform" in October 2004. They reiterated that political reform is not only a prerequisite for the progress of democratic moves but also for economic, social and cultural development.[6]

The declaration confirmed that political reform goals include good governance, transparency, fairness, accountability, the rule of law, expanding the base of political participation, increasing the participation of women and youth, establishing pluralism in politics and political parties, developing electoral systems in harmony with international principles on holding free and fair elections, founding independent national authorities to supervise elections, providing funding for political parties to spend on their electoral campaigns, and stipulating a financial ceiling for campaign spending. The declaration also observed that while elections constitute the fundamental pillar for building democracy, it is not sufficient by itself, as conducting them requires guarantees for various fundamental rights.

An important positive aspect of the international reform initiatives is that it has driven Arab governments, which were earlier indifferent to the reform demands of national public opinion, to pay attention to this issue, if only in words. For the first time in the history of Arab League summit meetings attended by Rulers and Presidents of the member states, the issue of reform, democracy and human rights imposed itself on the agenda. The governments of Egypt and Yemen took the initiative of convening two conferences on reform—one in Alexandria as mentioned above and the second in Sana'a in January 2004. The second conference, the Inter-Governmental Regional Conference on Democracy, Human Rights and the Role of the International Criminal Court issued the Sana'a Declaration.

Reform in Palestine

Several Palestinian reform initiatives have been proposed over the past years. They include the report of the General Control Office of the Palestinian Authority (1997), the reform document issued by the Palestinian Legislative Council (May 16, 2002), the One Hundred Days Plan of the Palestinian government (June 23, 2002), the statement of the government of Mahmoud Abbas in April 2003, and the plan of the National Reform Committee, which was founded in 2003. These initiatives reiterated the need to reform the political system by approving the Basic Law and creating the position of Prime Minister in 2003, and also the need to modify the elections law and conduct municipal, legislative and presidential elections.

The "Roadmap" plan to further the peace process in the Middle East has asked the Palestinian National Authority to adopt the following reforms:[7]

- appointing a Prime Minister to form a government which enjoys executive authority and is accountable to the Legislative Council
- real separation between the powers of the executive, legislative and judiciary
- writing the draft constitution of the Palestinian state stipulating the foundation of a democratic, parliamentary state and a government headed by a prime minister who enjoys authority, and getting it approved by specialized institutions
- forming an independent Palestinian Elections Commission
- reviewing the electoral law by the Legislative Council
- conducting free and fair Palestinian elections
- unifying the security forces.

After the speech of the late President Yasser Arafat before the Palestinian Legislative Council on May 15, 2002 and the issuance of the Council's reform document, a new government was formed. The government, in its turn, prepared a plan for reforming the institutions of the Palestinian Authority. The plan included a pledge by the government to execute a series of reforms within one hundred days of approving the plan on June 23, 2002. The plan confirmed the principle of separation of powers, the rule of law, the independence of the judiciary, the restructuring of ministries and formal institutions, and preparing for the presidential, legislative and municipal elections.

In 2002, the Basic Law (the constitution, which was later amended in March 2003) was approved and the post of Prime Minister was created. The Prime Minister was made accountable to the Legislative Council.

Palestinian civil society organizations were involved in the reform process and issued a document in which they confirmed that the Basic Law, as a temporary constitution, is the basis for the functioning of the

Palestinian Authority and its institutions. They also reasserted the need to enhance democracy by reconstituting the Central Elections Commission, finalizing the law of general elections by adopting proportional or mixed representation and conducting elections at all levels: trade unions, associations and all civil society organizations.

The Palestinian Legislative Elections of 2006

Since mid-2002, several meetings were held with all the civil society organizations, political parties and independent personalities in order reach consensus on a new democratic electoral system that would lay the foundations of an independent state.

More than 60 civil society organizations issued a memorandum on October 17, 2002 demanding that the Legislative Council seats be increased from 88 to 120. These seats were to be divided into two categories. In the first category, 60 seats were to be assigned for individual constituencies, with one seat for every 27,000 people (with 1.6 million eligible voters in the West Bank, including Jerusalem and the Gaza Strip). In the second category, 60 seats were to be allotted to various party lists based on the principle of proportional representation, with the whole country being regarded as one electoral constituency. Seats would be allotted only to those parties that polled more than 2 percent of the total votes cast in the election.

The proposal was presented as a bill to the Legislative Council and was approved as law in the first reading in February 2005. The law provided for allocating two thirds of the seats for the constituencies and one third for proportional representation. The Palestinian territories were to be regarded as a single constituency and the number of seats was raised to 132, with 88 allotted for the constituencies and 44 allotted for proportional representation, with a 2 percent minimum vote requirement. The women's quota was abolished together with the financial support for the lists, and the age of nominees was set at 30 years.

At the start of April 2005, President-elect Mahmoud Abbas (Abu Mazen) announced his adoption of the system of one constituency and total proportional representation. The National Committee for Monitoring Elections (which consists of more than 350 institutions and more than 3700 observers of local and general elections) welcomed the President's position and demanded quick approval of the electoral law so that elections could be conducted on schedule. The Committee demanded the adoption of the total system of proportional representation or the mixed system, reducing the age of the nominee and the allocation of a women's quota (20 percent of the seats of the Legislative Council).

Following this, the National Campaign for Electoral Reform asked President Mahmoud Abbas to use his constitutional authority and return the electoral law, which was approved in the second reading, and to object to all the articles that contradicted national consensus as expressed in the "Cairo Declaration" of March 18, 2005 and the memoranda of parties, the different civil society organizations and social and economic actors. The campaign asked the government to amend the law in accordance with the national consensus, adopt the system of total or mixed proportional representation on the basis of at least 50 percent and also guarantee the fair representation of women with at least 20 percent of the total seats.[8]

Based on the amendment proposed by President Abbas, the Legislative Council agreed on June 18, 2005 to adopt the mixed system: 50 percent of the seats to be allotted by proportional representation to parties on the basis of the whole country being a single constituency (with a minimum eligibility requirement of 2 percent of the actual votes cast), and 50 percent of seats to be allotted for various constituencies, with 16 approved electoral constituencies.

The Basic Law was amended in accordance with the amendments of the Elections Law No. 9 for 2005, increasing the seats of the council from 88 to 132, as well as stipulating the holding of presidential and legislative elections every four years.

President Mahmoud Abbas issued a decree declaring January 25, 2006 as the date for the legislative elections. He also issued another decree in which the 66 seats intended for the constituencies were distributed as follows:

- 4 seats for Jenin
- 1 seat for Tubas
- 3 seats for Tulkarm
- 2 seats for Qalqilya
- 1 seat for Salfit
- 6 seats for Nablus
- 1 seat for Jericho
- 5 seats for Ramallah and Bira (one seat reserved for Christians),
- 6 seats for Jerusalem (two seats reserved for Christians),
- 4 seats for Bethlehem (two seats reserved for Christians)
- 9 seats for Hebron
- 5 seats for North Gaza
- 8 seats for Gaza City (one seat reserved for Christians)
- 3 seats for Deir el Balah
- 5 seats for Khan Yunis
- 3 seats for Rafah.

The Central Elections Commission continued election preparations and reopened registrations, especially after the Legislative Council cancelled the civil register and approved the electoral register for those seeking to participate in the elections through nomination and voting.

As many as 1,350,000 citizens, both males and females, registered to vote in the elections—a number that constituted 80 percent of all eligible voters. This reflected a high percentage considering the difficulties posed by the Israeli closure and siege. Occupation troops prevented the Central Elections Commission teams from registering Palestinians in Jerusalem. For this reason, a regulation was issued stipulating that all Jerusalem citizens, who carried blue cards, would have the right to participate directly in the elections. This reaffirmed their right to choose their representatives in the Palestinian Legislative Council.

[51]

At the start of December 2005, the Central Elections Commission began to register nominees and approve the electoral lists of those parties taking part in the proportional representation system. Eleven such electoral lists were registered.

Under the constituencies system, the nominees numbered 414, including 15 women. As many as 1,042,424 voters actually participated in the elections. This number constituted 77 percent of registered voters, a high level compared to several neighboring countries. The valid votes cast numbered 1,000,246 (95.95 percent). Six of the party lists met the minimum percentage requirement (2 percent of the actual votes cast). The Central Elections Commission issued the final election results.

The Islamic Resistance Movement (Hamas) gained 74 seats (29 proportional representation seats and 45 constituencies). The Fateh movement won 45 seats (28 proportional representation seats and 17 constituencies). Proportional seats allotted to other winning lists were: three seats for the Popular Front for the Liberation of Palestine, two seats for the Alternative List (a leftist coalition comprising the Democratic Front for the Liberation of Palestine, the Palestinian People's Party, Palestine Democratic Union and independents), two seats for the Independent Palestine list (independents headed by Mustafa Al Bargouthi) two seats for the Third Way list (academics and businessmen headed by Salam Fayad) and four seats for independents. All these results were declared under the proportional representation system. Ultimately, Hamas gained 20 additional seats under the constituencies system at the expense of Fatah and other party lists, as the presence of several nominees in the latter resulted in a scattering of the votes.

Had the system of total proportional representation been followed, the results would have been as follows:

- 58 seats for Hamas
- 56 seats for Fatah
- 6 seats for the Popular Front

- 4 seats for the Alternative group
- 4 seats for Independent Palestine
- 4 seats for the Third Way.

The total proportional representation system necessarily reflects the size of all political groups and parties on the basis of the votes cast in their favor.

Under the current mixed electoral system, Hamas got 44 percent of the votes and 56 percent of the seats. Fatah gained 42 percent of the votes but only 34 percent of the seats. The leftist democratic forces got 13 percent of the votes but only 7 percent of the seats. Hence the electoral law must be changed from a mixed system to total proportional representation. The law relating to political parties must be approved after incorporating the following general principles:

- Confirming the right of citizens to participate fully in elections and form political parties
- Guaranteeing total equality of political parties within the law
- Encouraging political parties to organize participation by women and youth and formulating the necessary framework for such participation
- Stipulating clearly in its charter the party's commitment to the following principles and conditions:
  - the rules of the Basic Law as amended in 2003 and the document of independence announced in 1988
  - the principle of political pluralism in the realms of thought, opinion and organization
  - respecting international charters on human rights, especially the Universal Declaration of Human Rights (1948) and the International Covenant on Civil and Political Rights (1966),
  - working toward achieving the ultimate goals of the Palestinian people with regard to freedom and independence, protecting national unity, condemning the use of violence in resolving internal disputes and avoiding discrimination against citizens

- o allowing citizens to join and leave the party voluntarily
- o maintaining transparency and openness with regard to sources of party funding and avenues of spending
- o forming and electing party caucuses on democratic and modern foundations
- o holding periodic general and auxiliary conferences.
- Funding assistance by the Palestinian Authority for political parties based on principles of justice and level of participation, especially for the purpose of conducting election campaigns.
- Forming an independent committee to register parties, or approving the Central Elections Commission
- Establishing avenues of cooperation and solidarity with related and friendly parties on the basis of parity and common interests.
- Ensuring equality in the use of the official media by political parties
- Forming a special court to resolve issues relating to political parties and politics.
- Preserving the unity of the Palestinian people both within the country and among the diaspora.

Conclusion

To conclude this presentation on the issue of reform in the Arab world, I would like to make the following observations:

- Calls for internal reform have frequently been subject to confusion. Historically, the role of external powers, especially western democracies has contributed to this confusion, by officially supporting and forming alliances with existing regimes against opposition movements and forces. The dual standards of Western powers on issues of international legitimacy and their related decisions, especially with respect to the Palestinian issue, explain why external calls for reform are greeted with suspicion. These calls are seen as a means of containment and hegemony, aimed at reconstituting the region to facilitate total Israeli dominance in the Middle East. Civil society forces, parties and organizations have also been viewed with suspicion and have suffered for decades from persecution and imprisonment owing to the lack of democracy and freedom in the Arab countries.

- Arab societies are highly sensitive to the idea of change imposed from abroad owing to the long colonial history of the international powers that are urging such change. This sensitivity also arises from the sheer neglect of local opposition forces by the international forces at a time when the former were subject to tyranny by the existing authorities and security institutions. Till 9/11, reform and democratic change did not figure on the agenda of the western governments, which were content to pay homage to some opposition leaders, especially from the radical reformist factions. Also, the American administration's subsequent approach to tackling so-called "terrorism," the selective definitions of that term by the same administration, the blatant military invasion and occupation of Iraq outside the framework of international legitimacy, coupled with the fact that Iraq has now become a fertile ground for violence and instability have heaped suspicion upon the external model of reform and democracy.

- Some Arab regimes have exploited the hostility of nations towards US policies to cast doubts on or even abort the democratic reforms necessary for modernization in these countries. This in turn has isolated the internal forces that have relied on the international climate favoring reform. These forces are now being accused of being agents of the West.

- International calls for reform and democratic change can gain credibility and become effective if they collectively address the real problems confronting the people of the region, primarily poverty and occupation, and if they respect and implement the decisions of international law pertaining to regional crises, the foremost being the Palestinian issue.

- The absence of political and social freedoms, the weakness of civil society organizations and the state dominance over them, corruption within official political structures, the spread of poverty, illiteracy and repression have all helped to reinforce the role and position of fundamental forces. Aided by funding and the effects of government policies, these forces have presented themselves as alternatives to these regimes, by projecting themselves as forces hostile to imperialism and US policies in the region and by playing on national and religious feelings. They have also managed to penetrate the social fabric through their charity organizations and by exploiting increased social needs. They have begun to infiltrate all social institutions and trade unions. At the same time, the official authority has stifled political and media activity and the forces of civil society.

- The premises of reform, change, democratization and modernization involve reinforcing political life, protecting the free functioning of civil society organizations, facilitating real rotation of power through the separation of powers, forbidding the army and security forces from intervening in society and its diverse activities as well as separating the state and its institutions from the ruling party and applying the motto that the state exists for all its citizens.

To stimulate reform in the Arab world, the following measures must be adopted:

- Encouraging official and civic reform initiatives
- Benefiting from international reform initiatives as long as they do not undermine national sovereignty and the rights of nations to self-determination
- Boosting political and democratic life by developing the laws that support democracy building, especially the laws pertaining to parties and elections

- Respecting the particularity of Arab countries but not using this as a pretext to refrain from political, economic and social reform
- Crystallizing an Arab strategy for reform, formulated jointly by official institutions, political parties and civil society organizations
- Activating the mechanisms of cooperation between official and civic institutions to serve the objectives of reform in the Arab world
- Exchanging expertise and successful reform experiences in the Arab world
- Encouraging the participation of women and youth in the political process, especially in parties and elections
- Developing the work of civil society organizations dealing with issues of reform and democracy
- Liberating the media from official patronage
- Developing Arabic constitutions and ratifying international charters on human rights
- Emphasizing the close link between the processes of political, economic, social and cultural reform.

As for the Palestinian situation in the aftermath of the legislative elections, in order to overcome the crisis due to the Israeli occupation and the siege imposed on the people because of the election outcome, there is a need for a comprehensive national dialogue to form a broad national coalition government. This government should work in accordance with the program of the Palestinian Liberation Organization, which is aimed at founding an independent Palestinian state within the existing borders on June 4, 1967. The government should also approve the Arab initiative agreed at the Beirut Summit of 2002, adhere to the decisions of international law (UN resolutions 242, 338, 1397), reject all unilateral solutions (including the isolation plan of Israeli Prime Minister Ehud Olmert) and call for an international peace conference to embark immediately upon final status negotiations.

3

Iraq as a Model for the Spread of Democracy in the Arab World

Dr. Adnan Pachachi

The issue of democracy has commanded great attention not only in Iraq and other Arab countries, but also throughout the whole world. Currently, Iraq is experiencing difficult circumstances, as it is undergoing a phase that witnesses huge and diverse political, security and economic challenges.

On March 16, 2006 I had the honor of inaugurating the first session of the Iraqi Council of Representatives, a significant step along the path of Iraq's democratic experience which has stumbled and faced obstacles from time to time due to various internal and external difficulties and influences.

In this chapter, I will address democratic transformations in Iraq from both the theoretical and practical perspectives. Theoretically, democracy is founded on several principles and bases. First, respect for the freedoms of opinion, expression and religion, as well as the rights of association, demonstration and the formation of parties, unions and civil society organizations, under the rule of law, an independent judiciary and full equality of all citizens, regardless of their social background and their nationalist, religious and sectarian loyalties. Second, separation of powers with checks and balances maintained between them; third, conduct of free, periodic elections to ensure the peaceful transfer of power; fourth, subordination of the armed forces to the democratically elected civil power; and fifth, prohibition of armed militias operating outside the authority of the state's regular army.

The question that arises is: How are these principles applied in today's Iraq? The spread of the free press, the creation of scores of TV satellite channels and radio stations and the establishment of hundreds of political parties, associations and civil society organizations are clear evidence that Iraqis are enjoying and exercising their fundamental rights and freedoms.

Notwithstanding these positive accomplishments, the political process has suffered a number of setbacks. To start with, the judiciary has lost its independence and integrity, and is now employed to intimidate the public and tighten the grip of authoritarian rule. Despite the fact that the new constitution provides for the legal protection of the Iraqi citizen, such a safeguard hardly exists. Arbitrary raids and detentions are still carried out, torture has become a familiar practice, and prisons are overcrowded with detainees who have yet to be interrogated and charged. Since this is the most important problem for which people need an immediate solution, the new government is called upon to take urgent measures to reform and revitalize the judiciary as the ordinary citizen's shield against oppression and injustice, especially since Iraq has a host of efficient and impartial jurists and legal scholars.

Moreover, although the separation of powers and the mutual balance between them do exist, some flaws are still evident in the executive branch as the Prime Minister enjoys far greater powers than those accorded to the President. Therefore, a constitutional amendment is needed to restore the balance between the powers of the two leaders.

Although the new constitution has banned the formation of militias outside the structure of the Iraqi military, the ground reality is completely different. Private militias are active throughout the whole country and cannot be deterred from indiscriminately committing crimes such as murders and kidnappings. Again, this is a highly complex problem that has to be thoroughly eliminated, as no state can survive if sects and parties were allowed to maintain forces that rival the regular armed forces.

Since the collapse of the former regime, 2005 alone has witnessed the election of members to the Transitional National Assembly and local councils (January 30), the Constitution referendum (October 15) and the election of members to the Council of Representatives (December 15). Generally speaking, the electoral experience proved a huge success despite some violations and acts of fraud during the polls owing to inadequate numbers of international observers due to deterioration in security and interference by certain militias and religious figures to influence the voters' choices.

The two elections above demonstrated that sectarian and ethnic considerations overwhelmingly determined voting trends. However, no democratic system can survive and flourish if the public continues to elect representatives according to their religious, ethnic and sectarian loyalties, instead of their political attitudes and orientations. Nevertheless, in my judgment, this is only a temporary drawback, and once security and order are restored and economic conditions are improved, Iraqi voters will almost certainly elect those candidates who advocate their political preferences and priorities.

Other obstacles that might disrupt Iraq's democratic process are the main disputes over specific articles of the Constitution involving three major issues. The first is the question of federalism since the new constitution has endorsed the right of the Kurds to create a federal region in northern Iraq. Indeed, this endorsement represents continued recognition by the Iraqi state, from its inception, that the Kurds must be granted special status together with some political and cultural rights. For the last fourteen years, the Kurds have established their own government that has been known for its seriousness and efficiency. Accordingly, the Constitution has approved the continuation of this federal experience in the north.

[61]

Nevertheless, differences exist over the application of federalism in other parts of the country. As many fear that such federalism could result in dividing Iraq, this issue will be tackled when certain constitutional amendments are to be examined by the special committee of the House of Representatives. Owing to the fact that the Constitution has granted the governorates far-reaching powers, the main point in the question of federalism is to ensure that the powers of regional governments do not exceed those of the central government.

The second contentious issue is that of the natural wealth and resources. Although the Constitution has stated that these resources constitute the property of all the Iraqi people in every governorate, it also granted the producing governorates a special status that allows them to join the central government in the management and distribution of the country's riches. Thus, the contradiction is evident in handling this matter, and we hope that a constitutional amendment can possibly be reached to resolve this issue.

The third matter disputed by the Iraqi political factions is the so-called "de-Ba'athfication" and the relevant committee set up for this purpose. Indeed, this issue was inherited from the foreign authority that was in charge of Iraqi affairs immediately after the war. Many Iraqis now believe that it is high time this committee was abolished because it has been exploited for political ends.

We believe that these basic issues can be settled through the constitutional amendments that the Council of Representatives is expected to endorse pending the report of the special committee set up to examine these amendments.

To sum up, if the Arab states want to benefit from the lessons of the Iraqi experience, they must respect their peoples' fundamental rights and freedoms, consolidate the independence of the judicial system and the peaceful transfer of power through free elections, and subordinate the military to the civil, democratically-elected leadership. At the same time, these states must avoid the afore-mentioned disadvantages of the Iraqi experience, the most important being the formation of political parties on a religious or sectarian basis because they will almost certainly create divisions among the citizens of any single country. At any rate, according to Winston Churchill, democracy is a bad system but all other systems are much worse!

In conclusion, despite all the problems and difficulties, Iraqis are determined to move forward in developing their democratic experience since they have no other choice. The fundamental freedoms and rights that Iraqis enjoy currently are very precious, and as many constitutions have been employed to support the rise of dictatorships to power, it is the peoples, not constitutions, that preserve and protect these freedoms and rights. In view of their bitter experiences, the people of Iraq will not permit anyone under any pretext whatsoever to confiscate those freedoms and rights that have been achieved through great suffering and sacrifice.

4

The Imperatives and the Logic of Arab Economic Reform

Dr. Atif Kubursi

From the Atlantic Ocean to the Arabian Gulf, the real wealth and hope of the Arab countries are embodied in its people—men, women and children. People represent the real "renewable" resource and constitute both the basis and the objective of Arab development. The Arab people, simply on humanitarian grounds, have a fundamental right to a decent life that fulfills their basic needs. Such development is being identified increasingly with the process of expanding people's choices and providing them with opportunities to realize their potential unencumbered by hunger, disease or oppression.

Over the 1970s and 1980s and more recently, the "success" of many Arab economies was based on deriving a huge rent from oil exports, which masked many structural problems and allowed the Arabs to glide into the 2000s. Oil revenues may allow them to coast for a few more years without having to restructure or reform their economies to improve their productivity. However, the harsh economic realities of the new millennium will leave the Arabs with no option but to adjust and confront the challenges of the globalized economy or face the prospect of being left behind. Ultimately Arab success will depend on the extent to which they can engender meaningful, concerted action to meet these challenges and how their governments, businesses, investors, workers and communities respond to them.

The global economic and technological environments are changing rapidly, leaving little room for delay and sluggish action. National and geographical boundaries have been transcended and perceptions of space have changed, with places becoming interconnected, regardless of their physical location and time zones. The new information and communication technologies (ICT) are reshaping the ways in which people live, work and interact with each other. Governments are in retreat and more political and economic space is left to the market and the private sector. Global competition is intensifying and competitors are only a fraction of a second away from each other instead of being thousands of miles apart.

Technology and politics are two equally important factors that have acted in combination to transform the classical international economy. The new economy in its most fundamental arrangement is now *global*, just as the classical economy was in its essential aspect *national*.

Successive rounds of trade liberalization under the General Agreement on Tariffs and Trade (GATT) and the World Trade Organization (WTO) and cross-border investment and financial deregulation have led to major changes in world trade, finance, investment and the rise of transnational corporations. The world financial markets are an integrated network that works on a 24-hour basis. When Japan's Nikkei stock index is about to close its operations, London's FTSE will be opening and by the time it is about to close, NYSE will open. Today, a widow in Brazil can invest in New York and trillions of dollars cross national boundaries on daily basis.

Ironically, the most advanced countries have consolidated their markets and moved to integrate their economies more deeply and extensively, while Third World economies remain disjointed and economic integration among them is still limited, superficial and lacking in cohesion. Of course, there are exceptions such as the GCC, but these are rare and unusual. Regional trading blocs dominated by the United States, Japan and the European Union are expanding and consolidating

[66]

their markets and strengthening their competitive advantages. Newly industrialized countries, such as South Korea, Taiwan, Singapore and many others are rising again. China has practically become the factory of the world, putting greater competitive pressures on many industries and activities and threatening local and traditional comparative advantage in many areas.

A new competitive dynamic has emerged in which countries are expected to open up their markets and to restructure their economies with greater emphasis on exports and become more welcoming and hospitable to foreign direct investments. This is precisely what the advanced countries of the past did not do when they embarked on their industrialization process. This has led many economic historians to charge the First World countries with "kicking the ladder" so that no new industrial countries can emerge after them. Arab economies, particularly those in the Arabian Gulf region will have to confront these challenges at a time when many basic structural weaknesses hamper their ability to adjust to global change. By and large, the Arab economies are still at "a very low entry point into the Information Age."

Arab Economic Vision for Change

Meeting future challenges requires vision and a successful development strategy that guides and controls the reform process. The issues are not as much about picking winners as identifying a winning strategy and being guided by the correct vision. There is a critical and definite need to establish a broad-based Arab consensus on what it takes to succeed in the global economy. Arab states need to be encouraged, guided and provoked into a common sense of purpose and a shared vision that will help them to raise their economic productivity, improve their global competitiveness, build efficient and sustainable structures, set up transparent institutions, raise the overall standard of living of the common people and protect their values and uniqueness. State action is necessary but not sufficient. This will always be small and insignificant in today's global markets characterized by colossal trading blocs, giant transnationals and ideological hype. A regional perspective and regional institutions are indispensable to the success of this effort.

Arabs need a collective, co-operative and innovative economic and social policy as part of a broader economic and social renewal agenda for the New Millennium. This effort is not about setting out elaborate blueprints for the economy, nor about establishing an array of expensive government programs. Rather, it is about providing a framework, an understanding and a reform strategy that enables all segments of society to work realistically together as partners. Grand schemes and large, uncoordinated government programs in the past have not borne the expected fruits in the Arab region. Indeed, while some of these blueprints and grand schemes were necessary at the earlier stages of Arab development, they are no longer workable. Arab sustainable development is too complex a process and no single sector or scheme can carry it forward.

Arab economies must overcome some severe structural problems and build sustainable sources of income. It is necessary to raise awareness among member states about the dangers of heavy dependence on non-renewable resources, scarcity of water, late entry into the new economy and the emergence of tough new competitors.

The following is a short list of critical actions to be taken:

- New competitive advantages must be created and attention must be given to illuminating these new advantages. The broad outlines of feasible future scenarios have to be drawn.
- Critical masses must be established in strategic domains. This presupposes the existence of regional and collective identification of these strategic domains.
- Sustainable development should be anchored in human development, a regulated entry into the new economy, improving the transformative

capacities of the state and co-operation on joint Arab strategies. Future research, conferences, experts and expertise should be focused on this sustainable perspective.

- A comprehensive indigenous reform agenda should be drawn up with the full participation of all segments of society.

The Logic of Reform

Reforming Arab economies is no longer a matter of choice. The options have narrowed considerably and the choice is stark: Arabs can mount their own reform process or have it imposed on them by other parties or under duress. If reform is to be self-initiated and self-propelled, then it pays to be proactive and pre-emptive. In this way, Arab choices and unique characteristics can be protected and used as a basis for building a new economy.

Without being trite it seems that an accurate diagnosis of the problems facing the Arabs will help to solve 70 percent of the problem. It is equally relevant to recognize and come to terms with the nature of the process and its outcome. First and foremost, it is necessary to distinguish between reform that deals with the economy as a set of mechanisms or as an organism that needs to be replaced by a new one. If the old economy is seen as an organism, then it is crucial to realize that it will develop antibodies, fight and thwart any feeble attempt to introduce piecemeal reform. Those that benefit from the status quo will fight any change. However, changing organisms may be drastic, as the new organism may not survive in the new circumstances and destroying old organisms may leave the economy lifeless. China's reform process is typically described as evolutionary where networks and mechanisms were changed slowly, cumulatively and carefully. On the other hand, the Soviet system was reformed using shock therapy that brought massive and simultaneous changes without developing proper institutions and support personnel.

With hindsight, it is clear that the Russian reform proved too rapid and drastic and therefore developed a host of problems. In many respects, the depth and pace of reform were so much that they backfired and a new, immature system replaced the older and more mature system. There was not enough time to train the proper heirs of the *ancien regime*. The new *apparatchiks* were neither sufficiently prepared nor properly selected to lead and shepherd the reform agenda. In fact, the Russian economy still suffers from the brutal marks of its rebirth.

The Arab reform agenda should assess carefully and thoroughly the reform episodes in Eastern Europe and Russia and learn from the mistakes of others. It is rarely the case that economists have the chance to develop their theories in a laboratory setting. The historical experiment that developed after the downfall of the Soviet System is an incredibly valuable phenomenon from which to appraise, learn and distill best practices.

Invariably Arabs are facing strong pressures for reform and there is no dearth of blueprints and formulas. Unfortunately most of these formulas are couched in oppositional dichotomies and irrelevant binary choices: market vs. government, free trade vs. protectionism and so on. The West is asking the Arabs to use models, policies and visions that they themselves did not employ at similar junctures in their own economic histories. There are also pernicious suggestions that the only way the Arabs can develop is to discard their culture and adopt western values and practices. This flies in the face of history. The Arabs of the 12th and 13th centuries have proven that their culture and religion were quite consistent with scientific discovery and economic success. Reform is about reverting to Arab roots, developing and building upon the great Arab traditions and values that sparked the "Golden Age of Baghdad," a time when its libraries contained more books than the rest of the world combined. It seems that the reason for present failures in the Arab world lies, partially at least, in having moved off course and abandoned cultural trends.

Structural Challenges

Today, several underlying structural weaknesses in Arab economies and societies hamper their ability to make the transition to a new and productive economy. This transition is contingent upon the development and the optimum use of Arab intellectual capital and pursuit of the knowledge economy. A brief account of the most salient problems is presented below:

- *Dependence on oil revenue:* A heavy direct and/or indirect dependence on the rent derived from natural resources, especially oil, is still a dominant characteristic of the Arab economies. This dependence has propagated an "Arab Disease," manifested by over-priced domestic currencies that served to deter the development of manufacturing exports, as well as by inflated costs of production that partially undermined local industry and agriculture. Domestic markets are typically flooded with cheap imports that have ultimately compromised the balance of payments of even the richest Arab states and have earned them the dubious distinction of sustaining the highest per capita imports in the world. Although it is true that the direct dependence of GCC countries on oil has declined to less than 35 percent of GDP, this direct dependence is still very high and indirect dependence on oil is perhaps twice as much as direct dependence.

- *Unsustainable high consumption patterns:* These patterns are divorced from high production and are characteristic of most Arab economies, including some non-oil economies. Investment/GDP ratios are relatively high in the Arab World but a good part of these investments are made in large real estate or infrastructural projects that have often been not as productive as contemplated and have tended to be duplicative, ultimately leaving the domestic economies with large maintenance costs. Yanbu, Jubail and few industrial cities around are examples to the contrary. However, few if any, have proven their economic worth independent of large subsidies and government support.

- *Bloated government bureaucracies*: The transformative powers of the state are hampered by bloated government bureaucracies with overlapping rings of rent seekers, a set-up where merit and work discipline are not given sufficient focus.

- *Incomes linked to oil:* Incomes of people are quite often divorced from production and are highly related to the state of the oil market and oil rents.

- *Exposure to global oil market fluctuations:* Domestic economies are exposed to the wide fluctuations of the global oil market over which the Arabs have limited control. Oil and natural gas exports still account for over 70 percent of total Arab exports.

- *Weakness of Arab scientific structures and innovation*: There are also a number of telling indicators of the weakness of Arab scientific and innovative structures and performance. Less than 35,000 Arabs are engaged in full-time research and half of them are working in Egypt. There are only 3.3 researchers holding masters and doctoral degrees for every 10,000 persons in the Arab labor force. This is less than 10 percent of the corresponding share of developed countries. There are only 50 technicians for every one million persons in the Arab world. The comparable figure in industrialized countries is over 1000.[1] Very few engineers and scientists work on research and development in the Arab world.

- *Limited transfer of technical knowledge:* The Arabs have shown a perverse tendency to pursue "turnkey" technological projects with limited or no potential for the transfer of technical knowledge to the local labor market. Slow adoption of new technologies is a tendency that is observed in the Arab world.

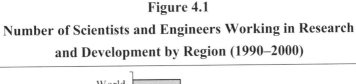

Figure 4.1

Number of Scientists and Engineers Working in Research and Development by Region (1990–2000)

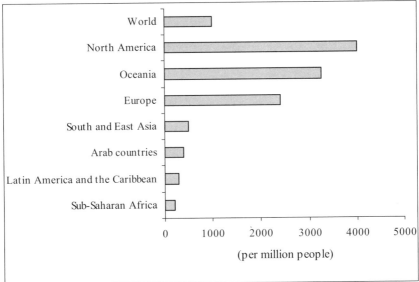

Source: UNDP, 2002

- *Fragmented industrial structures:* The Arab countries lack a well-established nexus or clusters of firms. It is becoming widely recognized that over the long run, sustainable competitive advantages develop in clusters of linked industries. Arab industrial structures are typically fragmented and implemented weakly. There have been some successful attempts in large industrial cities (for example, Yanbu and Jubiel in Saudi Arabia), but much more is needed than just building on technical affinities in resource-dependent industries.

- *Shortage of medium-sized and large firms with a home base in the Arab world:* Branch industrial organizations set up by multinationals have often resulted in poor local skill development and fewer spin-off industries being developed in the Arab region as compared to other regions of the world. Small firms are incapable of massive efforts in

[73]

research and development and are too fragile to compete in increasingly globalized world markets.

- *Under-investment in training and slow adoption of flexible workplace organizations:* Compared to other more advanced developing countries, there is under-investment in training and slow adoption of flexible workplace practices. There are also glaring deficiencies in the provision of adequate financing for technology and export-oriented companies. Labor markets are characterized by high unemployment rates. The Arab region suffers from an overall unemployment rate of over 12 percent and youth unemployment in the region is the highest in the world at 25 percent.

- *Widespread income and wealth inequality:* Such income and wealth inequality exists both within and between Arab states, and manifests itself in limited domestic purchasing power. This, in turn, reduces the capacity of the local market to sustain local production and also undermines health and education opportunities for the masses, which in turn, hampers labor productivity growth.

- *High illiteracy levels and low education levels of the labor force:* Adult illiteracy rates in the Arab world are relatively high. Total adult illiteracy is about 47 percent, which is significantly higher than the corresponding rates in low and middle income countries, in South East Asia, Latin America or in the developing countries of Europe. When female illiteracy rates are singled out, the Arab world shows a relatively worse record. Lebanon, Jordan and Syria show relatively lower rates of illiteracy than the rest of the Arab countries, rates that are comparable to the rates of some of the NICs.

- *Low life expectancy at birth in the region:* Only South Asia and Sub-Saharan Africa have lower values than the Arab world. Fertility rates are very high and exceed all other corresponding rates. People who are 14 years and younger represented over 43 percent of the Arab population in 2000; the corresponding share for low and middle-income countries is 35.3 percent. Only the Sub-Saharan Africa region has a higher percentage.[2]

- *Relatively lower mean years of schooling in the Arab world:* Participation rates in education, at every education level, have risen dramatically in the Arab world between 1965 and 2005. There is still room for improvement particularly when Arab indices are viewed against those in the Pacific Rim or Europe. Mean years of schooling in the Arab world are still relatively lower than those in East Asia and the Pacific, Latin America and the Caribbean. Moreover, very few students enroll in scientific and mathematical areas.

- *Lower educational attainments:* The educational attainments of the Arab labor do not prepare it adequately for international competition. In 1992, the average years of schooling of Arab labor was equal to 3.6 years while the 2010 forecast is for 4.5 to 5.5 years. In comparison, in China it was 5.2 years in 1992 and the 2010 forecast is for 5.4 to 6.1 years. The poor performance of Arab countries is particularly obvious when one considers that mean schooling in East Asia and OECD in 1992 exceeded the 2010 forecasts for the Arab world. In 1992, mean schooling in East Asia was 6.9 years, while the corresponding OECD average was 9.2 years.[3]

- *Lopsided industrial structures:* The lopsided industrial structures of many economies in the Arab world compromise their ability to sustain stable investment environments and provide opportunities to local labor. Arab economies are still primarily based on the "old" economy. The Arabs have not ventured seriously enough into the new economy. Primary manufacturing production still dominates the Arab production structure. The Third Industrial Revolution is rooted in solid state electronics and information and communications technology (ICT). The Arab countries have not yet been able to develop even a rudimentary base in these industries. Conversely, newly industrialized countries in Southeast Asia have successfully developed an export-oriented electronics industry. Employment in agriculture in the 30–70 percent range is still the mainstay in the most populated Arab countries. One also sees a high level of employment in services, which reflects basically inefficient bureaucracies. For example, employment in services in the Gulf Co-operation Council countries represents 65 percent of total employment and in Jordan it constitutes 76 percent of the total employment.

Figure 4.2
Ratio of Students Enrolled in Scientific Disciplines in Higher Education in Selected Arab Countries and S. Korea (1990–1995)

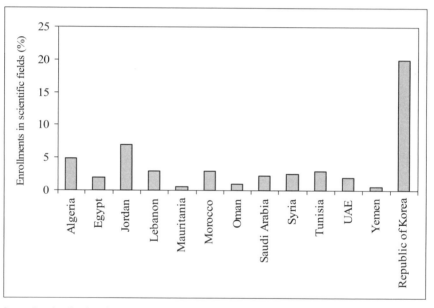

Source: Based on data from the World Bank, 1998.

- *Manufacturing activity is still relatively modest:* Most of the Arab states seem to depend rather strongly on primary production or downstream oil processing. With the exception of few oil-producing countries, Arab manufacturing activity has remained limited or stagnant. Notably, though, the North African countries show higher manufacturing value added per capita than their counterparts in the

Arab East excluding the oil economies of the Gulf. Per capita manufacturing value added (MVA) in US$ in the year 2000 shows Egypt with $281, Syria with $282.8, Jordan $229.6, Kuwait with $1969.9, Saudi Arabia with $621.3, and Tunisia with $370.7. Malaysia shows a total MVA per capita of $1,262 and Chile $704.8 in the same year.[4]

- *Heavy reliance on export of primary products:* Primary products accounted for over 98 percent of the Arab exports in 1965. This share declined to 87 percent in 1990 and to 75 percent by 2000. However, this is still an excessive share and symptomatic of the heavy reliance on the export of natural resources and the limited share of manufactured exports. Machinery and equipment constitute less than 1 percent of total exports in 1965 and in 1990. Chemicals and refined petroleum exports increased as did textiles and clothing, but these export increases remained modest, particularly in comparison with other successful developing regions. Actually, exports of machinery and transport equipment increased in most regions between 1965 and 1990 except in the Arab world.[5]

- *Greater specialization in resource-based industries:* Classifying industries by their technological sophistication and using UNIDO's designations of Medium and High Tech (MHT), and Low Tech (LT) and Resource Based (RB), we find that in the year 2000, most Arab countries still show a heavy specialization in RB categories. A few Arab countries, particularly Egypt and Jordan have developed a good standing in Medium Tech industries. The following shares, obtained from the UNIDO database indicate that Egypt's manufacturing was split 45.3 percent in MHT, 20.5 percent in LT and 34.2 percent in RB. Jordan's shares were 30 percent in MHT, 13 percent in LT and 57 percent in RB. Kuwait shows 8.8 percent in MHT, 10.5 percent in LT and 80.7 percent in RB. The break-up in Tunisia indicates 24.4 percent in MHT, 36.6 percent in LT and 38.8 percent in RB. Syria's shares were 9.3 percent in MHT, 55.9 percent in LT and 34.8 percent in RB.[6]

Figure 4.3

Mean Years of Schooling (Population 25 Years or Older) by Gender For Selected Arab Countries and Three Asian Tigers (1960–2000)

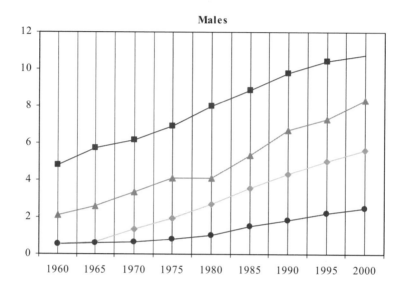

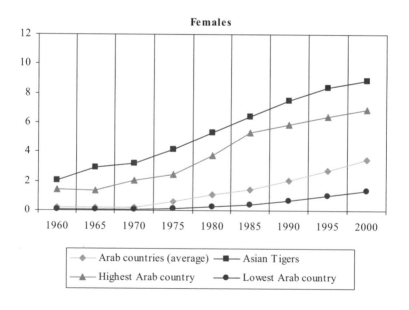

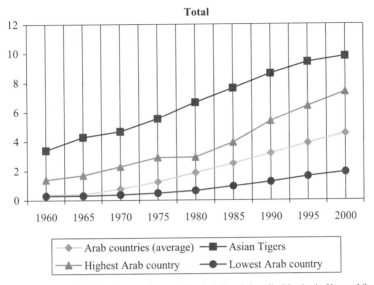

Total

Note: Countries with no available data include: Comoros Islands, Djibouti, Somalia, Mauritania, Yemen, Libya, Saudi Arabia and the United Arab Emirates.

Source: UNDP, 2002.

- *Technological exports heavily biased towards LT and RB:* Of Egypt's exports in the year 2000, 24.9 percent and 37.8 percent were LT and RB respectively. Kuwait's exports in the same year were predominately RB with over 42 percent of its exports being oil-related. Jordan's exports show a fair share of MT, constituting about 18.2 percent. Tunisia's exports are primarily in the LT category with 49.4 percent. Textiles, clothing and chemicals are three dominant manufacturing products of the Arab world. Machinery and transport equipment manufacturing shows very low shares. By all standards, Arab manufacturing activity is traditional or resource-based and the shares of the modern sector and products are low.[7]

- *Low share of High Tech exports:* The shares of High-Tech exports in the total exports of Arab countries are more telling. Egypt shows a 2 percent share, while most other Arab countries show very low percentages varying between 0.1 and 0.3 percent. Israel on the other hand has a share of 29 percent and South Korea has 33 percent.[8]

[79]

- *High exposure to foreign trade:* For all practical purposes the Arab economies are all export-oriented economies and show very high foreign trade percentages (exports + imports as percentage of GDP). Arab oil producers typically show export share levels exceeding 70 percent. Non-oil Arab economies are also highly exposed to trade. This exposure, which is measured by the share of goods exports or non-factor incomes in GDP is also relatively high. In this regard, exposure means that a major source of income is dependent on foreign sources over which the national economy has very limited influence. It is perhaps important to note here that the high share of exports to GDP is more the result of non-factor incomes than the exports of merchandise.

- *Decline in exports:* While exports from East Asia and the Pacific grew at 9.8 percent between 1980 and 1990, they declined in the Arab world at the rate of 1.1 percent per year. Between 1990 and 1995, the two regions exhibited an even starker disparity. While exports in East Asia grew at 17.8 percent per annum, Arab exports fell by 4.7 percent per annum. Using 1987 as the base year, the terms of trade (ratio of export prices to import prices) declined from 130 in 1985 to 96 in 1990. While the terms of trade have improved slightly in the mid-1990s, the region has still not counteracted the reverses suffered in the 1980s. Indeed, while most regions of the developing world experienced declines in their terms of trade, none were as severe as those of the Arab world.[9]

- *Dependence on external sources of finance:* This dependence on external finance is manifested by the high indebtedness in the Arab world. In 1990, Egypt's public foreign debt was put conservatively at $34.2 billion, having risen from less than $1.5 billion in 1970. This debt is twice as large as that of South Korea. By 1990, Kuwait had accumulated a total external debt of $34 billion. In 1995, resource-strapped Sudan had a debt of $18 billion while Morocco's external debt was calculated at $22 billion. In the same year, Syria's debt stood at $21 billion and Jordan's at $8 billion. Iraq's external debt before

[80]

occupation was rumored to run over $100 billion. For the Arab world in 2000, external debt as a ratio of exports was over 180 percent. It constituted 52.6 percent of the region's GNP in the same year. The latter ratio is the highest for all developing regions except Sub-Saharan Africa. Servicing the debt is exacting a heavy toll on these economies. Measured as a percentage of exports it exceeded 14.9 percent in 1995. The debt-service demands were even higher in 1990, being 24.6 percent. It is due to debt-restructuring and forgiveness, lower international interest rates and some regional growth that this figure has dropped. Nonetheless, interest payments on this debt alone are absorbing 8.1 percent of the export proceeds of the region.

- *Fall in factor productivity:* Total factor productivity and partial factor productivity have fallen drastically in the Arab world between 1960 and 2000, while in most other developing countries average total factor productivity increased. In East Asia and in the OECD countries it grew by over 1.5 percent per year.[10]

- *Lack of an adequate science and technology system:* Until now, no Arab state has established an adequate science and technology system. Although there are more than 10,000 consulting firms and over 100,000 contracting firms in the Arab world, these remain small and narrowly specialized in civil engineering fields. A number of constraints impede these consulting and design organizations. There are little or no financial services provided to these institutions on par with their OECD competitors. They typically undertake projects in their home base and rarely venture outside because of the lack of access to risk coverage. While Asian countries that are seriously seeking to develop domestic technological capabilities have emulated OECD practices, the Arab countries have not.[11]

- *Low scholarly output:* In 1995, Arab scientists and professionals published over 7,077 articles and papers in international refereed journals. About 80 percent of this published research was carried out in academic organizations. The two leading fields covered are applied chemistry and clinical medicine. The Arab world's scholarly output in 1995, as measured by the number of publications per million inhabitants was 26. By way of contrast, Brazil had 42, France 840, Switzerland 1,878 and South Korea 144. To compare the advancement of South Korea relative to the Arab World, it may be noted that in 1985, the scholarly output of the whole Arab world was equal to that of South Korea at 15 per million inhabitants.[12]

• *Limited output by professional researchers:* In 1995, more than 1,000 Arab organizations published one or more scientific papers. It is estimated that the number of full time researchers working in research centers in the Arab world is about 10,000. In the same year, the departments of basic and applied sciences in Arab universities were staffed with 50,300 faculty members, 32,200 of whom held a Ph.D. degree in science and technology. Antoine Zahlan estimates that there are roughly 50,000 Ph.D. professionals in science and technology in the Arab world. However, their output and their effectiveness are limited, on account of low research and development (R&D) budgets and the absence of science and technology (S&T) systems.

• *Inadequate production of scientific publications:* In 1995, 33 percent of all scientific publications were produced in the GCC countries, which constitute only 9 percent of the Arab population. Egypt accounted for 32 percent with 25 percent of Arab population. The Maghreb region accounted for 18 percent of the publications, with 31 percent of the population. Lebanon, Syria and Jordan accounted for 8 percent of the publications with 9 percent of the population. Only 29 organizations published 50 or more scientific papers in refereed international journals, and only 5 organizations published 200 or more papers. King Saud University (Riyadh) had 422 publications and was the leading research organization in 1995. Cairo University was next with 330 publications. King Fahd University of Petroleum and Minerals (Dhahran) had 320 publications.[13]

- *Low levels of research and development:* Low R&D levels and slow rates of technological diffusion are evident in most Arab countries. Egypt is one Arab country that has mounted a credible research and development program, but it under-performs its competitors in the Third World and spends far below the record of developed countries on R&D. While advanced countries such as the United States, Japan and Sweden spent on average 3.7 percent of their GNP on R&D, the Arabs spent less than 0.2 of 1 percent. More disturbing is the fact that the largest proportion (89 percent) of this limited expenditure is made by the public sector.[14]

- *Fewer patent applications:* There are very few patent applications, grants of patents or patents in force in the Arab world. In 1990, Algeria had 185, Egypt 789, Iraq 322, Tunisia 144 and Saudi Arabia 455. By way of contrast, Netherlands had 53,514, South Korea 31,387, Israel 3,908 and Japan had 376,792.

- *Wide disparity in telecommunication lines:* There were 4.9 main lines per 100 Arabs in 1996 as compared to 0.8 lines in 1975. This is about the same level as that of Southeast Asia but below Latin America with 10.2 lines per 100 inhabitants. However, the disparities between the various countries of the region are staggering, with 7.5 main lines per 100 in Egypt (1999), 24.02 in Kuwait (1999), 30.2 in the UAE (1998), 8.98 in Tunisia (1999) and 1.3 lines in Yemen (1996). Most of the telecommunication industries are public utilities operating under monopoly conditions. Only Morocco and Tunisia have opened the door to foreign investment in these sectors.[15]

- *Prohibitive rates for use of cellular phones:* Mobile phones are widely used in the GCC countries, Lebanon, Jordan, Morocco, Tunisia and Yemen. They are typically very expensive to use and the initial subscription fees are prohibitive. In Saudi Arabia, the subscription fee is $800, the highest in the world. In Saudi Arabia, number of cellular phones per 1000 inhabitants is over 63.6 in 2000, while the corresponding figures were 212.5 in Lebanon, 58.31 in Jordan and as low as 5.84 in Tunisia. When compared to averages in other countries such as Turkey with 245.6, Chile with 222.2 and Indonesia with 17.3 cellular phones, the average Arab numbers are rather comparable. However, it is difficult to determine precisely the business/ consumption divide in the use of cellular phones. There are considerable grounds to suspect that in the Arab world, cell phone use is higher in terms of consumption rather than in business [16]

Figure 4.4

Number of Phone Lines per 1000 Persons*

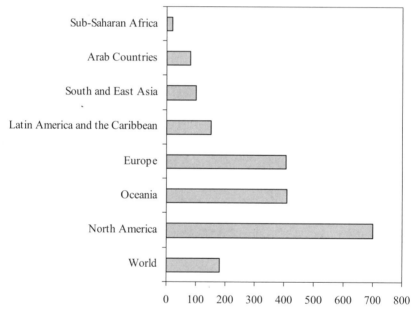

* The average is taken as the country-specific likely average (based on population size in 2000) of basic phone data extracted from UNDP HDR 2002. Data on 173 countries (out of a total of 179) includes 19 Arab countries.

Source: Based on UNDP HDR, 2002.

- *Limited Internet connections or users:* Unlike mobile phones, Internet connections or users are limited and these countries are at the initial stages of usage. Syria and Saudi Arabia have only recently permitted limited Internet connections. In 2000, the highest rates of connectivity were in the UAE and Kuwait and then only at the rate of 1.8–2.14 hosts per 1000 inhabitants. There are 0.094 hosts in Jordan, about 0.35 in Egypt, 0.146 in Lebanon and Morocco, 0.3 in Algeria, Tunisia and Syria. This compares to 0.06 in Southeast Asia and 0.35 in Latin America. In the year 2000, Internet users per 1000 people show 1.27 for Syria, 2.98 for Egypt, 18.51 for Jordan, 52.75 for Kuwait, 61.81 for Lebanon, and 14.35 for Saudi Arabia. In 2001, Internet users in the Arab world reached 4.5 million people or 1.6 percent of the population.[17]

Figure 4.5

Internet Penetration in Arab Countries: Users as Percentage of the Population (2001)

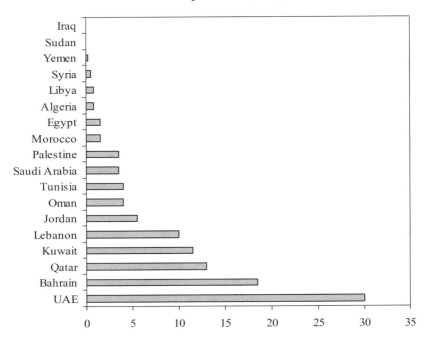

Source: World Markets Research Centre, 2002.

•   *Computer ownership much below global average:* Computer ownership is relatively high in the Arab region, compared to Latin

America and Southeast Asia. The UAE has 6.5 personal computers per 100 inhabitants, followed by Saudi Arabia with 6, Lebanon 5, Oman 3, Jordan, Egypt and Tunisia 2.2, and Syria 1.5. In Latin America, the average per 100 inhabitants is 2.4 and in Southeast Asia is 0.45. However, there are only 18 computers per 1000 inhabitants in the Arab world versus a global average of 78.3 per 1000 inhabitants.

- *Lower proportion of GDP spent on education:* Arab countries spent about 4.5–5.5 percent of their GDP on education. This is about the same as most low-to-middle income developing countries spend on education, but significantly lower than the expenditures of advanced and newly industrialized countries (NICs). Furthermore, the Arabs spend heavily on tertiary levels of education (four times more than on primary and secondary levels).This is a significantly higher ratio than other developing countries spend on this level.[18]

- *Low proportion of Mathematics and Engineering students:* Between 1990 and 1995, in the 20–24 age group, 0.1 percent of Egyptians studied mathematics and computer science and 2.5 percent studied engineering. The corresponding numbers were 0.8 percent and 2.5 percent for Algeria, 0.6 and 1.1 percent for Lebanon, 0.3 and 0.5 percent for Saudi Arabia, 0.3 and 0.8 percent for Tunisia, 0.1 and 1.0 percent for Syria, and 2.5 and 3.1 percent for Jordan. This compares with 2.8 and 13.5 percent for Korea and 1.2 and 2.7 percent for Mexico and 2.7 and 4.2 percent for the United States.[19]

- *Low competency of the education system:* A recent study in Egypt showed that competency in language and mathematical skills is 30 per cent and 40 per cent, respectively. In an international study of comparative educational achievement in 1996, Kuwait, which was the only entrant from the Arab world, was ranked 39th out of 41 countries. A year earlier, Jordan had been placed in the last position.[20]

Figure 4.6
Personal Computers: Arab World and Other Regions

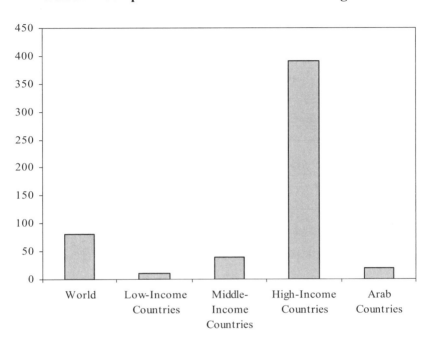

Source: World Bank, 2002

- *High unemployment rates*: The unemployment rates in the Arab world (with 15 million unemployed), are rather high, particularly among university graduates (30–35 percent). This may be due partly to the lack of synchronization of the educational system output with the skills required by industry and government.[21]
- *High levels of job creation required to match labor supply:* More than 30 million new jobs were required by the year 2005 simply to employ the expected increase in labor supply. This would have required at least a 6 percent real annual rate of growth. Although the recent rates of growth topped this target, they were unfortunately unaccompanied by any perceptible increase in employment.

Conclusion

It is not difficult to envisage the broad outline of necessary reform. It covers a wide spectrum of issues and areas. First and foremost, the reform would be conceived within an enabling, free and responsive policy environment for developing and utilizing the full human capabilities of all citizens. It will involve the courage to unleash talent and creativity in all age groups, especially the young. The Arab countries have the resources to eradicate poverty and build human development (HD) provided a solid political commitment is made to build HD objectives through the following measures:

- Building a society that fosters freedom and knowledge
- Working towards a future built by all for the benefit of all
- Fostering a culture that values quality and openness
- Building a society that encourages dialogue and cross-cultural accommodation
- Having representative parliaments, with more representation for women
- Setting up independent judiciaries, supported by well-functioning legal systems
- Instituting transparent regulatory systems
- Implementing public sector reforms to reduce high transaction costs and eliminating monopolies
- Providing efficient public services and establishing cohesive organizational structures
- Building an active, empowered and socially committed civil society
- Broadening political participation, ensuring accountability and transparency in government
- Protecting freedom of the press and inculcating respect for human rights
- Empowering women politically through far greater participation

- Mainstreaming gender equality in national development strategies and plans and thereby boosting greater female participation
- Establishing and implementing a timetable to eliminate legal discrimination
- Reversing the feminization of unemployment by effectively addressing gender gaps in the quality and relevance of education, skill-training programs and jobs
- Reforming educational content and quality and redressing gender disparities
- Instituting informal and in-service vocational training and encouraging lifelong learning
- Matching educational output with job market demand
- Networking with well-qualified Arab expatriates
- Investing more in applied R&D and building dynamic linkages among scientists, researchers and investors
- Establishing policies, info-structure and public–private partnerships to boost ICT access and uptake and reduce costs
- Focusing on increasing the Arabic content for web & general knowledge
- Considering higher education as vital as primary education
- Providing incentive packages to foster private sector growth; encouraging entrepreneurs to invest, take risks, open opportunities and expand markets and jobs
- Establishing sound and coherent government economic policies
- Developing efficient, equitable and accountable mechanisms for the allocation of public expenditure
- Creating and maintaining efficient infrastructure and skilled workforces, reducing red tape and fostering attractive and hospitable investment regimes
- Mainstreaming human development and poverty reduction within national economic policy

- Upholding the transparent rule of law
- Putting legal reform at the core of institutional reform
- Ensuring citizens' rights are compatible with fundamental human rights
- Activating the voice of the people by the following measures:
  - Strengthening institutions of local governance
  - Liberating civil society organizations
  - Fostering free and responsible media
- Providing for more effective participation by local communities, especially the poor and under-represented
- Re-orienting societal incentives, leading by example, promoting attitudinal change towards knowledge & achievement, and building dialogue among civilizations
- Supporting Arab integration measures, which are critical to survive and compete—such as the implementation of the GAFTA and its transformation into a common Arab market
- Pursuing active and preventive development; building social cohesion, tolerance and respect for minorities and other cultures
- Pursuing a just, durable and comprehensive resolution to the Arab-Israeli conflict
- Building Arab economic and trade cooperation; promoting freer mobility of knowledge, people and resources
- Supporting inter and intra-regional cooperation.

While the foregoing points may appear to be a long list of wishful measures, they are increasingly becoming the essential ingredients of an indigenous reform package that can sow the seeds of a brighter and more stable future for the Arab world—one that is free from outside impositions and reflects the region's deep-rooted traditions and glorious history.

Section 2

POLITICAL ORIENTATIONS IN ARAB SOCIETIES

5

Moderate Islamists and Reform in the Arab World: Case of the Muslim Brotherhood in Egypt

*Dr. Amr Hamzawy**

Contemporary Islamist political movements in the Arab world share three major characteristics, which are listed below:

- Islamists are critical of prevailing societal conditions in Arab countries, which they describe as being decadent, underdeveloped or unjust.

- Islamists blame authoritarian ruling elites for these societal conditions and consequently consider the promotion of political change as the first crucial step toward altering Arab realities. Religious political movements in Arab countries differ from other collective religious actors such as missionary groups and charity organizations, which seem to understand change as a gradual, long-term process of Islamizing societies taking place outside the political realm.

- Islamists legitimize their practices and create popular appeal for their movements by basing them on religious norms and values, which serve as the ultimate ideological frame of reference for society and politics.

Within the broad category of Islamist political movements, groups can be differentiated on the basis of their attitudes toward violence and their political perceptions. Militant groups such as the Egyptian Jihad and the

* The first part of this paper is based upon the author's study "The Key to Arab Reform: Moderate Islamists," Policy Brief No 40, July 2005, published by the Carnegie Endowment for International Peace © 2006.

[93]

Algerian Armed Jammaa Islamiyya employ violence and seek to establish theocratic states as the sole means of changing conditions in Arab societies. They draw inspiration either from idealized interpretations of past phases in Islamic history or contemporary models of Islamic republics, whether in Iran, Sudan or even in Afghanistan.

Moderate Islamists reject the use of violence and support competition through pluralistic politics, and it is such groups whom Western governments should now seek to engage. Saad Eddin Al Uthmani, leader of the Moroccan Justice and Development Party (PJD), and Muhammad Mahdi Akef, leader of the Egyptian Muslim Brotherhood, best respresent the moderate Islamist position. They exclude radical strategies as options for political transformation and view gradual democratic openings as the only viable way to challenge repressive authoritarian regimes in the Arab world.

Mapping the Islamist Spectrum

This is a relatively new position. In the 1980s and 1990s moderate movements still had not accepted the value of democratic governance. Caught in the iron grip of state oppression and continuous radicalization at the outer edges of the Islamist spectrum, these movements were either forced out of the official political sphere (Egypt's Muslim Brotherhood) or violently banned and denied the opportunity for any public role (Tunisia's Al Nahda Party). In Morocco and Jordan, where Islamists were partially integrated into the political process, their preoccupation with rhetorically sound though politically unattainable goals – such as the implementation of Islamic law and the Islamization of educational systems – did not help them to overcome general doubts about their real objectives. Instead, their doctrinal purity reinforced the generally negative perceptions of Islamists as traditionalists who showed scant interest in tolerating the diversity of Arab societies or accommodating political pluralism in any serious way.

The Algerian civil war and the Islamist insurgency in Egypt, which erupted in the first half of the 1990s, affirmed this image of the "Islamist threat" and ultimately blurred the distinction between radical and moderate movements and violent and non-violent strategies. By the end of the 1990s, Arab Islamists had failed to alter political realities in their homelands despite considerable popular support. This failure prompted various revisionist trends that gathered momentum in the aftermath of September 11, 2001. Consequently, moderate movements have become increasingly receptive to democratic procedures.

Although moderate Islamists continue to urge the establishment of Islamic states across the region, this has increasingly become a matter of symbolic language and traditional metaphor. These ideals are subordinated in real politics to the priorities of liberal democratic reforms. A new consensus has emerged within movements such as the Jordanian Islamic Action Front (IAF), the Yemeni Reformist Union and the not-yet-legalized Egyptian Center Party (Al Wasat), that the ideals reflected in the utopian Islamic state can best be realized in the contemporary Arab world by each country adhering to the principles of democracy, the rule of law and human rights.

The meaning of democracy and the rule of law within the moderate Islamist spectrum does not differ much from Arab secular views. Universal citizenship, peaceful transfer of power, checks and balances, citizens' participation, neutrality of public authorities in relation to various religious and ethnic identities, and tolerance of diversity are principles that are as well accepted among moderate Islamists as they are in liberal circles. Certainly, Islamists will never use the adjective "secular" to describe the neutrality of public institutions, but they convey identical connotations when they assert the "civility" of the public sphere. Nor should Islamists be expected to drop their rhetorical emphasis that the teachings of Islam should guide all action, because this emphasis maintains the distinctiveness of religion-based political perceptions and sustains to a great extent the popular appeal of the Islamists.

[95]

The embrace of pluralist politics does not mean that moderate Islamists are surrendering their religious legacy and becoming wholeheartedly the new liberals of the Arab world. Rather, the crucial issue is that promoting democratic reform and pragmatism are being added to the existing central components of the Islamist agenda. Recent Islamist rallies in Rabat, Cairo and Amman as well as public opinion surveys indicate that the constituencies of the Islamists are inclined to support this shift.

Furthermore, the new pragmatism of moderate Islamist movements creates an atmosphere of relative openness toward US and European policies in the Arab world and an initial willingness to engage Western countries less ideologically. This change gives the United States and Europe the potential opportunity to reach out to Islamists in the Arab world and develop strategic ties. The possibility of Islamists becoming key players in countries such as Morocco, Egypt, Jordan, and Yemen through processes of substantial political transformation and the ballot box cannot be ruled out.

Any effort to deal objectively with moderate Islamists in the Arab world cannot avoid highlighting the less liberal zones in their positions and practices. Issues such as gender equality, civil and political rights of non-Muslim population groups, religious freedom, and modernization of educational systems have been highlighted as examples of the illiberality of Islamist views. Although there has been some progress in relation to the status of women and non-Muslims in a number of movements, especially in Morocco and Egypt, the majority of moderate Islamists continue to be trapped in discriminatory illiberal stances on vital socio-cultural issues.

These attitudes should not be ignored, but neither should the absence of perfection be the enemy of the good. Democratic developments within the Islamist spectrum will be a long and uneven process. A key step in this process is the inclusion of the Islamists in the political sphere in a way that confronts them with the real challenges of managing contemporary societies and gives them space to experiment in public with different moderate views on socio-cultural issues. Exclusion and repression never lead to sustainable momentum for an embrace of liberal trends. Instead, exclusion and repression push those who are silenced to uncompromisingly reassert their distinct identity by refusing to change.

Moderate Islamists and Arab Political Reform: Assets and Liabilities

Authoritarian regimes such as those that rule in the Arab world would never reform fully or voluntarily. They would have to be pushed by those indigenous actors who enjoy the sustainable support of large segments of the populace. Oppositions that lack wide support cannot prevail because ruling elites can outmaneuver them. Without the formation of far-reaching opposition alliances, autocrats ruling across the Arab world will outlast Western pressures by either inventing a "theater of democratization" based on cosmetic reforms or discrediting US and European calls for democracy as foreign aggression against the national sovereignty of Arab countries. The mobilization of popular domestic opposition is necessary to achieve the political reform that the United States and others now perceive as necessary both for humanitarian reasons and for stemming the sources of terrorism.

It would be convenient if liberal democrats among the Arab intelligentsia could form the vanguard of political reform, but they are too few and too disconnected from their bodies politic to compel resistant autocrats to open the way for representative government. However, there are good reasons for the United States and Europe to support liberal parties and secular non-governmental organizations across the region. Normatively and politically, Arab liberals have embraced the Western political value system of universal citizenship, democracy and the rule of law. Their objectives are identical with Western aspirations for tolerant, pluralist Arab societies. They speak a language that US and European policy and intellectual communities understand and admire. Unfortunately, though, Arab liberals are marginalized back home. Celebrities in the West, Arab liberal actors remain incapable of reaching out to considerable constituencies in their home societies or influencing political developments substantially. With ruling elites determined to preserve their power and liberal democrats too weak to wrest power away, the only way for the United States and Europe to promote democracy in the region is by working with more representative forces on the Arab political scene.

Moderate Islamists are well rooted in the social and cultural fabric of Arab countries. It is precisely because Islamists are popular that ruling regimes seek to repress or contain them. In Morocco, where the Justice and Development Party (PJD) is legal and enjoys parliamentary representation, the government constantly attempts to limit its political participation. Prior to the legislative elections in September 2003, the PJD was forced to reduce the number of its candidates and submit to the dictates of the Ministry of Interior as to which electoral districts it could contest. In October 2004, King Muhammad VI announced new legislative proposals covering political parties. This bill sought to ban religious references in party platforms and expand the power of the executive to dissolve political parties. It was primarily designed to curb the popular PJD and minimize its political influence but the bill was blocked by the Moroccan parliament.

The current relationship between the Jordanian government and the Islamic Action Front (IAF) is similar. In the legislative elections of June 2003, Islamist politicians, facing various governmental restrictions, won about 15 percent of the seats, down from 20 percent in 1993 and 27 percent in 1989. Since September 2004, Jordanian authorities have arrested several IAF members on unspecified charges of threatening national security. A new draft law barring Islamist-dominated professional associations from engaging in politics was approved by the Jordanian cabinet on March 6, 2005.

Even as Morocco and Jordan put authoritarian pressure on legal non-violent Islamist movements, these two states as well as Kuwait and Yemen are positive exceptions in the degree to which they allow Islamists to participate. In Tunisia, President Ben Ali banned the Islamist Awakening Party (Al Nahda) in the first half of the 1990s and forced its leading figures into European exile. In Egypt, the Muslim Brotherhood remains excluded from the political sphere and subjected regularly to acts of repression by the regime of President Hosni Mubarak. Islamist-led initiatives to establish political parties are normally blocked in Egypt's government-controlled Political Parties Affairs Committee.

In spite of their continued containment and exclusion during the past few years, moderate Islamists have not questioned their strategic choice of gradual political reform. On the contrary, they have launched different reform initiatives to increase the momentum for change in the Arab world. On March 3, 2004, in Cairo, the Egyptian Muslim Brotherhood announced its reform plan, which called on the government to rescind the emergency law and other restrictions on political activities and embark on the road to democratization. Although the regime has since ignored the Muslim Brotherhood's initiative, its significant impact has been to position Egypt's Islamists within the emerging reform consensus and among liberal opposition movements and to help bridge the Islamist-secular divide as a prerequisite for forging broad alliances for democracy. Analogous developments can be seen in Jordan and Yemen.

Arab regimes have long invoked the nightmare of anti-Western fanatics gaining power through the ballot box to alarm the United States and Europe into implicitly supporting the repressive measures of these regimes toward Islamist movements. Ben Ali, Mubarak, and other autocrats still play this game to minimize Western pressures on their regimes. However, Arab politics has changed a great deal since the beginning of the 1990s. At present, excluding non-violent Islamists from the political sphere weakens the chances of democratic transformation in the region.

Arab liberals recognize this reality and in the past few years, have been gradually reaching out to moderate Islamists and engaging them in reform campaigns. Secular-religious national alliances for democracy are instrumental in contesting the authoritarian state power and articulating popular consensus over the need for political transformation. Islamists, on their side, have seized the integration opportunity and positioned themselves at the heart of growing opposition movements across the region. In Morocco, Lebanon, and Egypt, differences between liberals and Islamists remain relevant, but the degree of convergence of liberals and Islamists over national priorities is systematically growing. These are steps in the right direction. Democratic opposition platforms are by far more effective with Islamist participation than without it.

Any democratic opening across the Islamist spectrum needs to be promoted and pushed forward via further engagement. Continuous debate about the degree of the Islamists' commitment to democracy and the real intentions behind Islamists' new inclinations, best summarized by the catchy allegation "one man, one vote, one time," are misguided to a large extent. Such debates represent the residual ideology of past decades and ought to be revisited in the light of recent developments.

Without the active participation of moderate Islamists, calls for political transformation in the Arab world are bound to remain whispers among closed communities, irrelevant for the larger social fabric, and harmless to authoritarian regimes. If initiating and managing the first reform steps remain the prerogative of ruling autocrats and require their backing, the degree of the rulers' strategic commitment to democratic change will depend on the existence of sustainable popular opposition alliances. To this end, the contribution of Islamists is indispensable.

The Egyptian Case: Muslim Brotherhood and Political Reform

In 2005, after more than a decade and a half of stagnation, Egyptian politics witnessed two dramatic elections. The first election, held on September 7, was an unprecedented multi-candidate race for the presidency, held pursuant to a May 26 constitutional referendum that had established direct popular election of the President and also set up a Presidential election commission. The second election, spaced over three separate days: November 9, November 20 and December 1, was a regularly scheduled balloting to fill the 444 popularly elected seats of the 454-member People's Assembly, the lower house of Egypt's bicameral parliament. The most remarkable development to come out of this election was the surprising rise to prominence of the still formally banned Muslim Brotherhood (MB), which refused coalition offers from other opposition groupings, ran 144 nominally independent but de facto MB candidates by itself, and won 88 seats—a nearly six-fold increase from the 15 seats that it had controlled when going into the elections, and by far the strongest showing by any Egyptian opposition party in the last half-century.

Each election had its own distinct set of dynamics. Hosni Mubarak, now 77 and President since the 1981 assassination of his predecessor Anwar al-Sadat, held on to his office by winning 88.6 percent of the vote in an election that was non-competitive (despite the ten-candidate field) and whose conduct clearly violated democratic norms. Even accounting for the effect of election-day irregularities, opposition performance was poor. Ayman Noor of the newly formed Ghad (Tomorrow) Party was the runner-up with just 7.6 percent of the vote, while Noman Gomaa, the candidate of the older liberal New Wafd Party (NWP), took just under 3 percent. The remaining candidates, meanwhile, mustered less than 1 percent between the seven of them.

The presidential election showed the limits of regime-led political reforms as well as the marginality of Egypt's non-Islamist opposition. President Mubarak pledged during his campaign that he would introduce substantial reforms that at least touched on most of the major popular demands regarding the political process. He committed himself to replacing the state of emergency with a more specific anti-terrorism law, amending the constitution to limit the powers vested in the presidency, granting more autonomy to the judiciary, putting more oversight capacity in the hands of the legislature, and initiating a new round of national dialogue on reform. As of mid-2006, none of these measures has been implemented.

The secular opposition, meanwhile, watched as all its candidates failed to make much of an impact, and as the voter boycott urged by the Egyptian Movement for Change (Kifaya) and others failed. Turnout on September 7 was estimated to be 23 percent, relatively robust by Egyptian historical standards. While the race represented neither a historic breakthrough, as the government claimed, nor a major shift in the state–society relationship, as the pro-Mubarak and state-run media claimed, it did help to inject a new liveliness into the political scene and somewhat reduced the apathy toward politics that most Egyptians feel. It also normalized the public perception of the presidency by opening it to pluralist contest and by forcing the incumbent President to reach out to citizens during his election campaign.

The parliamentary balloting that began two months later took place amid a sense of urgency among Egypt's diverse opposition groups, ranging from secular leftists to Islamists such as those of the MB. Their decision to participate led to a vibrant election campaign, which however witnessed a higher degree of bias in the state-run media for National Democratic Party (NDP) candidates as compared to the presidential elections. While no one believed that Mubarak's ruling NDP would actually lose its large Assembly majority, the extent of its victory and the size of opposition representation seemed uncertain.

In the event, the NDP wound up with 311 seats (down from 388 in the previous Assembly) after padding its total by persuading winning candidates who had run as independents to join or rejoin its ranks. Moreover, as compared to the presidential election, the NDP had found itself forced to resort more to its traditional mix of violence and manipulation to secure its continued preeminence. In particular, the MB's gains in the first stage of the elections (November 9) resulted in outright regime repression of its candidates and voters. In the end, the regime still wound up facing a large and convincingly popular MB caucus in parliament—in 70 percent of the cases where an MB candidate had squared off against an NDP candidate for the same seat, the MB candidate had won.

The shifts that set the stage for the still-unresolved drama of 2005 did not happen overnight, of course, but have been in motion for some time. In order to understand what has been transpiring in Egypt over the last year or so, a somewhat fuller consideration of the country's recent past will be helpful. For the last decade and indeed the last quarter of the twentieth century, Egypt was—or so the official version would have it— toiling down the road to political democracy and a market-based economy. In reality, however, neither Egypt's soldiers and policemen nor its technocrats favored more than a limited political pluralism. They violently marginalized whatever opposing alternatives—regardless of ideological coloration—seemed as if they might find serious public favor. Such reforms as did take place were minor and marginal. The constitutional and legal system and power relationships remained essentially unchanged and decidedly semi-authoritarian.

The regime resorted to different mechanisms to ensure its dominance over society. The 1971 Constitution vests enormous authority in the president and empowers the executive branch over both the legislative branch and the judiciary. While Article 85 authorizes the People's Assembly to impeach the president by a two-thirds vote, the NDP's continual hold on the legislature has rendered this provision moot. Since 1980, Egypt has had a bicameral parliament chosen through popular elections, but the NDP held almost 90 percent of all seats throughout the 1990s, regularly manipulated elections in its own favor, and kept Mubarak securely at the head of both state and party.

The result of this system was an authoritarianism favoring the intermingling of state and party structures. Opposition political parties, if not co-opted and fully controlled by the authorities, have been highly restricted in their activities. The Emergency Law enacted after Sadat's murder in 1981 and extended several times since then by the People's Assembly) banned parties from holding public meetings without government permission and subjected them to direct supervision by state security forces. Public efforts to criticize the regime or to articulate alternative political views were met with official dismissal as either the chattering of isolated intellectuals or the dangerous work of Islamist "elements" bent on seizing power.

Islamist movements, which probably had the largest constituency among the Egyptian public, were forbidden to organize political wings by the Political Parties Law of 1977, which outlawed parties based on religious or ethnic identities. Thus, the MB has remained banned as a party organization, though its members have been able to run for parliament either in ad hoc alliances with legal parties or as independents. The legal framework regulating non-governmental organizations (NGOs) has remained restrictive, most recently under Law No. 84 of 2002, which reins in the organizational and financial autonomy of civic associations through a series of registration and reporting requirements.

In each of these areas, the 1990s brought little or no improvement. The major legitimizing strategy for the Egyptian model of "democratization" continued to consist of systematically evoking the mantra that economic reforms must come before political reforms, and consistently maintaining that the populace must be "prepared" for democracy before reforms can take place. It was difficult to find much difference between the defenses of restricted pluralism common in the 1970s and 1980s and the approach of the allegedly reform-oriented cabinets of the 1990s. The one-sided emphasis on economic modernization has never wavered. The notion that "Egyptians need bread, not freedom of association" was the credo that the regime used while portraying itself as the legitimate representative of Egyptian society and its "true" needs.

The government's neo-liberal economic policies, however, marginalized large segments of the population. Privatization was posited as the sole key to growth, while issues such as joblessness, poverty, gross disparities in wealth, and the increasing marginalization of the middle classes were not discussed. In the 1990s, according to the UN Development Program's Human Poverty Index, 30.9 percent of Egyptians lived below the poverty line. Under such conditions, the custom of ignoring the social circumstances needed to underpin a market economy eroded the legitimacy and popular support enjoyed by Egyptian governments. The transformation to a socially responsible market economy was just as problematic and ambivalent as the democratization process had been. Since 1976, the state had been retreating from the economic sphere and attempting to consolidate privatization and liberalization. However, aside from the first half of the 1990s, Egypt's economy was deteriorating during this time as inadequate regulation, lack of vision, and divergent perceptions and interests within the ruling elite permitted an "anything goes" form of capitalism to spring up.

In defending its approach in the political, no less than the economic sphere, the regime depended on the notion of Egyptian exceptionalism. Leading regime figures continually mouthed formulas about the "Egyptian way to democratic transformation" in order to paint minor, cosmetic steps as the gradualism needed to introduce democratization to an Arab-Muslim society whose majority does not demand such a thing. Yet a go-slow approach with more slow than go, no clear timetable, and no clear resolve to do things such as to amend the constitution and abolish restrictions on parties remains a corrupt defense of authoritarianism.

In addition to government restrictions, both opposition movements and civil society actors faced various internal dilemmas. Although the party system was fundamentally established and showed a moderate degree of fragmentation, the NDP dominated it with its strong hold over the legislative and executive branches. Even the major opposition parties of the 1990s – the liberal NWP, the leftist Progressive National Unionist Party, and the Arab Nasserist Party – were structurally weak and lacked mass constituencies. Smaller parties made even less difference.

While there were approximately 16,000 registered civic associations, the diversity of vital social interests was still under-represented as the poor, the weak, the marginalized and the rural constituencies remained excluded from the system. In the 1950s and 1960s the state had acted as the major representative of these groups, but with the onset of Sadat's Open Door Policy in 1976, the state retreated from various social spheres with no viable substitutes taking its place. Representation of interests had become a monopoly of powerful political and economic elites—a dangerous situation considering that the exclusion of large segments of the Egyptian population had always resulted in an unstable mix of political apathy, radical ferment and social unrest.

Civil society groups met with both state restrictions and popular distrust. Through an efficient conglomerate of legal and political measures, the state controlled the scope and content of activities performed by civic organizations, which tended to remain focused on cities and the middle class. Opposition parties, NGOs and intellectuals managed to retain their ability to criticize authorities and to keep a small space open for fairly free political discourse. The existence of these critics and this space was what set Egypt somewhat apart from other Middle Eastern authoritarian states in the 1990s.

In contrast to secular NGOs, traditional and modern Islamist networks such as charity organizations and cultural centers were better rooted in the social fabric and thus a greater potential source of social-capital formation than other non-governmental actors could be. In a contrast with the situation in other countries of the region, the political salience of radical Egyptian Islamism declined during the 1990s. The last wave of radical-Islamist violence can be dated to the first half of the 1990s. Government counter-violence and repressive policies destroyed the power base of the radical groups. Later in the 1990s, the rise of questions about the use of violence could be detected among members of radical factions such as Al-Jama'a Al-Islamiyya and Al-Jihad, which contributed to the decrease in religiously motivated attacks. More moderate forces, especially younger members of the MB and the New Wasat (Center) Party, were gaining ground towards the end of the decade. Yet they lacked the legal and institutional tools needed to generate effective political capital.

Moreover, democratic norms and procedures were contested in the Egyptian public sphere and did not enjoy a relatively high degree of acceptance. Thanks in part to the government's persistent misuse of them, concepts such as democracy, good governance, and pluralism evoked at least partial distrust among most Egyptians. Also contributing to this alarming reality were the continuing appeal of religion-based perceptions of society and polity, which ultimately stood for an alternative normative order, and a political culture going back to the 1950s in which habits of fear and submission to the ruler were paramount. A series of polls conducted in the 1990s by, among others, the Al Ahram Center for Political and Strategic Studies in Cairo showed that almost 60 percent of Egyptians viewed democratic norms and procedures as less important than combating poverty, campaigning against corruption, and improving the

[107]

public education system. Egyptians seemed less ready or eager to fight for their democratic rights.

In recent years especially, the NDP government began responding to changing regional conditions and international pressures (primarily from the United States) by initiating cautious reforms. The cabinet was newly formed in July 2004 and contained a significant injection of mid-career technocrats and businessmen, added with a view to the modernization of state structures. This trend was strengthened in the latest cabinet reshuffle in December 2005. The backbone of intra-regime reformism is a class of mostly young professionals, businessmen and university staff members clustered around the President's son Gamal Mubarak.

However, like the rest of the government, this reformist group ignored the consensus, widely held outside official circles, that Egypt's democratic transformation will never have a chance until three conditions are met:

- the constitution is substantially amended beyond the May 2005 adoption of direct presidential election
- the Chief Executive is subjected to term limits and boundaries on executive power
- laws that obstruct freedom of assembly as well as the free functioning of political parties and professional associations are repealed.

Preserving the state's control over society has continued to be the basic priority of the Egyptian regime.

In the context of this stalemate, Mubarak's decision to put the question of direct, multi-candidate presidential elections to the voters came as a revitalizing development. It came amid modest domestic pressures by non-Islamist and Islamist opposition forces, which, inspired by political openings throughout the Arab world, put forward reform demands. Government sources like to point out that the Amendment 76 referendum, which passed with an 83 percent majority, was preceded by a package of political reforms that included the establishment of the National Council for Human Rights and the abrogation of emergency courts. Also, laws pertaining to political rights and participation, and the electoral system were changed in 2005. Thus they project an image of an Egyptian government committed to a gradual democratic transformation that will not disrupt stability or security.

Opposition parties and protest movements such as Kifaya, which appeared on the scene in 2004, have been skeptical. They see another chapter in the Mubarak regime's record of coupling largely cosmetic changes with systematic repression of opposition forces. The opposition points out that the May 2005 amendment will raise considerable barriers to ballot access for independent and opposition presidential candidates, even as it neglects to provide for fully independent electoral supervision, opting instead for a ten-member commission comprising five judges who are presidential appointees and five public figures who are named by the NDP-controlled parliament.

Second, the government has not acceded to opposition demands to lift restrictions on forming political parties and on freedom of assembly. Rather, it has increased its repression of opposition movements, in particular the Muslim Brothers, nearly one thousand of whom were arrested in the first months of 2005, including leadership figures such as the MB spokesman Issam al-Irian. In addition, there were beatings and sexual assaults of activists from Kifaya and other movements on the day of the constitutional referendum.

Despite their doubts and concerns about the NDP regime's sincerity, its violations of democratic standards during the presidential balloting, and its continued repressive bent, oppositionists by and large embraced with gusto the task of campaigning for parliament. There were several reasons for this enthusiasm. First, US pressure for political reform, while viewed skeptically by participants across the political spectrum, was combined with greater international attention and emerging international standards for conducting elections to ensure that the behavior of Egyptian officials would come under far closer scrutiny than before. Second, the regime seemed confused, with the outlines of a succession crisis already beginning to appear. Third, freedom of expression had been expanding since the last elections held in 2000. The regime still showed far less tolerance for free association than it did for free expression, but livelier public discussions led to the perception that political "red lines" in general – always vague and contested – had become cloudier still and might be modified. Fourth, new voices – the boisterous but peaceful Kifaya's most prominent among them – were making themselves heard. The contribution of Kifaya (whose name means "enough" in Arabic) had less to do with its (thin) popular support than with its willingness to push free expression to its limits and to challenge the prevailing, cynical notion that working for political change would be futile. Finally, the squabbling among judges for their shares of election-oversight authority boosted confidence that any electoral manipulation would not go wholly unchallenged.

The sense that change was possible moved opposition groups to do their best to face the regime with a united front. Since the rebirth of multi-partyism in the 1970s, opposition parties had periodically discussed common electoral lists and strategies, but deep ideological and personal divisions always sank such efforts. This time, the net was cast wider. Not only were legal opposition parties included but also the Kifaya movement and respected non-partisan public figures. The National Front for Change and Reform brought together most major secular opposition movements around a detailed program of political reform and an agreement to coordinate campaign efforts. The glaring absence was that of the MB, which shrewdly stayed out and went on to win a number of races by itself, while National Front candidates performed dismally.

This is not to say that the secular opposition tried especially hard to bring the MB on board. At least one leftist leader made clear his deep distrust of the MB. Some liberals and leftists preferred secular semi-authoritarianism to the prospect of Islamist rule. Still others suspected not that the MB was too extreme, but that the authorities would find it all too willing to cut a separate deal while shutting out the rest of the opposition. And all opposition leaders cast a wary eye on the MB's extensive organizational structure and fund of experience. MB leaders returned the distrust, recalling how few secular oppositionists had protested state repression aimed at Brotherhood members, and calculating quite correctly that the narrowly based secular opposition parties had little of electoral value to offer anyway.

Much remains to be seen in terms of how the situation in Egypt will play out. However, the MB's rise to parliamentary prominence is the biggest development so far, and needs to be explained. Three factors appear to be at work. The first is the movement's sheer organizational and political acumen. Most MB voters chose as they did because they saw the movement as a viable political alternative. To be sure, the MB's slogan of "Islam is the solution" and its religious discourse drew voters who want Egyptian society to return to what they see as a truer Islam and a re-Islamized public life. Yet, the MB's appeal comes more from its intensive presence in a variety of social spheres and its ability to base itself on a variety of organizations providing grassroots services.

The MB is connected to a broad social movement, segments of which work in the fields of healthcare, education and poverty alleviation. The gradual and uneven withdrawal of Egyptian state institutions from these areas since the mid-1970s left a vacuum that religious forces have filled using their money, organizational capacities and experience in charitable activities. In the process, new social networks based on trust among citizens have been created. While these networks, both urban and rural, are not driven primarily by political concerns, the MB has nonetheless been able to use them to turn out supporters effectively for demonstrations, professional-association elections and parliamentary campaigns. In a sense, it was precisely the success of such MB mobilization efforts on the three days of the 2005 parliamentary balloting that prompted the government to resort to force and fraud. Yet at the same time, the scale and efficacy of the MB's labors counterbalanced the official repression and manipulation enough to allow the Brotherhood to register its surprising electoral gains.

The second factor explaining the MB's success involves Egypt's other parties. The NDP provoked protest votes, but the remarkable weakness of the country's registered opposition parties drove such votes in the direction of the MB. The opposition parties, from the staunchly leftist and secular National Progressive Unionist (Tajammu) Party to the liberal NWP and Tomorrow Party, lacked an effective presence in Egyptian society. Even those, such as the NWP, that had once shown some organizational capacity had atrophied. Their platforms, campaigns and strategies were poorly developed, and showed few signs of serious planning. Beyond blaming their failure on the limited political pluralism of the last two decades or the regime's containment strategies, fault must also be found with the inner workings of the secular opposition parties themselves. Unless they undertake an honest self-assessment and devote far more attention to internal development, they are destined to disappear.

Without its access to state power, the NDP might well be in the same boat. After the relatively poor showing of its parliamentary candidates in 2000, the ruling party began to talk a reformist game and work on its internal structures, but to no electoral avail. In 2005 as in 2000, the party saw its candidates succeed only about 40 percent of the time and had to patch together a majority by embracing large numbers of "NDP independents" who won election despite the party's refusal to nominate them. More distressing still for the NDP leadership was the dismal performance of their candidates in head-to-head contests with the MB members The NDP – with a corrupt old guard and a bewildered young guard – cannot find widespread public acceptance and must rely on power to prop up its hegemony.

The third factor explaining the MB's strong performance was the unprecedented local and international attention that the 2005 elections drew, and which cramped the NDP's accustomed freedom to rig results. While a more active judiciary, local monitors and independent media could not stop all abuses, they did make possible a marginally more credible election. The NDP's response, particularly on the second and third days of balloting, was to call in the security forces to block voters from the polls. Only through the open use of force and terror in contested districts could the NDP prevent the MB from challenging its two-thirds majority.

Ultimately, nothing could stop the MB from emerging as the only credible opposition to the regime. However, those who voted for MB candidates were not casting mere protest votes. There were, after all, candidates from the Front and the Tomorrow Party (which had stayed out of the Front due to a personality dispute) who might also have drawn protest voters but instead attracted almost no voters at all. The MB's strong showing can be traced to its willingness to spend years creating a nationwide social and political network and the ability of its cadres to cultivate an image of personal rectitude and dedicated service to the public. For the time being, at least, the Egyptian political system is bipolar. For the next few years, the shape of politics and the fate of political reform will be determined in no small part by how the MB uses its position as well as by the relationship that develops between the movement and the regime.

The MB's 2005 campaign platform, in keeping with the movement's rhetoric over the last few years, clearly embraced political reform as a priority. The MB's stated ideas about reform are the same as those advanced by secular oppositionists. All these opposition parties call for an immediate repeal of the emergency law, an end to the limits placed on the formation of parties and civic associations, the abolition of restrictions on political freedoms, stronger guarantees of judicial independence and a more active oversight role for parliament. These steps are aimed at producing a qualitative transformation in the relationship between citizens and the state. Moreover, the MB's vision mirrors that of other opposition groups in framing the steps of political reform in terms of a comprehensive set of constitutional amendments to provide for democratic alternations in power. The MB also demands the protection of public freedoms, including those of belief, opinion and expression.

However, the common reform ground shared by the MB and the secular opposition should not obscure some essential differences between their platforms. Even though the MB has made a strategic decision to stress political reform, it still has a social and cultural agenda that can come into conflict with its liberal political priorities. The MB's election platform is characterized by some notable internal contradictions, some of which are noticeable in its stress on its Islamic *marja'iyya* (source or reference point). The platform states that "the *marja'iyya* upon which we base our program for change is an Islamic one with democratic means in a modern civil state." Elsewhere in the platform the movement calls for "a civil state founded to implement the *shari'a* and govern within the boundaries established by the Islamic religion." The platform does not expand on its conception of an Islamic *marja'iyya* when it treats the issue of political reform, nor does it do so when it discusses the traditional issues stressed by the MB in the 1980s and 1990s, such as the application of *shari'a* and the Islamization of public life. By its use of very broad but seemingly pragmatic terms, the MB's rhetoric provokes some genuine doubts. The question about how much its principle of an Islamic *marja'iyya* remains in conflict with its acknowledgement of the civic nature of the state is a crucial issue and cannot be left to general statements that fail to spell out the details.

The potential for contradiction is strongest when it comes to such matters as the conception of citizenship, the rights of non-Muslim Egyptians, and the degree to which religious concerns can serve as grounds for the restriction of public freedoms. For instance, there are small but significant differences in the various statements made by movement leaders regarding Egypt's Coptic Christian minority. The deputy head of the movement, Muhammad Habib, recently stressed that Copts should have all rights of citizenship except for assuming the position of head of state, whereas 'Abd al-Min'am Abu al-Futuh, another prominent leader, claimed that the movement has no objection to a Copt as President. However, other statements from various election candidates that call on intellectuals and opinion makers to respect the "Islamic feelings" of Egyptians, deepen the doubts regarding the compatibility between the MB's liberal politics and its less liberal cultural and social preferences.

In the face of ambiguous and conflicting statements from the MB, one way to assess its likely course as a political actor is to analyze its recent behavior. The MB is frequently accused of being insincere when it proclaims itself committed to democracy, non-violence, pluralism and election-driven alternations in power. Yet the MB's record in elections to professional associations, club faculties and student unions over the last several decades suggests otherwise. In those cases, MB members honored the results of the balloting whether favorable or not, as long as the electoral process was reasonably clean.

In the last parliament, the small MB bloc (the 17 members elected in 2000 dropped to 15 after the government overturned the election of two deputies) did put forward a series of parliamentary questions and interpellations of ministers that focused on the compatibility of some laws with the Islamic *sharia* as well as a set of moral and cultural issues. Yet the MB deputies also expressed concern about economic and social issues, especially corruption and unemployment. In the last two years, they joined the prevailing trend in giving priority to political reform and to confronting the NDP on questions of political rights, parties, and the manner of choosing the President.

Although the MB made a tactical decision to stay out of the Front, its willingness to entertain seriously the possibility of joining showed a respect for pluralism, which has helped the MB to position itself at the heart of the movement for political reform. Indeed, it defended the rights of its secularist reform allies. In the campaign, the MB was accused of conspiring against non-Islamist candidates in the parliamentary elections, but this charge was an attempt by secular opposition forces to rationalize their failures and avoid facing the fact of their own parlous condition. Although it is true that the MB candidates did seek to assure their own victory, even if it meant defeating other members of the opposition, any criticism of its behavior on this score seems to be based on confusion between politics and philanthropy. The MB did not renounce its gains, but this can hardly serve as a realistic standard of its commitment to democratic principles. The overall picture that emerges is of a movement which can be a force for serious political reform if efforts are made to incorporate it into the political system, but also one whose social and religious agenda continues to raise questions. The impact that the MB will make on the Egyptian political system depends largely on how the regime decides to respond to the movement's electoral performance. In addition, choices made by the MB itself and by external actors can deeply affect the political outcome.

Mubarak and the Muslim Brotherhood: Prospective Scenarios

The Mubarak regime faces now three choices in dealing with the rise of the MB. First, it can try to suppress the movement. Should it choose this path, it would not necessarily have to take the same kinds of extreme measures that the Algerian regime used in the early 1990s. In the Algerian case, the Islamic Salvation Front stood on the brink of a parliamentary majority, while Egypt's MB holds only about a fifth of seats in parliament. Instead of a sudden crackdown, the regime could use

[116]

gradually escalating repressive measures in order to squeeze the MB as quietly as possible. A series of steps to harass the MB – such as those the regime used against it during much of the 1990s – might be capped by a dissolution of parliament. Selective arrests, targeting of activists, exclusion from official institutions, and closures of Islamist institutions could all inhibit the MB's operational capacities. If deftly executed, such a strategy might avoid international criticism and pressure, especially if the regime can exploit the specter of an Islamic takeover. Such an approach might attract support from Copts and secularists who fear the MB more than they resent the regime. However, the strategy could have real costs as well—not only in the form of violence and international opprobrium but also in the return of a political stalemate such as characterized the 1990s.

The second possible scenario for the regime is to accept the new role of the MB in the political space and to accommodate it in somewhat the same way that the Jordanian monarchy has moved to include certain of its own Islamists in selected ministerial posts. This approach might bring the regime the twin benefits of partially co-opting the MB while forcing it to accept a measure of responsibility for how Egypt is governed. This path of outright inclusion is less likely in Cairo than it was in Amman, however, since the Mubarak regime mistrusts Egyptian Islamists more than the Hashemite monarchy mistrusts their Jordanian counterparts. Indeed, portions of the ruling elite fear that the MB will never settle for a mere share of power, but aims instead at total domination.

The third scenario open to the regime is cautious accommodation. This would begin with accepting the current composition of the People's Assembly and searching for common ground with the MB, perhaps by accepting a measure of political reform in return for MB cooperation on issues related to presidential succession. After all, some of Mubarak's advisors and a few others within the NDP see the moderation and pragmatism of the movement, especially its restrained tone in addressing leading officials, as attributes that might be encouraged if the movement becomes accommodated as a loyal opposition group with a significant but contained parliamentary role. This scenario offers the most promising possibilities for transcending the current polarization of the Egyptian political system by means of introducing genuine political reform.

The MB also has different options in this new political landscape. Should it choose to continue in its flexible and pragmatic approach, avoiding direct threats to the regime or any words or actions that would tend to deepen fears among the opposition or segments of the broader population, especially the Coptic and business communities, it would help foster a political environment capable of integrating it as a legitimate political actor. This option would require a continued use of moderate rhetoric toward the regime and a strategy of self-restraint such as the MB displayed when it put up candidates for only about one third of the seats in the parliament. Nor can the MB abandon its partial alliances with other opposition forces in support of political reform.

This option, if reciprocated by a regime engaging in cautious accommodation, might entail the eventual formal legalization of a political party for the MB in the context of rather broad understandings between the regime and the movement. Given the MB's new status as the dominant opposition bloc and the conviction of some of its leaders that they have successfully challenged the regime in the parliamentary elections, the movement might be tempted to press for immediate political gains, primarily legalization as a political party. If the MB pursues this path in a confrontational way – by mobilizing its supporters and attempting to intimidate rather than negotiate with the regime – polarization will increase. One of the major implications of this scenario would be that other opposition actors, though extremely weakened, would move away from the MB and possibly join regime voices in calling on the state authority to eliminate or control the movement, which would make it easier for the regime to follow a gentler version of the Algerian path.

In contrast, if President Mubarak were to instruct his government and the NDP to open discussions on his reform promises with the MB and other opposition forces in the new People's Assembly and to articulate specific timelines for their implementation, the dramatic events of last year might one day been viewed as the start of a new stage of political change in Egypt.

6

Causes of Terrorism in the Arab World and Ways to Counter it

H.E. Dr. Mohammed Bin Ali Kouman

This chapter seeks to address a number of issues pertaining to terrorism such as the definition of terrorism, the difference between terrorism and resistance, the causes for the spread of terrorism in the Arab world and the ways to counter it.

The Definition of Terrorism

The definition of terrorism at the international level poses great difficulty owing to the lack of consensus on what constitutes terrorism and what amounts to legitimate resistance. The political orientations of countries and their position towards the struggle against occupation constitute a stumbling block to an internationally acceptable definition of terrorism.

One acceptable definition of terrorism is stipulated by the Arab Convention for the Suppression of Terrorism, which was signed in Cairo by the Arab Interior Ministers Council and the Arab Justice Ministers Council in April 1998. Article 1 of this Convention defined terrorism as follows:

> Any act or threat of violence, whatever its motives or purposes, that occurs in the advancement of an individual or collective criminal agenda and seeking to sow panic among people, causing fear by harming them, or placing their lives, liberty or security in danger, or seeking to cause damage to the environment or to public or private installations or property or to occupying or seizing them, or seeking to jeopardize national resources.[1]

This definition coincides with the *Shari'a* definition of terrorism as included in the decision of the Islamic Jurisprudence Council of the Muslim World League in its sixteenth session, held from 5–11 January, 2002. The gathering defined terrorism from the *Shari'a* perspective, as including all acts of aggression unjustly committed by individuals, groups or states against human beings, including attacks on their religion, life, intellect, property or honor. The definition includes "any act of violence or threat…designed to terrorize people or endanger their lives or security" as well as "damaging the environment and public or private facilities and endangering natural resources," and also covers actions such as waging war, murder and banditry.[2]

The Arab Convention for the Suppression of Terrorism clearly distinguishes between terrorism and the struggle to resist occupation. Article 2 (a) stipulates:

> All cases of struggle by whatever means, including armed struggle, against foreign occupation and aggression for liberation and self-determination, in accordance with the principles of international law, shall not be regarded as an offence. This provision shall not apply to any act prejudicing the territorial integrity of any Arab State.[3]

A clear criterion that distinguishes terrorism from resistance is the nature of the goal each seeks to achieve. Resistance intends to liberate land whereas terrorism seeks to achieve political agendas by evoking terror and creating turmoil and chaos. It must be reiterated that targeting innocent civilians and terrorizing society under any circumstance, is not condoned by the revealed religions or international charters.

Terrorism is not restricted to the Arab world because terrorist acts cover all the countries of the world. Until very recently, the Italian Red Brigades, the Spanish separatist organization ETA, the Irish Republican Army (IRA) and others used to capture the attention of the global media and public opinion. Why has attention been focused solely on what is termed by some western circles as "Islamic terrorism"?

[122]

In my view, there are four reasons for this particular focus. First, there is an actual increase in terrorist acts occurring in the Arab and Islamic worlds. Second, most perpetrators of these terrorist acts justify their heinous deeds by claiming alleged religious or nationalist motivations. Third, the western perspective confuses terrorism and legitimate resistance and labels the struggle against occupation as terrorism. Fourth, the Arab world commands international attention for several reasons, the most important being that the region contains much of the world's oil and gas reserves.

Causes of Terrorism in the Arab World

In my view, the exacerbation of terrorism in the Arab region has stemmed from several causes—political, economic, religious, civilizational, social and psychological. These causes will be dealt with at length in the subsequent sections.

Political Causes

There are several political causes behind the emergence of terrorism in the Arab world. The first cause is embedded in the political goals that the terrorists seek to realize through their acts. These goals involve the pursuit of power by creating a sense of state failure, evoking unrest in order to control national efforts in confronting this unrest, which diverts significant resources away from development programs. Such a situation can reduce government popularity and reveal its shortcomings in terms of increasing security and providing prosperity for citizens besides creating circumstances that necessitate measures to tighten security and hence limit personal freedoms.

Terrorism is also associated with the focal points of tension in the Arab world, which stem from occupation. The Israeli occupation of Arab territories with the blessing of some western countries indirectly breeds terrorist acts that are radically different from the legitimate resistance to

[123]

this occupation carried out for instance, by the Palestinian people and the resistance forces in southern Lebanon. The term "terrorism" here refers to those acts committed to confront Israeli occupation and which extend to western interests in Arab countries and lead to killing innocent citizens or subjects of some western countries. Both religious duty and international customary law require protecting the latter. Undoubtedly, a just settlement of the Palestinian issue and abandoning double standards in dealing with it would greatly reduce acts of violence in the Arab world.

Moreover, one cause for growing violence in the Arab world is the contradiction between the sublime principles underlying international law and the practices of the international order, when it manipulates these principles on occasion, or even negates them by giving precedence to the political and economic interests of major powers. This situation leads to the escalation of violence by stirring up feelings of political injustice in some people. This feeling is confirmed by the UN failure to solve international conflicts peacefully and to apply the criteria of international legitimacy justly and universally. Such failure is evident in the so-called "war on terrorism" that has deviated from the realm of law to that of politics and from the field of security cooperation to that of deploying military force.

Finally, there is a political cause of a historical nature pertaining to the Afghan-Arabs. These are Arab citizens who volunteered to fight on the side of Afghan fighters to liberate Afghanistan from the Soviet occupation. Many of them returned to their original countries after the Soviet troops withdrew from Afghanistan possessed by the mentality of war. This makes them an easy prey to any one who tries to direct their energies towards acts of violence.

Religious Causes

The religious causes of violence arise from the fact that many terrorist theoreticians confuse terrorism with *Jihad* because they misinterpret the verses of the Holy Quran. For instance, they view "terrorism" as a *Shari'a* duty since the Holy Quran has ordered Muslims to prepare their might to threaten the enemy of Allah and their own enemy as in the verse:

> And make ready against them all you can of power including steeds of war (tanks, planes, missiles, artillery, etc.) to threaten the enemy of Allah and your enemy, and others beside whom you may not know but whom Allah does know, And whatever you shall spend in the Cause of Allah shall be repaid unto you, and you shall not be treated unjustly.[4]

This interpretation is mistaken because the idiomatic meaning of terrorism today has no relationship with *Jihad or* terrorizing the enemy. Rather, it is spreading terror and panic among people, destroying public installations and exposing a nation's resources to danger. Hence it is akin to acts of war against the state and spreading of corruption on earth. Both these are condemned by Islam, which severely punishes those who engage in them. Allah has specified heavy punishments for those who wage war against the state, highway robbers and those who spread corruption on earth. The Holy Quran states:

> The Recompense of those who wage war against Allah and his Messenger and do mischief in the land is only that they shall be killed or crucified or their hands and their feet be cut off on opposite sides, or be exiled from the land. This is their disgrace in this world, and great torment is theirs in the Hereafter.[5]

This is the current understanding on the phenomenon of terrorism because it is tantamount to waging war against the state and spreading corruption on earth and reputed scholars have concurred with this. The Council of Senior Ulema in the Kingdom of Saudi Arabia gave their authorization to Fatwa No. 148 in 1988 under the title, "A Statement on the Punishment of One Who Engages in Sabotage Acts." The statement imposes the death penalty, if in accordance with the rules of *Shari'a*:

> Anyone is proved to have carried out acts of sabotage and corruption on earth, which undermines security, by aggression against persons and private or public property, such as the destruction of houses, mosques, schools, hospitals, factories, bridges, ammunition dumps, water storage tanks, resources of the treasury such as oil pipelines, the hijacking or blowing up of airplanes, and so on.

[125]

The punishment for those who carry out acts of sabotage and corruption is death because the above mentioned verses tell us that such corruption requires spilling the blood of the corrupter. The danger posed and the harm caused by those who commit acts of sabotage exceeds that of highway robbers who assault people, kill them and take their money. Allah has sentenced them in accordance with what is mentioned in *Al Haraba* verse (waging war against Allah and the state)[6]

The above-mentioned confusion also stems from a failure in the religious education imparted within the culture of fanatic groups and their followers. A statistical survey carried out on some such groups in one Arab country demonstrated that only a small minority of group members is affiliated to universities that teach religious sciences while the vast majority is enrolled in general universities for their higher education.[7]

Also, this confusion in interpretation is attributed to a juristic failure among most theoreticians of terrorist acts even if they follow a culture derived from *Shari'a*. This failure is embodied in the absence of an important branch of Islamic jurisprudence—that relating to state politics and the questions of authority and Imamate, the relations of Islamic countries with others, and the approach in dealing with non-Muslim communities. Unfortunately, this branch of the *Shari'a* has not received the same kind of attention given to the jurisprudence of worshipping rituals, transactions and *Hodoud* [the penal code of *Shari'a*]. In my view, the most important source from which to infer the appropriate path to follow is the history of the first Islamic state, which was keen on signing and respecting peace treaties, taking care of non-Muslim communities and respecting their rights, as well as preserving peace and uprooting the causes of unrest and *Fitnahs* [a heretical uprising in Islamic usage, and a 'trial' or 'test' in Arabic].

Other religious causes of the phenomenon of terrorism include excessiveness and extremism, whether in terms of creed or jurisprudence. Many perpetrators of terrorist acts do not accept the views of other Islamic

[126]

groups and do not acknowledge independent juristic opinions approved by other doctrinal schools. A glaring example can be found in those who are obsessed with apostasy, and level this charge against anyone whose behavior differs from their own, or who interprets sources of legislation in a manner inconsistent with their own preferences. It is well known that independent juristic opinions guarantee the constant renewal of Islam and its suitability for all milieus and times. God has pronounced that disagreement among religious scholars shall be a source of clemency for Muslims because this gives effect to the freedom of choice that distinguishes Islam.

Civilizational Causes

Arab-Islamic civilization is confronting a relentless campaign waged by certain western quarters that are subservient to Israeli politics and Zionist lobbies. This campaign takes several forms such as accusing Arab and Islamic civilization of failure and resistance to modernity, denigrating Arab-Islamic culture using several labels: the culture of violence, backwardness and inability to cope with the age.

What is really unfortunate is that terrorists contribute directly to kindling the western campaign against Arabs and Muslims, by abusing their own religion through their criminal acts, thus causing wide segments of western public opinion to confuse Islam with terrorism in their minds. Regrettably, this western campaign deliberately desecrated religious sanctity as evidenced by the publication of offensive caricatures of the Prophet (PBUH). Hence it was to be expected that Muslim reactions to such provocations would be violent.

Economic Causes

Terrorism is also rooted in economic causes represented by poverty and unemployment, which generate a feeling of being deprived of a dignified lifestyle. Specialized studies have strongly linked poverty and unemployment with the commission of crime. It is now clear that most cases of aberrant behavior punishable by law involve individuals at the very bottom of the social ladder. These include the truly impoverished individuals, with low educational and economic levels and living standards.[8] Several field studies on the link between unemployment and crime in the Arab world have shown a direct connection between greater levels of unemployment and high crime rates.[9] Studies conducted on a sample group of criminals have concluded that 21 percent were unemployed. It should be noted that the average level of unemployed persons in the Arab world is about 20 percent and this proportion is concentrated mainly in the 15–29 age group.[10]

It is ironic that the same terrorists who hold their governments responsible for economic crises carry out criminal acts that serve to undermine the economies of their countries by shattering the confidence of foreign investors who cannot risk investing in unstable environments. They also do so by targeting vital economic sectors that rely on sustained security and stability for their success. This includes the tourism sector, which represents an important sector of the national economy in many Arab countries. It may be recalled here that criminal acts have targeted foreign tourists in a number of Arab countries.

Socio-Psychological Causes

The socio-psychological causes of terrorism are represented by the lack of proper social adjustment whether in the family or other institutions of society. It is well known that family upbringing has a significant role in forming personality and determining psychological tendencies. There are several indicators that link response to terrorism to certain psycho-social factors. One of these is the age group, which constitutes a crucial factor for terrorist organizations. Studies have shown that the great majority of persons committed to extremist Islamic groups, like the *Jamaat al-Islamiyya* in Egypt, belong to the category of young people between 18 and 37 years.[11] This is attributed to the youthful, teenage phase characterized by rebellious attitudes against society and the tendency to reject prevailing values.

Another indicator is the social circle from which most terrorists originate. Studies have shown that "the majority of arrested terrorists, prior to joining their terrorist groups, had spent most of their lives in highly deprived and impoverished areas."[12] Another indicator is the fact that terrorists generally belong to low vocational circles such as making handicrafts and practicing traditional arts. Moreover, terrorism is linked to urban migration and the fact that most terrorists hail from shanty towns bred by migration to cities.

As for the psychological determinants of terrorist inclinations, they are linked to a number of psychological deviations primarily represented by frustration, a sense of loss, an identity crisis, superiority complex or persecution complex. One study has pinpointed the main psycho-social causes of the phenomenon of terrorism as follows: [13]

- *The educational flaw:* The most important aspects are bad role models in educational institutions, cultural chaos in society, individual misjudgment of mental and personal capabilities, the inability of society to respond to the needs of young people, and rapid social changes.
- *Lack of family harmony*: Aspects of familial disintegration include weak parental control over children, abuse of personal freedom, faulty social adjustment and lack of confidence in others.
- *Rejection trends among the young:* These are represented by the desire to rebel against authority, feelings of frustration, the inability to adjust to reality, the urge to show off and an aspiration to be different from others.
- *Psychological problems:* These relate particularly to those experienced by young people.

- *Conventional social problems:* These include generational differences of opinion between fathers and sons as well as ignorance and illiteracy.

The same study has demonstrated that young people are exposed to contradictory cultural currents and unstable educational values and attitudinal criteria at the individual, family and societal levels. This is accompanied by political and economic developments that breed an atmosphere of uncertainty, which cannot be tolerated by these young people, who eventually surrender, withdraw or become extremists.

In my view, these are the most important causes that lead to terrorism in the Arab world. However, there is another factor that helps to spread terrorism although it is not a direct cause: namely, media coverage of terrorist operations and the platforms provided by the media, especially television channels, for advocates of violence and extremism. Such media coverage can encourage weak-willed people to commit terrorist acts just to gain media attention.

However, the greatest danger from media coverage is allowing terrorists to achieve their basic goal—attracting attention to their so-called cause and spreading terror on a wide scale. It is well known that spreading terror and panic is the first objective of the terrorists and the intention to terrorize and intimidate is the major motivation behind terrorist acts.

Having pinpointed the most important causes of the phenomenon of terrorism in the Arab world, it is necessary to examine this phenomenon, which is extraneous to Arab culture and traditions and very far removed from the tenets of the gracious Islamic religion—the faith that preaches temperance and moderation, urges tolerance and rejects violence and terrorism.

Measures to Counter Terrorism in the Arab World

It would be a truism to say that terrorism, with its offshoots, manifold aspects and various causative factors, requires a multi-pronged treatment and comprehensive approach—to deal with the political, religious, economic and social circumstances underlying the phenomenon. In this approach, the efforts of several government and non-governmental bodies must converge. These include civil society organizations and institutions and the citizens themselves, who constitute the primary target of terrorist operations. The confrontation with terrorism is divided into two aspects— a security confrontation and a non-security confrontation.

The Security Confrontation of Terrorism

At the outset, it is necessary to outline briefly what has been done in the context of the Arab Interior Ministers Council, in the field of Arab security cooperation in tackling terrorism. The Council accorded intense and incessant attention to confronting terrorism in all its forms. This confrontation has been divided into two parts: on the one hand, combating terrorist acts, tracking down their perpetrators and bringing them to justice, and on the other hand, preventing terrorism by raising security awareness through campaigns that employ all available methods, particularly television.

Countering Terrorism

Arab cooperation in fighting against terrorism has led to several steps being taken in different spheres, which include the following:

1-General Politics

Measures undertaken in the sphere of general politics includes strategies, plans and agreements as follows:

CODE OF CONDUCT FOR MEMBER STATES ON COUNTER-TERRORISM

This code was approved by the Arab Interior Ministers Council in 1996. In accordance with this code, Member states adopted a number of charters pertaining to cooperation in combating terrorism, pledging to deny any kind of support to terrorists and also to prevent their territories from being used as a launch-pad for terrorist acts.

ARAB COUNTER-TERRORISM STRATEGY AND ITS PLANNED STAGES

This strategy was adopted by the Council in 1997. It included a group of constituents, whose aim is to coordinate the counter-terrorism efforts in Arab countries and promote cooperation with international organizations and agencies concerned with this issue. The implementation of these strategies is carried out through planned stages, each lasting three years. The Council approved the first in 1998 and is currently working on completing the programs intended for the third stage, due to end in 2006. Each plan consists of a series of programs, the implementation of which is entrusted to the Secretariat General (the administrative and technical apparatus of the council) and the Naif University for Security Sciences (its scientific apparatus).

ARAB CONVENTION FOR THE SUPPRESSION OF TERRORISM

This Convention was signed at a joint meeting of the Councils of Arab Interior Ministers and Arab Justice Ministers in Cairo in 1998 in accordance with a desire by Arab countries to promote cooperation in counter-terrorism. A joint ministerial committee set down the necessary procedures and executive models of the Convention in 2000. The Arab Bureau of Criminal Police, which is affiliated to the Secretariat General of the Arab Interior Ministers Council, was given the task of following up the implementation of the Convention by Arab countries and preparing an annual report on this matter to be submitted to the ordinary session of each council. The Bureau was assigned to follow up the procedures and executive models of the member states. In the light of security developments, the two Councils were keen on developing the Convention and its executive procedures and in 2003 the Convention was amended in order to criminalize the lauding of terrorism, the raising of funds under the guise of charity organizations or similar methods of support. In 2005 the executive models and procedures of the Convention were developed after being tested over five years from early 2001.

GUIDING STATUTES IN THE FIELD OF COUNTER-TERRORISM

The Arab Interior Ministers Council was keen to provide guiding legal frameworks for consultation by Arab countries while enacting or amending legislations intended to counter terrorism. With this in mind it approved two model statutes in 2002 pertaining to counter-terrorism: the Arab Model Law for Counter-Terrorism and the Arab Model Law for Arms, Ammunitions, Explosives and Dangerous Materials. On the other hand, the Council took great care to compile the counter-terrorism legislations in Arab countries and to apply them generally for common benefit. In this context, two compilations were published: the collection of laws in operation for counter-terrorism in Arab countries and the collection of Arab mutual and multilateral agreements signed in the sphere of counter-terrorism.

MODEL PLANS FOR DEALING WITH TERRORIST ACTS

The Secretariat General has prepared a set of model plans to deal with terrorism in its different forms. These have been applied generally in the member states for their benefit. They include:

- Two model plans to deal with terrorist acts (2000), the first focusing on legal aspects and the second concentrating on practical field aspects.
- A model plan to deal with the hijacking of airplanes and free hostages (2001)
- A model plan to conduct raids against organized criminal gangs (2001).
- A model plan to deal with terrorist acts on means of transport (2002).

[133]

- A model plan to protect public installations against rioting (2002).
- An Arab security plan to tackle terrorist acts on steamers and ships (2003).

2-Conferences and Meetings

Under the aegis of the Secretariat General of the Arab Interior Ministers Council, an annual conference for counter-terrorism officials in Arab countries has been convened since 1998. These conferences, of which the eighth was held in 2005, provide a forum for Arab counter-terrorism officials to exchange experiences and expertise. They also provide an opportunity to study the different aspects of this phenomenon and propose suitable solutions.

Concern over terrorism is not only confined to the annual conference of the counter-terrorism officials. Terrorism issues are discussed in other conferences convened by the Secretariat General, especially the annual session of the Arab Interior Ministers Council, the annual conference of Arab Police and Security Commanders, as well as the annual meeting of the Commission on Novel Crimes, which is formed every year by a number of specialists to study new crimes and propose suitable solutions. In the context of this Commission, the issue of terrorism has been discussed in several aspects, such as the rehabilitation of misguided persons and those involved in terrorist acts.

3-Research, Studies and Publications

The Arab Interior Ministers Council has commissioned a number of research studies and diverse publications on counter-terrorism. These include, "Mechanisms for Dismantling Terrorist Cells," "The Role of Youth Institutions in Resisting Terrorism," "Information Terrorism and Techniques to Counter it," "Discovering Sources of Financing for Terrorist Operations and the Means to Counter Them," "Links Between

[134]

Terrorism and Organized Crime," and "Managing a Security Crisis in Tackling a Terrorist Operation," in addition to a quarterly report on terrorist crimes committed in Arab countries.

4-Procedural Aspects

The Secretariat General, through its specialized Arab Criminal Police Bureau and in coordination and cooperation with the relevant authorities in Arab countries, undertakes a number of measures and arrangements necessary to track down terrorists and follow up and monitor their movements. These include:

- Enhancing cooperation between member states to prevent and counter terrorism, especially by exchange of information on the activities and crimes of terrorist groups, their leaders and elements, main locations, means of funding, weapons, ammunitions and explosives. They also consider common issues, coordinating plans for tackling terrorist acts and techniques to develop cooperation in these matters.
- Activating cooperation between Arab countries in searching for, investigating and arresting persons who have committed terrorist crimes and are on the run.
- Promoting coordination between Arab countries in exchanging visits, sharing experience and information on terrorism issues.
- Receiving and circulating requests for initiating and halting search operations and dealing with requests relating to fugitives who are accused or convicted of terrorist crimes.
- Establishing a database in the Arab Criminal Police Bureau on the phenomenon of terrorism in all its forms and types, as well as providing Arab security services with available information and continuously updating this database to keep pace with new developments in this field.

- Collecting and analyzing information and data on terrorist groups and acts, successful experiences in confronting them, monitoring new counter-terrorism techniques, and providing specialized agencies in member states with all this information.
- Issuing blacklists of plotters and perpetrators of terrorist acts and updating them periodically in coordination with the relevant authorities in the member states.
- Forming subordinate anti-terrorism task forces comprising geographically neighboring member states in order to enhance procedures for Arab cooperation in counter-terrorism operations.
- Organizing and encouraging the exchange of scientific and technological expertise and experience; conducting educational and training programs in dealing with and confronting terrorist groups; ensuring the security and protection of land, air and sea transport; and implementing security procedures in ports, airports, railway stations and public venues.
- Encouraging the exchange of research studies analyzing terrorism, recording its development and monitoring its activities, proposing suitable solutions as well as preventive measures and circulating these studies to member states for their benefit.

5-Reinforcement of Arab Security Capabilities

The Naif Arab University for Security Sciences in Riyadh holds training sessions, scientific symposiums, cultural lectures and specialized exhibitions to promote the competencies and capabilities of Arab security services in countering terrorism. The most important achievements in this field are briefly summarized below:

- *Training Sessions:* The University has organized a number of training sessions for the benefit of Arab security services involved in counter-terrorism. These sessions included training in negotiating techniques with hostage-takers and hijackers, ensuring the safety of civil aviation against terrorist operations, carrying out laboratory analysis of bomb residue and debris, dealing with explosives and booby traps and learning ways to defuse them.

- *Scientific Symposiums and Seminars*: The University organized a number of scientific symposiums and seminars. The most important of these focused on laws to combat terrorism in the Arab world, exchange information on combating trans-border terrorism through Arab and international covenants, terrorism and human rights and other matters.

- *Cultural Lectures*: Specialists at the University delivered nine lectures in foreign countries to depict the true picture of Islam and Pan-Arabism and reveal how they condemn violence. They also held nine lectures in Arab countries on the phenomenon of terrorism, its dangers, causative factors and ways to counter it.

All these important measures undertaken by the Arab Interior Ministers Council indicate how it is countering terrorism. However, the Council, based on its conviction that the security confrontation alone is insufficient to eradicate terrorism and in accordance with the principle that prevention is better than cure, pays great attention to preventing terrorist crimes and works on raising awareness regarding their dangers and eliminating its root causes.

Prevention of Terrorism

Preventive measures against terrorism comprise several dimensions, the most important of which is heightened awareness. Realizing this goal involves information security and strengthens the relationships between the security services and the media to protect society against all forms and types of crimes.

[137]

The Council's move to enlist the media in countering terrorism stems from the appreciation of its important role in influencing public opinion and the recognition of the societal benefits to be gained from raising awareness through the media about the dangers of crime in general and terrorism in particular.

Measures taken in this regard are based on the information security policy drawn up by the Arab Information Strategy for Security Awareness and Prevention of Crime, which was approved by the Council in 1996. In the context of this and the Arab strategy for countering terrorism, the following measures have been undertaken:

1-Media Awareness Campaigns: Under the guidance of the Secretariat General of the Council, media awareness campaigns have been formulated and circulated for the benefit of member states. These include:

- An awareness plan to highlight the basic concepts of Islam and correct the misleading concepts marketed by advocates of violence and extremism (1992).
- An Arab model plan for raising security awareness and preventing crime (1998).
- A universal Arab model plan to make Arab citizens aware of the dangers of terrorism and building up their resistance through spiritual, moral and educational values (1999).
- A universal model media plan to make Arab citizens aware of the dangers of terrorism (2000).

2-Producing Awareness-Raising Films: In the context of the Arab Information Security Office, which is affiliated to the Secretariat General, films that warn against the dangers of terrorism and urge citizens to cooperate with the security services to counter it, have been produced as follows:

- An awareness film on terrorist crimes and their dangerous impact on the security and stability of the Arab world (1998).
- An awareness film on the dangerous impact of terrorist crimes on Arab security and stability and encouraging different individuals to cooperate with the police against terrorism (1999).
- A film raising the awareness of citizens regarding the importance of their role and the scope of their responsibility in confronting terrorism and acts of violence.
- A film encouraging citizens to support the efforts of security services in confronting terrorism (2004).

3-Issuing communiqués: No session of the Arab Interior Ministers Council has been held without a communiqué stating the position of the Council on terrorism. This position condemns all terrorist acts, regardless of their causes and motives, whether committed by individuals, groups or countries and rejects the commission of such acts under cover of religion. This attitude distinguishes between terrorism and the legitimate struggle of nations for liberation and for resisting aggression. These communiqués, which are transmitted via different media, help to raise awareness of the dangers of terrorism and counter the allegations made by advocates of terrorism.

The Council is eager to promote cooperation and coordination with different kinds of media to guarantee wide dissemination about the dangers of terrorism and create an Arab public opinion that remains aware of this phenomenon, its dimensions and its negative repercussions for the Arab world, and is not swayed by the false claims made by advocates of terrorism. In this connection, the joint meeting of the Councils of Arab Interior Ministers and Arab Ministers of Information was held and constructive coordination has been established between the Secretariat General of the Council and the business and communication sector in the

Arab League, as well as the Arab States Broadcasting Union. The objective of this coordination is to prevent the media from being used as platforms to promote feelings of hatred and envy or thoughts of violence and extremism. Based on this, the Secretariat General prepared a mechanism of cooperation between security services and the media in 2004 in order to prevent terrorist organizations and elements from employing the media to spread their extremist ideology.

The security battle against terrorism in the Arab world has been fruitful as a number of terrorist networks and cells have been dismantled, several terrorist plots have failed and many terrorists have been brought to justice owing to the positive cooperation between countries through the Arab Interior Ministers Council and the interest of Arab countries to give all misguided persons the chance to repent and withdraw from terrorist acts, provided that all counter-terrorism measures take place within the framework of the law and full respect for human rights.

However, regardless of the need for the security confrontation and the capabilities made available, this approach alone cannot conclusively eradicate terrorism. The efforts of several authorities must converge to confront this phenomenon at the religious, political, economic and social levels.

Non-Security Confrontation with Terrorism

The first field of non-security confrontation with terrorism must be that of religious thought where the claims made by advocates of terrorist acts are refuted and the falsehood of their religious standpoints that seek to justify their criminal acts is demonstrated. The responsibility for this falls on the shoulders of Muslim scholars as the heirs of the prophets and the custodians of the *Shari'ah*. Allah has authorized them to deliver the message of Islam and sincerity is a religious duty. According to the proper collection of *Hadith* by Muslim:

[140]

Abu Ruqaiya Tamim bin Awas ad-Dari (May Allah be pleased with him) related that the Holy Prophet (PBUH) said:
"Religion is sincerity."
We submitted, "Oh Prophet of Allah! For whom?"
He said, "Sincerity to Allah, His Book, His Messenger and for the Imams and general Muslims.[14]

Hence these scholars are required to express the correct teachings of Islam, especially with regard to its freedom of choice as a religion, its moderation and rejection of violence, fanaticism and extremism, as well as the tolerance and mercifulness of Islam and its dedication to the protection of the human soul—with its illegal extermination being regarded by Allah as an extermination of all humanity, whereas its rescue according to Allah is like imparting life to all humanity.

The heavy responsibility of national scholars becomes even more critical because most deluded terrorists believe strongly that by committing their crimes they are seeking to please Allah and serve His cause and they invoke Allah's blessings, convinced of the legitimacy of their acts. In the face of this reality, security measures serve no useful purpose because those suffering from such delusions are ready to die for their beliefs.

In the political sphere, attention must be paid to democracy in the Arab world from a religious and social perspective, and solutions must be found to the current focal points of tension in the Arab world. Moreover, Arab efforts must be intensified to hold an international counter-terrorism conference and find an international definition of terrorism that distinguishes it from genuine acts of resistance to occupation and aggression.

It is necessary to bridge the gaps between the Arab-Islamic civilization and other civilizations. Such bridging can be done through constructive dialogue, adherence to the values of tolerance and condemnation of violence, hatred and envy to project a clear picture of this civilization to global public opinion and to demonstrate its beliefs to all humanity. No doubt this will help to clear up the confusion existing in some minds between terrorism and Islam.

In the economic sphere, attention must be paid to enhancing development and providing job opportunities to the greatest possible number of citizens, employing degree holders, eliminating financial corruption, and creating development projects in villages and rural areas since this will limit migration to cities and its attendant security problems.

On the social and psychological side, more efforts are required to reinforce sound social adjustment, promote family welfare, fight negative social phenomena such as addiction to alcohol and drugs[15] and take care of weaker social classes, develop more impoverished regions and provide social and psychological services to all segments of society.

The success of these efforts is only possible through a principled media that gives priority to national interests and the coming generation rather than to scoops and public attraction. Such a media will carefully find the way to cover terrorist acts without compromising press freedom which is sacrosanct and cannot be treated with indifference. The media must not allow advocates of terrorism to use media channels to disseminate ideas of violence, extremism and hatred and must give prominence to scholars with vision who seek to promote morality and national good.

Structural Transformations in Arab Countries: Growing Legitimacy of the State and the Shrinking Role of Governments

Dr. Ahmed Jameel 'Azm

There is a common assumption among some Arab intellectuals that there has been no real reform in the Arab world and that such reform requires particular structural transformations. In fact, the very presence or absence of reform is a controversial issue. In my view it is too early to say whether or not real reform is evolving in the region. Nevertheless, it is necessary to consider the fact that there are actual transformations taking place in the Arab world, which amount to a level of structural change that cannot be overlooked. In this chapter, the focus is on four major transformations that have created actual change irrespective of whether or not these lead to real reform in the ultimate analysis.

The first three transformations have occurred in the spheres of economics, Islamic movements, information and communications. All these spheres help in the transformation to a more liberal society where individual freedoms and roles are promoted. The fourth transformation points towards a different direction and threatens to abort the first three by thrusting the region into internal struggle and conflict. This transformation involves the dangerous escalation of sectarian tension within the region.

Before discussing these transformations, it is worth noting that reform processes in general and studies on this subject have greatly restricted the use of analytical material to transformations and changes taking place at higher political levels (or what is called "high politics"), such as elections, major state institutions and political authority. However, there are other levels and spheres, which are not any less important and deserve in-depth analysis. For instance, despite several studies on the impact of the media and the spread of satellite and information technology on Arab society, these have focused mainly on the news channels, specifically Al-Jazeera and subsequently Al-Arabiya. In my view, there is a need for a more comprehensive and general interpretation of the different kinds of channels and for research into the economic, psychological and social impact of media factors on a broader scale.

Therefore, in order to understand the direction and extent of the societal transformations taking place, it is necessary to examine certain aspects of socio-political life that may be termed *soft politics*. This term denotes issues that seem directly unrelated to political authority and distribution of power, but have a considerable impact on transforming society.

Economic Transformations in Arab Countries

The first sphere to consider is that of economic transformations in the region, which can change much of the realities of socio-political life, specifically the trend towards privatization, permitting foreign direct investment, allowing property ownership by citizens and foreign investors in spheres which, until recently, remained a monopoly of governments and state investment institutions or available only to the citizens of the state concerned.

Such transformations lead us to the concept of theoreticians and thinkers such as Francis Fukuyama who maintains that "the state in a liberal democratic system is by necessity a weak state; preserving the rights of the individual means by necessity reducing its authority."[1] While it may be too early to speak of liberal Arab democratic states, it is possible, in the light of the following examples, to speak of growing individual rights and the relative shrinking of state authority.

In late 2005 and the beginning of 2006, subscription in the Gulf to company shares recorded extremely telling phenomena. One is represented by the large numbers of GCC citizens who moved from one country to the other to respond to public share offers and the related interactions and controversy. The UAE witnessed this in the initial public offering (IPO) of the Dana Gas Company in October 2005 and the scenario was repeated in Qatar in the case of the Al Rayan Bank IPO in January 2006.

In the case of Dana Gas, for instance, company sources have confirmed that the public offering attracted 288 billion dirhams whereas the amount required was less than 2.1 billion dirhams. In other words, the offering was covered 138 times! The subscribers numbered 413,000 while 398,000 citizens from the GCC states attempted to subscribe to the offering. Some 56 percent of the subscribers were citizens of GCC states other than the UAE.[2]

In fact the phenomena that accompanied the public subscription are perhaps more significant than the actual figures. The UAE's land and air entry points witnessed an influx of thousands of Gulf citizens, especially from Saudi Arabia, who sought to subscribe to the company's share offer. All seats on incoming flights from Saudi Arabia were booked. Crossing points at the land border were congested in an unprecedented manner. Many of the visitors who came as potential subscribers were unable to find rooms in the crowded hotels. Despite extensive prior preparations by the banks assigned to handle the process, confusion prevailed due to the unexpectedly high number of subscribers.[3] It may be noted that the news of this subscription stirred much public discussion and interaction among citizens of the six GCC states, who participated in the offer.

Another indicative phenomenon is represented by the proceedings of the annual general meetings (AGM) of major companies. One instance is Emaar, the UAE-based public joint stock company, whose shareholders number between 40,000–50,000 persons. It is considered the largest real estate company in the world, with a market value that exceeds 146.9 billion dirhams (according to the 2005 year-end data). In March 2006, its AGM took place. The Chairman of the company, Mohammad Ali Alabbar, was involved in a heated discussion on company policies that lasted two and a half hours. Although the 33 percent stake owned by the government of Dubai determined the final voting in the session, it was described by the UAE's *Al-Ittihad* newspaper as the "mother of annual general meetings" for the discussion it raised regarding the basis for profit distribution and other issues concerning the company's future. Voting on some issues was repeated more than once amid demands by some shareholders to exclude the Dubai government from the right to vote. Such interactions indicate changes in the economic structure and the related network of social and political relations and reveal the growing role of individuals within the Gulf states.

It must be admitted that economic transformations have not occurred in a parallel way in all the Arab countries, since the Gulf states are witnessing faster transformations than the others. Generally speaking, this trend enables them to lead transformations in the Arab world. One of the indicators of accelerated change in the Arab Gulf states is their economic growth. Experts estimate that if the current rates of growth continue, the GCC states with its population of 90 million persons, will collectively become the sixth largest economy in the world by 2025.[4]

For Arab countries outside the Gulf region, the withdrawal of subsidies for major goods and petrol derivatives, cessation of free education and subsidies for education in the majority of these countries, and privatization moves are all matters that constitute a structural transformation, which embodies the collapse of the *rentier* state concept.

[146]

The expansion of the private sector, especially privatization based on the general contribution of the citizens of different states has ushered individuals into different economic sectors and gave them control, authority and roles in the administration of companies and their boards of directors. Such roles are relevant and significant with respect to the scope of state power and the extent of its jurisdiction. As the Arab state shifts, albeit slightly, towards being more liberal, with political authority playing a lesser role and civil society assuming a greater one, this will have an impact on employment policies and job opportunities and subsequently affect the relationship between the government and the citizen.

Such a trend is evidenced in Jordan by the Executive Privatization Commission (EPC), which acts on the following presumption:

> ...privatization redefines the roles of both the public and private sectors because the government reduces its role in the direct activities of production and focuses on its main agendas relating to organization, legislation and controlling and providing social services.[5]

In the UAE, H.H. General Sheikh Mohammed bin Zayed Al Nahyan, the Crown Prince of Abu Dhabi and Deputy Supreme Commander of the UAE Armed Forces, has stated as follows:

> The program of privatizing companies and factories has for its point of departure a clear vision that asserts the need to distribute wealth through a wider ownership base and the participation of the private sector in joint ventures along with the public sector. This vision has helped to bring about substantive changes in the march of development and is expected to accomplish even more in the future.[6]

A similar view has also been expressed by Hussain Al Nowais, Chairman and Managing Director of Emirates Holdings and Member of the Abu Dhabi Council for Economic Development. He admits that the role of the private sector in public projects in the Emirate of Abu Dhabi is still limited, the reason being is that its "capabilities are still modest compared to the private sector in the world." However, he states that Abu Dhabi is currently undergoing a process of restructuring, which might take up to 25 years.

> What is occurring today in the process of building up the economy sketches the final features of the future role of the government, making it legislative and supervisory while assigning the task of implementation to the private sector. [7]

It is noteworthy that as privatization grows, opportunities expand for communication between companies and the business sector, without government involvement and this illustrates the scope of the corporate role in integrating the region with economic globalization. For instance, in early 2006, the World Bank announced changes in its Arabian Gulf policies with a view to enhancing its relationship with the private sector. These policy changes were indicated by Mahdi Al-Jazzaf, the Managing Director of the World Bank in the Middle East region when he announced that the bank had allocated $300 million for loans to companies operating in the GCC states.[8]

The transformations occurring in the region – related to issues of wealth distribution, control over the economy and building and reconstruction projects – have profound implications insofar as the interests of citizens are concerned. These implications can be summarized as follows:

- The private sector has become a point of entry allowing individuals to participate in decision-making and has ended state control over economic decisions and wealth monopoly. This in turn means that the economic role of individuals has expanded and subsequently, their political and social roles have also been enhanced. It reflects the fact that the state is gravitating towards some measure of liberalism where the role of governments has been reduced while that of the individual has grown. Successively, the traditional structures of authority and society are giving way to new structures based on wealth, achievement and individual endeavor.

- Private sector and investment opportunities have both become avenues that help to integrate and activate citizens of different countries. This

[148]

has created a bond based on economy and investment. Despite its economic nature, this link also guarantees socio-cultural interaction. This means that what official regional institutions have failed to achieve – whether at the Arab level as represented by the Arab League and its agencies or at the Gulf level as represented by the GCC – has been achieved when the private sector and individual investors have been given opportunities. There is integration and economic overlapping between the GCC states through their citizenry and stock markets.

- Past and present interactions and difficulties encountered in trans-border processes involving small scale investment – as mentioned earlier – led many ordinary individuals to discuss trans-border issues such as travel procedures across different countries, the basics of currency exchange between one state and the other, the conditions for investment and the obstacles to its liberalization. Consequently, the discussion of such issues has been transferred from Arab/Gulf summits, their institutions and bureaucratic circles to popular circles. In other words, the dream of unity, which was expressed earlier through high sounding ideological slogans, is now expressed more quietly, without much ideology and slogans.

Islamic Movements and Groups

A second variable worthy of consideration involves changes in the realities affecting civil society. It is related specifically to the role of Islamic movements in this society. In the beginning, there was a general tendency within and beyond the Arab world to divide Islamic Movements into two major types—violent groups and non-violent political groups. There are several indicators that non-violent groups generally gravitate towards becoming part of the process of "building legitimacy" in the Arab countries although they might adopt some slogan that trancends their

[149]

national borders—for example, their quest to found a super state in the form of a Caliphate or a greater Islamic state.

These groups do not adopt a practical program against the legitimacy of present structures and their projects revolve within the framework of existing states. Thus, groups (such as the Muslim Brotherhood) differ from terrorist organizations (such as Al Qaeda) and from other non-violent organizations (such as the Islamic Liberation Party). The latter organizations have in common a "project" that goes beyond current states and political structures. Therefore, Islamic movements can be divided into first, non-violent movements working within the legitimacy of the existing state, and second, other violent and non-violent movements working towards the destruction of existing institutions of society and state and the creation of new ones.

Theoretically, in terms of texts and slogans, there is no difference between the ultimate goals of the two sides of the Islamic movements, insofar as founding the unified Islamic state or the Caliphate, and they both "offer a program for society and humanity because *Jahiliyah* (ignorance or barbarism in Islamic tradition) pervades the world, including Islamic societies."[9] However, political groups that participate in elections are placed in a different category by Manuel Castells in his book *The Power of Identity*, in which he discusses the term "identity of the project." According to Castells, this identity denotes that of the state and society and is based on the concept of civil society, which in turn is based on finding a group of organizations, institutions and social forces that generate an identity acceptable to the whole group. Sometimes, this occurs with some degree of struggle and conflict. At times, it may also involve a change in the nature of the force controlling the group or state and lead to a rotation of power. All this is conditional upon the fact that civil society continues to act within its own general framework as well as the framework of state identity.

Civil society is conducive to some kind of continuity and communication between the societal institutions and state authority in a relationship that centers round an identity whose most important constituents are citizenship, democracy, politicizing social change and restricting the use of force to the state and its affiliates. There must not be a quest to disintegrate or divide the state or integrate it with a wider surrounding universe.[10] It is increasingly clear that an important segment of Islamic movements is committed to such a quest. This does not negate the fact that more time is needed for the full maturity of the transformation and more conditions are needed to guarantee that there will be no relapse that hinders total transformation.

In fact, the difference in means between all the violent fundamentalist groups and the Islamic movement groups is one of the most important reasons for their parting company. The difference in means often leads to a different development from the viewpoint of the state, its institutions and methodology of governance. The following points reinforce the assumption that political Islamic groups are actually moving towards becoming a part of the process of building a civil society that strengthens the existing legitimacy of different countries and their identities.

Distinction from Terrorism

Many theoreticians and representatives of what was termed "Islamic awakening" in the 1970s and the 1980s felt they must acknowledge the gravity of not rejecting violent or what is called *jihadistic* (derived from the term *jihad*, meaning "struggle" or "battle") interpretations of Islam. Consequently, they chose, or were forced to side with the existing social and political system and rejected violence as a means of change. In other words, they accepted a commitment to respect the boundaries of law in their quest for change and thus became a part of the process of building civil society, which is an aspect of reform, thereby rehabilitating the state and developing its special identity.

In the Kingdom of Saudi Arabia, for instance, Sheikh Salman Al 'Ouda, one of the most popular preachers in the country, has adopted a discourse condemning *"jihadistic"* interpretations of Islam. Through his weekly program *Al Hayat Kalima* (Life is a Word), on the MBC channel, he provides a varied discourse that touches on daily issues, such as the issue of beauty. This broadcast has stirred criticism of Al 'Ouda among conservative Saudi circles. The cause of Al 'Ouda's transformation is unclear: "whether it is because of his own detention, the suicidal tendencies of the jihadists, the 9/11 attacks or the more liberal attitude adopted by Abdullah, then Crown Prince well before he came to the throne."[11]

In his turn, Sheikh Abdul Mohsin al-'Obeikan, one of the "traditionalist" Saudi Sheikhs, admitted some mistakes had been committed in the 1990s, specifically the attitude taken towards enlisting the support of foreign troops to expel Saddam Hussein's troops from Kuwait. He announced his readiness to engage in debates with Osama bin Laden and terrorist group theoreticians such as Abu Muhammad al-Maqdisi and any person who defends the thinking of Al Qaeda or seeks to justify it.[12]

One cannot be absolutely certain that the parting of ways between Islamic political groups and the methodology of violence is total and absolute. This possibility has been expressed in a study published by the Carnegie Endowment for International Peace. The study observes that "most of the region's electorally-oriented major Islamic movements have never been involved in violent political activities or have repudiated them if they were." However, this does not negate the fear of small groups affiliated to primary Islamic movements getting involved in such acts. Also, the demarcation between resistance and terrorism in the thinking of these groups stirs questions and ambiguity.[13]

[152]

The death of Abu Musab al-Zarqawi, the leader of the *jihad* base in Iraq, proved to be a real test to the Muslim Brotherhood in Jordan insofar as its attitude towards violence is concerned. Four representatives of the Islamic Action Front (the political wing of the Brotherhood) offered their condolences on the occasion of the death of Al-Zarqawi, with one of them, Mohammad Abu Faris, describing him as a martyr and *Mujahid* (a Muslim waging war to spread Islam). This elicited a furious reaction from a segment of the Jordanian public as well as the government, and these four representatives were arrested.[14]

This visit stirred real anxieties about the credibility of the orientation of the Jordanian Muslim Brotherhood, which is embodied in condemning violence, especially since it is one of the Islamic movements that is more moderate and favored because it has maintained good relations with Jordan's governing system since its foundation almost 80 years ago.

The action against the four representatives by the Jordanian government might have been prompted by political expediency, as claimed by the Muslim Brotherhood. However, the visit reflects the lack of a firm and clear attitude towards terrorism. Nevertheless, it is difficult to consider the visit an expression of a strategic attitude of the Islamic group. If the reactions of other leaders of the group are considered, there is near consensus that the visit was a mistake, and that the methods of Al-Zarqawi were worthy of condemnation. However, there is also a rejection of any condemnation against the four representatives. This is evidenced by the statement of 'Azzam al-Hunaidi, head of the parliamentary bloc of the Islamic Action Front in the Jordanian parliament, in which he said that what Abu Faris had said "is personal and relates only to him." He went on to add:

> I say that Abu Musab al-Zarqawi went the wrong way, first by targeting civilians, and second, by adhering to the notion of charging others with apostasy. We do not approve of this. We have rejected this in the strongest terms and condemned the criminal terrorist operations in Jordan and the targeting of civilians. This is our standpoint, attitude and strategy.[15]

It transpires that while there are several signs of transformation in the Islamic movements towards commitment to democracy, there are justifiable fears of the existence of pockets within these movements that might adopt attitudes serving violence and terrorism in one form or another.

Engaging in the Political Process

With the exception of the Algerian experience which began in the early 1990s, the participation of Islamists in a number of democratic experiences in countries such as Kuwait, Egypt, Jordan and even Lebanon, signals their integration with social institutions and their willingness to engage in the political process even though matters are not always in favor of these movements. Sometimes laws are compromised and acts of violence are committed against the supporters of these movements in order to constrain them and reduce their influence. Instances include the "one man, one vote" system in Jordan and the phenomenon of *"baltaja"* (riotous acts) in Egypt where violence was used by supporters of the ruling party against supporters of the Muslim Brotherhood. Also, hundreds of supporters of the latter were arrested during the legislative elections conducted in 2005.

If the Turkish model is a progressive one as a pattern of Islamic secularism, other models support the theory of democratic transformation in the thinking of Islamic movements. In Egypt, the leadership of the Muslim Brotherhood, during the last legislative elections, confirmed that its famous slogan "Islam is the solution" is a mobilization slogan intended to polarize voters. Although this assertion is neither clear nor convincing, it reflects a readiness to admit the general nature of the slogan and the need to spell out detailed social programs. The confirmation by the leaders of the Muslim Brotherhood including Issam al-Irian, aimed at reassuring the Copts about the Brotherhood's commitment to the principle of "citizenship"[16] is another sign of a change in the practices of the Islamic movement. Moreover, after the relatively high number of seats won by the Brotherhood, Al-Irian stated that the movement seeks "a democratic, parliamentary republic" and supports "freedom of expression."

The American researcher Bruce Rutherford notes in the Egyptian context, that the Muslim Brotherhood in the aforementioned election campaign focused on matters of daily life such as public services, education, corruption and the accountability of the government.[17] Even in Palestine, where it is logical for resistance slogans to dominate the political discourse, it was the developmental and reformist discourse that was prominent in the poll campaign of the Islamic Resistance Movement (Hamas) for the Legislative Council elections held in January 2006.

In reality, the Turkish model itself has started to find increasing acceptance among Islamic movements. For instance, Ali Sadreddin el Bayanoni, the "General Guide" of the Syrian opposition Muslim Brotherhood, said that his movement "considers itself moderate and closer to the ruling Justice and Development Party in Turkey, and that it will not seek to impose *Sharī'ah* (Islamic laws) in Syria." [18]

Transformation into Islamic Liberalism

Recently, the terms "liberalism" and "liberals" have gained significance in a number of Arab countries, but in different contexts. In the Kingdom of Saudi Arabia, for instance, the terms still trigger reservation and controversy. Hence many people are keen on identifying themselves as "Muslims and liberals."[19] The reality is that instances of linking liberalism to Islam and reviewing antipathy to secularism are growing.

The secularism intended in the Islamic context is summarized in the separation between religious institutions and the state (and not necessarily between religion and life), confirming respect for the rotation of power, accepting the majority view and abandoning the imposition of many

Sharī'ah rules pertaining to personal freedoms, whether by violence or the force of law.

The separation between religious institutions and the state is the rectification of a historical mistake. When Islamists defined secularism as the separation of religion from life, they were confusing the religious institution with religion itself. The former comprises persons, groups and institutions, which are prone to both right and wrong. The latter is not coercive, belongs to all and is subject to different interpretations. In addition, they were confusing the political institution with life in general.

Actually issues such as rotation of power and acceptance of the majority view have been subject to a lengthy discussion among Islamists. The failure of Islamic movements to attain power and the repeated accusations on the part of elites and governments that if Islamists attain power they would turn their backs on democracy prompted some reviews. These included reviewing the concepts of violence, the *Jahiliyah* of society, governance, pluralism, and democracy. Sheikh Rachid Ghannouchi, leader of the Tunisian *Al-Nahda* (Renaissance) movement, says in his book *Al Huriyaat al 'Ama fi al Dawla al Islamiya* (Public Freedoms in the Islamic State):

> Rejecting democracy, despite its shortcomings, might be a kind of a leap
> into the unknown and a free service to dictatorship, the greatest enemy of
> the nation and the formidable obstacle on the road to its prosperity.[20]

In this context, Turki Ali al-Rab'iu observes in the *Al Hayat* newspaper as follows:

> Despite all the shortcomings of democracy…as conceived of in the Islamic
> discourse, the acceptance of it has become a reality and a methodology for
> many parties, especially the Muslim Brotherhood, which has engaged in
> the game of democracy before the others, and the political sphere in
> general which has to be founded on political pluralism, based in its turn on
> citizenship and equality.[21]

Pluralism now reaches other levels of thought and opinion. In Egypt, for example, a religious leader from the Muslim Brotherhood's Guidance

Bureau visited Nagib Mahfouz and condoned the republishing of his novel *Children of Gebelawi*, which had been banned in the country nearly half a century ago on religious grounds. Here there are two facts to ponder. First, the republication of the novel was permitted. Second, there was no protest by the persons and groups who generally file lawsuits and move the media to prevent the production of films and artistic works. These facts show that an important wing of the Islamic movement has been convinced of the need for dialogue and acceptance of other views. The late novelist Mahfouz had stipulated that in order to approve the republication of the novel, the introduction must be written by an Islamic leader. The introduction written by the prominent Islamist Kamal Abu Al Majed covers important points although it was first written and published in the form of an article in 1994. The introduction reconciles itself with the novelist's view as follows:

> The controversial character in the novel (Gebelawi), whom many thought was meant by the writer to symbolize "Allah" is not so. It symbolizes religion and the final conclusion of the novel is that science as embodied in the character of "'Arafa," who was followed by many, is no substitute for religion.[22]

At first glance, this interpretation seems to favor religion but the introduction implicitly makes it a subject of discussion and admits that there is some measure of deviation in the practices and acts of exploitation carried out in the name of religion. What is more important is the agreement to make religious phenomenon subject to discussion and human interpretation.

In addition, Islamists have accepted that some issues pertaining to personal freedoms will not be imposed, whether by coercion, democratic compulsion or the force of law. Notwithstanding the Turkish experience, which many might believe unsuitable for standardization and generalization, there is also the Jordanian experience. For instance, Ishaq Al Farhan, the former Secretary General of the Islamic Action Front in

Jordan, occupied high political and academic positions whether as a Minister of Education or President of the University of Jordan, the largest university in the country. However, he did not attempt to impose the rules of Muslim Brotherhood on these institutions. This applies also to the participation of the party in the government in the early 1990s. Though some trends indicated that the Islamic perspective was being applied, this aspect remained limited. The Brotherhood, which for a long time urged a ban on co-education in universities, resorted to the same when its leaders founded the Zarqa Private University in Jordan.

In Kuwait, the National Assembly decided by a majority to grant women their political rights to vote and nominate themselves to the Assembly. Islamists across the spectrum had to accept this as a *fait accompli* and abide by the opinion of the majority. This happened after some measure of controversy and protracted rivalry that involved public rallies in the street, using different competitive techniques and political protests such as *fatwas* (formal legal opinion), political maneuvers, holding forums and mobilizing demonstrations.

In the Palestinian case, after winning the majority in the Legislative Council in January 2006, Hamas leaders confirmed that they would not resort to issues such as imposing the *hijab* (veil) and banning alcohol by the force of law. Maryam Salih, a Hamas representative, said that the group "will not force women to wear *hijab*, and will not oppose women working." She stated that "there is no system of radical religious governance in Islam" and that the "Hamas movement wants a civil state whose laws are derived from its primary source, *Sharī'ah*."[23]

Though debates are still taking place within the Islamic movement and there is a tug-of-war between different trends in the movement, there is a strong faction within the movement that calls for a radical review of its thought. Perhaps the following comments from Ibrahim Gharaiba, the journalist and researcher who is closely associated with the Islamic

Movement in Jordan, express how far the movement might go if the domestic transformation reaches its full flow. He observes as follows:

> Generally, the Islamic Movement will change into parties closer to secularism. The state of 'Islamism' might end because it will be common to most people, represent a public base of all societies and therefore not distinguish any particular movement or group. The basis for forming parties and groups, and the differences between them, will be the programs pertaining to people's needs, taxes, freedoms and resources, and choosing between these groups and parties will be done on the basis of their detailed programs, and not their ideas and general ideologies.[24]

Gharaiba might appear to have a Utopian vision but it is based on premises and events which reinforce its probability as a scenario. In the light of the tensions and dilemmas that emerged in the experience of the Brotherhood, specifically in the Jordanian case, but which might also be true of other cases, Gharaiba observes as follows:

> It would have been better (and still there is a chance to reconsider) if the Brotherhood had given its members and supporters the freedom to join all political parties and had not committed itself to joining with any particular party. This way it would have activated political life generally and could also be a partner of all political currents and parties in the country, thus enriching electoral competition in parliamentary and municipal elections and subjecting it to social and public monitoring and accountability.[25]

Distinction between Political Islamic Movements

There is a distinction between political Islamic movements, even those affiliated to the Muslim Brotherhood in different countries, based on the differences in the political interests and realities in each country. For instance, the Iraqi Islamic Party (which is closer to the Muslim Brotherhood) engaged in the political and electoral process whereas most Islamic movements outside Iraq opposed such engagement while still under occupation.

On the other hand, political Islamic groups within the same country exhibit differences. In Sudan, for instance, animosity abounded between the wing led by Hassan al Turabi (the Popular National Congress, PNC) and factions in the ruling party. The gravity of these divisions is revealed in the exchange of criticisms between the factions. Such criticisms undermine the sanctity of the viewpoints expressed by the leaders of Islamic movements and differentiate their views from the rules of the *Sharī'ah*. Such criticism encourages these Islamic leaders to engage in the political process and enhances the aforementioned separation between religion and religious institutions on the one hand and between religious and political institutions on the other.

Finally, it must be remembered that one reason for the ascendancy of "religious fundamentalism" in the Middle East is the failure of the nation-state model, which was formed in the wake of World War I, in achieving modernity, economic development and equal distribution of the fruits of economic growth among the people.[26] This is in addition to the failure in meeting external challenges, the foremost being the Israeli occupation of Arab territories and the subsequent turning of millions of Palestinians into refugees.

More precisely, the current fundamentalism in the Middle East is the outcome of a particular paradigm of modernity followed by Arab countries in the 1950s and 1960s. It produced classes of educated people and led to migration from rural to urban areas, creating intellectuals, employees and educated people who later changed their focus and formed the base of Islamic movements. This shift occurred when economic modernization projects failed in the 1970s and 1980s, since the economy of the Arab world failed to keep pace with the requirements of global competition and the technological revolution that followed. Highly educated elites created by the first modernization wave were angered when their expectations remained unfulfilled, the economy began to falter, and new forms of cultural subordination started to appear. People who migrated from rural areas to the cities joined these elites because developmental imbalances weakened the agricultural sector.[27]

Of course, these movements were also reinforced by the failure to meet the Israeli challenge, the spread of corruption, restriction of freedoms, and imbalance in education systems. If real economic reforms are realized and the Islamists become part of the reform process, this will compel them to face the responsibilities of administration, governance and reform and cause them to veer away from fervent discourse in favor of rationality and realism. They will assume positions of responsibility and accountability and hence become more engaged in civil society.

The foregoing analysis does not mean that Islamic movements have been totally transformed to become a part of the modern state. To know the direction of events, it is necessary to monitor the performance of several actors: the Islamic groups, the ruling regimes, the international forces that observe elections and monitor reforms in the region, and the progress made in settling regional issues, especially that of Palestine and Iraq.

The Media in the Arab World

The development of the media via satellite channels and the emergence of a parallel media represented by the Internet are among most important features of the current wave of globalization. Perhaps the media and their affiliates in the Arab world have a deeper effect than in many other regions of the world. In 2005, the number of Arab satellite channels was estimated at 50 satellite channels.[28] Based on 2004 year-end data, Dubai Media City alone hosted about 80 different satellite channels with more than half of these being Arab channels.[29] This new media scene has generated several regional effects, the most important of which may be discussed below.

Common Arab Issues

In their bid to attract the greatest number of viewers, Arab satellite channels have to address issues that command the attention of Arabic-speaking people around the world. By virtue of technological development, the targeted audience constitutes tens of millions and hence the need arises to raise common issues affecting all. Naturally, in the initial stage, issues that unite this audience were chosen. Unification against the "other" was the most significant common issue. Therefore, the Palestinian question, followed by the Iraqi issue, proved to be the best subjects to attract the greatest number of viewers.

If the political content manifested common issues, the program content for the common Arab audience went beyond politics to include art, song and even quiz programs. For instance, song programs or talent-spotting programs for the young have now become generally Arab in character, after initially being country-specific. One cannot separate the political and cultural facets of programs such as "Superstar" in Future TV and "Star Academy" in the LBC and similar programs. Market considerations imposed multiple nationalities on the participants in order to attract the greatest number of viewers and voters and hence achieve larger financial returns. In addition, these programs made participants formulate their aspirations within an Arabic framework, and consequently created a common sphere of thought and interaction. In one form or another, this might reflect a move closer to the concept of a common Arab sphere of daily life, which serves to further Arab bonds. Yet, it could also mean that the individual's concerns and daily activities are no longer linked to governments nor do they necessarily occur within national borders.

The Role of the Private Sector

The development of satellite broadcasting and its huge potential enabled the private sector to emerge as a dominant player by establishing private sector-affiliated Arab channels that form a major component of the Arab media. This move has weakened the grip of state authority over the Arab media. It has become obvious that many Arab governments have been compelled to exercise greater openness with regard to the media. Controlling what the citizen can and cannot know has become virtually impossible. What the local media fails to convey is revealed by the satellite channel being broadcast from a neighboring country, or the newspaper published on the Internet. There is now greater openness to the world and the press in general. All this has constituted a driving force for reform, manifested in different forms, including the abolition of the Ministry of Information in several Arab countries.

This change caught the attention of French journalist Alain Gresh, Editor of *Le Monde Diplomatique*, who compared his visit to the Kingdom of Saudi Arabia in 2002 and his visit a few years later, in 2006. He makes the following observation:

> A few years later, journalists enjoy much greater freedom to travel across the country and meet anyone they wish, even intellectuals the authorities have forbidden to speak to the press.

It may be noted that for several years the Saudi newspapers have been regularly presenting social problems such as unemployment, poverty, drugs, and others.[30]

This openness will entail repercussions, including the fact that there is now greater courage to adopt a critical social discourse. Any person advocating change can find different platforms to deliver his message. Relevant instances include the novel *Banat al Riyadh* (The Girls of Riyadh), which was a bestseller among Arabic books in 2005 and was reprinted more than once. The novelist, Rajaa al Sanea, found a publisher in London. She was warmly welcomed by television stations outside the Kingdom of Saudi Arabia and was also introduced to the Saudi public and the Arab public in general. Her novel recorded the highest circulation in Saudi Arabia although not formally approved by the official "censor" in the Kingdom. What is more, the novel treats a subject regarded as 'taboo' in Saudi society—love and human relationships between the two sexes.

[163]

The foregoing developments indicate the vitality created by the media and the atmosphere of political openness, which leads ultimately to a kind of social liberalism. This is quite different from a conservative, strict atmosphere where the margin of expression and movement is limited, not only for political reasons but also due to social considerations.

Therefore, it may be said that the Arab media has weakened the authority of governments, created a sphere for common interaction, and helped to promote trans-national political and cultural ties and build solidarity for national issues such as Palestine and Iraq. All this has not been accomplished through any action program calling for consolidated political unity. In other words, the new media has helped to reinforce the diverse identities of the different Arab countries rather than try to create a single state with a composite identity.

The Growth of Sectarianism

While many factors have contributed to bringing countries closer to liberalism and encouraged the emergence of a civil society, there are many obstacles along this path—the most important being the danger of sectarian divisiveness. The sectarian problem in several Arab countries is not a new subject but one that has historical roots. The examination of these roots is beyond the scope of this chapter. However, there are two new factors that have served to further escalate sectarian tension in the region.

The first factor is the sectarian dynamics in Iraq that permitted the issue of sect to become a major pillar of political life in Iraq. This fact helps to transfer sectarianism to neighboring countries. One of the known and established rules in the literature of conflict management is that sectarian conflicts in one country can cause groups in other countries to adopt extremist claims. The extent of sectarian polarization in a country, or the success of a particular sect in one country may increase the level of polarization in other countries and encourage ethnic or sectarian groups in other countries to show support for those sects. They may try to adopt the same methods and pursue similar gains, or lift historical injustice, or drive sects, minorities or ethnic groups benefiting from the status quo to adopt precautionary policies to stop sectarian convulsion from spreading to their sphere. Sometimes this happens in a negative way in the form of tense and spasmodic reactions leading to the escalation of sectarian conflict. Also, sectarian conflict in a country may revitalize historical and religious issues that highlight the sectarian issue generally in social, economic and political activity.[31]

The second factor that has currently caused an escalation in sectarian issues is the increasing level of foreign intervention in internal Arab affairs. In the post 9/11 period, issues relating to religious and sectarian freedoms and human rights have become matters of concern to the major powers, especially the United States more than ever before. This external effect takes two forms: the first is the push exerted by internal groups that are propelled by external support, or at least the perception of it, that renders the group more capable of disrupting the old balance of power and raising issues and claims that were not possible earlier. The second effect, in contrast to the first, is the perception by particular sectarian groups, of being targeted by major external powers or being vulnerable because the new configuration of international interests has deprived them of the protective shield provided earlier by certain major powers.

Sectarian unrest is evident in more than one Arab country, from Egypt through Lebanon (especially after the withdrawal of the Syrian troops), to the Gulf Arab states, particularly the Shiite issue in the Kingdom of Bahrain, the State of Kuwait and the Kingdom of Saudi Arabia. There are many instances of escalating sectarian tension in these countries.

In the Bahrain and Kuwait the press on different occasions expressed official worries regarding the relations between Shiites in these countries and Iran. In Kuwait, news circulated about meetings that Shiite leaders held in April 2004 with Iranian embassy officials. The Kuwaiti press published articles criticizing Iran for these meetings. Against the backdrop of these meetings, Sheikh Sabah al Ahmed, the then Kuwaiti Prime Minister, met Shiite representatives and leaders in May 2005 and confirmed that Shiite problems would be solved and dealt with in accordance with legal frameworks. He clarified that Kuwait had never known any distinction between Sunnis and Shiites throughout its history.[32]

However, on more than one occasion, Sheikh Sabah repeatedly voiced his fears over the repercussions of sectarian violence in Iraq on the neighboring countries. In May 2004 he warned against attempts to stir civil strife between the Sunni majority and Shiite minority in Kuwait. He stated as follows:

> We have noticed that aspects of civil strife have become evident after events occurred in Iraq. Our geographical location is sensitive and we must be always cautious...If sectarianism is ignited, it will first burn the one who has ignited it and then burn everybody else.[33]

Some observers think that the government has "punished" Shiites for the meetings with the Iranians by refraining from appointing a Shiite minister in the government after the resignation of Mohammad Abu Al Hassan, the Minister of Information, in December 2004. Shiite personalities responded by holding a meeting to discuss this matter in November 2005 and Deputy Yusuf al Zalzala observed to journalists that "some groups of Kuwaiti society have been excluded from many leading positions."[34] The sectarian factor has become more prominent in Kuwaiti political life, in the municipal and parliamentary elections and within the National Assembly itself. For instance, in some cases of interpellation in the Assembly, the sectarian loyalty of ministers being subjected to interpellation and the representatives requesting it are linked.[35] He stated on more than one occasion that Shiites in Kuwait intend to form a special political bloc of their own.[36]

In Bahrain there is comparatively more tension than in Kuwait. There are permanent differences over issues like "naturalization." A stormy

[166]

session in May 2005 was devoted to the protest by Shiite members of the *Shoura* (Consultative) Council against what they described as "random naturalization." Shiite representatives along with a group of liberal representatives protested against the 'random naturalization' policy, leading to social unrest. Shiites in Bahrain "view 'random naturalization' as an attempt to change the demographic structure in favor of Sunnis."[37] Shiite protests and demonstrations recurred on several occasions and at times escalated to the level of fights with the police.[38]

Generally, however, despite cases of sectarian tension in Arab countries, especially between Sunnis and Shiites, there are signs that this can often be contained rationally. The assumption is that the Arab world is passing through a transitional phase on the sectarian issue. The war in Iraq and so-called reform moves have led to public controversy over sensitive issues. This phase may help to confront some problems although it could also raise tension during the transition. However, in the long run, it helps to create better communication and an environment that provides the thrust necessary to solve problems.

Frank discussion of the sectarian issue in the press and parliament in both the Kingdom of Bahrain and the State of Kuwait has been limited to official channels so far. The current signs of openness in Saudi Arabia also involve the sectarian issue. It is no longer addressed behind closed doors but forcefully presented and may lead to a dialogue to change perceptions. This aspect is referred to by Hassan al Safar, a religious Saudi Shiite who lived in exile between 1980 and 1995 for political reasons and returned to the country after an agreement with the Saudi government. He says, "The national dialogue has certainly demolished some barriers between Sunnis and Shiites but we are still on the level of discussion." He believes that there are conservative religious circles impeding the development of relationships, observing that "we need common initiatives to steer the desired development, whether among Sunnis or Shiites."[39]

In the ultimate analysis, the sectarian issue is one of the most important current challenges affecting the progress of Arab societies. However, managing this issue in a rational and logical way may lead to a positive outcome based on reinforcing the issue of citizenship by giving citizens, regardless of their religious and doctrinal affiliations, the right to equal opportunities as long as they fulfill the duties of citizenship, including the duty not to owe any allegiance to elements in another country.

Conclusion

Sectarianism and issues such as Palestine and Iraq are all subjects that stir tension in Arab societies and prevent their democratic and social progress towards greater openness, liberalism and pluralism. At the same time, the shift of many Arab regimes in this direction is still not serious, driven by external and internal predicaments and pressures and by a desire to buy time. Yet there are many serious planned and unplanned transformations, which result from responses to external challenges and pressures, or a conscious decision on the part of elites in different countries.

The Arab Gulf states in particular, and in varying degrees, apart from other Arab countries, are adopting new economic systems and laws, which may open ownership of real estate, investment and the like for both their citizens and foreigners. In the past, these spheres were limited to the governments. This openness makes the investor and citizen involved in economic decisions and consequently in social and political decisions as well. In the same context, the rise of the private sector as a major player in the ownership and management of the media sector in the Arab world has resulted in freeing the media, to a great extent, from the control of governments. This has also given the elites in the fields of finance, culture, writing and art a bigger role in daily discourse and in forming public opinion.

In addition, there is a clear intellectual transformation in the Arab street. Terrorist operations, media freedom and the election challenge in

[168]

more than one country have made commitment to democracy and pluralism an issue for serious discussion. Political Islam movements are the largest organized political blocs in the Arab street and the primary party that will attain power if fair elections are conducted. These movements face questions regarding their commitment to intellectual, political and social pluralism and the extent of their respect for individual freedoms, peaceful rotation of power, rule of law, and working under the umbrella of the nation-state. There are many indications that there is an important Islamic movement involved in an intellectual review, which is moving towards accepting political and intellectual pluralism.

In the final analysis, several factors are leading to a new equation being experienced by countries in the region. For instance, the legitimacy of the nation-state is being reinforced by promoting state efficacy and the reform process and making larger segments of society participate in the decision-making process and the ownership of wealth and investments. All this is being enhanced by the corresponding retreat of the concept of integral Arab unity and the increasing economic interaction between the citizens of these countries. In opposition to this trend, the role of government is shrinking in favor of the expanding role of individuals.

This means that the nation-state in the region is following the same track as the nation-state at the global level. It is in a position that may be described as follows: "the power of the state is derived from its weakness." In other words, there is a difference between the recession of the state in terms of its exercise of power, authority and role, and in terms of its symbolic value, in favor of new kinds of roles and tasks, and the redistribution of these roles within the state. This is the situation in many Arab countries. However, the attempt of many ruling elites to stem the process of change in order to maintain their own authority and gains, coupled with the regional tension resulting from the Iraq and Palestine issues, hinders the fruition of this process into a fundamental historical transformation in the region.

COMPARATIVE EXPERIENCE OF POLITICAL REFORM

8

Modernization and Political Transformation: The Turkish Experience

Dr. Metin Heper

The origins of modernization in Turkey go back to the last decades of the eighteenth century. In the late sixteenth century, when the Ottoman Empire began to face defeat in the armed confrontations and wars with its adversaries in Europe, the formula adopted for the empire to regain its past grandeur was that of reviving the institutions and practices of the "golden years of the Empire," the zenith of which had been reached in the early sixteenth century. Three centuries later, the formula in question changed and it was thought that "the infidel could be defeated only by its own weapon." This thinking led to the adoption of the policy of Westernization.[1]

Not unexpectedly the first institution to be modernized was the military. In 1826, the traditional Janissary Corps was dissolved and replaced by the so-called New Order (*Nizam-ı Cedit*).[2] Since a modernized army needed to be supported by an equally modernized civilian institution, the next to be reformed was the civil bureaucracy. There was another reason for having a modern civil bureaucracy. In the nineteenth century, the Ottoman reformers had come to the conclusion that Islamic institutions had blocked the necessary reforms and that in the future the state policies should be formulated along secular lines.[3] The emergence of a relatively Westernized bureaucracy as well as an intelligentsia (the most prominent members of the latter were journalists), in turn, gave rise to aspirations of ending the absolutist rule of the sultans.[4] In the 1860s, the newly Westernized cadres in question asked for a more representative government. However, their view of who should be represented was rather limited—it comprised only them and excluded the people at large.[5]

The First Constitutional Monarchy inaugurated in 1876, which lasted until 1908, was the end result of such aspirations on the part of the newly Westernized elite.[6] However, during this period, Sultan Abdülhamit II (who ruled from 1876–1909), taking advantage of Article 113 in the 1876 Constitution, which granted him powers to banish persons anywhere in the empire, was able to prorogue Parliament and establish his personal rule. He pursued a pan-Islamist policy for preventing the Muslim elements of the Empire from adopting an exit strategy. In the process, the new Westernized elite were to a great degree rendered ineffective.[7]

However, while Abdülhamit II put an end to the influence of one set of Westernized elite in imperial affairs, he inadvertently prepared the ground for another set of Westernized elite to flourish in the Empire. It was during his reign that several institutions of higher learning were opened to educate future bureaucrats, officers, doctors, and other professionals.[8] The Sultan's aim was to salvage the Empire, which at the time was tearing apart at its seams. He realized that the project required educated cadres in all walks of life. However, what he failed to realize was that such cadres, in particular officers and civil servants, would also want to reclaim the Ottoman administration from absolutist sultans like him. The post-1909 Young Turks did exactly that.[9] The new set of Westernized elite in question constituted the founding cadres of the Turkish Republic established in 1923.

The Republican Period

Westernization

At the turn of the century, the Turkish sociologist Ziya Gökalp had suggested that the Ottomans should borrow *technology* from the West, but retain their own *culture*.[10] Instead, Mustafa Kemal (later Atatürk),[11] who led the liberation of the country from foreign occupation in 1919–1922 and served as President of the Republic from 1923 to 1938, opted for total Westernization.[12] Consequently, he and his close associates carried out what is usually referred to as the *"cultural* revolution"[13] and what was, in fact, a *cognitive* revolution. In practice, Islam was presented by the Ottoman-Turkish theologians as a set of dogmas closed to change, the Turks were now to be transformed into citizens who would use their own reasoning faculties for decision-making and not turn to various interpretations of Islam offered by religious personages. In the ultimate analysis, the new Republic aimed at having citizens who "would think logically."[14]

Approach towards Islam

As already implied, the founders of the new Republic did not seek to target Islam itself. The *fez* headgear was proscribed, but not women's *chador*. The obligation for men to wear European-style hats was merely intended to get people accustomed to change. As for the *chador*, Atatürk thought that in a "civilizing country" it was not appropriate to enforce it. Yet he did not think it proper to take legal action against its use, as he had done in the case of the *fez*.[15] Atatürk's closest associate İsmet İnönü, Prime Minister from 1923–1937 (except in late 1923 and early 1924) and 1961–1964, and President of the Republic during the 1938–1950 period, carried in his pocket a small edition of the Holy Quran, although he too, like Atatürk, was a strictly secular person. In later years, when his Republican People's Party was in opposition, his party members, on one occasion, had requested him to mention the name of Allah at least once in his speeches, so that their party "would garner more votes in the elections." İnönü obliged, but only by uttering the word '*Allahaısmarladık*' at the end of a speech.[16] In Turkish, this word means "I leave you in the good hands of Allah" and is used interchangeably with the word "good-bye." Thus for many people in Turkey, it is not a conscious reference to Islam.

Secularization

Such a sympathetic but firmly secular approach towards Islam on the part of the state founders must have helped secularization reforms to take root in the country. These reforms included the abrogation of the Caliphate, striking out the provision that the state religion was Islam from the 1924 Constitution, not providing religious education at schools between 1933 and 1947, replacing the Arabic script with the Latin script, moving the rest day from Friday to Sunday, using only the Gregorian calendar (which had been used since 1917 alongside the Lunar calendar), and adopting the Swiss civil law, the Italian penal law, and the German commercial law in their entirety. Attempts were also made to transform the people from being *pious* members of a *religious community* to *patriotic* members of a *secular republic*. For this purpose, the young were offered a strictly secular education and certain measures were introduced, which included saluting the flag, singing the national anthem, taking part in state parades, and introducing non-religious holidays to mark national anniversaries.

Here it should also be mentioned that the Ottoman state was not a theocratic state[17] and this antecedent regime type, too, must have facilitated the consolidation of secularism in Republican Turkey. The Ottoman ruling stratum governed a population that was divided along ethnic, religious and even sectarian lines. Under the circumstances, the state could not afford to impose one particular faith upon this human mosaic. Moreover, the empire was a large and complex entity that needed elaborate sets of secular laws and regulations, particularly for the public space, which Islamic provisions did not fully cover. As a result, from the fifteenth century onwards, secular legal codes took their place alongside the *Shari'a* law.

As with secularization reforms, in the case of Westernization reforms, too, the founders of the Republic took care to render the momentous changes involved as palatable to the people as possible. They did not actually talk of "Westernization." The word they had chosen for this purpose was "civilization." They designated the goal of the Republic as that of catching up with the "contemporary civilization and even surpassing it." They pointed out that civilization was the property of all humankind and that, along with other peoples, the Turks, too, had contributed to its development. [18]

Attitudes toward the West

An important fact was that the makers of the Turkish revolution took care to see that the country did not develop any hostility towards the West.[19] In the process, their own sympathy towards the West was not generally resented either by the elite or the people themselves. Here, too, the founders' hand was strengthened by a number of factors. First, as already implied, the policy of Westernization went back to the late eighteenth century. It was not an innovation introduced initially by the founders of the new Republic. The latter had only extended its scope, however, with far greater determination and resolve. It should also be pointed out that for more than two centuries, at least the elite who had become Westernized, appreciated the benefits that this had brought to their country. Second, as already noted, it was the Turks themselves who had opted for Westernization—it was not *imposed* upon them by the Europeans. Third, the Turks had not always been the losers against their European adversaries. In fact, in earlier centuries, some European rulers had asked the Ottoman Sultan's help against other European rulers. It is true that from the late sixteenth century onwards the Ottomans had continuously lost territory to European countries (as well as to Russia). Moreover, in the second half of the nineteenth century, when it could no longer pay its debts to the European countries, the Ottoman state had to transfer the control over some of its revenues to those countries. It is also a fact between 1919–1922, in the aftermath of the First World War and the signing of the Treaty of Sèvres, Greek forces landed and took over parts of Anatolia with the backing of some European countries. However, Turkey was never a colony under the direct or indirect rule of a foreign country. Moreover, the Turks won a stunning victory against the Greek forces at the Battle of Dumlupınar in 1922. This brings us to the fourth reason. At a very critical moment in history, the Turks had a charismatic leader in the person of Atatürk who led Turkey to victory in 1922. Another key figure was İsmet İnönü, Atatürk's close associate and loyal supporter.[20] İnönü diligently carried out the important reforms that Atatürk had introduced, when the latter began to immerse himself in some other state matters.[21]

Cognitive Revolution

The success of the Westernization efforts and the related secular reforms were critical for the Turkey's next two revolutions—that of the democratic revolution in the mid-1940s (the transition to a multi-party system) and the economic revolution in the early 1980s (the adoption of an export-oriented economic policy in place of an import-substitution economic policy). Turkey could achieve the last two revolutions because its "cultural revolution," which was a prerequisite for the last two, has indeed been a success story. This fact has been shown by a number of empirical studies carried out from the early 1960s onwards. First, it has been found that the Turks, who only forty years ago identified themselves as either "Muslims" or "non-Muslims," have been gone through an identity transformation. In the 1960s, 50.3 per cent of the workers in a textile factory in the city of İzmir (Smyrna) on its Aegean coast perceived themselves as "Turks" and 37.5 per cent as "Muslims."[22] In a 1994 nationwide survey, 69 percent of the respondents identified themselves as "Turks," 21 per cent as "Muslim Turks," 4 percent as "Muslims," another 4 per cent as "Kurds," while 2 per cent expressed other identities.[23]

Second, the Turks *had* started to go through a significant cognitive secularization process. In 1964, a nearby town or even a city was no longer viewed by villagers as "a conglomerate of humanity profaned by infidels."[24] A 1969 survey has found that among the migrant employees at the Middle East Technical University in Ankara, there was a weak correlation between the frequency of religious practice and the belief that religion should not be separated from politics.[25]

Having gone through an identity shift from being a "Muslim" to being a "Turk" and a thorough cognitive secularization process whereby their own reasoning rather than Islamic principles they are presented with started to inform their decisions,[26] the Turks in general came to support the Republican reforms. In a nationwide survey in 1993, 77 per cent of the respondents agreed with the statement that Republican reforms made Turkey modern, 8 per cent did not think so, and 15 per cent had no idea. It was not therefore surprising that the Turks in general were against the notion of a state based on Islam. The 1993 survey has also found that 67 per cent of the respondents opposed the idea of religion regulating state affairs, 10 per cent approved it, and 23 per cent had no idea.

The Turks had also developed rather relaxed views about other Muslims' attitudes towards religion. The 1993 survey further indicated that 86 per cent of the respondents thought that a person who believes in Allah and Prophet Mohammad [PBUH] can still be considered as a Muslim even without performing daily prayers. However, that percentage dropped to 82 when that same person did not observe the necessary religious fast. Similarly, in the same survey, 85 per cent of the respondents held the view that if a woman believes in Allah and Prophet Mohammad [PBUH] she can be considered as a Muslim even if she does not cover her head. The same tolerant attitude was shown by a majority of the Muslim Turks towards non-Muslims and even atheists. In the 1993 survey, 42 per cent of the respondents agreed with the statement that "If they have not displayed sinful behavior, the non-Muslims too, can go to paradise," while only 29 per cent disagreed, and another 29 per cent had no idea. Along the same lines, 53 per cent of the respondents agreed with the statement that "Those who do not believe in God too, may be nice and kind people," only 35 per cent disagreed, and 12 per cent had no idea. [27]

In the post-cultural revolution period, a typical Turk was someone who on one hand, performed at least some of the five daily prayers and fasted during the Holy Month of Ramadan, but on the other hand, obtained loans from a bank and paid interest on them, and even had a couple of alcoholic drinks in the evening. The typical Turk did not criticize others if their conduct as Muslims differed from his/her own and was generally reluctant to vote for a political party just because it was a religiously-oriented party. In recent decades, although there was a general revival of Islam in Muslim countries, including Turkey,[28] the votes of the religiously-oriented parties did not increase in a parallel manner. In fact, sometimes from one election to another they went down. [29]

Turkish Islam

In the whole of Turkey, Islam had become a private matter—a belief system between the individual and Allah and a source of ethics for the individual concerned. In addition, Islamic tenets continued to linger as part and parcel of the cultural heritage of the Turks. For instance, a cognitively secularized Turk could still consider not turning the light off when leaving a room as "sinful behavior" and not just a "waste of resources."[30] Not unexpectedly, Islam also continued to influence at least implicitly some of the policies pursued by the state. This had been so even during the single-party years (1923–1945). The Republican People's Party governments of the 1920s agreed to an exchange of population with

Greece whereby Turkish-speaking Orthodox citizens of Turkey (except those living in Istanbul) were obliged to leave Turkey for Greece and, in return, Greek-speaking Muslim citizens of Greece were to come to Turkey. Similarly, in the 1930s and later, governments allowed non-Turkish speaking Muslim Bosnians to immigrate to Turkey, but not the Gagauz Turks in Romania who spoke Turkish but who were Christians.

It is true that the 1924 Constitution adopted civic nationalism so that a person who professed to be a Turk was considered so, regardless of ethnicity and creed. However, sociologically speaking, the Turk was someone who had embraced Turkish culture and not unexpectedly, the values and attitudes derived from Islam constituted an important dimension of that culture. It was for the same reason that according to the Lausanne Peace Treaty signed by Turkey and the Allied Powers at the end of the Turkish War of Independence (1923), only the non-Muslim citizens of Turkey were attributed a "minority" status, and were thus granted both group and cultural rights – for instance, the right of being educated in their own language and celebrating their sacred days, respectively.

However, the instances when Islam continued to have some such lingering effects in Turkish public space constituted an exception rather than the rule. During the consolidation phase of democracy in Turkey from the year 1945 onwards, when for most people democracy gradually became the "only game in town," Islam was not allowed to interfere with the secularization process. By the time the religiously-oriented political parties were allowed to compete in the national elections (from 1970 onwards), the electorate had become adequately secular so that they would not vote for a political party just because of its religious orientation. Moreover, even in the case of the leadership cadres of the religiously-oriented political parties, religion on the whole, played a role basically at the individual level and only to some extent at the community level. In the case of these rulers, too, religion did not play a serious role at the state level.

Trials and Tribulations of Democracy

If Atatürk was the leading spirit behind Turkey's Cultural Revolution of the 1920s and 1930s, İnönü was the leading spirit in the country's democratic revolution, which started in 1945. There was no societal pressure on government for a transition to a multi-party system in the early 1940s. Celal Bayar was the leader of the Democratic Party (DP), which was established in 1946 and which in the 1950 national elections defeated the Republican People's Party. Years later he admitted that İnönü as President could have closed the DP simply by sending two gendarmes, and nobody could have opposed him. [31] One also cannot explain the opening of the political system in Turkey in the mid-1940s by the victory of the democratically-inclined Allied Powers, because as early as 1939, President İnönü had given the first signs of his intention to introduce democracy to Turkey. In his opinion, when so many countries already had democracy, it was a shame that Turkey did not have a democratic system. [32] From 1939 until 1945, he undertook some piecemeal measures to democratize the political system and after the Second World War, he allowed the formation of opposition parties. [33]

İnönü belonged to the group of the early Republican elite who had become not only the object but also the subject of modernization. That elite generation as a whole had become supporters of Westernization. For them, an important dimension of the Western way of life was democracy. Atatürk had endeavored to develop the cognitive prerequisite for democracy, for he believed in the inherent capacity of the people for progress. He pointed out that when people progress they could influence the government and when necessary, even direct it toward the right path. [34] İnönü thought there was a need to make the transition to democracy as soon as possible, because one could learn from past mistakes, as he himself did. [35]

Since both Atatürk and İnönü favored Westernization and thus supported a cognitive revolution and because the original impulse for the democratic transition had not come from societal elements, the democracy that Atatürk and İnönü had envisaged was "rational democracy." As later defined by Giovanni Sartori,[36] rational democracy is based not on interests, but on ideas. It is a democracy in which the *educated* would be engaged in a *debate* in order to find out *what is best for the country.*

Rational democracy must have been perceived by the founders of the Republic as another measure against personal rule, which was considered by Atatürk and his associates as a trademark of the late Ottoman period and consequently, one which the Republican elite wished to avoid. However, in the hands of the post-Atatürk intellectual-bureaucratic elite, "Atatürkism" as an outlook, which is essentially a technique of how to think, was converted into a political manifesto—an ideology of *what* to think.[37] The intellectual-bureaucratic elite seemed to have loaded "Atatürkism" with such a meaning in order to retain the influential role to which they were accustomed during the single-party period. Not unexpectedly, this particular attitude on the part of the intellectual-bureaucratic elite brought them into a collision course with the political elite of the multi-party period. The latter thought that the *vote* rather than *Atatürkism-as-an-ideology* should be the ultimate criterion of political legitimacy. The consequences of this state of affairs were the 1960 and 1971 military interventions.[38]

The fact that democracy in Turkey had been perceived by Atatürk, İnönü and their followers in the ensuing decades, including the military, as a derivative of Westernization had two consequences. On the one hand, rational democracy, which was a consequence of the cognitive revolution, has given rise to a conflict between the post-Atatürk "Atatürkists" and the "democrats." On the other hand, it has led to democracy being perceived as an *end* rather than as a *means*. In Europe, democracy was seen by various "interests" as a *means* to promote their particular interests at the expense of others' interests. As a result, a serious threat to the interests of the propertied classes could cause some political regimes on the continent to drift toward class-based authoritarianisms. In Turkey, because democracy was perceived as an integral part of Westernization, thus as an *end*, the problems that democracy encountered were attributed to the politicians and not to the democracy itself.[39] Consequently, the Turkish military's interventions were carried out to save democracy from the "democrats," not for establishing long-term military-based authoritarian regimes in the country.

Indeed, in Turkey, the military intervened to render "*stumbling democracy*" into a *viable* democracy. When they intervened, officers always mentioned "the ills of democracy" as the reason for their intervention. They tried to deal with those problems to the best of their ability, and then voluntarily returned to their barracks. They acted in this manner because they viewed democracy as the ideal regime for Turkey to adopt, and therefore, concluded that they should resort to military intervention only when all other options were exhausted. At least prior to the 1971 and 1980 interventions, officers sent warning signals to the politicians, sometimes several times, urging politicians to get their act together and effectively deal with "the threats the country faced."

Following the 1961 military intervention, an effort was made to institutionalize rational democracy in Turkey so that the country would not again face the "politics of the absurd." This was sought to be achieved via the "mixed" 1961 Constitution. That constitution divided the exercise of sovereignty between Parliament and a number of bureaucratic agencies such as the newly created National Security Council (NSC), the Constitutional Court, the Council of State (with new powers granted to it during the interregnum), the autonomous Radio and Television Corporation and equally autonomous universities. The NSC was to advise governments on security and related matters. The Constitutional Court was to test the constitutionality of the legislation enacted by Parliament, in particular by acting in a vigilant manner concerning secularism. The Council of State was to protect civil servants against being removed from their posts (line duties) for political or other such "inappropriate" reasons. The assumption was that civil servants were the indispensable guardians of secularism and consequently, there was a need to reinstate them in their posts should they be subjected to "unjust treatment" at the hands of politicians. The autonomous Radio and Television Corporation and autonomous universities were expected to shape public opinion in a Republican direction. The 1961 Constitution also expanded the scope of the basic rights and liberties so that individuals could have safeguards against arbitrary government actions. Another measure taken against any possible resort to authoritarianism by a government was the introduction of proportional representation, with the purpose of making the formation of majority governments as difficult as possible.

However, the political developments that followed the restructuring of the political system along the lines summarized above were not those anticipated by the makers of the 1961 Constitution. The liberal provisions of the Constitution, in effect, lifted the lid on a Pandora's Box. The 1960s and 1970s witnessed the emergence and proliferation of anti-system political parties, associations and their militant auxiliary entities, which subscribed to ethno-nationalistic, Islamic, Leftist and/or Rightist ideologies. The situation was one of polarized political life and politicized bureaucracy. These developments took place when Parliament and governments were deprived of some of their powers and could not effectively grapple with the critical issues that the country faced. The end result was a tug-of-war between the state elite and the political elite and among the latter themselves. This state of affairs further sapped the energies of the political elite when they had to grapple with serious economic problems and armed clashes among several illegal organizations.[40]

The Military and Democracy

For this reason, following the military interventions of 1971 and 1980, efforts were made to trim "the excesses" of the 1961 Constitution vis-à-vis basic rights and liberties and to further bolster the agencies that acted as the guardians of "the long-term interests" of the country, but not Parliament and civilian government. The basic rights and liberties granted by the 1961 Constitution were significantly curtailed while the powers of the Presidency and the NSC were bolstered. The 1980 interveners also attempted to restructure the political landscape in the hope that Turkey would have a better functioning democracy in the future.

With this notion in mind, officers banned the pre-1980 political cadres from active politics for several years. In the case of the leadership cadres, the ban was imposed for ten years. They saw the need for a new generation of politicians who would hopefully act "with greater common sense." They amended the Political Parties Act, among other things, granting greater powers to the rank-and-file in the political party vis-à-vis the leadership cadres. Their assumption was that where necessary, the rank and file would prevent the leadership cadres from pursuing policies detrimental to the long-term interests of the country and the political regime. The interveners also prohibited the political parties from having auxiliary units. It was hoped that this ban would stop the former being adversely affected by overtly politicized civil societal entities in the future.[41]

Not unexpectedly, these efforts to legislate away the long-consolidated political culture and praxis that they opposed could not succeed. It seems that it was not the attempted political engineering, but the intervention itself that brought about fundamental changes in Turkish political culture and praxis. The 1980 intervention started a learning process for many people in Turkey. One early sign of this process was the development of a *modus vivendi* between the military and the Motherland Party under

Turgut Özal in the post-1983 period. Initially, the leader of the 1980 junta-turned President, General Kenan Evren, made some political statements that did not befit a constitutionally neutral head of state in a parliamentary system of government. However, Prime Minister Özal did not make a capital case out of such a behavior pattern on the part of President Evren. Then, gradually Özal began to exercise his full powers as Prime Minister and this time, Evren did not question Özal's assumption of powers that should have belonged to him in the first place.[42] Then, in 1999–2002, a coalition government among the Democratic Left Party of Bülent Ecevit, the liberal Motherland Party of Mesut Yılmaz, and the Nationalist Action Party of Devlet Bahçeli functioned quite harmoniously, thanks particularly to the efforts of Ecevit and Bahçeli, which included taking courageous economic decisions that would have cost them votes. That government also maintained harmonious relations with the military.

Since 2002, Turkey has been ruled by the majority government of the Justice and Development Party (JDP) headed by Recep Tayyip Erdoğan. This party was formed by politicians who formerly belonged to religiously-oriented political parties. For this reason the JDP is also considered a religiously-oriented political party by a great majority in Turkey, although the party defines itself as a "conservative-democratic" party and so far (March 2006) the JDP government has acted accordingly. However, initially the past affiliation of Erdoğan and most of his close associates with religiously-oriented political parties made the secular establishment, including President Ahmet Necdet Sezer and to a lesser extent the military top brass, rather suspicious of the former's "ulterior motives," that is, whether or not they have in mind the idea of "one man, one vote, only once." However, as time passed, the JDP government's relationship with the military became more harmonious. On different occasions, both Prime Minister Erdoğan and Chief of Staff General Özkök changed course when requested by the other. It is true that the government's relationship with President Sezer has remained tense.

[187]

However, those relations continued to be at least correct and mutually respectful.[43]

The military's more favorable attitude towards the JDP may be explained to a great extent in terms of the pattern in which the civil–military relations developed in Turkey. The Ottoman state was founded by a warrior stratum, which played a significant role in the administration of the realm, so much so that the ruling group was actually referred to as *askeri* (military).[44] This particular Ottoman antecedent saddled the military with a sense of responsibility for the long-term welfare of the country. In addition, from the end of the nineteenth century onwards, the military became both the *object* and the *subject* of modernization. Initially, the military itself became professionalized gradually and thereafter, it sought to modernize the country and act to safeguard the modern features of that country, in particular secularism. On the other hand, during the tumultous years of the Committee of Union and Progress period (1912–1918), the military became very much involved in day-to-day politics.[45] This involvement detracted from its efficiency and effectiveness and Atatürk, who at the time was a member of the Committee, resigned from it in an act of protest. Following the proclamation of the Republic in 1923, Atatürk asked those parliamentarians who were also commissioned officers, to choose between the army and Parliament.

These developments created a serious dilemma for the military. Whenever the military concluded that the country's long-term interests were in jeopardy, officers felt the urge to intervene. At the same time, officers were restrained on the one hand, by the fact that Atatürk had asked them to stay above politics, and on the other hand by the fact that they too had subscribed to the goals of Westernization and democracy. Their inclinations were also bolstered by the Western-type education they received, which convinced them that a modern political system could only be based on democracy. That explains why in the late 1940s, a military faction made up mostly of young officers who received Western, secular education, tended to support the Democratic Party who were criticizing the Republican People's Party for the latter's "authoritarianism." [46] During recent years, Turkey's aspiration to acquire full membership of the European Union has also obliged the military to further withdraw to the sidelines. [47]

The fact that the officers had these tendencies, which had been at cross purposes with each other, goes a long way to account for their views on military interventions and their praxis as interveners. Officers in Turkey have not been enthusiastic about their intervention in politics. As already noted, they only intervened when they came to the conclusion that there was no other option left. They did not intervene just for the sake of intervention or for staying in power indefinitely. Whenever possible, following an intervention, they gave a date for their return to their barracks and tried to keep their promise.

Their reluctance to intervene became apparent when the 1971 and 1980 military interventions turned out to be intervention by generals in contrast to the 1960 military intervention which was an intervention by colonels. They did not want a repeat of the 1960 intervention, thinking that those at the lower ranks might be more adventurous than those in the upper ranks. Whenever possible, they avoided taking power directly into their own hands. They acted in this manner following the 1971 intervention. More recently they chose not to act alone when they felt that Turkey again faced a grave threat. In 1997, when the military thought that the coalition government between the religiously-oriented Welfare Party of Necmettin Erbakan and liberal-right True Path Party of Tansu Çiller were not acting diligently enough against the "threat of political Islam," they decided to mobilize civilian opposition against that coalition government. [48]

It should also be noted that in all interventions, except the first in 1960, there were several meetings among the top brass on whether or not the military should intervene. In some cases, the decision to intervene was adjourned to a later date if a particular development occurred after fixing the intervention date that could have ameliorated the "crisis situation." The self-questioning on the part of the military concerning their interventions continued even after two years in the case of the 1980 military intervention. That intervention was carried out by four generals and one admiral who together had constituted the top brass. In 1982, on one occasion, the admiral in question asked the author and his colleague, Professor Üstün Ergüder, whether or not their intervention in 1980 was really called for.[49]

Even more significantly, since 2003, the military top brass started to question the very wisdom of military interventions. In 2003, the Chief of Staff General Özkök admitted that none of the military interventions in Turkey (1960, 1971 and 1980) had been successful. He pointed out that if those interventions had been successful the politicians banned from active politics after an intervention could not have been able to return to active politics after a while, which they did. Özkök arrived at the conclusion that military intervention should no longer be looked upon as panacea for Turkey's ills and that the military should put more trust in the people. Furthermore, keeping in mind that all military interventions in Turkey have been carried out in the name of Atatürkism, Özkök also suggested that "the Atatürkist way of thought, which is free from dogmas and based on reason, can and should be reinterpreted."[50]

Islam and Democracy in Turkey

The fact that since 1999, Turkish political life seemed to discard many of its earlier features that could be referred to as the "politics of the absurd" must have contributed to the military's growing preference for staying on the sidelines. Here, one other factor must have also played a role. That was the increased tendency, from 1970 to the present, on the part of religiously-oriented parties to turn themselves into system-oriented parties, that is, into political parties that do not challenge the basic premises of the political regime in Turkey, including its secular character, and thus play the democratic game according to its established rules.

Even in 1970, when the first religiously-oriented political party, the National Order Party (NOP, 1970–1971), was founded, political Islam was not the impulse behind the establishment of that party and those of its successors. The initiative for forming the NOP came from the Sheikh of a religious order[51] who thought that Turkey needed new generations of people who would be patriotic, self-sacrificing and well-educated so that Turkey would be a leading country in the scientific, technological, and civilizational race. Accordingly, the NOP and its successor National Salvation Party (NSP, 1972–1980) perceived Islam not as an end in itself (a religious goal), but also as a means for material development (a secular goal).[52] In turn, the Welfare Party (WP, 1983–1998), [53] which was the successor political party to the NOP and NSP, pursued the goals of political stability and economic development, aiming to achieve those goals by bringing about a "just order" (adil düzen)—a social order that was "rational" (a basically secular notion) as well as "just" (a secular and religious notion). All this was not surprising, since the religiously-oriented politicians in Turkey had also received a secular education.

However, all three political parties simultaneously followed a policy of appeasement toward their radical members and supporters by attempting (although unsuccessfully) to carry out certain measures such as turning a well-known former Byzantine Church in Istanbul (the Haghia Sofia) into a mosque;[54] rendering Friday a weekend day; and objecting to the eight-year compulsory secular education, which was recommended by the National Security Council. They also were sympathetic to the so-called "National View" (Milli Görüş) developed by certain religiously-oriented groups in the 1970s. The proponents of this view emphasized the significance of certain moral and spritual values. Islam, although not mentioned, was clearly implied. They also set their goals as industrialization, closer ties with other Muslim countries, and a just economic order. [55] In the event, all three parties were closed – the NOP and the WP by the Constitutional Court and the NSP by the 1980–1983 interveners on the grounds of "tinkering with the secular premises of the Republic."

These party closures revealed to the religiously-oriented politicians that the secular establishment was a great barrier not only against Islam-derived policies but also against the carrying of Islam-derived values and attitudes to the public space.[56] They also realized what has been noted before—that the great majority of people in Turkey do not vote for political parties just because they are religiously-oriented political parties. Thus, the discourse and praxis of the religiously-oriented parties went through a transformation from the 1970s to the end of the century. Some examples will serve to illustrate this point. Whereas earlier the dominant discourse was one of seeing a basic incompatibility between Islam and the secular state, later that discourse was replaced by one of "neither should interfere in the affairs of the other." Similarly, while in earlier decades even veiled women could not participate in party activities, in later decades, even those women who did not wear the veil and who publicly consumed alcoholic drinks, could be elected to Parliament.

However, such transformations in the religiously-oriented political parties were not adequate to convince the secular establishment that such parties would no longer be engaged in the Islamic *takiyye* (dissimulation), or hiding one's real intentions until the time is ripe for their disclosure. Consequently, both the Welfare Party and its successor the Virtue Party (1997–1998) were closed.

Currently, Turkey has two political parties, which are successor parties to the five religiously-oriented parties referred to above. Those two political parties are the Felicity Party (FP) and the Justice and Development Party (JDP or AKP), both established in 2001. The FP has no objections to its being referred to as a religiously-oriented party. Its discourse on the whole reflects those of its somewhat "reformed" predecessor parties.[57]

In contrast, the JDP, which won the 2002 national elections and formed a majority government, calls itself a "conservative-democratic" party, and rejects the label "religiously-oriented." The leadership cadre of the JDP, led by Prime Minister Recep Tayyip Erdoğan, point out that they are Muslims who prefer secular politics. They conduct politics in accordance with that maxim. Among other things, the JDP made strenuous efforts to make Turkey a full member of the European Union and ultimately got the membership negotiations started. Furthermore, the JDP government pursued economic policies in tandem with the relevant International Monetary Fund (IMF) formulas, and endeavored to maintain close but correct relations with both Muslim and non-Muslim countries. Prime Minister Erdoğan stated that there is no conflict between democracy and republicanism and that both, in fact, complement each other.

It must be as a result of such policies that the party has strong support among the populace, while the FP has very weak popular support. In the 2002 national elections, while the JDP obtained 34.2 per cent of the votes, those of the FP remained at 2.4 per cent. Opinion polls indicate that the party continued to enjoy strong support even after three and half years in office. The party's staying away from Islamic discourse and praxis in particular and its emphasis on harmony in political life in general has contributed to the ongoing strength of democracy in Turkey.[58]

Concluding Observations

In the Turkish revolution, Westernization played a crucial role. It began two centuries ago and still continues, as borne out by Turkey's ongoing efforts to become a full member of the EU. Westernization was palatable to the Turks because they opted for it themselves and it was not imposed upon them. It was also possible because Turkey had never been colonized by a Western country, and in fact, had its days of glory vis-à-vis the European countries. Accordingly, the Turks did not harbor a deep hostility to the West and could easily adopt Western ideas, instutitions and praxis.

Until the founding of the Republic in the early 1920s, Westernization emerged as a partial process. It was turned into total Westernization by the founders of the Republic. This became possible because the transformation was attempted by a charismatic leader beloved and respected by this people. Another contributory factor here was the manner in which this charismatic leader converted partial Westernization into total Westernization. The project in question was introduced to the Turks as the adoption of a new "civilization" and not as "Westernization" along with the complementary argument that the civilization in question was the product of all humankind, including the Turks. The idea was probably not too far-fetched for the Turks because the country had its golden ages as well as military victories over the Europeans. The transformation was helped by the fact that the founders of modern Turkey did not oppose Islam as such, but they were only against certain retrogressive interpretations of Islam, which they thought had contributed to the demise of the Ottoman Empire.

This favorable attitude toward Islam and the absence of hostility towards the West combined with the fact that in the Ottoman Empire non-religious rules had always been promulgated alongside religious ones, enabled the founders of the Republic to make secularism one of the most important premises on which the republic was founded. This accomplishment in turn paved the way for the success of the cognitive revolution project.

The cognitive revolution in question had a number of significant consequences. First, Turkey came to have a staunchly secular establishment. Second, even the leadership cadres of the religiously-oriented political parties turned out to be basically secularly-oriented politicians rather than religious personages. Third, Islam became a private matter. At the individual level, it emerged as a personal belief system and a source of morality. It continued to play a role at the community level to a certain degree, but one that was not anti-Republican. It played virtually no role at all at the state level. The lower *cihad* as against the higher *cihad* was absent, except those occasionally attempted by some marginal groups, which were easily suppressed. Consequently, there was generalized support for the Republican regime and there was very little support for a political party if its credentials were merely limited to being a religiously-oriented party.

This state of affairs created a convenient milieu for the transition to democracy. The adoption of a multi-party regime was possible because among other things:

- The elite in Turkey considered democracy as an indispensable dimension of Westernization
- That same elite believed in the inherent capacity of the people to progress as had been apparent by the cognitive revolution they were undergoing
- There was a generalized absence of hostility towards the West and therefore, towards Western ideas and practices.

Not only did the Turks make a transition to a democratic way of life but they also managed to consolidate democracy. This was possible for the following reasons:

- When the political life drifted to the "politics of the absurd," as it did several times, paradoxically, it was the officers who saved democracy from the "democrats."
- The saviors in question did not toy with the idea of staying in power indefinitely because they continued to subscribe to Westernization and considered democracy as an end and not as a means. Thus, in times of crises, they blamed politicians, not democracy itself.

Despite the rather rosy picture drawn in this chapter, Turkey, until the end of the twentieth century experienced several political crises, which led to three-and-a-half military interventions. However, what those with clout tried to do was to restructure democracy to make it viable and they did not intend to do away with democracy indefinitely.

The twenty-first century seems to have opened a new page in Turkish political life. From 1970 until the end of the twentieth century, the religiously-oriented political parties in that country had gradually become more system-oriented. Furthermore, in the twenty-first century one off-shoot of the twentieth-century religiously-oriented political parties totally denied its religious identity and acted accordingly. Here, the realization by the leadership cadres of that party that the Turkish people would never vote for a political party just because of its religious orientation and that the secular establishment would never allow political Islam to flourish in the country must have been the primary contributory factors. As noted earlier, the twenty-first century is also witnessing the deepening of democracy thanks to the *acquis communautaire* (accumulated body of law) of the Euopean Union, which Turkey is trying to join as a full member. However, that is another story which is beyond the scope of the present chapter.

Is it possible to draw certain lessons from the Turkish experience that may be useful for the Arab world? It is a well-known fact that every country has a past that is to a great degree unique to it. Consequently, giving concrete advice to other countries on how to proceed in their efforts to bring about particular types of modernization and political transformation may not be appropriate. However, it may be useful for other countries to focus their attention on the grand strategy adopted in a country such as Turkey, where such efforts are considered to have been relatively successful.

Assuming that Turkey has been relatively successful in its efforts at modernization and political transformation, the grand strategy behind this evolution may be summarized as follows. Turkey itself decided to start the change process before it was forced to do so by others. Turkish leaders quite successfully persuaded their citizens that what was being adopted was not completely alien, because at some point in history, Turkey had also made a contribution to what was being adopted. In their efforts to transform their country extensively, Turkish leaders also benefited from the fact that in the past, even for a short period of time, their country had had an edge over the countries or the constellation of countries, which were now being emulated.

Moreover, the Turks did not try to alter everything at once. Their starting point was to achieve a cognitive revolution, an important dimension of which was secularization. However, secularization was not allowed to lead to atheism. Although Islam no longer played a role at the state level it continued to have significant functions at the community and individual levels. These developments prepared the ground for political opening.

In the second stage, an effort was made to bring about a careful balance between republicanism and democracy; democracy was not allowed to be a means of infringing upon the basic premises, such as secularism and civic-cum-cultural nationalism, upon which the state was premised.

The final revolution was that of an economic revolution. That revolution turned out to be a transition from a policy of import-substitution and state intervention to that of export-orientation and the dominance of market forces. The dynamics of democracy did not permit the new economic system to make life unbearable for the have-nots. The new economic system, in turn, enabled Turkey to have a healthy economy, compete in international markets, and earn adequate foreign exchange. In the process, the country came to enjoy a certain degree of autonomy from other countries, and was able to develop into a regional power.

9

The Principles of the American Republic in a Revolutionary Century

Dr. Gary Hart

A merican democracy is characterized by certain principles embodied in its founding documents, especially its Constitution, history and political culture. These principles, according to scholarly consensus, are derived from the philosophy of humanism associated with the Age of Enlightenment and represent today the most advanced evolution in political thought. A number of these principles are shared by all democracies, Western and otherwise, but some are more closely identified with the United States than any other nation. Over its almost 225-year life, the United States has not applied its principles consistently either at home or abroad. Though most Americans choose to believe that the country is unfailingly faithful to its highest ideals, cycles of principle and pragmatism characterize its complex history. Therefore, any account of US principles, particularly one that emphasizes principle as a component of strategy, must acknowledge inconsistency and imperfection in application.

Principles of American Democracy

The United States believes, above all else, in freedom—the principle that none should suffer from political oppression but all should have the liberty to pursue their best individual destiny without interference from the state or from others. The United States believes that democracy is the best system to guarantee that freedom through its reliance on an open participatory process, political equality and elected representation. The principle of meritocracy, the opportunity to achieve one's personal goals, is central to US democracy. The supremacy of the rule of law, equal status under the law and protection of a just legal system, is a US principle. Other US principles embrace the sanctity of property and the protection of private property from intrusion and confiscation. The United States believes absolutely in the right and necessity of protecting the country from attack. And finally, US principles dictate that the country will resist, selectively it must be admitted, oppression by others without seeking to exert its power over others.

Put more immediately and directly, these principles may be described as follows:

- The American people are protected by a written Constitution from coercion by the state. Those "unalienable rights" are most clearly articulated in the Bill of Rights but are interpreted and expanded by judicial interpretation according to the changing realities of the ages.
- Americans are entitled to vote for their representative leaders ("deriving their just powers from the consent of the governed" in the words of the US Declaration of Independence) and they are accountable to the public for assuring the equality in which all people were created. These procedures are, significantly, contained in the first and second Articles of the Constitution which provide, also significantly, for the removal from office of members of Congress and the President.
- Americans can achieve whatever their talents permit without interference. Though not specifically a constitutional guarantee, the removal of artificial or political barriers to achievement is implicit in the US Constitution and laws.
- American laws do not provide special status for the wealthy and powerful over the poor and powerless (though economic disparity

offers clear advantage). A central purpose of the Constitution itself was to "ensure justice." Any question concerning "the equal protection of the laws" was removed by the adoption of the Fourteenth Amendment.

- American land and possessions cannot be taken from their owners even by the state, except under public necessity and even then, not without just compensation. The Fifth Amendment provides due process of law, protection of private property and the requirement of just compensation for property taken for public use.

- The American people will defend themselves from attack whether against citizens or the nation. The Constitution was enacted, in part, to "provide for the common defense" and provides for "calling forth the militia...to repel invasions." Fundamental rights of individual and collective self-protection, however, require no further constitutional guarantees.

- Americans do not seek to dominate others and will resist those who seek to do so. Likewise, this principle arises more from the nature and history of the United States than from any explicit constitutional provision.

Who in the world would not wish to live under a political system based upon such principles? They represent the noblest ideals of human political aspiration. The power of these principles rests in their inherent attractiveness to others not so fortunate and in their consistent incorporation into American foreign policy. The difficulty lies in their implementation, both at home and abroad, and in those cases when they are not consistently followed.

Applying American Principles Abroad

Let us explore the ways in which these principles might be extended by application through US international relations.

[201]

- The United States will ally with free societies and oppose oppressive ones
- The United States will encourage other nations to adopt democratic structures, systems and processes
- Those nations and societies that the United States favors and aligns with will provide opportunities for all their people
- The United States favors a world characterized by the rule of law
- All nations should promote and protect private property rights
- The United States will permit no one to attack the country with impunity
- The United States will resist hegemony but will not seek it.

These principles are neither so unrealistic nor so impractical as to be readily dismissed. They may, however, prove inconvenient to implement. And therein lies the crux. In an age of *realpolitik*, imperial ambition and power politics, principles become inconvenient. Convenience is only a short step away from expediency. Nations, like individuals, cannot simultaneously claim principle and behave expediently. In the revolutionary Information Age, where deception finds little room to hide, this is truer than ever. Additionally, to adopt expediency in US foreign policy, that is to say to abandon the standards that Americans claim for themselves as the easiest or quickest means to achieve a desired or favorable result, almost always requires either deception of the American people or their willing acquiescence in unprincipled international conduct. Either way, national pride is sacrificed and a price is paid in terms of national embarrassment.

It must be emphasized that the argument here is not strictly for principle over power in foreign policy. It is a more positive brief for incorporation of the highest US principles into the range of powers, together with the more traditional military, economic and political powers, applied to achieve an early 21st century US strategy. Where some have seen the nation's ideals as an inconvenience at best and an outright hindrance to the exertion of US power abroad at worst, I argue here for core US principles, its canon of beliefs to be considered as a fourth power, a positive advantage, in achieving the nation's larger purposes in the new century.

What the United States is gives the country its strength. The United States possesses certain natural advantages in the world, given the desire of virtually all the world's peoples to share its norms, albeit in their own cultures if possible. People do not want to become Americans. They want to share what Americans have, what they have achieved, as much as possible under their own terms and conditions. They readily understand that the prosperity and material success of the United States are largely the product of its political system, political standards and beliefs. However, when the United States abandons its principles for short-term political or economic advantage, it abandons one of its greatest strengths. For the United States to act imperially, expediently, or ignobly, is to weaken rather than strengthen itself. I argue here for the principles outlined above, or some version thereof, to become nothing less than a national code of conduct, a compass, a set of reference points, for the achievement of America's strategy in the 21st century.

Accordingly, the United States must consider, at all points and on all occasions, how to turn the natural appeal of its principles and beliefs to the achievement of its larger purposes. Rather than be viewed as a hindrance to policy, US principles should be seen as its greatest natural advantage in today's world. And, almost as a law of political nature, when the United States neglects, sidesteps or denies those principles and ideals that define it—the country weakens itself and lessens its chances of achieving larger national purposes.

Thus, the argument here is as much a pragmatic one as it is an idealistic one. The United States has much greater chances of becoming what it wants to be, of uniting peoples of goodwill, of leading permanent coalitions of democratic societies, of achieving a more just and perfect union, by adhering to its principles rather than seeking ways to evade them and then covering its tracks by denying that it has acted contrary to its principles.

America is different, or at least Americans believe themselves to be. The difference is rooted in American ideals, beliefs and principles. Few, if any, other nations make the similar claims for a more noble or principled approach to international interchange. However, with the emergence of the United States as a dominant power, the nation has been increasingly faced with opportunities to exert its power. However, these opportunities require a choice between US principles and ideals on the one hand and what are perceived to be its "interests" on the other. Those "interests" often have to do with acquiring support in ideological struggles, protecting resources, achieving regional "stability," protecting or promoting the interests of allies, or in the age of terrorism, preempting those perceived to be threats. The United States has supported dictators and oligarchs against its principle, in each of these causes. Thus, in each instance, the nation has left a message that when its interests and principles clash, it will choose its own interests over principles.

Policies based upon a country's interests have characterized national conduct throughout human history. There is nothing new in that approach. On the best of occasions, principle and interest coincide. In such cases, nations do what is right because it is also in their interest to do so. However, when interest-based policy collides with the notion of principled, exceptional conduct, then hypocrisy, or even downright ignorance of such collision surfaces. It is bliss for a great nation to believe itself to be exceptional and to behave in an exceptional manner. However, to claim one thing and to do another is confusion at best, and cynicism at worst. Here there may be a divide between US leaders and the American people. If the American people believe that their country acts according to its principles when in fact it does not, then the people are either deceived (that is to say, they are lied to by their leaders) or they are willing participants in deception.

Either way, where interest prevails over principle, the power of principle is sacrificed. The near universal appeal of the principles underlying the US political system is undermined by the nation acting contrary to its claimed beliefs. If the historic principles of the United States constitute one of its greatest strengths, their casual erosion by the expedient exercise of power weakens, rather than strengthens the nation in the long term.

The principles of the United States flow from the democratic nature of the republic created by the founders. The US government's nature is inseparable from its founding principles—as defined by its democratic republican character. To abandon, suspend or evade those principles is to alter the very nature of the Republic. Therefore, it is argued here that US principles are a power to be applied to its larger strategic purposes but that evasion of those principles erodes the power they represent and makes it harder rather than easier to meet its objectives. To preserve core US principles is to strengthen the Republic, and to restore the Republic, as argued in the conclusion, is to strengthen the nation's ability to achieve its strategic objectives.

Terrorism and the US Response

Against this constitutional backdrop, and in the decade following the Cold War, the United States and its friends and allies suddenly confronted a new threat carried out by ancient methods. This threat came quickly to be called "terrorism," which is a method that has been used throughout history by weaker powers against greater powers. Terrorist methods are often used not by a nation-state but by stateless nations. The authentic threat was *jihad*, a war declared by Al Qaeda and affiliated organizations against the United States and its allies.

This was a threat that the United States was unprepared to counter. The country had configured its security forces for nation-state wars—

World War I, World War II and the Cold War. US force structures and weapons systems were not configured to defeat Al Qaeda, and thus its intelligence services were caught totally off-guard on 9/11. Thus the United States and many of its traditional allies were suddenly required to re-think the very nature of security and how best to achieve it.

This new threat and the re-thinking of security required Americans to review the constitutional history upon which the nation was founded. This would seem obscure to those in the Middle East and elsewhere in the world, but understanding US constitutional structures, especially provisions for security, raises issues at the very heart of what the nation is and what it believes.

For example, few Americans know that their nation has two armies and that both are acknowledged by the United States Constitution. One is the military that people know best—the regulars, the United States Army and Navy, later extending to the Marines and the Air Force. The other army, originally known as the militia, is now called the National Guard.

Why would the American Founders invite confusion and duplication by creating two separate military establishments? The answer is quite simple and dates back to the earliest city-state republics in Greece. Throughout 2800 years of republican theory and practice, a standing army has always been considered a threat to republican liberty and a potential instrument of tyranny. Educated in the classics and familiar with both Greek and Roman republican history and culture, the Founders were keenly aware of this danger. This led to one of the bitterest struggles in the establishment of the new American Republic for it was the language and values of the republic that animated the Founders of the United States. Alexander Hamilton and the Federalists saw the future of the United States as a commercial republic, with expanding trade frontiers and intricate political and business alliances. These would, from time to time, be threatened by circumstance, whether local political unrest or jealous commercial rivals. American commercial interests would have to be

[206]

protected by land and by sea and, therefore, in Patrick Henry's memorable and sarcastic formulation, "a standing army we shall have also, to execute the execrable commands of tyranny."

As glorious as such an army might be, it would also be expensive and politically dangerous, Henry's Anti-federalist allies believed. They were only partially relieved by the Constitutional provision limiting military appropriations to two years and by ensuring civilian command and oversight.

Though neither Federalist nor Anti-federalist, and largely absent (as ambassador to France) during the Constitutional debates, Thomas Jefferson urged his ally James Madison and others, at the very least to isolate domestic politics from the standing army and its international commercial concerns by providing for a separate army, a distinct military establishment, to protect and defend the American homeland. This separate military force already existed in the form of State militia.

Following ancient republican precedent and history, as well as radical Whig ideology, the core of this homeland militia would be citizen-soldiers, the successors to the Greek farmer-warrior. The militia would remain under the command and control of the respective States, except as provided for in Article I, Section 8, of the US Constitution. Congress would have the authority "to provide for calling forth the militia to execute the laws of the union, suppress insurrections and repel invasions," and "to provide for organizing, arming and disciplining the militia, and for governing such part of them as may be employed in the service of the United States..."

Article II, Section 2, provides that the President shall be Commander-in-Chief of the militia of the several states "when called into actual service of the United States" just as he was to be Commander-in-Chief of the regular forces.

In his first inaugural address, Jefferson counted among the Government's essential principles, "a well-disciplined militia, our best reliance in peace, and for the first moments of war, till regulars may relieve them...." He went on to observe in the same address: "These principles form the bright constellation which has gone before us and guided our steps through an age of revolution and reformation..."

Quaint as it seems now, Jefferson turned modern defense on its head: citizen-soldiers would repel invaders until the regulars arrived, rather than regulars invading elsewhere, as today, with the National Guard (militia) relieving them. In his case, Jefferson's philosophy of the role of the military in American society remained constant. In his eighth and last annual message to Congress and the American people he wrote: "For a people who are free, and who mean to remain so, a well-organized and armed militia is their best security."

Oddly enough, this topsy-turvy view of regulars and militia was reversed once again on September 11, 2001. Prior to the terrorist attacks on the World Trade Center towers and the Pentagon, the US Commission on National Security in the 21st Century, having warned that terrorists would in fact attack America, strongly recommended that the National Guard be trained and equipped for the homeland security mission, its original Constitutional purpose. Though not yet adopted as the official policy of the United States government or even debated comprehensively, this issue needs to be addressed.

The question of which army should defend America's homeland is already being raised, albeit obliquely, in the post-9/11 period. Not too long after the terrorist attacks, voices in Congress and the Administration raised the ancient issue, whether realizing its rich history or not, by urging reconsideration of the so-called Posse Comitatus Act. Senator John Warner, Chairman of the Senate Armed Services Committee, and Undersecretary of Defense Paul Wolfowitz, have both urged "reconsideration" of the Act to permit a greater role for the standing military in defense of the US homeland.

This is a crucial issue, though not so far recognized as such by opinion leaders and public alike. The Posse Comitatus Act was passed by Congress in the wake, ironically, of the threatened use of military forces following the last razor-thin national election in 1876. The term *"Posse Comitatus,"* according to Black's Law Dictionary, is simply "the power or force of the county," the entire adult population whom the sheriff may summon and deputize to guarantee the peace. The Act itself forbade regular military forces from occupying or conducting operations on American soil:

> From and after passage of this act it shall not be lawful to employ any part of the Army of the United States, as a posse comitatus, or otherwise, for the purpose of executing the laws, except in such cases and under such circumstances as such employment of said forces may be expressly authorized by the Constitution or by act of Congress.

That infamous date, "9/11," now raises a fundamental Constitutional issue, hitherto largely ignored or evaded. Which United States army should have the primary responsibility to protect the security of America's homeland? Should it be the regular army or the militia, the professional or the citizen-soldier? Does the age of terrorism justify overturning a 225-year American belief system and reversing a 2800-year history of the republic?

This is the question being raised, once again obliquely, by those who wish to "revisit" the Posse Comitatus Act. And it just might be the most important issue raised by the age of terrorism. For it could well determine how and by whom US constitutional rights and civil liberties will be protected on domestic soil in the future, whether indeed the American people must sacrifice those liberties to protect their security, and even what kind of nation and people the Americans are. If the Pentagon becomes the principal public safety agency, if uniformed standing soldiers guard US streets, if the principal domestic guardians are professional military forces, then the American Republic, whose flag the people salute and to which they pledge allegiance, will no longer exist as such.

Should a major catastrophe strike the United States, few would argue that the organization, manpower, and strength of its military forces should not be employed. Clearly, in a time of great national emergency, the nation will call upon all its resources to protect itself and respond in every conceivable way to all the demands of that emergency. US military forces have communications, health, transportation, and other systems – almost all to one degree or another mobile and portable – that could prove critical in an emergency. It would be folly to argue that, based upon an abstract political theory, these forces and systems should not be deployed to help affected communities, regions or the nation at large.

However, that is not the issue. According to the ideal of the historic republic, and particularly the principles of the American Republic, the front line of defense of the homeland is composed of the citizen-soldiers who formed the original militia, and for whom the Second Amendment was designed, and who now form the 50 State National Guards. This was their original Constitutional mission and one for which the National Guard must be urgently trained and equipped. Only when their homeland security training, equipment and resources prove inadequate – when a disaster or attack is of the greatest magnitude – are the regular forces to be called upon. In a word, under the Constitution and history the standing army is the last, rather than the first resort for ensuring domestic security against terrorist attack.

Further, as a practical matter, the National Guard is "forward deployed" in hundreds of communities, including in all major cities, across the country. The Colorado National Guard and its equipment, for example, have much more immediate access to the urban areas of Colorado than most major standing army units. The one exception is the Fourth Army division stationed at Fort Carson, Colorado. However, this is the exception that proves the point. If Colorado were to be attacked, the front-line forces are the Colorado National Guard, which are to be supplemented and back-stopped, if necessary, by the regular Army.

One of the great perplexities of post-9/11 America, however, is the lack of urgency about homeland security generally and the preparation of the National Guard particularly. This lack of urgency is made even more inexplicable by a statement made to a National Guard unit by President George W. Bush less than 30 days after taking office:

> As threats to America change, your role will continue to change. The National Guard and Reservists will be more involved in homeland security, confronting acts of terror and the disorder our enemies may try to create. I welcome the important part you will play in protecting our nation and its people."

Nevertheless, this lack of urgency prevailed and was documented more than a year after the first major terrorist attack (almost all experts agree there will be others) in a task force report by the Council on Foreign Relations entitled: "America—Still Unprepared, Still at Risk." That report, following the recommendations of the US Commission on National Security in the 21st Century, urged the President and Congress to take all actions necessary to train and equip the National Guard for the homeland security task:

> A year after September 11, 2001, America remains dangerously unprepared to prevent and respond to a catastrophic terrorist attack on U.S. soil...An aggressive approach to revamping the capabilities of National Guard units designated to respond to domestic terrorist attacks can in the short term provide a more robust response capability while states and localities work to bring their individual response mechanisms up to par.

To date, that has not been done.

Indeed, now that the United States seems bogged down in Iraq for the foreseeable future, possibly a number of years, it will be even more difficult to assign this mission to the Guard. Now Guard units are deployed, in some cases for many months, in reconstruction, peace-making and peace-keeping chores in Iraq, Bosnia, Afghanistan, and quite soon, probably in Liberia as well. This will prevent preparing the citizen-soldiers, now quasi-permanent expeditionary forces, for the more crucial and urgent task of defending US home shores. Jefferson, and possibly even Hamilton, would be dismayed.

If one were to refer to the Sage of the Revolution, Benjamin Franklin, on this basic issue one might appreciate both his foresight and his wisdom. It was he, of course, who responded to the question of a concerned citizen outside the Constitutional convention as to the nature of the new nation by describing it as "a republic, if you can keep it." However, almost twenty years earlier, he wrote: "They that can give up essential liberty to obtain a little temporary safety deserve neither liberty nor safety." Doubtless today Franklin would conclude that by seeking domestic security through the deployment of a professional army on America's homeland and in its neighborhoods we would be giving up essential liberty to obtain safety and would be taking a giant step toward losing the republic.

Formulating a Grand Strategy

Thus, the "Age of Jihad" has caused the United States to return to the very nature of its republican heritage. It also requires the country to adopt a totally new strategy for a revolutionary age. Indeed, it requires Americans to adopt a new grand strategy.

Grand strategy has to do with the application of power and resources to larger national purposes. In the case of the United States, its power in the 21st century is economic, political and military in nature. In each of these categories its powers are greater in magnitude than those of any other nation – friend or rival – and, in the case of military power at least, greater than several of the next strongest nations combined. America possesses a fourth power, the power of principle, which may turn out to be its greatest strategic asset in the 21st century. Much depends on whether and how this asset is employed.

[212]

Today the United States, the world's greatest power, possesses abundant, even historic power but lacks a grand strategy. It does not have a coherent plan to apply its powers to achieve broad national purposes or even a consensus as to what these national purposes are. The United States is much clearer about the extent of its power than about how it should be used and what ends it should serve.

There are general objectives – peace, prosperity, and so forth – to which all Americans subscribe, but these are abstractions and relative ones at that. Whose peace? How much prosperity? Being in favor of a "strong national defense" was such a common political catchphrase during the Cold War that it became a cliché. No one actually favored a weak defense.

The Cold War had the curious advantage of offering a larger national purpose – containment of communism – and a simple, understandable one at that. It was a kind of central organizing principle around which policies could be shaped, resources mustered, and the public engaged. For the period between 1946 and 1991, it became the grand strategy for the United States and its allies.

Strategically, all was well until the virtual overnight collapse of the Soviet Union and with it, the threat of communist expansion against which containment was structured. Suddenly, containment of communism as a strategic focus lost its relevance. The United States, now the world's sole superpower, found itself triumphant but strategically adrift. Overnight it lost its large national purpose and any coherent notion of how to apply its economic, political, and military power in order to achieve it.

During the last decade of the 20th century it was not as if the triumph of democracy – the "end of history" it was called – brought with it a utopian golden age. Trouble abounded, although some of it was repressed during the bipolar ideological struggle of the second half of the 20th century. Artificial states, such as Yugoslavia, collapsed in turmoil. African tribes slaughtered each other with machetes, and warlords chased the world's greatest power from Somalia. Drug cartels undertook to govern Colombia. An epidemic of new conflicts spawned by ancient grievances stimulated nostalgia for the strategic simplicity of the Cold War.

Then came the events of 9/11. Nineteen suicidal young men armed with tradesmen's tools turned four commercial aircraft into guided missiles killing 3,000 Americans. At the very least, this event signaled the resumption of history, albeit in a new form. However, unlike communism's threat to Europe, Asia, Africa and Latin America, this event failed to provide a new central organizing principle equivalent to the containment of communism.

For the time being, the "war on terrorism," with its overthrow of the government of Afghanistan and invasion of Iraq, has sufficed to fill the vacuum of national purpose. However, few would argue that this war represents an American grand strategy – the application of its powers to broad national purposes – worthy of a great nation. Rather, terrorism and the responses it demands might best be seen as a metaphor for an emerging age for which a new grand strategy must be created.

The first step in erecting the framework for such a new grand strategy must be an understanding of the historic realities characterizing our age. In contrast to the stagnant and linear second half of the 20th century, the early 21st century is revolutionary in terms of several dimensions. Globalization, the name given to the internationalization of commerce and finance, is fundamentally transforming markets and is challenging the authority of central banks and national financial and regulatory structures. Capital flows and multinational corporate entities operating complex cross-border transactions are defying national constraints.

Simultaneously, the Information Revolution, the equivalent of the Industrial Revolution in the early 19th century, is transforming the economies of the advanced world and expanding the divide – in this case a digital divide – between the developed and the underdeveloped worlds. The advent of the silicon chip and miniature processors has transformed productivity, revolutionized the workplace, and expanded communications explosively—at least for those on the positive side of this digital divide.

Both these revolutions have gradually eroded the authority of the nation-state, the fundamental political building-block since the mid-17th century. Not only have national financial regulatory structures suffered from the internationalization of commerce, but tribalism, fundamentalism, privatization, and other forces of disintegration have begun seriously to challenge the authority of the state to guarantee social and economic stability. Moreover, non-state actors, especially terrorist organizations, challenge the state's monopoly on violence and its compact with its national citizens to provide protection in exchange for loyalty.

This phenomenon, terrorism, represents the fourth 21st century revolution, the transformation of the nature of conflict. Not only do states no longer control when, where, and how violence or war is to be conducted, in accordance with established international rules, but terrorism and its antecedents, which include Mafias, cartels, tribes, clans and gangs, do not owe allegiance to any state, often have no political objectives, and directly target civilian society.

Thus, globalization, the Information Revolution, eroding nation-state authority, and the changing nature of conflict all represent the foundation of 21st century realities. The framework for an American grand strategy should be constructed upon these realities and should be in response to them. To neglect these new revolutionary realities, to assume the new century will be merely a linear extension of the last, is an invitation to folly and failure.

A further and equally dangerous error is to assume, because of its unrivaled power, that the United States is at liberty to do as it wishes, that it can flaunt its power, bully its inferiors, and unilaterally exercise its own will. In addition to recognizing the revolutionary realities of the 21st century, the United States' new grand strategy must also recognize its constraints—those resulting from US membership in the world community, its lifestyle and patterns of resource consumption, and access to instant information.

More explicitly, the United States is a member, and often the leading one, of a number of 20th century organizations and alliances both bilateral and multilateral in character. The North Atlantic Treaty Organization (NATO) is the most prominent of these, but dozens of others bind the United States, so long as it agrees to be bound, to certain cooperative commitments. In the early years of the new century, the current US government is either directly challenging those commitments or assuming it is at liberty to act as it wishes regardless of their terms. Nevertheless, strategic planning requires that those obligations and commitments either be acknowledged and taken into account or formally abrogated, with the acceptance of all the attendant consequences.

An additional constraint on strategy is America's continued dependence on foreign natural resources, especially petroleum supplies, to fuel its increasing energy demands. This dependence requires a coherent national strategy to acknowledge and take into account this dependence, either to support it militarily or reduce it. A 21st century grand strategy is obliged to deal seriously with this dependence, which is so central to the American way of life.

Further, the United States is constrained by its increasing demand for foreign investment to finance its debt and even to pay for its defenses. This constraint is most graphically illustrated by America's huge trade or balance of payments deficits and by its reliance on foreign public and private investors to the extent of hundreds of billions of dollars. Like other constraints, the implications of this dependence must be explored further as the search for a new national strategy is pursued.

Finally, though by no means exhaustively, America is, or at least ought to be, constrained by its own Constitutional heritage, its espoused beliefs and ideals—in short, its principles. Cold War exigencies led the United States to erode and sometimes violate those principles in its perceived

[216]

need to protect itself. The historic antecedents for abandonment of its highest principles were often characterized as *realpolitik* or justified as *raison d'etat*. Of all the constraints under which the United States operates in the new 21st century, the one that most requires attention in devising a grand strategy and offers the most compelling challenge, is the country's adherence to its own principles. This is particularly true if one accepts the premise offered here that America's fourth power, its principles, represents its most potent asset, and if one accepts the further premise that the exercise of this fourth power, the power of principle, inevitably conditions the exercise of the three traditional powers of economics, politics, and the military.

Arguably, strategy would be simpler if it were played out on the horizontal plane – as many suppose it to be – of using power, particularly military power, to deter or respond to threats, to achieve dominance, or to obtain national objectives, such as securing oil supplies. However, America's larger purposes must embrace opportunities as well as threats, possibilities as well as constraints, and progress as well as decay. In short, larger national purposes and the resources applied to achieve them must include clear-eyed, practical and realistic ways of alleviating the human condition, both for its own sake as a humanitarian ideal as well as a strategy to reduce the conditions and causes of violence and the widespread resentment of American wealth. People with the hope of a better life seldom seek out the terrorist's camp.

Twenty-first century strategists will consider economic and political power as being equal in importance to military power and, in some instances, credit the former with even more effective influence. A potential threat that never comes to fruition is a victory won. If a standard principle of military strategy is the concentration of maximum force at the decisive point of impact, the same must be true of economic development, financial investment, diplomatic attention and benign political influence.

Thus, grand strategy becomes a multi-dimensional chessboard much more than a war game table, a relief map of peaks, contours and depressions rather than a flat surface. In addition, the powers and resources brought to bear on the objective represent values that change with circumstances—a pawn today, a knight tomorrow. Thus on the one hand, Special Forces might point laser designators at distant mountain caves to guide ordnance to the target but on the other hand, humanitarian relief workers might feed starving refugee children. On the one hand, cruise missiles might be fired from unmanned aircraft destroy a chemical weapons dump but on the other hand, wells might be drilled and irrigation systems built to grow food for drought-stricken villagers. A serious strategist will appreciate the importance of both approaches, indeed of a multitude of approaches, some never before conceived, to help in the defeat of terrorism and to further US interests.

These examples illustrate yet another characteristic of strategy, the distinction between means and ends. If the purpose is to defeat terrorism, means other than or in addition to force must be employed. This is especially true in a new century in which revolutionary realities do not lend themselves to purely one-dimensional military response.

It would, therefore, be especially troublesome, and possibly even dangerous, for the "war on terrorism" to be mistaken for a national strategy. This is even more true of the recently-introduced doctrine of preemption, the self-proclaimed right to initiate a military attack on a nation or set of actors perceived to represent an imminent threat. Leaving aside complex and troublesome questions of national morality and international law, to elevate a doctrine such as preemption to the level of strategy, let alone grand strategy, is to misunderstand the strategic enterprise.

Preemption in this context is little better than an organic impulse—"I'll strike you before you strike me." Such an impulse, or doctrine if you wish, falls far short of grand strategy. To declare a policy of anticipatory self-defense may, at best, be seen as one doctrinal facet of a greater military strategy. Even so, it is just one of many options open to policy makers and military commanders to carry out much larger objectives contained in a serious grand strategy of a major power.

Likewise, much the same could be said of notions such as containment. Containment in the Cold War context might rise to the level of national strategy, in that its historic context was an epic struggle involving one great bloc of nations resisting a perceived hegemon represented by a distinctly aggressive ideology and another great bloc of nations. Yet, containment of terrorism as a strategic concept falls far short of the strategic principle of applying national resources to achieve broader purposes.

Surely, in this new revolutionary age, America's larger purposes may include, but must go much beyond mere containment or even elimination of terrorism. Terrorism constitutes both an immediate threat and a symptom of greater challenges. Those challenges include widespread resentment of American power, foreign policy and commercial culture. They include threats to increasingly fragile oil supplies. They include intricate and complex international financial systems vulnerable both to cyber attack and global recession. They include failed and failing states and the challenge of the forces of disintegration, such as tribalism, on traditional nation-states.

These are examples of a much greater phenomenon, the revolutionary world of the 21st century, a world requiring not only new approaches but a new mentality that appreciates the interrelationship of these new challenges and the interrelationship of the responses to them. This is the response to those who might ask, Why the need for a grand strategy? During the unstructured, post-Cold War 1990s, the President's National Security Advisor was heard to disclaim any notion of an overarching strategy and to advocate an ad hoc approach to the crises that might (and did) arise.

[219]

Certainly, this reactive approach is an alternative to grand strategy. The current government's theological approach to security issues – the "axis of evil"– is another. Arguably, both qualify as "strategy" in the most prosaic sense of the word. However, grand strategy, in the classic sense used here, is a systematic, ordered, coherent enterprise that takes into account the nation's total resources, its capabilities and constraints, and its traditions, culture and values to achieve great objectives that include, but are not limited to, its own security. At least to the degree that the two political parties represent consensus thinking in America and the potential to implement that thinking, the two "strategic" options available for consideration are the reactive approach and the theological approach.

This essay challenges these two current approaches on two grounds: they are inadequate as coherent guides for the kind of American action that is required to address the new realities of the 21st century; and they are not strategies in any meaningful sense of the word. More traditional strategies of containment, unilateralism, hegemony and isolationism must also be analyzed for their potential relevance to 21st century realities. In each case, however, the four revolutions of globalization, information, sovereignty and conflict challenge their relevance.

A Strategy Based on the Power of Principle

A grand strategy centered around the fourth power of principle and the application of economic, political and military powers based on national principle must directly address these four revolutions and thus, they will be discussed with some specificity in that context. By definition, a grand strategy must be relevant to be meaningful, and this relevance must be gauged by its applicability to the realities it must address. The test is not coherence in the abstract sense but implementation in the context of the concrete realities of the times.

- First, the United States needs to examine the revolutionary realities of the times in structural terms. What kind of world do we now live in? Is it sufficiently new and different to require new strategic thinking?

- Second, the powers, resources and assets of the United States need to be assessed. What are the national strengths available to the United States? In this connection, some attention will be paid to unconventional US strengths and assets.

- Third, constraints on the exercise of US powers and the employment of its resources ought to be more fully analyzed. What are the genuine limits on US powers?

- Fourth, traditional concepts and US policies that now pass for strategies should be critiqued for their relevance to new 21st century realities. Important terms such as "security" and "preemption" must be defined with some precision. Is current thinking adequate to deal with new 21st century realities and does it take account of both US strengths and limitations adequately?

- Fifth, on the basis of this foundation, considerable attention should then be paid to US goals and purposes. What are the definable US goals in the new century and what priority does the nation give to them?

The answers to all these questions will provide the framework for a grand strategy for the United States in the early 21st century. We will attempt to propose how the United States should apply its powers to achieve its larger national goals.

However, the world now faces the most important reality of the post-Cold War world, the US occupation of Iraq. The Bush administration does not wish to call it an "occupation," but that is the way it is seen by jihadists and critics of the United States alike. Even as the United States attempts to address the revolutionary world of the early 21st century, the nation must have a much more comprehensive plan for Iraq than merely "victory," defined by the Bush administration as a stable, self-secure Iraq.

[221]

Several steps are required to be taken in Iraq and these are outlined below:

- The United States should establish negotiations with Sunni Arabs to agree to a mutual and speedy draw-down of forces. The US should then pull an agreed number of troops out of an occupational role in exchange for insurgent disarmament and completely withdraw such forces whenever the insurgency abandons the use of force and joins political discussions.
- Shia and Kurdish forces, as well as former Sunni insurgent elements should be tasked with the role of isolating and expelling jihadists from outside, most of whom are Saudi in origin.
- The United States should declare that it does not intend and will not construct permanent military bases in Iraq.
- US occupation forces should be replaced with NATO peacekeeping units which will oversee the training of Iraqi police and military units and move those trained units into the principal security roles, especially border control missions to seal Iraq off from outside jihadists.
- A genuine, international reconstruction program should be organized for the benefit of Iraq, with European and Asian contracting companies involved in competitive bidding for major infrastructural projects— such as water, waste management, transportation and communications.
- A Bank for Iraqi Reconstruction should be established, funded by all Western democratic governments, to finance national reconstruction.
- A new Iraq oil company should be created as a consortium of the Iraq Ministry of Oil and major international oil producers to build modern production and distribution facilities and allocate revenues fairly to all Iraqis.

These steps are illustrative of a more concrete approach to Iraqi independence. However, they also require a formal declaration that the United States does not intend any long term military presence in Iraq. If the United States constructs permanent military bases and encourages the new Iraqi government to invite the US troops to stay, this will convince people in the Middle East that the neo-conservative agenda is still alive.

Beyond Iraq, the United States must now restore its republican principles, make those principles the centerpiece of a new approach to international relations, and collaborate with all people of goodwill to address the new agenda of the 21st century—proliferation of weapons of mass destruction, climate change and global warming, massive South–North migrations in Europe and North America, failed and failing states and the threat of pandemics such as avian flu.

None of these new realities can be solved by military means and none can be solved by a single nation, not even by the United States acting in isolation. Thus, the 21st century will require greater international cooperation, including concerted efforts by nations of the Middle East, than at any other time in human history.

ROLE OF INSTITUTIONS
IN THE PROCESS OF CHANGE

10

Managing Challenges to Sovereignty in an Era of Regionalism: Asia and the Arab World

Dr. Amitav Acharya

This chapter examines the changing relationship between regionalism and sovereignty in Asia and the Arab World. The purpose here is not to make a case for the defense of sovereignty. Whether sovereignty needs to be "protected" and if so, from which threats, are issues that generate much controversy. An excessive deference to state sovereignty has been implicated in some of the worst human tragedies of our time. The issue is not whether absolute sovereignty is to be safeguarded at all costs, but how the international community, of which regional organizations are an integral part, can manage challenges to sovereignty in principled ways that would preserve international order. A related issue is to develop criteria under which regional organizations may depart from sovereignty for the sake of some higher collective good.

The chapter is divided into four sections. The first looks at the conceptual relationship between regionalism and sovereignty, especially the different ways in which regional institutions have dealt with or affected the institutions of sovereignty in international relations. The second section sketches the historical background to regionalism in Asia and the Arab world, comparing their approach to and impact on state sovereignty and its norms. The third section reviews the recent developments in world politics that have challenged the salience of state sovereignty, particularly in Asia, where regional institutions are under increasing pressure to alter their ways in dealing with common problems. In the fourth and final section, some thoughts are offered on the lessons to be drawn by the Arab world from the new trends in Asian regionalism.

Until now, most comparative studies of regionalism have considered Europe (be it the European Union or the Organization for Security and Cooperation in Europe) as the "mother" of all regionalisms and not only used it as the model for judging the progress of regionalism elsewhere, but also sought to apply its lessons to other regions.[1] In this chapter, it will be argued that Asia rather than Europe offers a more appropriate example of regionalism for other regions in the developing world, and that the recent experience of Asian regionalism may offer a better model for the Arab World, despite significant differences between the two regions.

Regionalism and Sovereignty

Scholars of international relations have long debated the relationship between regionalism and state sovereignty. Some of these debates revolve around the question of whether regionalism undermines or enhances state sovereignty. This constitutes a basic point of difference between post-Second World War European regionalism and regionalism in the developing world, including the Arab world and Asia. Other disagreements about regionalism relate to the specific ways in which regionalism can challenge state sovereignty.

In this chapter, four main pathways are identified by which regionalism and regional institutions have affected sovereignty. First, regional organizations may be the focal point for states to bargain away sovereignty for some common social purpose and collective good. Second, regionalism may be employed by states to preserve their sovereignty from inter-state disputes and intervention/interference by outside powers. Third, regionalism can be a tool in the hands of powerful states to create pan-national federations which challenge the legitimacy of nation-states. Fourth, regional organizations may resort to intervention for humanitarian objectives, or what has been called "humanitarian intervention." The following sections provide a brief elaboration of these pathways.

The role of the regional organization as a receptacle for the voluntary surrender by states of their sovereignty, or parts thereof, is the basic West European model, which evolved from the European Coal and Steel Community to today's European Union. The EU model has three basic characteristics: functionalism/neo-functionalism, inter-governmentalism and/or supra-nationalism. Functionalism implies that cooperation in areas of low politics can gradually spill over into cooperation in areas of high politics. Neo-functionalism, a variation on functionalism, means that cooperation cannot be an automatic or linear process because political interventions and the role of the governments in promoting the integration process are crucial. Inter-governmentalism and supra-nationalism are sometimes viewed as alternative ways of conceptualizing how the EU works, with the former giving a greater agency role to national governments in determining the outcomes of regional bargaining, while supra-nationalism places more emphasis on the role of a central bureaucracy, which stands above and over individual governments. In reality, both inter-governmentalism and supra-nationalism have been evident in the EU integration process, and what they both represent is that this form of regionalism is state-led, rather than market-driven.

Some argue that the voluntary act of surrender of sovereignty in the EU should not be regarded as an erosion of the nation-state as a fundamental institution of world politics. After all, the act of surrendering a part of one's control over areas of national decision-making itself represents a supreme exercise of sovereignty or a pooling of sovereignty.[2] The key drivers of the EU integration process are not coercion, but socialization and persuasion. Yet, the EU model of voluntary surrender of sovereignty has no parallel elsewhere in the world. The reason is not hard to find. The EU experience was possible because of the collective experience of the two World Wars and the widespread realization in Europe that the unbridled sovereignty of the nation-state was a major catalyst of these wars and thus had to be curbed. No such realization accompanied the impulse towards regionalism in the developing world. On the contrary, the achievement of nation-statehood and Westphalian sovereignty was seen by the developing countries in fundamentally moral terms, as emancipation and the attainment of formal equality. It should be recalled that under the colonial order, sovereignty was seen as an exclusive attribute of "civilized" peoples and thus the non-European regions were deemed unworthy of sovereignty and thus fundamentally unequal members of the international system.

With the decolonization process and the emergence of newly-independent countries as a political force, it was thus natural that the EU model of regional integration was seen as an unsuitable or even dangerous experiment to be emulated. Instead of seriously considering even a slight act of voluntary surrender of sovereignty for a regionalist project, developing countries have engaged in regionalism and used regional institutions primarily to accelerate national liberation and defend their sovereignty. This has meant different types of regional institutions, including security arrangements, none of which are based on the EU model of functionalism and intergovernmentalism/supra-nationalism.

The second pathway by which regional organizations have affected sovereignty in the international system is by acting as its bulwark, rather than challenging it. Instead of the EU model, what really found appeal in the developing world is regionalism and institutions that protect the nation-state by providing mechanisms for conflict-control, especially for the settlement of intra-regional disputes and reducing the scope for extra-regional, great power intervention. At the drafting of the United Nations Charter in San Francisco in 1945, regionalists from Latin America and the

Arab World, including members of the newly formed League of Arab States, debated with "universalists" from the Roosevelt Administration as to why regional organizations should share with the United Nations a role in the peaceful management of international conflict, especially in their own neighborhood. They own a partial but important victory, securing a role as first points of referral for regional disputes. This role in the pacific settlement of regional disputes and the creation of regional norms of non-intervention, such as those articulated at the Bandung Conference in 1955, have been the most common purpose of regional organizations in the developing world aimed at defending, rather than diluting state sovereignty.

One exception to this early-post World War II attachment of developing states to Westphalian sovereignty was the effort by some nationalist leaders in locally powerful states to imagine and pursue pan-national unions. This constitutes a third way in which regionalism has challenged sovereignty in the international system. Examples of this pan-regionalism can be found in pan-Americanism in South America, pan-Africanism in black Africa, and pan-Arabism in the Arab world. The basic motivation here is not functional cooperation for an objective common good or agenda, although there may be such specific goals, but the pursuit of a subjective or inter-subjective identity. This type of pan-nationalism is most evident in the early 20th century and in the early post-World War II period, but its appeal has progressively diluted ever since. Moreover, there is little doubt that in the struggle between the nation-state model with its attribute of Westphalian sovereignty and the pan-nationalist ideals in the developing world, the former has prevailed decisively. A major feature of these types of efforts is the central role of a charismatic personality, often ruling over a relatively powerful state in the region: Simon Bolivar in Latin America, Kwame Nkrumah in Africa and Gamel Abdul Nasser in the Arab world. Yet, precisely because of this, pan-nationalist schemes were thwarted by the inevitable suspicions of a large power by its smaller and weaker neighbors. Few newly independent states were willing to accept this new form of dominance after shaking off centuries of colonial rule. Moreover, the fact that in many cases, certainly in Nkrumah's Ghana and Nasser's Egypt, the aspiring leaders were not hesitant about using coercive means to propagate their regionalist visions added to the misgivings about these schemes and contributed to their eventual failure.

The fourth pathway by which regional organizations have challenged state sovereignty is a recent development: the idea of "responsibility to protect" and the practice of humanitarian intervention. NATO's role in Kosovo offers the most potent contemporary example of this role by a regional entity (although to many, NATO would count as a alliance or a collective defense organization, rather than as a regional organization under the UN Charter.) However, other regional institutions have begun to contemplate humanitarian assistance, if not "intervention" in weak or failed states, and experience significant internal conflict in their neighborhood. The African Union's recent initiatives in this regard are noteworthy. A variation of this role is the "democracy promotion" role of regional organizations, especially that of the Organization of American States (OAS). Common to these roles is a qualified transgression of the norm of non-interference in the internal affairs of states, under circumstances deemed to be exceptional. Theoretically, such interventions are supposed to be undertaken by legitimate authority, usually with the UN Security Council authorization. In practice, regional organizations have not fulfilled these criteria. Sometimes, they have merely rubber-stamped the intervention of a great power, such as the sanctioning of the US invasion of Grenada (for a geopolitical, rather than humanitarian motive) by the Organization of Eastern Caribbean States (OECS). NATO's intervention in Kosovo was undertaken without Security Council authorization, although a post-facto authorization was sought and obtained. The criteria for humanitarian intervention has been hotly debated, although the recommendations of the report of the International

[232]

Commission of Humanitarian Intervention and State Sovereignty, *Responsibility to Protect*,[3] have now found increasing acceptance in the United Nations as the basic criteria for such intervention, whether by the UN or by regional organizations. It should be noted, though, that the report and its follow-up documents show a distinct preference for such intervention by the UN, rather than by regional organizations.

Comparing Asian and Arab Regionalism: A Brief Historical Background

With the above points serving as a conceptual framework, one may turn to a brief overview of how regional organizations in Asia and the Arab World have dealt with the issue of state sovereignty. A comparative analysis also permits an exploration of the similarities and differences between the two regions when it comes to institution-building.

Such a comparison must begin by noting some important differences between the two regions. One key difference concerns the homogeneity of the two regions, no matter how we define them. The Arab world is one of the most homogenous entities in the world in ethnic, cultural, linguistic and religious terms, while Asia is perhaps the most diverse continent on earth. Here one has to be careful about regional definition. The two regions we are comparing are "Asia" on the one hand, and the "Arab world," rather than the "Middle East," on the other (my own preference would be for the "Arab world"). The term "Arab world" has until now not been used extensively in the literature on international regions, where the dominant notion of region has been "Middle East" or "Near East." Both "Asia" and "Middle East" were European constructs, and the term "Middle East" came into usage much later than the term "Asia" in European writings. The distinction between "Asia" and the "Arab world" is not always neat; some parts of the latter are sometimes subsumed under "Asia" (e.g. "West Asia"). However, there is little question that if the "Arab world" is a more homogenous entity not only in relation to the

"Middle East" (this in itself is a chief rationale for its usage instead of the latter), it is also much more so in relation to Asia. There is little doubt that the homogeneity of the holistic Arab world also exceeds that of any sub-regional configuration in Asia, such as "Southeast Asia," "South Asia" or "Northeast Asia," all of which are modern, arbitrary formulations inspired by colonial or Cold War geopolitics.

Two other differences between the Arab world and Asia may be noted. The former was the first among the two to develop a formal regional organization. The first Arab regional organization, the League of Arab States, was established in 1945, before the first Asian regional organization, the still-born Asian Relations Organization, was established by India in 1947. The first viable Asian regional organization, the Association of South East Asian Nations (ASEAN), did not emerge till 1967. A further point of contrast between Asian and Arab regionalism is that in the Arab case, there has been at least a notion of a common threat, Israel, around which regional identities and cooperation could be galvanized, at least theoretically. There has been no such consensus on a threat in Asia.

Yet, despite its greater homogeneity as a region, and longer history of regional organization, and the existence of a common threat, the regionalism in the Arab world has arguably made lesser headway in realizing its professed objectives than its Asian counterpart. Why?

This is primarily because Arab regionalists have set themselves a far more ambitious task than their Asian counterparts. To be sure, neither Asian nor the Arab world believed in or espoused the kind of visionary functionalist agenda as did Western Europe after World War II. India led Asian regionalism by convening the Asian Relations Conference in 1947 and the Conference on Indonesia in 1949 (also known as the Second Asian Relations Conference). However, neither of these conferences produced anything concrete in terms of economic or functional cooperation comparable to the European Coal and Steel Community, through which Jean Monnet and Robert Schuman hoped to render war unlikely by controlling its two most essential ingredients of weaponry. Indeed, European style economic cooperation, starting with a free trade area, and then moving into a customs union and a common market, was not been a feature of either Arab or Asian regionalism during the early post-war period; and it emerged in Asia only towards the 1990s through the sub-regional framework of ASEAN.

Indeed, up to a point, the interests and objectives of regionalists in the two regions converged. Nationalist leaders from both regions came together at the historic 1955 Bandung Conference. Although nominally it was an "Asia–Africa Conference," in reality, there were very few representatives and voices from sub-Saharan Africa at the meeting (Ethiopia and Ghana being notable exceptions, although the British successfully blocked Nkhrumah from attending, forcing Ghana to send more junior representatives, while Rhodesia turned down the invitation). By contrast, Arab leaders played a major role at the conference, with Nasser being the star attraction. This was his first international conference, and he clearly enjoyed the attention, being at his charming best, while playing a key mediating role to resolve stalemates. The Arab representatives were of course divided along Cold War lines, with Iraq (a member of the Baghdad Pact) Iran and Lebanon taking a strong pro-Western line along with Turkey. Nasser sided with the neutralists led by India's Jawaharlal Nehru, although he was far from being regarded as "lost" to the West at this time. His full-scale turn to non-alignment (as neutralism came to be known) came soon after, and Bandung was undoubtedly a major influence. Bandung also provided Nasser an opportunity to meet the Chinese leader, Zhou En-lai, another star of the Conference, and some analysts have suggested that it was at Bandung that Nasser conceived of an arms deal with the Soviet Bloc in consultation with Zhou. In any case, Bandung failed to produce a standing Asia–Africa organization, although it gave birth to the global Non-Aligned Movement

[235]

(NAM) in which Nasser was a founding member. More importanly, Nasser turned to an aggressive policy of pan-Arabism, promoting it with a highly interventionist policy towards his neighbors.

Herein lies a basic contrast between the trajectories of Asian and Arab regionalism as it pertains to the issue of sovereignty. Nasser's pan-Arabism, which assumed that the division of the Arab nation into sovereign states was but a temporary phenomenon that had to be overcome, had no Asian equivalent. Although Nehru and others championed Asian unity, they did so strictly within the framework of the nation-state and Westphalian sovereignty. There was no attempt to create a pan-Asian super-state. The nation-state, however arbitrary its physical boundaries and ethnic composition, was there to stay. Asians had no desire or hope for restoring the pre-colonial unity of even sub-regions, where it might have existed. It also reflected the greater physical and cultural diversity of Asia compared to the Arab world. However, by limiting expectations about what regionalism could realistically hope to achieve, Asia's subsequent regional institutions would achieve greater success than their counterparts in the Arab world.

Pan-Arabism was of course an institutional failure, producing only one short-lived union, the United Arab Republic. Gradually, the nation-state model came to prevail over the dream of a single Arab nation, as it had done in Africa in relation to pan-Africanism. The League of Arab States remained an association of nation-states, without any supranational institutions. Yet, the challenge of pan-Arabism took its toll on the League's regional conflict-control function.

Compared to Asia, the Arab world had an early start in providing a regional conflict-control mechanism. At inception, the League had established principles for peaceful settlement of disputes, and at least in theory provided for a collective defense mechanism against outside intervention. As noted before, Asia had no such regional mechanism, although regional conferences held in Asia and under Asian leadership, including the Bandung Conference, did articulate norms of non-interference for reducing intra-regional conflicts and great power rivalry. Arguably, however, these had a greater effect on the Asian security architecture even in the absence of a formal organization, than on the security dynamics of the Arab world, where as mentioned earlier, non-interference was frequently flouted (for the sake of Arab nationalism). Moreover, the theoretical availability of a collective defense mechanism did not provide the Arab world any greater immunity from outside intervention. The fact is that both regions suffered from external penetration, with the Cold War acting as a common framework for such interventions. However, this seems particularly ironic in the Arab case, where the common aversion to the intrusive presence of Israel in the region should have served as an additional basis for coordinating security policies against external intervention. In reality, the Arab-Israel conflict was as much a divisive factor in the regionalist politics of the Arab world as a unifying force.

While the weakening of pan-Arabism as a political force meant the alternative model of a Westphalian inter-state system defined the Arab world's security architecture, it did not translate into strength for the Arab League and its institutions. Asia experienced greater success in this regard, but not necessarily at the regional level. It was through a sub-regional organization, rather than ASEAN, that some Asian actors were able to use regionalism to safeguard their sovereignty. They did so not by creating and resorting to formalistic and legalistic mechanisms, but through a set of informal practices which have come to be known as the "ASEAN Way." The key ingredients of the ASEAN Way, especially its processes of consensus-seeking and inclusiveness, were helpful in reducing intra-regional tensions in Southeast Asia, providing an avenue for the management of regional conflicts such as the Vietnamese invasion of Cambodia, to a much greater degree than the regional institutions in the Arab world, not just the League itself, but also sub-regional organizations such as the Gulf Cooperation Council (GCC). A comparative analysis of ASEAN and the GCC, will illustrate this contrast.

Comparing ASEAN and the GCC[4]

Both ASEAN and GCC belonged to the second wave of regional organizations which emerged in the developing world.[5] ASEAN was formed in 1967 and the GCC in 1981, after the original continental regional organizations, Organization of American States, The League of Arab States, and the Organization of African Unity, which dominated regional cooperation in the developing world, had declined. ASEAN could claim a little credit for being a regional pioneer, because for all practical purposes, it was the first regional organization in Asia, while the GCC members had belonged to the Arab League. Nonetheless, ASEAN's emergence was possible because earlier attempts at pan-Asian regionalism, spearheaded by nationalist leaders such as Jawaharlal Nehru of India, had failed in the face of the continent's enormous physical, cultural and political diversity, and the divisions brought about by the Cold War.

This leads to one comparative advantage of smaller regional groups, an advantage that applies more to the GCC than ASEAN. These groups were geographically more compact, culturally less heterogeneous and their members politically more like-minded than the membership of continental groups. Moreover, there were three striking similarities in the conditions and manner of their establishment.

First, both consisted of conservative regimes facing a revolutionary neighbor which threatened to export its revolution and thereby aggravate their members' existing internal security problems. Thus, the ASEAN members, already faced with the danger of communist insurgency, perceived the threat to become much greater with the communist takeover in Indochina and the unification of Vietnam under communist rule in

1975. The GCC members were threatened by the overthrow of the Iran's pro-Western Shah regime and the advent of a radical Islamic regime in Teheran, which made no secret of its desire to export its revolution around its neighborhood.

Second, both ASEAN and GCC members had to contend with a regional power within their own ranks: Indonesia in the case of ASEAN and Saudi Arabia in the case of the GCC. Although both these regional powers took a restrained approach to their respective neighbors (ASEAN after the changeover from the Sukarno to the Suharto regime), it nonetheless meant that regional cooperation would only be viable as long as the regional power remained internally stable and externally moderate and was willing to provide leadership in building regional cooperation. ASEAN would realize the importance of this factor the hard way after the overthrow of the Suharto regime in 1998.

A third similarity between ASEAN and GCC at the time of their inception was the security dependence of their members on the United States. Although both professed regional autonomy, with the GCC calling for the "Gulfanization of Gulf security" and ASEAN adopting the framework of Zone of Peace, Freedom and Neutrality (ZOPFAN), this apparent neutrality served to manage the reality of dependence on the US security umbrella.[6] There is little doubt that some degree of long-term security autonomy was a sincere goal of both groupings, especially after the credibility of the US security commitment in their respective regions could no longer be taken for granted (ASEAN after the US withdrawal from Vietnam and GCC after the Carter administration's perceived failure to support the falling regime of the Shah).[7] However, achieving a modicum of security independence called for an activist diplomatic track in managing existential threats to regional order and developing a long-term diplomatic capacity for intra- and extra-mural conflict management.

And here the parallels between the two groups end, especially in their subsequent evolution as regional security actors.

ASEAN adopted a much more vigorous diplomatic approach, both at the United Nations and at the regional level, in managing the Cambodia conflict from 1980 to 1991 than did the GCC in dealing with the Iran–Iraq War, the outbreak of which in 1980 was itself a catalyst for the GCC's formation. More importantly, ASEAN from the beginning maintained an inclusive approach to Vietnam, promising eventual reconciliation if and when Vietnam was to end its occupation of Cambodia. The GCC's role in seeking a diplomatic solution to the Iran–Iraq War was not pronounced by comparison.[8] A major difference between the security approach undertaken by ASEAN and GCC was with respect to defense cooperation. ASEAN, disillusioned by the South East Asia Treaty Organization (SEATO) experience, shunned defense cooperation except at the bilateral level.[9] It focused its energies on diplomatic networking and developing political habits of conflict avoidance and management. The GCC developed a more formal approach to military cooperation, to the extent of creating a joint force called the Peninsula Shield.[10]

Against this backdrop, the GCC could not, and did not develop a serious *modus vivendi* for long-term reconciliation and partnership with Iran and Iraq. Its greater sense of common cultural identity proved to be more of a liability in dealing with Iran, a non-Arab state, than ASEAN's more contrived but functional regional identity which reflected the region's historic tolerance for ethnic, religious and cultural diversity. In contrast, soon after the Cold War ended, ASEAN moved quickly to reward Vietnam's withdrawal from Cambodia by conferring its membership upon the former. Pursuing a "one Southeast Asia" concept, ASEAN during the 1990s became synonymous with the whole region of Southeast Asia.[11] No one can seriously envisage renewed conflict between Vietnam and the non-communist ASEAN members now.

Meanwhile, the GCC's relations with Iraq worsened, posing serious security challenges to its members.[12] To make matters worse for the GCC, the Saddam Hussein regime in Iraq continued to hold its members in contempt despite receiving generous aid from them till 1988, during its war against Iran. Bolstered also by Western support during the Iran–Iraq War, Saddam revived Iraq's irredentist claims on Kuwait, resulting in its disastrous invasion of the country in 1990 and the subsequent US-led war in 1991.

Another major difference between the approaches taken by the two groupings to regional security concerns their relationships with external powers. From the outset, ASEAN had developed a close economic and diplomatic relationship with the major Western powers. After the Cold War ended, this relationship was extended to Russia, China and India. In effect, ASEAN acted as a healer for the Cold War divide in its own region. It also played a key role in the development of wider and inclusive regional institutions, such as the Asia Pacific Economic Cooperation, ASEAN Regional Forum, the ASEAN Plus Three and the East Asian Summit. This cooperative security approach has paid dividends in fostering a more constructive relationship with China, the region's emerging power, which has the potential to become a regional hegemon. Indeed, many of the new regional institutions are based on the ASEAN model, and have ASEAN in the driver's seat. Compared to ASEAN, the GCC has remained a relatively inward-looking regional organization.

Sovereignty Challenges in Asian Regionalism: Lessons for Arab World

As the foregoing discussion shows, out of the four main approaches of regional organizations toward state sovereignty, integration through functional cooperation was seriously pursued neither in Asia and nor in the Arab world. The second pathway, pan-national unity, was attempted only in the Arab world, but could not prevail over the Westphalian nation-state model. Both regions pursued the goal of enhancing sovereignty through regional conflict control. In the Arab world, it was done macro-regionally through the Arab League and sub-regionally

[241]

through the GCC. While Asia initially did not have a macro-regional grouping undertaking this role, ASEAN as an Asian sub-regional organization was quite effective in reducing intra-regional tensions. And with the end of the Cold War, ASEAN became the basis for a wider Asian regional conflict control framework.

Neither the Arab world nor Asia has seriously attempted regional intervention or endorsed the notion of human security and the "responsibility to protect." Whether this will change or not will be the subject of the next section, which discusses the pressures facing Asian regional organizations to adopt more flexible notions of sovereignty in order to address new dangers and challenges and the relevance of their responses to these challenges for rethinking regionalism in the Arab world. Neither Asia nor the Arab world has come to terms with the idea of humanitarian intervention. Neither region is keen to embrace NATO-like regional institutions that can provide a military mechanism for humanitarian intervention. Neither has seriously considered adopting the principles of "responsibility to protect" that would legitimize collective regional action against acute cases of genocide or loss of lives caused by state repression or state failure. The UN Secretary-General's High Level Panel on Threats further refined the principle of Responsibility to Protect and the United Nations at its 2005 summit moved to secure further recognition to this norm. Existing regional organizations in Asia and the Arab world have stayed out of this growing international consensus around humanitarian intervention. Whether this will change or not would depend at least partly on the fate of state sovereignty, which has come under increasing pressure but which continues to cloud the future of Asian regionalism, despite some of its recent successes.

The challenges to the centrality of sovereignty in Asia's regional organizations come from several fronts. At least five are noteworthy. The first comes from new and emerging transnational threats. Since 1997, the region has been confronted with a series of common dangers; the Asian financial crisis in 1997, the terrorist attacks on Bali in 2002, the SARS outbreak in 2003, and the Indian Ocean tsunami in 2004. The fear of bird flu is now haunting the region, which could become the center of a pandemic. These challenges do not fit the traditional conception of security threats such as aggression, as they are neither purely domestic nor inter-state. These threats may arise from the domestic milieu of one or more states, but quickly spread across national boundaries. Another feature is the relative suddenness and unpredictability of these dangers. Asian governments increasingly accept that such threats cannot be contained nationally, no matter how sound the coping mechanisms and how plentiful its resources might be. Hence, they have called into question the tendency to respond to security threats through national security frameworks, and the principle of non-interference which marks their approach to regional order.

The Asian economic crisis led to the advocacy of a limited form of intrusive regionalism in Southeast Asia, including a call for ASEAN to depart from its non-interference doctrine and adopt a policy of "flexible engagement" to deal with transnational dangers. While this advocacy failed to find widespread support in ASEAN as an official doctrine, it did not fade away. The terrorist attacks, and the SARS epidemic renewed calls for new approaches to regional cooperation which made "intrusive regionalism," albeit in limited form, more acceptable to ASEAN members.

A second challenge to the Westphalian-mindset of ASEAN is democratization. The downfall of the Suharto regime in Indonesia led to the relaxing of Indonesia's attitude towards sovereignty. Jakarta became less sensitive to outsiders' interest and involvement in its internal security issues, as reflected in its welcoming of outside mediation in the Aceh peace process and in the enforcement of the agreement to settle the conflict. Indonesia has also called for respecting human rights in the region and for recognizing democracy as a regional norm.

[243]

A third challenge to sovereignty in Asian regionalism comes from the civil society groups advocating human rights. Their original target was East Timor, but since the latter's independence from Indonesia, Myanmar has become the main target. Increasingly, civil society has challenged ASEAN's policy of constructive engagement towards Myanmar, which was an excuse for inaction.

Fourth, at the sub-state level, terrorist organizations also challenge Westphalian sovereignty. The Jemmah Islamiah group, Southeast Asia's most powerful terrorist network, had developed a blueprint for an Islamic super-state, which comprises territories from several existing nation states in the region. How do states in the region counter this within the framework of the non-interference doctrine?

Finally, sovereignty in Asia faces the challenge of the Bush administration's "war on terror," which includes such policy instruments as "limits to sovereignty," preemption and regime change. These policies are less visible in Asia than in the Arab world's neighborhood, with the exception of North Korea, which is a designated member of the "Axis of Evil." However, Asian governments are nervous about their cumulative impact in undermining the global Westphalian order. As such, many have openly challenged the Bush Doctrine. Incidentally, the Bush administration's "limits to sovereignty" thesis, originally articulated with respect to Afghanistan and later applied to Iraq, seeks to "graft" onto the prior advocacy of humanitarian intervention. For example, Bush officials have said that the doctrine of preemptive or preventive war against terrorism, including states which knowingly or unwillingly harbor terrorist groups, was based on the same logic as intervention to protect lives from genocide or state collapse. Notwithstanding the contradictions in this rationalization (especially when the United States would not accept the criteria for such intervention, which includes multilateral action), this has aggravated existing concerns among Asian nations over the issue of humanitarian intervention and their unwillingness to endorse the "responsibility to protect." Although humanitarian intervention and the notion of human security on which it is based have yet to be adopted by any Asian regional organization, the need for multilateral action to combat terrorism, natural disasters and pandemics has led to an unprecedented level of regional cooperation in Asia and advanced the agenda of intrusive regionalism in Asia.

Is there any relevance of these responses to regionalism in the Arab world? Like Asia, the Arab world also faces a number of transnational dangers. Being less globalized and less dependent on foreign investment gives the Arab world a certain degree of immunity from the volatility of world financial markets and currency manipulators which brought about the Asian financial crisis in 1997. However, the Arab world also faces transnational terrorist organizations whose conception of a Caliphate (which the United States sees as emanating from strife-torn Iraq) at least theoretically challenges the Westphalian state. There is an interesting parallel between this challenge and that of Arab nationalism of the earlier era, but the chances are high that the Caliphate idea will meet with the same fate as the idea of a single Arab federation.

Yet, to a much greater degree than Asia, the Arab world is the central focus of the Bush administration's regime change and preemptive war strategies (directed at Iraq). In addition, the Bush administration's agenda of democracy promotion is essentially confined to the Arab world, given its courtship of Pakistan's military dictatorship and its indifference towards the Myanmar regime. The challenge of democratization to sovereignty in the Arab world is thus very different than that in Asia. In Asia, democratization in key countries like Indonesia has led to a greater willingness to promote democratization in the region and allow outside mediation in internal conflicts. However, democratization itself was not induced by external pressure, especially by a foreign power, although IMF conditions did play a part in toppling the Suharto regime in Indonesia. In the Arab world, democratization is being driven by an outside actor. Thus, although no one would view democratization in Indonesia as a result of outside pressure, in the Arab world it will be seen as an integral part of an interventionist agenda by the United States.

How should regional organizations in the Arab world respond to these challenges? If there is one lesson to be learnt from the Asian experience, it would be to step up regional efforts to stabilize the Arab world. This is not the same as advocating a "regional solution to regional problems." That cliché does not necessarily imply asking external powers to leave the region or denying them any role in regional affairs. That is neither practical nor desirable. What it really means is that regional countries should make a concerted effort to address regional issues to the best of their ability and external involvement should be invoked and used primarily for the benefit of regional countries, rather than for the selfish or unilateral interest of an outside power. Hence, the essence of regional action would be to manage the involvement of outside actors so that it conforms to the interests and identities of local actors. The problem is not that Asian countries want the United States to leave the region, but that they expect and hope that the US treats regional players as equals, respects their voices instead of dictating to them and remains engaged in regional multilateral institutions as a constructive and responsible actor. The problem with the US approach in Asia has been that it has shown scant regard for such multilateral processes and institutions. In the Arab world as in Asia, the US and Europe should be welcomed as participants in a regional multilateral framework designed to address the region's problems, but this should not lead to capricious or unilateral action on the part of Washington. It is in this context that the GCC should build its relationship with the United States.[13]

Any meaningful regional action in the Arab world would thus require a new multilateralism, and this multilateralism would mean going beyond traditional Westphalian sovereignty, if not the outright creation of a single

Arab State or reviving pan-Arabist concepts. Here too, Asian regional organizations can offer useful lessons for the Arab world.

An Arab Security Community? Relevance of the Asian Experience

In recent times, with the civil strife in Iraq, the Hamas victory in Palestine and the nuclear crisis involving Iran, renewed attention has been given to the need for a new security architecture for the Arab world. Some have argued that it is time for the Arab world to develop new multilateral approaches to regional security.[14] Two pathways to multilateral security have been suggested.

The first, advanced by a RAND Corporation study,[15] may be called a *concert* model, because it calls for the US, the EU, Russia and the UN to jointly manage the core security issues facing the Gulf today, ranging "from helping to build a new Iraqi state, to encouraging reform and moderation in Iran, to convincing the Gulf Arabs to change."[16] However, the concert model proposed by the Rand Study faces several obstacles. A concert is essentially a great power club. It marginalizes weaker states. While the notion of regional solutions to regional problems might not have worked in the Arab world, this does not justify assigning the primary responsibility for regional security to a club of outside powers. The Rand study argues that the United States "will clearly be the dominant player in building and backing a more stable balance of regional power."[17] But without a significant involvement by the regional countries themselves, any framework for regional order proposed by outside powers in a top-down manner would lack legitimacy in the region.

This brings us to an alternative model of regional security cooperation, one proposed by a group of policy analysts in a recent article in the *Washington Quarterly*.[18] This may be called a *cooperative security* approach, not the least because it explicitly refers to the ARF, Asia's main multilateral security grouping as the model for the proposed security architecture for the Middle East (their regional concept). The authors refer to the informality of the ARF, the importance of comfort level in its security dialogues and "process over the product" approach to security cooperation. They also highlight the three-stage approach undertaken by the ARF: confidence-building, preventive diplomacy and conflict resolution, as an approach which could be applied to a similar regional system for the Middle East. A Stanley Foundation Report similarly argues that both ASEAN and the six-party talks involving North Korea could also be potential models for a Gulf security dialogue leading to the establishment of a security regime binding the GCC states and Iran, Iraq and Yemen.[19]

Asia does hold important lessons for regionalism in the Arab world. The Asian experience in state-building and the security predicament of Asian states have more parallels with the Arab world than with Europe. The stress on informality and consensus-building which are hallmarks of Asian regional institutions also make them easier to adapt to the Arab world than the legalistic mechanisms of the Organization for Security and Cooperation in Europe (OSCE) or the latter's supra-national character. Moreover, for historical reasons and owing to the distinctive nature of their security situations, both Asia and the Arab world are unlikely to create a NATO-type organization in their own regions.

While the cooperative security is an attractive framework one for the Middle East, caution should be exercised in applying the ARF model to the Middle East. First, the ARF model and Asian regionalism in general faces many obstacles and its potential for transforming Asia's security environment is yet to be fully demonstrated. The ARF itself is based on the ASEAN experience, and the lessons and successes of the sub-regional ASEAN are not easy to reproduce at the wider Asian regional level. It is yet to move beyond a modest stage of confidence-building to more intrusive frameworks of preventive diplomacy and conflict-resolution. Regional institutions in Asia, the ARF included, have not yet addressed the region's long-term and most dangerous conflicts, namely, that between North and South Korea, China and Taiwan and India and Pakistan. While great progress has been made to socialize China through regional institutions, this may have unintended consequences, such as establishing a regional organization that provides a platform for Chinese dominance. The fear of Chinese dominance itself has made progress difficult in translating the idea of an East Asian Community from concept to practice.[20] Moreover, and this may be noted as a fifth limitation of contemporary Asian regionalism, the region today hosts a confusing and potentially competing array of proposals and fledgling institutions such as Asia Pacific Economic Cooperation (APEC) the ASEAN Regional Forum (ARF), ASEAN and the East Asian Summit, demanding the limited attention and resources of their overlapping membership. Last but not the least, the issue of sovereignty and how and under what conditions the doctrine of non-interference should be relaxed to permit collective action against transnational dangers has yet to be settled in Asia. As a result, the fourth pathway through which regionalism shapes sovereignty, has made limited progress in Asia.

A second challenge to applying Asia's cooperative security approach to the Middle East has to do with the core aspect of cooperative security, the principle of inclusiveness. The essence of the doctrine of cooperative security underpinning the ARF is "security with" as opposed to "security against" one's adversary. Cooperative security itself was the Asian version of the "common security" notion held by the Commission on Security and Cooperation in Europe (CSCE) or the OSCE. The Arab world must also adapt and localize the doctrine to suit its own security environment. Yet, whatever modifications to the doctrine are made must allow for the participation of Israel in any resulting framework. What it means is that while the Asian version of cooperative security lacks the elaborate, formal system of confidence-building found in the OSCE, such as advanced notification of military exercises, transparency in defense spending and weapon holdings, retracting military deployments away from international frontiers to avoid provocations and accidental conflicts, it does allow for dialogue and negotiations among all parties. The ARF brought together such formidable Cold War adversaries such as Vietnam and ASEAN, China and Russia (part of the Former Soviet Union) and China and the United States under a single umbrella. Today, North and South Korea as well as India and Pakistan, are members of the ARF. Only Taiwan remains outside the framework, owing to Chinese insistence. Yet, there is little doubt about the ARF's commitment to inclusiveness. The Arab world need not emulate all of the OSCE's multiple security mechanisms, but it must allow for the principle of inclusiveness found in both the OSCE and the ARF by developing some formula for engaging Israel.

The challenge is a daunting one and would require a major transformation of the mindset of long-established security policies not just of the Arab states but also of Israel. Indeed, Israel itself is likely to be a major obstacle to any such regional security framework. It is hard to see a survival-obsessed nation like Israel accepting the principles of defense transparency and adjusting its military deployments that would compromise its offensive and preemptive strategic doctrines. Yet, this may be precisely why proposals for a ARF-like structure may be useful to the Arab world, because if successful, even if partially, such a structure would get Israel, with its undisputed military superiority over any combination of Arab countries, to accept restraints which will enhance the security of the Arab world in general.

The Arab world would also need to make space for Iran's participation in the proposed regional security structure. The GCC could help this process by developing different types of dialogue relationships with non-member states, such as Iran. The GCC has not attempted such expansion in the past.[21] As with Israel, socializing a rising Iran with its nuclear ambitions would bring major strategic benefits to the Arab world. At least as a proposal, the security architecture of the Arab world must include provisions for nuclear confidence-building and disarmament.

Finally, when contemplating whether Asia's security framework may serve as a model for the Middle East and the Arab world, one must keep in mind Asia's conscious effort to promote intra-regional economic interdependence. It must not be forgotten that Asian regionalism is underpinned by a strong dose of economic interdependence and is hence fundamentally a market-led regionalism. Asian countries recognize the benefits of interdependence and have consciously tried to enhance regional interdependence through a variety of bilateral and multilateral measures, including free trade agreements. The commitment of the Arab World to the conscious promotion of intra-regional interdependence is yet to be demonstrated, despite the efforts of the GCC to promote free trade. The richer or more dynamic Asian economies such as Japan, China and India, possess greater diversity, human resources and indigenous technology bases than the most dynamic Arab economies, which remain critically dependent on oil revenues. Developing economic interdependence would require some concessions with respect to state sovereignty. In Asia, the initial reluctance to engage in European-style economic integration remains, but Asia is now moving in the direction of legalizing its informal mechanisms for dispute settlement and conflict resolution.

In this context, two recent initiatives of ASEAN deserve attention. ASEAN is developing a regional security community. A security community is a group of states which have developed long-term expectations of peaceful change and ruled out the use of force in problem-solving.[22] The ASEAN Security Community concept, while still modest in scope, and still some distance away from achieving the attributes of a full-fledged security community, does provide for new mechanisms, including dispute settlement mechanisms, and cooperation in dealing with maritime security threats, transnational dangers such as pandemics and terrorism. Long-term plans under this concept call for regional peacekeeping forces and human rights protection. ASEAN has also taken a stand to de-legitimize the unconstitutional overthrow of governments, through military coups.

[251]

A related initiative of ASEAN is the ASEAN Charter, which is supposed to serve as the constitutional basis for an ASEAN security community. This move to formulate a charter does not amount to drafting an EU-style constitution, which is now facing major obstacles. Although the Arab League and the GCC already have their charters, what the ASEAN move signifies is giving the regional body a legal personality which would facilitate the domestic implementation of regional initiatives, solidify mechanisms for dispute settlement and collective bargaining with outside countries and institutions. The adoption of the charter may require some adjustments to its non-interference doctrine, but the charter itself is unlikely to emulate the EU. This ASEAN charter may thus be a more suitable model for the Arab world than EU-style integration, as it suggests the possibility of advancing regionalism by adjusting, rather than transcending sovereignty.

The Arab world should certainly aspire to become a regional security community within itself by eliminating the potential for intra-Arab conflicts, before it can offer regional solutions to regional security problems, limit intervention by outside powers in the region and develop a stable and long-term peace with Iran and Israel. However, the road to creating an Arab security community will not be easy. It will require overcoming ideological barriers, ongoing territorial disputes, differences in political systems and memories of past conflicts. It means revitalizing the mechanisms of both the Arab League (and the GCC) for managing and resolving regional conflicts. The League should work on a new Charter for regional dispute settlement, mediations and peace-building in internal conflicts and humanitarian assistance. While embarking on a regional security community, the Arab world also needs to develop a process of dialogue with Israel and Iran. Here, the experience of Asian regionalism, especially in relation to ASEAN and the ARF, will be instructive.

11

The Role of Non-State Actors in Promoting Change

Dr. Marina Ottaway

In any country, non-state or civil society actors play an important role in the process of political, social and economic transformation. Following the demise of most socialist regimes, North Korea and Cuba are among the few countries in the world where the government continues to exercise control from the top over social and economic spheres, in addition to the political sphere. Everywhere else, even in still-communist China, the state has ceded an increasingly large role to civil society, particularly in the economic and social fields.

Notwithstanding their enormous importance, civil society actors have never been, and never will be, the only or even the major agents of transformation in any country. Even in the most democratic, free enterprise-oriented countries, it is the government that provides the framework within which most activities unfold. Such a framework is provided by political institutions as well as by-laws and regulations affecting all aspects of life—including how non-state actors can and cannot operate. Unless the institutional and regulatory framework is altered, there can be no real transformation in a country. However, governments are more likely to tackle the transformation of institutions and regulations when they come under pressure from organized citizens, that is, by non-state actors. Therefore, the transformation of a country is the result of combined action by state and non-state actors. If the relation between state and non-state actors is antagonistic, the transformation is likely to involve conflict. If the relationship is reasonably cooperative, conflict will be limited. Nevertheless, it is important to keep in mind that a degree of tension between state and non-state actors is inevitable not only in countries that are undergoing rapid change, but even in well-established systems. Not only is there tension between state and non-state actors, but among different non-state actors as well.

The role of non-state actors in the transformation of a country can be either positive or negative. Non state-actors can promote the modernization of the country and its political system and open up avenues to participation that will make the government more accountable and responsive to the needs of the citizens. Yet they can also be a source of conflict as well as of social and economic disruption. Many organizations of civil society, for example, promote democracy and human rights, or lobby for more educational opportunities for children and better health care for all. However, civil society organizations can also support rising dictatorship, as it happened in Germany under the Weimar Republic, when many non-governmental organizations backed the rise to power of Adolf Hitler.[1] Furthermore, non-state actors can also include terrorist groups, militias and drug cartels.

This chapter will focus only on non-state actors that act within the boundaries of legitimacy, if not always of legality, to bring about the transformation of their country. The concept of legality is used here to denote conformity with the laws of a specific country. The concept of legitimacy, on the other hand, is used to denote conformity with the broader principles of universal rights embodied in the United Nations Universal Declaration of Human Rights (UDHR). This distinction is needed because non-state actors that are perfectly accepted and legal in one country can be banned in another. For example, some countries allow political parties to operate while others do not. This chapter will discuss the role of political parties, even if they are not legal in all countries, because they are legitimate organizations on the basis of the right of association recognized by the Universal Declaration of Human Rights. However, terrorist organizations are not discussed because they are not legitimate actors by any definition, since no country or international convention justifies the use of indiscriminate violence against unarmed civilians.

Although there is no universally accepted classification of non-state actors, analysts frequently differentiate between two major types—those operating in the domain of civil society and those in the domain of political society. Civil society organizations are those that seek to influence government policy, but do not aspire to control the government or form part of it. In contrast, political society organizations are those that seek a direct role in government. For example, an environmental organization that lobbies the government for the enactment of more stringent emission control laws is a civil society organization but a "Green Party" that tries to further its agenda by competing in elections in the hope of becoming part of the government is a political society organization.

Three types of civil society organizations will be analyzed—advocacy NGOs, business organizations and the media. The analysis will highlight their potential role in the transformation of a country and also discuss the more problematic aspects of their activities. The chapter will also examine the second broad category of non-state actors that often play a salient role in the process of transformation—political society organizations and more specifically, political parties.

Civil Society Organizations

There is little agreement among scholars about what really constitutes civil society. The term is laden with theoretical assumptions, unsolved problems and value judgments. According to G.W.F Hegel's oft-cited but ultimately unsatisfactory definition (laid down in his book *Philosophy of Right,* 1821), civil society comprises the realm of voluntary organizations that lie between the family at one end and the state at the other. While superficially clear and logical, the definition is abstract and difficult to use. The result is that very few scholars, and virtually no practitioners of democracy promotion, now accept such a broad definition in practice, even if they cite it in theory. Scholars still debate whether organizations that do not seek to influence government policy should be considered part of civil society—is a football club an organization of civil society in the same way as a human rights group? They debate what constitutes a voluntary association—there is a grey area of groups in which membership is not formally compulsory, but is not completely a matter of free choice, either. For instance, many people belong to a religious group simply by birth, rather than by voluntary choice.

Other disagreements about the meaning of civil society are of an ideological or political nature: which groups should be recognized as legitimate civil-society organizations? Is the US National Rifle Association (NRA) which advocates the right of all citizens to own weapons, a civil organization? Ideology comes into play in the answer to such question. Moreover, politics comes into play when governments decide which organization to recognize. Few governments object to recognizing the legitimacy of organizations that provide services to needy populations—for example free vaccinations for children from poor families—not only because they provide needed assistance, but also because many have no political goals. However, many governments object to the establishment of organizations they suspect of having political goals. In particular, human rights groups are controversial in many countries because they are often critical of government actions.

Finally, there is also disagreement whether organizations formed voluntarily in order to protect the financial interests of their members should be truly considered part of civil society—some analysts, but not this writer, do not consider business associations to be legitimate members of civil society.

Despite these and many other complications that give rise to endless and often fruitless debate, in practice it is relatively easy to reach a working definition of what constitutes the realm of civil society organizations that can play a role in the transformation of a country. Such organizations are voluntary; legitimate although not necessarily legal in all countries; independent of the government but not necessarily antagonistic to it; and they pursue goals that cannot be satisfied without interaction with the government and without influencing government policy. Some areas of uncertainty always exist when trying to decide whether a specific organization is a state or non-state actor—a question that often arises is whether women's organizations that function under the patronage of a Ruler's wife are part of civil society or are governmental institutions. However, in practical terms there is, generally speaking, a high degree of agreement about which organizations belong to civil society in a given country.

The dominant, pragmatic definitions of civil society tend to focus attention on what may be called formal civil society organizations, thus overlooking entirely the informal organizations or at least dismissing them as of secondary importance. However, such informal organizations often have stronger roots in a society. In this writer's experience, a researcher who starts enquiring about civil society organizations in a given country is supplied with lists of organizations formally registered with the appropriate ministry, with full time people on the payroll and real offices. Rarely is the researcher guided to informal organizations, often referred to as "community-based organizations" or CBOs. Yet such CBOs can play a crucial part in people's lives, particularly in poor countries with weak and under-funded governments, where they address needs that are not met in other ways—from educating children that cannot find a place in government schools to bringing water to neglected neighborhoods.

[257]

The neglect of community-based organizations is a problem primarily in countries where international organizations, bilateral donors, or international NGOs fund civil society in order to promote social and political change. Foreign actors by definition favor formal over informal organizations, and above all they feel most comfortable dealing with groups that most resemble Western ones in their governance structure. The reason is simple: when financial support is provided—something uncommon in the Gulf countries, but routinely done elsewhere, including other parts of the Middle East—aid agencies require organizations to follow accounting practices that will satisfy their standards and procedures. They thus favor "modern" organizations with formal structures, which are usually directed by educated people who speak the language of the donors. As a result, discussions of civil society organizations tend to be biased in favor of modern organizations. Unfortunately, the neglect of the informal or traditional civil society sector has resulted in scant knowledge about how this sector functions, how extensive it is and what its real and potential contribution may be to the transformation of the society.

The three types of organizations that will be discussed here – advocacy NGOs, business associations and media – all belong to the formal sector, as lack of information makes the discussion of other organizations much more difficult. These three categories are potentially very important to political and economic transformation, while other groups are often more important from a social and humanitarian point of view. Service NGOs in particular are crucial as direct providers of assistance to populations in need. Service organizations sometimes become politicized, however, acting as advocacy NGOs or becoming affiliated with political parties. In the Middle East, many Islamist parties owe much of their popularity to networks of charitable organizations that provide services and help to consolidate a perception of the political movement as being both compassionate and efficient. Moreover, in countries that ban political parties or at least severely restrict their numbers and activities, organizations of civil society sometimes become the center for the organizing of political forces.

Advocacy NGOs

Advocacy NGOs are organizations of civil society that seek to influence government policy on a particular issue or issues. Among the most common organizations in this category are those involving human rights and women's rights, both of which tend to play an important role in a period of transition.

Human rights and women's rights organizations usually receive the most attention in countries in transition, but there is an endless variety of advocacy NGOs in well-established democracies with highly pluralistic political systems. Some of these groups advocate policies they believe to be in the interest of the majority of the population—for example, human rights or environmental groups. Others cater to the narrow interests of a specific group—for example, neighborhood organizations formed with the express purpose of convincing the town council not to locate a power plant or an oil refinery nearby. Finally, there are advocacy organizations, normally referred to as lobbies, which seek to promote the interests of businesses or other interest groups. Lobbies usually employ paid specialists to advance their goals, so they are not normally included among civil society actors and advocacy NGOs. However, it is important to note that the distinction is not always clear-cut. In the United States, for example, large non-profit organizations, ranging from environmental groups to major universities, also employ paid specialists to further their interests. Despite such differences among advocacy NGOs, they all share one characteristic, namely that they want to influence government policy but are not interested in taking on governmental responsibility.

Several factors determine the number and importance of advocacy NGOs in a country. The most important are the legislation governing the registration of NGOs and the availability of funding to support their activities. These two factors are not completely independent of each other, because legislation can affect the availability of funds. Certainly, culture also plays a role. For some countries, the very idea of voluntary, non-governmental organizations other than religious charities is relatively new. It is important to note, however, that culture changes with changing conditions. In the case of the Eastern European countries and even the successor states of the former Soviet Union, it became evident that societies which did not previously have a culture of voluntary organizations, because none had been permitted, responded quickly and enthusiastically once the laws changed and funds became available.

All countries, even established democracies, have laws that require NGOs to register. Informal, unregistered organizations also exist and occasionally become very influential. The most notable case is that of the International Campaign to Ban Landmines (ICBL), an international network of NGOs that convinced many governments to sign an international convention against the use of land mines. The organization operated informally until it won the Nobel Peace Prize in 1997 and discovered it could not cash the check without becoming a legally constituted entity.[2] Most governments, however, require NGOs to register officially, and in general NGOs seek such registration because it provides a degree of legal protection and above all gives them a legal persona that allows them to enter into contracts, receive funds and undertake other actions for which its official existence as an organization is a prerequisite.

Some countries make it easy for citizens to register an organization but in others it can be very difficult, if not impossible. In countries undergoing a process of transformation, legislation governing the registration of NGOs is often a matter of contention, with organizations pressing for an easier process and governments often insisting on tight controls to prevent

NGOs from becoming engaged in political activities. Laws regulating NGOs thus have a major impact on the number of civil society organizations. The easier the procedure for registering an NGO, the more numerous such NGOs are likely to be.

Availability of funds also has a major influence on advocacy organizations. Financial resources are not the only determinant of activity—good leadership, strong organization, and the ability to mobilize members to provide voluntary work are also very important. Yet it is obvious that organizations will not be successful if they cannot raise money. This reality puts non-state actors in very poor countries at a disadvantage, because their members, even if they are committed and mobilized, are not in a position to make much of a financial contribution. After the end of the Cold War, many governments in Central and Eastern Europe, Central Asia, Latin America and Africa opened up their political space to some degree and allowed their citizens more freedom to organize. The richer Central European countries were able to develop a large numbers of advocacy organizations, with some external funding but also through the efforts of their citizens. People in poor African countries also started developing advocacy organizations, but the NGOs remained almost completely dependent on funding coming from the industrialized countries.[3]

In addition to the wealth or poverty of a country, legislation is also crucial in determining the financial capacity of advocacy NGOs. In some countries, legally registered civil society organizations do not pay taxes. Furthermore, donations to civil society organizations can also be tax exempt—such donations are deducted from the donor's income before the taxes are calculated. Such tax regulations encourage people to give to NGOs and also allow NGOs to use their entire revenue, rather than paying some amount to the government by way of taxes.

Legislation also determines whether non-governmental organizations can receive funds coming from other countries. This is often a delicate political issue and in poor countries the way in which it is solved can make the difference between the existence of a vibrant civil society or its absence. Prohibitions against foreign funding greatly reduce the number and level of activity of NGOs in countries where the private sector is weak and citizens do not have much disposable income beyond the requirements for survival.

Registration and funding are major determinants of the number and types of NGOs in a country. Sound legislation is thus a necessary requirement for NGOs. Their effectiveness, however, does not hinge on funding alone. Equally important is their capacity to elicit support from citizens and the relationship that they develop with the government. An organization whose goals are not shared by many people in society is unlikely to have much impact on government policy. However, there are exceptions among some business associations, which can be very influential even without large membership, as long as they are economically significant. Here, it may be noted that voluntary organizations that take an antagonistic position vis-à-vis the government are usually unsuccessful unless they become quite large and influential.

As they need to convince other people of the importance and justice of their cause, advocacy NGOs face the challenge of translating their ideals and goals from abstract ideas to concrete demands that are immediately clear and appreciated by many people, even those without much education. The effectiveness of many advocacy NGOs is eroded by the difficulty encountered by leaders of the organization, who are usually educated members of society, in communicating their ideas. Human rights NGOs, for example, often encounter this challenge. The idea of protecting human rights can sound very abstract and not directly relevant to many people engaged in a daily struggle for survival. The idea of learning what should be done, and to whom to turn for help, if stopped by the police, or if a family member disappears, is a concrete manifestation of the same idea to which everybody can relate. Similarly, environmental protection is an abstract idea, but stopping the smoke from the nearby factory which people know is making it difficult for them to breathe is something very concrete. The most successful advocacy groups are those that manage to combine simple, immediately understandable goals into an overall strategy for change. Civil society organizations that spearheaded the struggle against apartheid in South Africa were extremely successful in turning an immediate concern of most people—the issue of fair access to urban housing and the high cost of paying rent to the government —into a tool for mobilizing people against an unjust regime.

Advocacy organizations differ greatly in their relationship to the government. In the idealized vision of civil society that is sometimes upheld by promoters of democracy, civil society organizations are presented as repositories of virtue, a sort of national conscience, which ensures that government and citizens consistently uphold high standards of behavior. For example, human rights advocacy organizations are seen as watchdog groups, ready to monitor violations and encourage all involved actors to take corrective measures. The reality is more complex. First, some civil society organizations do not uphold broadly accepted standards, but seek to defend narrow interests, worrying more, for example, about the location of a new correctional facility than about the treatment of its inmates. More importantly, from the perspective of understanding the role of non-state actors in a process of transformation, advocacy groups, particularly in rapidly changing societies, do not always uphold values and ideals that are widely shared in society, but are at the forefront of a battle to change those values. For instance, organizations advocating equality for women uphold values that are not shared by all— and not only in the Middle East.

Organizations that seek to promote change, rather than to uphold established values and norms, can do so either in cooperation with the government or by operating against it, depending on whether the goal of change is shared and also on the style of the organization itself. Change is

[263]

more likely to occur smoothly if the relationship between government and NGOs is cooperative, that is, if state and non-state actors share the same goals of transformation. Of course, a cooperative relation is not always successful, either because the government is resisting change, or because the type of reforms advocated by a civil society organization are more radical—or sometimes more conservative—than those advocated or upheld by the government.

In conclusion, advocacy NGOs are among the many actors that seek either to promote or prevent transformation in a country. Whether their role is positive or negative is ultimately a value judgment to be made about specific organizations in particular countries, and will always depend on the values of the person making the judgment. From the point of view of Americans who support the unrestricted right to bear arms, the National Rifle Association (NRA) is a very successful organization upholding a fundamental right of all citizens. From the point of view of citizens who worry, as I do, about the high rate of violent crimes in the United States and the easy availability of guns in the hands of potential criminals, the NRA is a non-state actor that has a negative influence on government policy. Both sides can agree, however, that the NRA is an influential non-state actor with the right to exist in a democratic system. Whatever the judgment reached on specific associations, it is important to recognize that the development of advocacy NGOs is an intrinsic part of the transformation of a political system in a more democratic and participatory direction.

Business Organizations, Professional Syndicates, and Labor Unions

Organizations set up to protect the economic and professional interests of their members can be extremely important non-state actors, but their influence varies depending on a country's economic system. Business associations and labor unions in particular tend to be more influential in countries with free market economic systems than in those where state control over the economy is more significant.

Such organizations differ from other NGOs in that they are set up specifically and openly to protect the interests of their members, rather than the "public interest" or an overriding universal right, as many NGOs claim they do. As a result, some analysts contend that such organizations should not be considered part of civil society. This argument holds little validity. These are voluntary organizations that engage with the state institutions. To argue that they are not part of civil society because their goals are particularistic and self-interested, rather than universal and noble, is to embrace an overly narrow and even distorted view of civil society.

Business associations and labor unions are prominent groups in all countries with at least a partially free-market system. The importance of professional syndicates varies widely. In Arab countries, professional syndicates have historically played an important political role, particularly in countries that have tried to restrict the activities of political parties. Thus, control over the leadership of professional organizations has always been a delicate political issue. For example, Egyptian professional syndicates during the 1990s became the battleground in a struggle for control between pro-government forces and the Muslim Brotherhood. By contrast, in the United States and European countries professional organizations can be important lobbies that further the interests of their members, but the issue of who controls them is a matter of the internal politics of the individual organizations, rather than of national politics. The unusual political role played by professional syndicates in the Arab world stems partly from the fact that in many countries they perform quasi-public functions, such as the issuing of professional licenses, and partly from the weakness or absence of political parties. In countries where political activity is unrestricted and political parties operate freely with few governmental restrictions, professional organizations are less likely to become political.

The role of business organizations also varies. In the United States, with its tradition of private entrepreneurship, business organizations are powerful actors, often consulted by the government prior to the formulation of policies that affect a particular type of business. Thus business associations not only influence but sometimes even draft legislation that affects the interests of their members. On the other hand, business organizations were absent in socialist countries, even those that allowed a limited degree of space for private business. In the Arab world, with its history of state control over many sectors of the economy, business organizations have had a relatively small impact most of the time. Indeed, many analysts who have studied the role of business organizations, or more broadly the role of business in Arab countries, tend to reach the conclusion that their influence is limited even in countries with an important private sector, for example in Tunisia.[4] Businessmen in the Arab world, studies conclude, tend to protect their interests by cultivating close ties to the government through personal relations, rather than by banding together in associations seeking to further the corporate interests of their members. As a result, business organizations are usually not among the most important non-state actors in Arab countries. Their influence may well increase, particularly in countries with rapidly expanding economies, but it has been quite limited so far in most countries. Thus, business organizations in the Arab world have not lived up to their potential as instruments for transformation.

The importance of labor unions also differs, not only from country to country but also from period to period. Historically, the growth of labor unions has been a product of the early Industrial Revolution, with its large numbers of often poorly paid blue collar workers. Labor unions were set up specifically to bargain for improved wages and working conditions at the level of the factory and industry, and to influence government policy on behalf of workers—for example to ensure the enactment of legislation to limit the length of the work day.

In recent decades, however, the influence of labor unions has been decreasing steadily around the world. First, socialist countries and other countries where government plays a central economic role established tight controls over labor unions, turning them into state rather than non-state actors. Second, although socialist regimes are becoming increasingly rare, technological and economic forces continue to contribute to the erosion of labor union membership and of their economic and political influence. Technological development has decreased the size of the workforce necessary to produce a given quantity of goods. Even in industries that are still labor intensive, such as the garment industry, the size of the workforce relative to levels of production has decreased steadily. For example, a Chinese worker equipped with a state-of-the-art industrial sewing machine is many times more productive than his American counterpart in the 1920s. Technological development has also led to the emergence of much more diversified labor forces, with fewer blue-collar workers, historically the backbone of labor unions and a growing number of service workers, a category that has always proven more difficult to organize. Finally, economic forces and particularly globalization have also weakened labor unions. In the past, when the domestic market was paramount and export was a minor part of a country's economy, strong union demands cut into the profit margins of companies. Today, when economies are globalized and exports are a dominant part of economic activity, the success of labor unions can put the entire country at a competitive disadvantage. As a result, even governments that favor private enterprise tend to be much more hostile to labor unions than they were in the past.

The decreasing importance of labor unions may be a factor in slowing down political transformation in some countries. Labor unions in the past contributed significantly to the politicization of their members. Often they developed close ties with political parties—many European countries, for example, developed rival socialist and Christian-democratic unions—and in any case they increased the probability that their members would become politically active citizens, voting in elections and possibly participating in party activities. Thus, the reduced role of labor unions may have a broader impact on political transformation in the future.

Labor unions still remain significant non-state actors in many countries, but not to the same extent as in the past. Given the importance of the technological and economic forces that have led to the decline of labor unions, it is unlikely that the situation will change, at least not in the foreseeable future.

Media

Independent media are among the most powerful non-state actors in any society. By providing information and often commentary, they have an impact on the way people think and sometimes act. Written media such as newspapers and magazines and, increasingly, electronic media such as radio and television are important in the transformation of any society. Access to information is a crucial factor of change.

This does not mean, however, that media can control change. There is a huge difference between making information available and controlling how people will act in consequence. Even when state or private media deliberately slant information to suit their own purposes, they cannot really control or even predict how people will act as a result. Until recently, governments in non-democratic countries sought to control their citizens' access to news, allowing only carefully selected information – or disinformation – to be disseminated. Despite such control over the media, governments could not completely manipulate public opinion, let alone behavior. Today, some governments still try to control information, but they face increasing difficulty in doing so because technological change has extended the variety of channels through which information can be disseminated, thus making it difficult to control its flows. Information is distributed through the press, radio, TV, the Internet and of course through unofficial channels such as the rumor mill, and is thus exceedingly difficult to control. There is still plenty of distorted news being circulated—by governments, by private media with their own agenda, by bloggers and advocates of various causes on the Internet. However, most people have access to far too many different sources of news for anybody to be able to control effectively what they hear and learn about. People who are not directly connected to the modern media, particularly the Internet, are exposed to much of the information circulated there, which eventually finds its way around through personal exchanges and the rumor mill—or what the French used to call the "sidewalk radio."

During the 1990s, some analysts concluded that the Information Revolution would become a powerful tool for democratization. We now realize that reality is more complex. Information technology is a tool that can be used by many different organizations, democratic and non-democratic, secular or religious, seeking to promote transformation or determined to prevent it. Thus, while we know that the Information Revolution has greatly increased the amount and variety of information available to all, we cannot reach any generalized conclusions about how the availability of information will affect processes of transformation in various countries.

However, the proliferation of sources of information makes it very difficult for either government or non-state actors to successfully use information as a tool of the political and social transformation they favor. Readers, and particularly listeners and viewers, may be subjected to selectively controlled news by their government or private sources, but in the end they choose which source of information they will believe.

The availability of multiple sources may frustrate even well-intentioned efforts to promote transformation by using mass media for educational purposes. For example, governments may well decide to broadcast educational programs to improve literacy among disadvantaged children, but if private channels choose to broadcast programs without educational value at the same time, this effort may be defeated.

In other words, various mass media can be powerful tools of social and political transformation, but not tools that either governments or non-state actors can easily manipulate for their own purpose.

Political Society Organizations

The years since the end of the Cold War have seen a proliferation of civil society organizations everywhere. For many countries and even regions, particularly those emerging from decades of socialism, this proliferation of civil society organizations was an unprecedented phenomenon. As a result, it attracted an overwhelming amount of attention from analysts. Representatives of civil society organizations, and in particular of international NGOs, contributed to this focus on civil society by casting NGOs as the real agents of democratization, the selfless, public interest-oriented organizations that represent grass-root mobilization and influence in the best sense of the word. For a while, as a result, the centrality of political society to any process of political transformation was ignored.

Certainly, NGOs do play a role in political transformation and democratization, but they are not the most important non-state actors. Rather, it is the organizations of political society—political parties or political movements—that are the indispensable agents of political transformation. The difference between political parties and movements is not clearly codified, but the term party tends to denote a duly registered, official political organization, while the term movement usually denotes a more informal, unofficial political organization. Political parties are central to democracy. Indeed, no democratic country has ever succeeded in preventing the formation of political parties, although some have tried at times. However, democratic countries differ considerably in terms of the role played by civil society organizations. For example, civil society organizations play a much more important role in the United States than in European countries.

It may be recalled that the difference between civil society and political society organizations is that the latter seek to place their candidates and members directly in positions of power, while the former merely seek to influence policy. It is their efforts to attain positions of power that make political parties indispensable in a process of political transformation, because political transformation is ultimately about the redistribution of power. This is true in the case of both democratic transformations, where power gets dispersed among various institutions and is subjected to public scrutiny and demands for accountability, and of authoritarian transformations, where power is simply transferred from one autocrat to another, as is usually the case when a country is transformed by a military *coup d'etat*, or from an autocrat to an authoritarian political party, as in the case of the Russian Revolution of 1917.

The fact that political parties openly seek power, either by following the legal electoral route open to them or by other means, makes them much more controversial than civil society organizations. Furthermore, political parties are partisan and divisive by definition. Except for ruling parties in single-party systems, they do not claim to speak for the entire population, but only for their followers. By contrast, NGOs in any country usually claim to defend certain universal rights to which all human beings are entitled—even a controversial group such as the US National Rifle Association claims to be defending a constitutionally guaranteed right to bear arms. It is thus easy for political parties to be cast as villains – selfish, divisive and dangerous – in contrast to the virtuous and selfless organizations of civil society.

[271]

Suspicion of political parties has always been rife in countries undergoing political transformations. The young American republic had a difficult time coming to grips with the reality of the divisions and conflicting interests found in any country. In delivering his farewell address when leaving office, President George Washington warned his countrymen about the danger posed by political parties, but within a few years the country had a well-established party system. Two hundred years later, some Middle East countries, particularly in the Gulf, are going through a similar process, beginning to allow elections to take place while at the same time banning the formation of political parties and requiring candidates to run as individuals, rather than representatives of political parties. Even countries that allow the formation of some political parties, for example Egypt, try to limit the number and above all the type of parties that are formed.

It is easy to understand why parties can be controversial. They openly seek power, so they pose a direct challenge to the incumbent government, and they bring out into the open the existing divisions in the country. Yet it is equally easy to understand why no country has ever succeeded in developing a democratic system without being forced to allow the formation of political parties. Citizens cannot be effective as individuals and must join forces in order to succeed—in a process that political scientists call "interests aggregation." Furthermore, the citizens of all countries are divided among themselves about what they want and unanimity of views does not exist anywhere. Political parties do not create divisions, but reflect those that already exist.

Historical experience shows that preventing the formation of political parties in a country with a political system that is undergoing transformation is ultimately futile. However, a much more interesting issue that arises is whether the character of political parties can and should be controlled. Some countries have taken the position that political parties that represent ideological and programmatic preferences or economic interests are permissible, even good, while political parties based on identity should be banned because they threaten the unity of the country.

The argument for avoiding the formation of parties based on ethnic or religious identities is strong in theory, but such a policy is both difficult and even dangerous in the implementation. In abstract terms, political parties based on ideology or economic interests are less divisive because their demands lend themselves to compromise. The gap between parties favoring drastic reduction in government expenditure and taxes and those favoring more social services and thus higher taxes, can be reduced by compromise—for example by a program calling for moderate tax cuts accompanied by some reduction in available social welfare programs. The gap between parties favoring the dismantling of state enterprises and those considering such enterprises as crucial to the country's development and sovereignty can also be bridged—the answer could be partial privatization. However, when it comes to parties based on identities, compromise is more difficult and positions tend to be more absolute. In Yugoslavia, compromise between Serbs who wanted to maintain the old Yugoslavia and Croat nationalists who wanted an independent Croatia was impossible and the result was war.

Some countries have responded to the threat of identity politics by banning political parties based on ethnicity and religion. Some implement this ban directly and explicitly. Egypt, for example, forbids parties based on religion. Other countries do it in a more subtle manner. Nigeria, which experienced a secessionist war in the 1960s and is still threatened by such possibilities, requires all parties to demonstrate they have balanced support in many different regions before they are allowed to register and compete in elections. Nigeria's approach, which forces political parties to develop a broad base of support, seems a more appealing measure than the outright ban on certain types of organization. Yet such an approach, which has served Nigeria relatively well, would probably not work everywhere. Nigeria's population is fragmented, comprising over 300 ethnic groups that are forced to come together because of their sheer number. If similar rules had been applied to a country like Bosnia, whose population is divided among three highly hostile groups, they would not have worked. Banning parties based on ethnicity and religion would have put a halt to all legal political activity, probably pushing the parties to become underground, armed movements, as they were before the end of hostilities.

In conclusion, political parties are non-state actors that will inevitably arise in a process of political transformation. Political parties (and the less structured political movements that form in countries where parties are banned) are much more challenging to the incumbent government than civil society organizations, both because they seek power and because they are usually relatively few in number, thus potentially more influential than civil society organizations, which tend to be numerous and fragmented.

Parties are controversial also because they are by definition partisan and divisive. However, it is important to keep in mind that political parties are not the cause of divisions that exist in a society, but simply a reflection of them. While a well-designed political party law may keep parties from aggravating the divisions, no institutional design can obliterate the tensions and differences that exist in all countries.

Countries embarking on a process of political transformation cannot expect to be able to set up a political system that allows political participation but bans the formation of political parties, because no country has succeeded in doing so, except perhaps in the very short run. Nor should they have any illusions that allowing the formation of civil society organizations will prevent the formation of political parties. The respective roles of civil society organizations and political society organizations are quite different and both are bound to emerge in countries undergoing transformation.

[274]

Conclusions

Non-state actors are an intrinsic part of any process of political transformation aimed at opening up the political system and allowing citizens to play a role in influencing government policy and holding officials accountable. Only authoritarian political systems have the power to prevent the rise of non-state actors. Indeed, even such systems ultimately fail to prevent their rise. Rather, they force them to become clandestine, making them potentially more dangerous, and certainly less cooperative than organizations that operate freely and communicate with the government.

This does not mean that non-state actors always play a positive role in transforming a society. Non-state actors can foment violence and civil strife, not just participation and democracy, as pointed out earlier. Terrorist organizations are non-state actors, although they do not fall in the category of legitimate non-state actors discussed in this paper. And in any case "positive" and "negative" are words denoting a value judgment that is unlikely to be shared unanimously by every citizen. Islamist parties in the Middle East play a highly positive role from the point of view of their supporters, but a negative one in the eyes of intellectuals who prefer secular policies or of governments that do not like the challenge posed by movements with a potentially large popular base.

Citizens and analysts will always disagree about how to judge the role of specific non-state actors, since such judgments are value-laden and different people uphold different values. Even government officials in any given country often disagree in their judgment of specific non-state actors. This is particularly true of countries in the midst of a transformation process, where government officials are usually quite divided about how, and how fast, to proceed.

If we move beyond the judgment about specific organizations, whether civil or political, it becomes easier to reach a degree of consensus about the role of non-state actors in a process of transformation. There is plenty of evidence that for non-state actors to play a positive role—that is to promote change and participation without leading to chaos-- there must be a balance between the power of state and non-state actors. This is an elaboration of an insight put forward by Samuel Huntington long before he became concerned about the clash of civilizations. In *Political Order in Changing Societies,* Huntington pointed out that all countries need a balance between "participation and institutionalization," or in the terminology of this chapter, between non-state and state actors.[5] This observation is as applicable to today's transformations as it was to the evolution of socialist systems that Huntington worried about forty years ago.

Non-state actors are the conduits through which citizens freely express their preferences, put pressure on the government, and hold it accountable. However, non-state-actors require the presence of state actors. Organizations of civil society and even political parties are no substitute for a government, as they cannot and should not do what state institutions must do in order to provide administration or governance. Political parties in some countries end up by carrying out governmental functions, blurring the distinction between state and non-state actors, but this identity of government and party is invariably an indication that the country is highly authoritarian.

In order to transform its political systems successfully, a country needs a government capable of making decisions, an administrative apparatus to implement them, and a variety of non-state actors to push for change, act as watchdogs to prevent government abuses, and be ready to step in and assume government responsibility if voters so choose. Governments and administrative institutions need to be strong and well organized. It is important in this respect not to confuse the strength of a government, in the sense of its capacity to reach and implement decisions and its authoritarianism. An ideal country has a strong, well-organized and capable government, but also one which is democratic. Such a government does not impose decisions unilaterally on the country without consultation but can take the multiple inputs from various non-state actors and state agencies and weave them into a coherent policy. An ideal country, in other words, is one where the government can keep the proverbial trains running on time, but also listen to non-state actors to make sure trains will go where citizens want to travel.

One of the dangers about periods of political transformation is that a country may swing from a situation in which the state is authoritarian but civil and political society are weak to one in which the growing strength of political and civil society overwhelms state actors and makes them ineffective. In the former case the result is authoritarianism, in the latter case the result is instability or even chaos. A tragic example of this is offered by Iraq. The authoritarian institutions associated with Saddam Hussein's state collapsed with the American invasion. In the vacuum thus created, the power of political factions and religious institutions grew disproportionately, threatening the state.

A jumble of political parties that are competing for power in the government and establishing parallel administrative and even security structures cannot replace the state. The challenge of political transformation is thus that of balancing the growth of civil and political society organizations with the growth of state capacity to absorb and process inputs, thus making and implementing policies successfully.

Both state and non-state actors have crucial roles to play in a process of political transformation. The state cannot bring about transformation single-handedly, but neither can non-state actors. There are no heroes or villains in a process of transformation. The state needs to be viewed as a crucial actor with the ultimate responsibility for policy making and implementation. However, the state also needs to be held accountable, to be forced to listen to the demands coming from citizens who form part of civil and political society organizations. In turn, civil and political society organizations need to operate freely, but also to be given a framework within which to operate by state institutions. Achieving a balance between these requirements is not easy. This is one reason why processes of political transformation are rarely smooth, but usually entail a lot of tension. Particularly in countries that experienced authoritarianism, citizens are often hostile to the state, seeing its repressive potential more readily than they see the need for the stability and mediating functions that only state institutions can provide. Governments unused to the presence of an active, organized citizenry expressing its demands and interests also often overreact to demands, slipping back into repression and making citizens even more suspicious. These are the growing pains of transformation. In most countries, they ease as state and non-state actors get accustomed to dealing with each other and establish the needed balance.

12

New and Future Leadership:
Implications for Change

The Hon. William S. Cohen

The topic I was asked to speak about is leadership and how the Arab countries can plan for the future. I come from the state of Maine, located in the north eastern part of the United States, and the state motto is "*Dirigo*" a Latin phrase that means, "I lead." Maine is not a large state but it has had an impact on the country's political structure. Back in 1964, Republican Senator Margaret Chase Smith of Maine was the first woman to be nominated by a major political party as a candidate for the US Presidency. Other prominent figures from the state of Maine include Senator Edmund S. Muskie, who also ran for the Presidency in 1972 and Senator George Mitchell who became the Senate Majority Leader from 1989 to 1994. Yet another personality is Senator Susan Collins of Maine who is currently serving in the US Senate. The point I wish to make here is that one does not have to come from a huge country or a big state in order to create an impact, but one should have a positive outlook and strive to achieve one's goals.

A few years ago, I had the opportunity to visit Kim Dae-jung, the former President of South Korea who left office in 2003. I went to his residence and we spent a few hours together talking about his life and his time in prison. Asked what those years were like, he said: "Well, I read a lot of the Bible and I also read a great deal of Alvin Toffler." I recalled the early 1970s when Toffler first published his book *Future Shock*. He wrote about a time when the world would see traditions, culture and heritage really shaken by the hurricane winds of change. He described how perceptions of time were being changed by the rapid pace of events and how technology would miniaturize the world. If one considers the impact of technology, it is clear that the world is shrinking and undergoing rapid change. Therefore leaders need to have not only a sense of the past but also a vision for the future because they will have to make decisions at a faster and faster rate. Hopefully, the decisions on which direction to take will be based upon a sense of history and culture.

I was reading a book by Thomas L. Friedman called *The World is Flat*. When Christopher Columbus set out to find the New World, he thought he was going to reach India but he ended up in America. Friedman said that he also set out to reach India and when he got there, he discovered that the world had become "flat." Friedman describes this important "flat earth" concept as "a global web-enabled platform for multiple forms of sharing knowledge and work irrespective of time, distance, geography and increasingly, language." According to Friedman's book, with cheap and instant telecommunications there are no longer any impediments to global competition in the flat world. An African proverb takes on relevance. "The gazelle wakes up every morning and knows that it must run faster than the fastest lion or it will die. The lion wakes up and knows it will have to run faster than the slowest gazelle or it will starve to death." It does not make a difference whether you are a "lion" or a "gazelle." When the sun comes up, you have to start running faster just to survive and maintain your position. We all know that we have to keep on moving but the question is: Do we move forward or backward or do we go around in circles? In other words, the best direction is what leadership needs to determine.

In Lewis Carroll's book *Alice in Wonderland*, the following dialogue takes place between the young heroine Alice and the Cheshire Cat:

[280]

Alice: *"How do I get out of here?"*

Cheshire Cat: *"That depends a great deal on where you want to get to."*

Alice: *"I don't much care where."*

Cheshire Cat: *"Then it doesn't matter which way you go."*

The point is that one must first know where one wants to go and only then can one choose the correct path to get there. What Friedman observes in his book is that around the time the Berlin Wall came crashing down, Bill Gates's "Windows" opened up. As a result of the Microsoft Windows system, it was possible to use Netscape, which allowed people to travel electronically throughout the world and absorb vast amounts of information. People can now interact globally without having to travel. One does not have to go to Europe or to the United States to learn. Instead, one could stay here in Abu Dhabi, Dubai or Riyadh and obtain the same information that anyone elsewhere in the world can get. What Friedman means by a flat world is that people everywhere form part of one interconnected world in which everyone can share information on an equal footing.

The world has acquired advanced technology, which brings with it the threat of terrorism on a scale that people have not had to deal with before. As a result of technological developments, someone like Timothy McVeigh was able to bring down the Alfred P. Murrah Federal building in Oklahoma City on April 19, 1995. On September 11, 2001, nineteen people destroyed the Twin Towers in New York and attacked the Pentagon. This is the new kind of terrorism where individuals can get their hands on modern technology and the necessary information to cause widespread destruction. Such incidents remind us of Churchill's observation: "We will one day return to the Stone Age as a result of science."

There are different kinds of threats prevailing today. I would like to take a moment to talk about national security in particular. Having served in the United States Senate, the Armed Services Committee and later as

Secretary of Defense in the Clinton Administration, my main focus has been on defense issues. When I think about defense issues, I recall the reflections of 13th century Turkish poet named Yunus Emre:

> To keep the realm needs many soldiers. To keep the soldiers you need many funds. To get the funds, the people must be rich. For the people to get rich, the law needs to be just. If any of these is left undone, all four will be lost.

All states need to preserve their national security and in order to do so there must be justice. Therefore, states need to decide on what constitutes justice. In the United States we believe that equality is of paramount importance. Unfortunately, African-Americans and women have not enjoyed equal status with others for much of US history. It took centuries for people to realize the need for a just treatment of all and the United States is still trying to achieve this. However, all societies need to ensure just laws so as to be able to preserve the four pillars that the Turkish poet spoke about.

The war on terror is not a war in any conventional sense, for it is not fought against an identifiable enemy or a specific country. It is an open-ended struggle because as mentioned already, any individual or group of individuals can get hold of the necessary information to launch a terror attack. From my point of view, it is more appropriate to use President Kennedy's words: "We are engaged in a long twilight struggle against Communism." Indeed, we are currently engaged in a "long twilight struggle" against terrorism. The question is how do we continue this struggle and how do we cooperate in order to achieve common goals? Let us disregard Iraq for the moment. This struggle needs to be carried out through better intelligence and shared information, which is required of every country. I have always said that there are no longer any safe places in the world. You cannot take a holiday in Bali, ride a train in Madrid, board a bus in London or visit either Riyadh or New York without risking danger. Terror has no designated battlefield and all places are vulnerable to an attack.

It is necessary to address the causes of extremism. Among these are sources of energy and the effects it has on international relations. There is also the issue of water, and the need to provide adequate supplies of this resource to all. It must be remembered that there are approximately one billion people living on less than $1 per day and there are approximately 2 billion people who do not have access to clean water. There are huge environmental issues facing the world today but there are prerequisites that must be provided for the people to enable them to face the 21st century. More and more scholars are convinced that a future flu pandemic will affect the world. How do we face these global challenges? I emphasize again the need for people not just to learn but to learn about each other. As pointed out in the welcoming remarks delivered at the start of this conference, information can benefit us all but it is a double-edged sword. It can be used either for beneficial purposes or misused for less benevolent reasons.

This is where leadership comes in and helps to educate people. President Bill Clinton often discussed such a leadership role. I traveled extensively and covered approximately 800,000 miles. In the 1980s I went to Moscow to try to persuade the Soviets of the merits of an idea regarding the reduction of nuclear stockpiles. I remember one Soviet official remarking that we should stay in contact lest we should forget each other and not recall each other's faces. If people know each other at a personal level and can recall each other's faces they might be able to avoid conflict through mutual understanding. Therefore, it is important to always stay engaged with other countries and peoples.

Civilizations are constantly undergoing change. The United States and its treatment of its black population is a good example. Each nation needs to review its own society and look back at history to assess where different societies have reached today and find ways in which its own society can reconcile itself to these dynamics. The leadership of a country must be open to the past, envision the future and judge what needs to be done for it to continue to prosper in the future.

John Gardner in his book *Recovery of Confidence* says: "Our institutions have become caught in a savage crossfire between unloving critics and uncritical lovers." On the one hand, there are those who see nothing positive in the US approach and want to destroy it and so they offer no constructive criticism. On the other hand, there are those who see nothing wrong with the US approach, do their best to maintain the status quo and remain completely uncritical. What any country really needs is well-intentioned criticism. Thus, people should play the role of loving critics and countries should always remain open to such constructive criticism. It would be arrogance on my part to tell you what should be done in your own countries. However, I would suggest that all of you begin act as loving critics towards yourselves and your societies, so that your countries can achieve even greater progress.

I would also stress that no country can achieve real progress without an egalitarian society that utilizes the full potential of all its citizens. It is worth recalling some of the characters from the old Greek and Roman myths. There was Sisyphus, who was condemned to the futile task of rolling a boulder uphill forever, although the rock would soon roll down again by its own weight. Then there was Tantalus who was punished for his crimes by having to stand up to his neck in water, yet was never able to satisfy his thirst. Instead of pursuing futile tasks and getting into frustrating situations, countries must try to ascertain their current limitations, use the combined potential of all their citizens and give them the opportunity to channel their energies constructively by ensuring a just society.

EDUCATION AS A BASIS FOR CHANGE IN THE ARAB WORLD

The Role of Education in Development

H.E. Sheikh Nahyan Mabarak Al Nahyan

Education has now become, more than ever before, the indispensable road to the future and the solid foundation for actual development processes, in their different manifestations and forms. I completely concur with those who perceive education as the most important pillar supporting the infrastructure in any modern society. No society can progress or develop without a strong and effective infrastructure capable of dealing with the impact of different economic and social factors that influence this age. Among these factors are the phenomenon of globalization, the growing importance of science and technology in human life, the position attained by knowledge as a major driving force of economic activity as well as global and regional competition and what this entails in terms of developing the spirit of initiative in all people.

It would be no exaggeration to say that necessity has turned the twenty-first century into the century of education. In this context, the logical question that arises revolves around the nature of education, its system and its various roles. We must have a serious dialogue on the abilities and skills necessary for the citizen to acquire in this age, as well as the competencies which will enable society to attain its due position among other societies. We must also accord full recognition to the role education plays in developing such abilities, skills and competencies.

In pursuit of this objective, we seek the kind of education that produces a citizen who is capable of making an intelligent contribution in different national economic, social and cultural activities and can participate fully in the affairs of his own society and those of the world around him.

We want a purposeful and committed education that instills in each individual some inspiring moral values, pride in identity and appreciation of the other. We want an education that preserves the values of tolerance and coexistence in society and opens up broad horizons of enlightened understanding and meaningful dialogue for every student.

We want an education that infuses culture into society and enables the country to attain its appropriate rank in the hierarchy of progressive nations so that it makes a genuine contribution to research and development and works assiduously to absorb and create modern technologies.

In short, we want an education that serves society as a tool in its transition towards sustained development and one by which individuals can form a clear and conscious vision of the future they seek for their homeland. Moreover, we want an education through which individuals can mobilize their efforts to turn that vision into a tangible reality—the kind that offers measurable outcomes and achievements that can be monitored in a clear and transparent way.

Today I want to reiterate very strongly the conclusions drawn by research and experimentation—that the desired education cannot be realized by merely enrolling in courses or by increasing the years of study. What is more important is the quality of education received by the student, for which there are certain prerequisites that need to be studied and known to all.

Education is a field of great concern to the nation's leaders— represented by H.H. Sheikh Khalifa bin Zayed Al Nahyan, the President of the UAE; H.H. Sheikh Mohammed bin Rashid Al Maktoum, UAE Vice President and Prime Minister and Ruler of Dubai; and H.H. Gen. Sheikh Mohammed bin Zayed Al Nahyan, Crown Prince of Abu Dhabi and Deputy Supreme Commander of the UAE Armed Forces, who personally chairs the Abu Dhabi Education Council. In fact, this concern reflects a real desire to develop the educational system in the country, which suffers from obvious problems—whether in curricula, methods of teaching, examination systems, use of libraries and modern technologies, working conditions of teachers, the quality of classrooms, the administrative and procedural systems or even the size of available budgets and resources.

Allah has bestowed a wise leadership upon the UAE, which is well aware of the fact that achieving quality in the educational system requires a primary focus on the students and their capabilities.

All students must necessarily develop the capabilities needed for the following tasks:

- To understand their Arab-Islamic heritage and Arab-Islamic civilization in all its dimensions, and also understand their position in the map of the world
- To study Mathematics and Science and be able to utilize and develop technologies, and to understand and discuss the important environmental and scientific issues facing the international community both in the present and future.
- To be prepared to work successfully in both the public and private sectors, and to join the workforce after becoming fully qualified in terms of academic, professional and social skills
- To comprehend what it means to be a leader and an innovator in the age of globalization and to become one, by being qualified and keeping abreast of the imperatives of life in this age, and taking an interest in the affairs of the world around.

As I have stated, education alone is not adequate. We must realize that in the twenty-first century, it is no longer sufficient to prepare the student merely for graduating or gaining employment. We must prepare the student to become a useful person in his society, rejecting terrorism or violence as a means of expressing his views and beliefs, and seeking to coexist with others in peace and amity.

In the UAE, this requires attention to a number of issues, the first of which is the commitment to achieve quality in all the constituents of the educational system. This requires good curricula, modern teaching methods, effective examination systems, libraries and rich educational resources, intensive and effective use of modern technologies, useful student and cultural activities, and concern for the teachers themselves. In addition, the buildings and study facilities must reflect advanced global standards and the general atmosphere in the school must encourage constructive initiatives and develop beneficial educational practices.

Second, we must always ensure that students understand and respect different cultures and civilizations. We must make our schools effective institutions to prevent youth from being attracted to violence, terrorism or hostile behavior towards society.

Ours is a youthful society dominated by young people. Over 50 percent of the citizens are less than 15 years of age. In fact, these young people constitute an important human resource. We must provide them with an environment conducive to real education and train them to shoulder responsibility, as well as provide job opportunities and accustom them to displaying initiative and innovation. We must help them to determine their identity in this changing world—an identity that offers them not only hope in the future but also the ability to formulate this future. I reiterate the fact that an excellent education is the primary and vital tool for achieving these goals.

Third, a prerequisite for establishing a developed educational system is comprehensive and collective effort by all segments of society, not just by the schools. Schools must be supported by the family, the business sector and the general social structure.

All segments of society must work concertedly towards the goal of making the educational system a success. For instance, we must ensure that the family understands wholly the importance of rearing youth who are disposed towards seriousness and dedication at an early age. Religious scholars and *do'aat* (missionaries) in the country are aware of their role in making our children understand that peace and tolerance are important principles in Islam and in urging students to focus their interest on education.

We also invite businessmen to give students an opportunity to acquaint themselves with the labor market by providing them with jobs during their summer holidays, conducting practical training, offering guidance and direction for the students and establishing a complete partnership between schools and the business sector.

We also hope that our schools, colleges and universities will find greater opportunities for students to work with their fellow students in other countries of the world through their participation in meetings and international conferences, as well as the use of the Internet and modern communication technologies. The mission of every school should be to go beyond the walls of the classroom and develop its own program of student activities both within and beyond the country.

We also urge the government departments to help develop qualified future leaders for this country through student training programs and other avenues so that students can learn the importance of governance and recognize available opportunities. This will permit them to play their role in improving the standard of services which the government assiduously seeks to provide to its citizens.

Finally, we invite social activists and those in other fields who share similar interests to sponsor constructive initiatives and constantly seek ways to help nurture competent leaders from among our youth. For instance, they should sponsor students and help them to travel abroad to acquire the characteristics and skills needed for leadership.

I urge all the conference participants to support the grand objective—that of nurturing and developing new and successive generations and shaping them into future leaders of tomorrow.

In particular, I invite business executives to contribute and cooperate in making the nation's educational system more innovative and responsive to economic imperatives, as well as more appropriate and capable of confronting the challenges of the twenty-first century.

After covering education in general, permit me to focus attention on higher education. At the outset, I would point out that universities and colleges in the country today are facing major tasks that may be summarized as follows:

The first task is to strive hard to achieve the highest levels of education and learning output so that the graduate is equipped with the knowledge and expertise that makes him a true leader of society, capable of making an effective and productive contribution in whatever profession or activity he practices.

The second task is that universities and colleges must focus attention on scientific research in all spheres of life and endeavor to study the problems of the age, tackle them intelligently and find solutions to them. These solutions should ensure that we are not isolated from the mainstream of human civilization and should turn our universities and colleges into abodes of expertise in the real sense of the term. The aim is not only to understand the realities and problems of society but to help social institutions and agencies to succeed and continually aspire to reach even greater heights.

The third task relates to the need to focus on developing the capabilities of citizens in the spheres of continuing education and lifelong learning. It is evident that we live in an age where available knowledge is subject to rapid obsolescence. At the same time, new knowledge is growing exponentially. Thus we are facing new challenges, including how

[292]

to prepare the citizen to keep abreast of new developments and help him to continuously understand all the influences revolving around him.

The fourth task relates to the fact that universities and colleges play an important role not only in training citizens, but also in preparing society to adapt to the Information Age by using advanced techniques to gather data and selecting whatever information is helpful for problem-solving and decision-making

The fifth task is to pay attention to an important educational dimension in the new century—the prospective role of education in raising the standard of living of individuals and groups and the need to expand this role in support of the wider processes of comprehensive socioeconomic development.

Perhaps the question to be posed is: Have our universities and colleges succeeded in achieving these tasks? Thanks to Allah, we have succeeded in achieving many of these tasks and consequently, our universities and colleges have become a successful regional model. Yet huge problems and difficulties remain, hindering the progress of higher education in the country; mostly due to the low budget allocations made for universities and colleges. It is no secret that there are many current plans to expand the role of higher education in society but these are threatened by the lack of funds necessary to support their implementation.

Certainly there is a widening chasm between the expectations and aspirations in the realm of higher education, on the one hand, and the budgets and available resources to achieve them, on the other. Thankfully, this situation is now gaining the attention and sponsorship of state officials. We hope that our universities and colleges obtain the necessary budgets to proceed with the implementation of delayed plans in order to achieve all the hopes and aspirations of society.

I am confident that as we look ahead into the future, our nation, represented by its wise leadership, will reassert that all citizens in this country, both boys and girls, will have an opportunity to receive a suitable education, which will enable them to develop their personal potential and abilities in an optimal way.

The country and its leadership will continue to provide all necessary support to develop education as a foundation for building a knowledge society in the UAE. Simultaneously, we must all commit ourselves to carry out the required tasks, such as good performance, constant review and follow up, in every possible way, so that our children and future generations are wholly equipped to lead a successful and productive life.

These thoughts on education have been presented in the hope of achieving the best for our beloved nation. Allow me to conclude by quoting our late Founding Father, H.H. Sheikh Zayed bin Sultan Al Nahyan who said, "The greatest enterprise of a nation lies in the level and extent of its achievement in education."

13

Education as a Catalyst for Social Change in the Arab World

H.E. Dr. Faisal Al-Rufouh

C hange is considered a universal norm and a deep-rooted phenomenon in the history of humankind. Dynamism implies mobility and active interaction, both of which are fundamental factors that shape the life of individuals and enhance their intellectual capabilities. This is also true of societies and nations as a whole. Since change is recognized as an inevitable process, its impact will certainly be felt in all aspects of human life, and will affect individuals, nations and the entire globe. Though various types of change usually transcend the national borders and influence almost all societies, the levels of interaction with and acceptance of change differ from one society to another, including Arab societies.

Education is the most important of many active, interlinked factors and dynamics behind social changes within societies, including Arab societies. Women, mass media, civil society organizations and communication technologies also play critical roles in this respect, with education being regarded as the umbrella under which all other related factors interact to advance the process of social change.

Education as a Catalyst for Social Change

An educated and enlightened individual may be considered an effective tool in the processes of change and sustainable development. No transformation can occur in any society without the participation and interaction of the individual as its basic unit, along with the other agents of social change. The process of building up a society depends essentially on human knowledge and experience, which forms the essence of the individual's creative capabilities.

Education offers three major, interdependent and complementary paths to social change: knowledge, reform and transformation. The individual's basic inclination to acquire knowledge, adhere to rationalism and recognize scientific phenomena has become an important component of their personalities, along with religious, doctrinal, ethical and spiritual values. Downplaying the role of these values in setting up the social structure could lead to imbalances in society and distortions in the educational system. Therefore, to instill and institutionalize ethical and religious values among the youth has been a major challenge for all societies, even those in the Arab world. The basis of education in modern Arab and Islamic societies emphasizes the role of ethical and doctrinal values. Any comparison of this basis with that of ancient educational systems would reveal obvious similarities in the standards employed, even though they differ in terms of their application according to time and place. For example, in ancient Rome, ethical values were made the foundation of the educational system, while in the Middle Ages, ethical upbringing was developed within the framework of a theocratic ideal and was shaped entirely by religious values.

Ethical philosophy underscores the fact that morals are based upon autonomy or in other words, on the self-legislation, self-determination and ontological self-sufficiency of a human spirit. In the words of Immanuel Kant:

> A person can achieve the philosophical depth of understanding of the essence of knowledge, and consequently the possibility of taking the place he deserves in the world by virtue of ethical criteria.[1]

This means that throughout human history, most educational systems, including those of Arab and Islamic societies have made the advancement of morals and ethical values the cornerstone of the educational system. Islam, the central component of Arab cultural identity, has emphasized the important role of ethical values in the construction of society, linking them to the educational system as a tool and mechanism of social change.

If ethical factors represent the most important components upon which individual personality is built, then the understanding by individuals of socially acceptable codes of conduct, their interaction with positively subjective, external societal phenomena and the harmonious integration of these into a constructive educational system, will arguably constitute the most effective means of social change based on rationalism and the achievement of clear goals of comprehensive social development. Hence, in order to bring about successful societal reforms, Arabs must interact with the various dimensions of different cultures, but in a manner consistent with the principal pillars of Arab-Islamic culture.

Western philosophy perceives the moral conscience as an individual characteristic formed and realized through his immediate daily experience. Martin Heidegger believes that the philosophical aspect of an individual personality is one of the most complicated human aspects due to its ideological reflection on the understanding of the individual's day-to-day life. Through their analysis of Plato's educational dialogue, classical scholars believe in the impact of the interaction of both realistic and idealistic criteria on the structural materialization of human philosophy and its contribution to shaping the individual's personality, culture and role in the social change process.[2] In my view the ethical dimension of Arabs in their respective societies is the product of interaction between their doctrinal upbringing – as represented in Islam as a religion and a way of life – with the established cultural norms and social dimensions of different Arab societies.

If it is to play a part in the process of social change, the educational system in Arab societies must ensure harmony between the reform programs that protect the nation's identity, culture and basic components, especially Arab-Islamic heritage and values on the one hand, and the prerequisites of a free educational process and interaction with others, on the other.

Jan Amos Komensky, who is regarded as the "Father of Modern Education," assumed that the educational system could be understood from the perspective of transforming the individual through sustained and focused learning processes into a public figure who can promote the role of the individual in society and contribute to the desired social change in keeping with the morals and values embraced by a particular society.[3] Both social reformers Jean-Jacques Rousseau and Leo Tolstoy emphasized the ideal of "free" education of the individual, though the modern concept and societal role of education differ in many aspects from their views.[4]

The views of the modern European Renaissance have been built on the principle of separation between scientism and methodology of the educational system and its role in social change and reform, on one hand, and the values, ethical standards and religious beliefs of any society, on the other. In contrast, Islam has designed many patterns of behavior, codes, general standards and regulations that cover an individual's entire life, including the system of education, without restraining freedom of opinion and choice of lifestyle.

Perspectives on Social Change

Social change is the outcome of alterations taking place in the relations among individuals, on the one hand, and the whole of society, on the other. The term has been understood and employed in different ways depending on the field of knowledge with which it is associated. While the history of social change is determined by reviewing and analyzing the social forces that led to historical events, economic science perceives change from the perspective of the concepts of economic development, growth and reforms. The politics of social change derives its standpoint from studying the cases of success or failure of different political regimes and examining phenomena such as globalization, political reforms, democratization and revolution, as well as their particular role in the overall process of social change.

Though the pace of transformation could be slow and gradual, it would lead to proper, well-established changes with the minimum loss, whereas rapid, radical and revolutionary steps might jeopardize the entire process by creating such political and social polarizations as the totalitarian regimes of East Europe experienced before the start of *perestroika* and the subsequent fall of Berlin Wall in 1989. Sometimes, the processes of social change are so potent and comprehensive that they affect most social segments and the minutest details of life, such as the changes that accompanied the advent of Islam. However, some changes could also be quite limited and affect only small numbers of citizens, such as those associated with military coups in Third World countries.

Historical diversities and differences also help to trigger and enhance processes of social change. In analyzing this phenomenon, W.F. Ogburn noted several similarities between concepts used in previous studies on this term, as well as the impact of both the educational system and cultural standards on the entire process. The same holds true for Alfred Weber's notion of social change.[5]

Karl Marx, the founder of Communism, argued that class and material struggles (Marx's historical and dialectical materialism) are the driving forces behind social change. Other scholars attributed social change to theories such as "annihilation" and exclusion, ethical changes, ongoing social progress and the transformation of different social patterns, including Darwin's theories on social changes.

The notion of social change differs from that of the social order or system. Generally speaking, the first focuses on the structural transformations and development of the social set-up, while the latter is concerned with exercising control over the norms and practices embraced by society.[6]

Viewing in these terms, social change seems impossible in those Arab societies with prevailing Islamic norms, values, customs and traditions, in which the outcome of cultural interaction with other societies is not taken into consideration.

Education and Social Change in the Arab World

Individuals are identified as the "nation's real wealth," and human development as the "process of expanding people's options." Amartya Sen, the Economics Nobel laureate regards these "options" as largely reflecting the freedom of peoples to follow paths that ensure and enhance their potential for progress. The rapid human progress achieved during the 20th century and early 21st century contributed to changes in patterns of social behavior, provided motivation for change and reform, and created many positive effects on human life in general, especially in the fields of healthcare and educational services.

Undoubtedly, progress goes beyond the health and education sectors to include basic social, political and economic freedoms, thus creating more opportunities to enhance productivity and creativity. Self-respect and observance of human rights have become uncontested international norms that cannot be breached or circumvented. However, education remains the principal driving force that plays an important role in activating all these factors and determining their part in achieving human progress.[7] The proper practical applications of the knowledge and outputs of the educational system is the most important tool of human development since it constitutes a vital factor to boost production and productivity rates. Therefore, the World Bank has adopted the "knowledge gap" not the "income gap" as the basic criteria for categorizing countries today.

In Arab countries, social change is advancing further than political changes. According to United Nations estimates, the population of the Arab world will double to 749 million by 2050, putting greater pressure on infrastructure and basic services in these countries. Consequently, measures must be taken to ensure harmony between social changes and ongoing political and economic reforms.

The Arab world has failed to deal with and capitalize on many academic and scientific advances in today's world, thus widening its knowledge gap with the West. This has added to the barriers hindering the development of Arab societies. The UNDP Arab Human Development Report of 2002 noted that knowledge represents the path to liberty and progress, especially with the advent of globalization and accelerated growth rates.[8] The educational system, in general, and the higher education sector, in particular, are still unable to satisfy the needs of Arab society, and even as public expenditures allocated to this system are declining, most other societies are exerting rapid and strenuous efforts to meet their educational requirements in accordance with population growth.

According to the Report, approximately 40 percent of the population in the Arab world is illiterate and two thirds of these are women. Today, the number of unemployed people in the Arab world is around 25 million. Over 50 million people throughout the Arab world will join the labor market in 2010, and 100 million will join in 2020. Hence 6 million new jobs will need to be generated per year by Arab governments. According to 2004 statistics, about one third of the entire population is living on no more than US$2 per day per person. To deal with this problem, Arab decision-makers will have to double economic growth rate to 6 percent per year.[9]

Higher education, especially at the university level, plays a distinctive and important role in the acquisition of knowledge that will lead to social change. However, certain factors, such as the deteriorating state of higher education in the Arab world – particularly in terms of quality and interaction with the knowledge era – the declining role of women in the educational field, the increasing rates of illiteracy and concentration on humanities and social sciences more than on scientific and applied disciplines, have limited and weakened the effectiveness of education in advancing the process of change.

Nevertheless, this situation does not apply equally to all Arab countries, as many have dealt seriously with this process, exerting strenuous efforts to find proper solutions for the negative phenomena associated with it.[10]

Around the mid-1990s, the percentage of female students in higher education ranged from 13 per cent in Yemen to over 70 per cent in Jordan, UAE, Qatar and Lebanon. The UAE has the singular distinction of registering the highest percentage of females in higher education in the entire world (77 percent). Despite the many obstacles to higher education in the Arab world, it is to be noted that female enrolment levels in the majority of Arab countries are higher than in Turkey, Iran and South Korea. Indeed, four of the Gulf countries (UAE, Bahrain, Qatar and Kuwait) surpass even the United States in the proportion of female students undergoing higher education.[11]

The recent years have witnessed a rapid growth in the field of non-governmental research centers and academic institutions, notably in Jordan, Tunisia, Palestine, Lebanon, Egypt and Morocco.

With the entry of the private sector into the field, the number of universities has doubled in the Arab world, first during the period 1985–1995, and once again during the years 1995–2005.[12] However, many problems still beset the environment for scientific research in many Arab and developing countries. Despite low expenditures allocated for this sector when compared to other sectors, the past few years have witnessed the emergence of some prominent Arab scientists and talented scholars, such as the Egyptian scientist Dr. Ahmed Zewail, Nobel laureate in chemistry.[13]

In addition, the four major problems affecting scientific research in the Arab world are: the lack of clear research visions and strategies; weak research performance and management; limited financial support; and absence of the objective and open-minded environment needed by researchers.

At the level of quantitative performance, the science and technology research sector is currently suffering from decline, especially in the ideological, normative, methodological, computing and statistical survey fields, apart from the weak linkage existing between scientific research and economic and social activities.[14]

In mid-1990s, expenditures allocated for scientific research in the Arab world did not exceed 0.2 percent of gross national product, whereas the level is estimated at over 3 percent in some developed countries, and between 5–7 percent in others. Moreover, these expenditures are disproportionate, considering the increasing numbers of university graduates and the ongoing progress being achieved in the higher education sector, not to mention the low level of investment in scientific research by the private sector. Despite the private sector's growing role in producing and enhancing knowledge, Arab researchers have not yet begun to see any concrete and serious results.[15]

In order to assess the role of education in the social change process, it is necessary to examine the influence of some relevant factors: women, media, communications technology and civil society organizations.

Women and Social Change in the Arab World

Women are regarded as one of the main elements that motivate and support positive social change. Education makes an immense contribution towards qualifying women who become advocates of change and reform.

In turn, their role in rearing children constitutes a fundamental factor in causing these changes. However, the high rates of female illiteracy represent a major obstacle that prevents women from fulfilling their desired role in the social change process in the Arab world.

Depriving women of equal rights and opportunities as those enjoyed by men reduces their role in societal changes. Women in several Arab countries have not yet been given their basic political, civil and social rights—not even the rights to education and employment. In some other Arab countries, additional constraints are imposed upon women due to certain traditional norms and social customs. To date, only ten Arab countries are parties to the international Convention on the Elimination of All Forms of Discrimination Against Women (CEDAW).

However, fundamental rights and freedoms granted to women vary from one Arab society to another. While 98 percent of Tunisian school-age children undergo primary education, the corresponding percentage is only 57 percent among Saudi Arabian children. Even though male pupils at the primary level outnumber their female counterparts in most Arab countries, the difference could be as low as 2 percent in Tunisia or 3 percent in Algeria. In Yemen, only 44 percent of female students enroll in primary education compared to over 76 percent of male students. It is a different case in Jordan, UAE, Bahrain and Qatar where the percentage of females is higher than that of males. At the secondary level, male students exceed female students in Jordan, UAE, Bahrain, Tunisia, Algeria, Syria, Qatar, Kuwait and Lebanon.

As for the higher education sector, the percentage of female students is more than that of males in six Arab countries. In Kuwait, for example, the enrollment in higher education institutions is only 13 percent for males but as much as 30 percent for females.[16]

After achieving success in the education and health sectors, Arab women have made also made considerable strides in the public life of many societies. Business and commerce have traditionally been professions open to Arab men and women alike. Arab women have followed the ideal example set by the "Mother of Believers," Khadijah bint Khuwailid (May Allah be pleased with her), the wife of Prophet Mohammad (Allah's blessings and peace be upon him), who was a successful businesswoman, in whose business the Prophet himself (PBUH) took up employment. Over the years, women have practiced business in various ways. Rural women used to buy and sell in the markets and on sidewalks while middle class women started businesses from home. Nevertheless, at present, female economic activity is estimated to constitute just 30 per cent of total economic activity in many Arab countries, including the informal services sector.

Despite the limited economic role that women play in the Arab world, they have managed to institutionalize effective Arab women movements, especially in Jordan, UAE, Saudi Arabia, Qatar, Lebanon and Egypt. Besides, Arab women have asserted their presence in many economic forums and meetings inside and outside the Arab world, such as the first Women in Business conference organized in Dubai at the end of 2003.[17]

The Media and Social Change in the Arab World

The mass media, through its radio, television and printed forms, has played a vital role in stimulating interaction and communication among different segments of society in the Arab world. In addition, it has created an Arab media dynamics that transcends national borders to reach Arab citizens wherever they are directly without official scrutiny or censorship, especially through satellite channels and their growing influence. Moreover, as a result of the massive development of different means of communications, globalization has made the world a small global village, thus creating positive effects in the Arab world. Political boundaries are no longer hindering interaction among Arab citizens in their respective countries where mass media in general, and satellite channels in particular, has boosted the demands of the Arab masses for change and reform.

For example, *Al Jazeera* and *Al Arabiya* news channels have helped to enlighten Arab citizens and provide them with the information they seek, thus playing a major role in creating a common media ground throughout the Arab world. However, this media could not have played such an effective and influential role in enlightening people without an educational system that could raise the awareness levels of Arab citizens and foster their interaction with relevant regional and international developments.

Information/Communication Technologies and Social Change

Information and communication technologies (ICT), especially the Internet, have assumed a prominent position in all societies, including Arab society. Thanks to their vast and diverse capabilities in finding and disseminating knowledge and information, these technologies have been highly effective in increasing public awareness and motivating people to urge change and reform. The slow reform pace adopted by Arab governments has been rendered meaningless in the face of the ICT role in attracting different segments of society to follow regional and international events and developments.[18]

As a result of the Information Revolution, all barriers between societal interactions at the political, economic, cultural and social levels have crumbled, and Arab society is no longer isolated from the impact of these developments. Indeed, even Arab government circles have invested these effects both in advancing development processes and fostering the legitimacy of their plans and policies. Improved international relations between the Arab world and the West over the past few years have also helped to facilitate the transfer of information technology.[19]

Non-governmental organizations (NGOs) also played an important role in strengthening interaction and communication between the Arab world and other countries, especially in the popular, informal fields. The smooth flow of capital and joint economic projects have helped create a healthy environment for cultural and trade exchanges and transfer of technology, globalization and free trade agreements concluded between some Arab and western countries, particularly the United States, have further bolstered developmental processes in the Arab world in the political, legal, financial, technological and social fields.

The free access to the Internet and computer technologies represented a qualitative stride towards greater interaction between Arab and other societies. Except for Iraq and Libya, the number of Internet hosts in the region has increased more than seven-fold from 1995–1998. It even further doubled several times during the period 1998–2005.

Scholar Ithiel da Sola Pool attributes the deep penetration of the Internet in Third World countries and the Arab world, to low cost and easy connections, rendering it a major requirement for individuals as well as for political, economic, societal and other activities. He also notes the role of NGOs in promoting positive channels of interaction among peoples in the world, particularly with respect to human rights and dialogue between different civilizations, cultures and religions.[20]

In Saudi Arabia alone, there are around 40 licensed Internet companies. In 2002, the number of Internet subscribers in the Arab world as a whole was estimated at about 12 million, 20–40 percent of whom are women, and the number has doubled in 2005. The higher numbers of female subscribers have reinforced their contribution to the advancement of change and processes of reform.

Arab authorities, either directly or indirectly, have helped to facilitate greater access to information technology and the Internet. Despite official censorship imposed on the print media in some Arab countries, there is relative freedom from scrutiny for the "electronic" media and communications technologies, thus permitting Arab citizens a greater degree of freedom in dealing with the Internet and other information networks.

Civil Society and Social Change in the Arab World

The customary societal activities undertaken by political, economic, social and cultural institutions will almost inevitably lead to the desired reforms and changes. In this connection, the effects of globalization in relation to reforms, democratization, human rights, political participation and economic freedom, have led the NGOs (the so-called "civil society" organizations) to shoulder a major, influential and institutionalized role in pressing political regimes, particularly in underdeveloped countries and the Arab world, towards introducing the required reforms and changes. These organizations are now undertaking tasks that would normally fall within the core obligations of states and governments.[21]

The sphere of activity of civil society organizations includes a set of complicated voluntary economic, social and cultural practices and operations.[22] J. Cohen believes that the role of these organizations goes beyond sponsoring orphans and providing relief to the needy and includes working in coordination with political parties and movements over a variety of national and international programs, setting up and influencing lobbies and interest groups, and mobilizing and forming public opinion.[23]

Such activities are usually carried out to fill the vacuum resulting from the failure of state departments and institutions in fulfilling their original responsibilities, especially in protecting the environment, promoting human rights, organizing religious research symposiums and providing health and other services, particularly during natural disasters (such as earthquakes and floods). These organizations often enjoy the respect and appreciation of individuals, political parties, human rights institutions, and other entities in recognition of their support for, and protection of the aspirations and interests of these segments of society.[24]

However, the role of civil society organizations remains insignificant in Arab public life, with the exception of some Islamic and nationalistic organizations. There is skepticism at both the official and popular levels regarding the intentions of most of these organizations because of their external connections. This has undermined the confidence of Arab citizens in their activities and practices, since many of these organizations pursue the interests of their respective countries through those of foreign states.[25]

Despite the generally limited role of Arab civil society organizations, the past few years have witnessed an expanding role for some efficient ones, particularly in defending human rights, women's right to political participation and advancing the reform process as such.[26]

The presence of such institutions varies from one Arab country to another. Most of them exist chiefly in Jordan, Tunisia, Lebanon, Morocco, Egypt and the Arab Gulf states. Developments in means of communication and the free flow of information have helped to boost and advance the societal role played by these institutions, thus expediting the process of reform and social change in the Arab world.[27]

Conclusions

Education is an important factor in the life of any society, and the most effective and influential means of social transformation. It helps to disseminate and develop the moral values of any community. The greatness of any nation, as well as its regional and international position, is measured largely by the academic and educational achievements of its population and the role of women in its society. Many western scholars and Orientalists have attributed the lack of development and social change in Arab societies to the "conservative nature of Arab-Islamic culture," ignoring either consciously or unconsciously, the realities of this culture and the role of foreign elements and challenges in putting constraints on Arab aspirations for change.

This chapter has sought to take an objective, unbiased look at the social conditions prevailing in the Arab community, and the role of education and its dissemination in bringing about social and economic changes in the life of Arab communities as a whole. It has focused on investigating the role of education in interacting with the realities of globalization and its forces, which are pressing for reform in all its aspects in the Arab world. It has also analyzed the vital role and potential significance of education for the future of Arab life, and examines the standards of academic knowledge in Arab society. It has studied the impact of the spread of education and the role of Islamic values on the formulation of different lifestyles and thought patterns of common people in Arab communities.

Education helps to define the real image of Arab women and reinforce their role in sustainable development. The spread of education has reduced the rate of illiteracy among Arab women, elevated their position and enabled them to play a pioneering role in the process of social change in the Arab world.

The rapid and effective spread of information through satellite TV channels, the Internet and other media outlets, has had a tremendous impact on the development of education and its outputs in Arab communities. However, it has also had a negative impact on the cultural values of youth, leading to the growth of many unacceptable phenomena in the Arab world. Viewpoints differ about the role of the media in education and its implications for comprehensive social change in the Arab world as well as the role of education as a catalyst for social change, viewed from the perspective of Arab-Islamic customs, traditions and values.

One Goal, Different Agendas: Expanding the Scope of Education in the Arab World and Addressing the Requirements of the Labor Market

Dr. Rafia Obaid Ghubash

In the second half of the twentieth century, higher education witnessed a quantitative and qualitative revolution. This happened both at the level of general education and higher education. The number of universities and institutions of higher education doubled and the number of university students at the global level increased from 13 million in the beginning of the twentieth century to around 100 million by 1960. This development in education stemmed from an increase in socio-cultural consciousness, as well as change in the local and global economic patterns. In addition, several countries undertook the task of democratizing education and ensuring equality in gaining advanced, high-grade education for all those qualified to do so.[1]

However, after the collapse of the Soviet Union and the disintegration of its system in the late 1980s, some western thinkers perceived the demise of an era of "ideological" interests and the rise of an era of utilitarian economic interests coupled with historically unprecedented opportunism. An analyst of western literature would find that the basis of these orientations existed previously, but in several, different formulas.

Hence, the call from industrialized countries to link education to the economy more closely than before gained momentum. This move was intended to serve the higher interests of these states by preserving their economic hegemony, and consequently their political and military dominance, in the global arena and give effect to this in accordance with new developments, both current and future.[2]

In the Arab countries, the echoes of this call have reverberated in different forms and for different reasons. Unlike the case of the industrialized countries in the Arab world, the motives for reforming education were not naturally linked to maintaining economic, political and military hegemony in the global arena. Rather, they were concerned with upgrading the standard of living of these nations and driving them forward. Therefore, many successive moves have emerged to reform education in the Arab world, which has come under a lot of criticism. For instance, Dr. Hamid Ammar, the mentor of Arab educationalists, maintains that education in the Arab world is low, both in quantitative and qualitative terms. These low standards are revealed through several indicators, which are summarized as follows:[3]

- *Percentage of Illiteracy:* The first indicator is the percentage of illiteracy among those over 15 years of age. According to recent statistics, at least 45 percent of the population of the Arab world can neither read nor write.

- *Average Years of Schooling:* The second indicator is the average years of schooling. Here, the average number of years that an Arab citizen in the age group of 25-plus has spent at school is no more than 5 years, whereas the average years of schooling for citizens in advanced, industrialized countries is 13 years.

In addition, the percentage of university degree-holders is only 6 percent of the total labor force in the Arab world, whereas it is 20 percent in Israel and between 13–15 percent in the East Asian "tiger" economies. Expenditure on scientific research in the Arab world does not exceed 0.5 percent of the GNP.

Some analysts think that education in Arab countries has contributed inadequately towards achieving universal and sustainable development when compared to education imparted in India, South Korea and East Asian countries, where growth is beginning to reach record levels. The East Asian countries have become members of the group of advanced countries referred to as "Asian tigers." This inadequacy arises because Arab schools suffer from the weak and superficial education imparted in the primary stages. Children undergo successive stages of schooling till they enter university but without really being qualified to study at this level. Arab universities, faced with such a huge number of weak students, cannot fail all of them. Rather, they are forced to give them all pass marks as they are all more or less equal. Students thus move from one year to another till they complete their university education, but their intellectual level does not exceed that of primary or intermediate school pupils. Hence Arab universities award degrees but generally fail to produce well educated people.

Needless to say, when advanced nations become concerned about their educational systems – as a result of the fierce mutual competition – they focus immediately on promoting more scientific curricula, introducing vocational training programs and finding ways to develop technological skills. In the 1980s, alarm bells sounded in the United States when it was discovered that many American students had moved away from the science stream towards the humanities stream because of their low performance in Mathematics and Science. Faced with a similar situation, South Korea began to direct its education and training towards meeting the requirements of the age and was consequently able to turn into an "Asian tiger," registering as many as 16,380 industrial and technological patents alone within just twenty years. In contrast, the Arab world could only register 170 patents, despite having many poets, men of letters and specialists in the Humanities.[4]

Others say that the Arab education system has aggravated the labor situation by qualifying persons who do not meet the needs of the labor market, thereby increasing the number of unemployed. This happens because there is no connection between the labor market requirements and their academic specializations, which are often theoretical, humanistic or impractical although these specializations are important in many realms of thought, creativity, innovation and the moral education of nations.

Other reports attest that in several parts of the Arab world the citizen does not gain the full and adequate rights provided for by international charters, such as his rights to life, liberty, health, work and education. This has been referred to by a report issued in 2001 by the Education Programs Administration of the Arab League Educational, Cultural and Scientific Organization. This report highlighted the following points: [5]

- Despite the efforts exerted by Arab countries in the last decades of the twentieth century to spread compulsory education and expand secondary and university education within the traditional system, the realities indicate a large educational deficit. This deficit is both quantitative and qualitative, making the right to education a privilege available only to those in power and making it a cherished dream for the children of the masses, those in remote locations or those who are socially, culturally and economically dispossessed and remain deprived of this right even at the lowest educational levels.

- Enrollment in secondary education in the Arab world does not exceed more than 60 percent in the 15–18 age group compared to 98 percent and 99 percent in advanced countries. This proportion drops to round 15 percent for those enrolled in university education in Arab countries compared to a corresponding figure of 65 percent in the United States.

- Those who enroll in graduate studies are not more than 5.2 percent of all students in Arab universities compared to 20–25 percent in the western countries.

- The number of students who had obtained the certificate of general secondary education in ten Arab countries but failed to join universities in the 16-year period from 1980–1996 was estimated at 3 million persons. These students were deprived of the chance to continue their education in a globalized, contemporary society that demands providing education opportunities at all levels to every individual throughout life.

As the above-mentioned report reveals, even beyond the framework of this school education, the governmental and civic efforts exerted in the latter half of the twentieth century have not managed to eradicate illiteracy among the 65 million Arabs living in this age of computer culture, information and media technologies.

Despite the concern shown by educationists, intellectuals, academics and tens of debates, workshops and publications, most Arab countries did not initiate educational reform based on their own policy decisions until external pressure was applied to change the curricula and the education system. However, such external pressure is only concerned about the vision and interests of those exerting this pressure and there has been a focus on weakening and dismantling the Arab-Islamic identity through certain curricula.

Education in the GCC States

In the GCC states, the quantitative development in general and university education during the last quarter of the past century reached record figures. The number of students in the stages of general education in the year 1970 was around 765,000 male and female students. This number reached 4,500,000 students in 1994 and 5,747,881 students in 2004. The spread of education in the GCC states was one of the most important and significant social developments in recent years, as it was general and encompassed all categories of people.[6]

[315]

The Arab oil producing states have used education as a basis to establish modern states after most of them gained independence in the early 1970s. They have employed education to qualify the employees needed to build their structure and institutions such as the army, the police, the government departments and the state apparatus. In this they have succeeded to a great extent. In addition, through the education system, they have created a labor force in the domains of banking, industries, imports and exports. Unfortunately, however, these states have greatly encouraged high consumption levels among their citizens, who have started to demand new goods and services. These goods and services have become necessities of life for local citizens. Some believe that the educational system has contributed to this situation.[7]

One study on this subject refers to the realities of education in the GCC states, reflected in the following features:

- Rapid quantitative growth at all levels of education has led to inability on the part of educational institutions to absorb this increase in demand for education, although the states are committed to providing free education for all members of society.

- The educational system in the Gulf states suffers from unilateralism, as the educational order is confined to one system, without attempts to diversify or find alternatives to remedy the flaws of the prevalent system. Moreover, technological and technical education, despite receiving more attention recently has not been able to compete with the general educational system or position itself as an alternative.

- Budget constraints imposed in order to provide for oil market fluctuations have led to a reduction in education expenditure and this has made budget allocations incompatible with the increased numbers seeking education.

- The reliance of the Arab educational systems on memorization and reproduction of information by students has resulted in the failure to develop their higher intellectual skills, equip them to solve problems, tackle novel situations, take initiative and shoulder responsibility.[8]

The GCC states have responded to major world developments, especially in the last third of the twentieth century and the beginning of the twenty-first century. Each state has started to review its educational programs on the basis of current political orientations. Generally, the following observations may be made about the progress made in developing and reforming education in the Arabian Gulf region:

- There is a general acknowledgement that the educational system is in a crisis and that it needs to be developed and linked to the labor market and new global developments, including the characteristics and features connected with globalization and its related outcomes and impacts.

- The GCC states have formulated strategic educational plans ranging between five-year, ten-year and twenty-year plans. All these plans are ambitious and are aimed at rectifying specific deficiencies. However, certain factors can impede these plans, such as the appointment of a new education minister who takes a negative attitude or obstructs the strategic development plans drawn up by the former minister or under implementation by him.

- In these strategies, there is greater concern about focusing on subjects connected with Science, Mathematics, the computer, and the English language and reducing focus on humanities and social subjects, despite the general importance of the latter in developing the psychological, moral, social and humanitarian attitudes of the students.

- In some strategies, there are also some attempts to introduce some topics relating to ethical education, globalization and intellectual skills (particularly innovative and critical thinking).

- These strategies focus on topics relating to the curriculum and the teacher (the educational environment, the basic system of education, and others).

- Greater attention is paid by these strategies to quality and reliability criteria and what they entail.

The Arab Education Bureau for the Gulf States held a major workshop to formulate the projects and programs for developing education in the member states. The workshop was held in Jeddah, Saudi Arabia from July 17–19, 2004. The development program that emerged from the workshop made a number of decisions and recommendations. These included the importance of arranging priorities based on the workshop documents, the approval of the framework document on developing education and the adoption of the following programs:[9]

- program to decide on a suitable model to professionalize education
- provision for the issue of licenses to practice the teaching profession and a system for their renewal
- program for sustained professional development
- The Teacher House program, establishing a center for the continuous professional development of teachers
- program for assessment of the learning process
- program to develop the culture of the educational institution
- founding an association for Mathematics teachers and another for Science teachers at the level of the member states
- program to establish an electronic network for developing learning in Mathematics and Science
- compensational program to reinforce basic skills among pupils of early classes
- program for setting up a Gulf Establishment for Educational Investment
- program focusing on scientific and engineering specializations
- program to set up an organizational mechanism for the approval of schools

Many proposed projects were discussed and the following were then presented again in a subsequent meeting:

- experimental program for the teachers' teachers and zonal supervisors
- organizational mechanism for coordination between major committees supervising joint work in general, higher and technical education
- installing mechanisms, organizational and administrative tools to implement the decisions of the Supreme Council and ministerial committees in the field of education
- training program for planning the social participation of schools
- the program for promoting joint institutional action between educational institutions and the business and production sectors
- founding joint national councils to bring together the education, training and employment sectors
- intensifying current meetings of corresponding authorities
- founding an educational center for the study of Arabic language
- unifying certain fields in the subjects intended for study.

The following section reviews briefly some of the plans and strategies for developing education in the GCC states:

The United Arab Emirates

The UAE has drawn up an ambitious strategy for developing education in the country till 2020. The plan was prepared by the Ministry of Education in cooperation with other concerned parties by examining and identifying problems in the field. The plan outlines material and financial requirements and the criteria for implementation and assessment of achievements. The most important constituents of this strategic vision are:

- Increasing the cohesion and interaction between the educational system and other societal systems in order to serve the purpose of overall progress and achieve sustainable development for the UAE citizens.
- Upgrading the level of professionalism and the skills of all those who work in the educational system.

- Increasing the contribution of the educational system in developing knowledge, fostering the growth of culture and civilization (technology), and encouraging the competitive mechanisms in the era of global economics.

- Completing and developing the infrastructure and institutions of the educational system in order to increase its economic, social and cultural returns.

- Increasing the scale of societal participation in planning, financing and managing education in accordance with the principle that education is the fundamental right of all.

- Realizing greater integration at all levels between the domains of education: general, technical, university and technological.

- Improving the quality aspects of the educational system by paying attention to the quality of inputs and processes, as well as the objectives, curricula and teaching materials, the teacher and his teaching capabilities, the methodologies, techniques and tools of assessment in order to train a generation that is capable of innovation and creativity.

The former UAE Minister of Education, Dr. Ali Abdul Aziz Al Sharhan, stressed this strategy on several occasions. Also, he pointed out that the aim of this strategy is that the UAE educational system achieves 26 objectives, some of which are listed below: [10]

- All personnel in different stages of education must hold university degrees in education.

- All school directors must have graduate degrees in education, and at least 50 percent of them must have a Master's and doctoral degrees in education management and educational supervision.

- The rates of *emiratization* must be raised among teachers, directors and administrators to more than 90 percent of the total number of those working in education, and the percentage of nationals among the support staff must reach 100 percent.

- Kindergartens should provide a computer for every 10 children whereas secondary schools should provide each student with a computer.
- Efforts must be made to eradicate adult illiteracy.
- The quality aspects of the educational system must be improved, openness to other educational systems must be guaranteed, and UAE students must be trained to participate in international educational competitions (especially the Science and Mathematics Olympiads).
- As "education is a universal right" it must be translated into equal education opportunities for both sexes and for children hailing from different regions in the state, besides offering diversified opportunities that take into consideration individual differences between learners.
- Innovation must be fostered by nurturing a generation of inventors who can help to advance civilization and contribute to progress, by providing enriching curricula for advanced and creative students and by using appropriate teaching methods.

Here, reference may be made to the fact that the UAE Ministry of Education aims to make the output of pre-university education more appropriate and consistent with these ongoing efforts. In addition, the Ministry plans to establish a council to deal with affairs pertaining to pre-university education. This council will establish an education fund to which all organizations of society, especially the private sector, will contribute in order to support and upgrade the educational process.

The Kingdom of Bahrain

The Ministry of Education has launched several initiatives and programs to develop education and upgrade its level. The start of the academic year 2003–2004 witnessed the formulation of a strategic vision for educational development, including several qualitative developmental programs and plans approved by the Council of Ministers. The Ministry will begin implementing this vision via specialized committees and civil society organizations. Also, an integrated program for building educational institutions will be drawn up, in addition to developing the work environment, founding centers for educational measurement and assessment, a center for talented students, adopting a plan for catering to special needs students, introducing information technology, and developing the idea of school councils to reinforce the principle of participation and 'democratization' of education. The Ministry has developed a program for preparing and qualifying teachers, as well as developing English language teaching, embarked on implementing the project for unifying academic courses in educational institutions, completed the teachers' salary scale project, opened some educational institutions such as the Sheikh Khalifa bin Salman Institute for Technology, founded two public libraries, and launched the King Hamad Schools of the Future project for electronic education, information technology and communications and other developmental projects.[11]

Several attempts have been made to reform education in the Kingdom of Bahrain beginning with the 1940s. Reform attempts include all the developments during the last third of the last century and up to the present time. In addition to the founding of the University of Bahrain and expansion in the sphere of private higher education, some of the ongoing initiatives and objectives are listed below: [12]

- Making the process of educational reform universal so that it does not focus attention on one aspect of education at the expense of the others, and does not focus on one level (primary, for instance) and neglect the others.

- As part of the reform process at the primary level, some graduates of the secondary schools were sent to the University of Bahrain to obtain university degrees in the class teacher system to upgrade the level of primary education.

- According importance to developing the learning curricula, addressing the welfare of the teacher and enhancing the personality of the student in terms of knowledge, emotions and societal matters.

- Introducing the credit hour system (courses) in the secondary schools where a student's work is no longer assessed on the basis of one final examination in the third year, but through continuous assessment over three years of secondary school, and focusing thereafter on a comprehensive education track.

- Considering individual differences between students in selecting an appropriate load of credit hours (between 12–18 hours) according to their personal abilities, inclinations and circumstances.

- Within the context of this system, according importance to Arabic and foreign languages and also allowing students to choose some optional subjects consistent with their inclinations and future aspirations.

- Attaching importance to school administration by stipulating that the Director must have obtained a Diploma in Administration prior to his appointment.

- Reinforcing the role of the school as an educational unit by establishing a council to run the school comprising the director, assistant directors and some primary education personalities, provided that half of the council comprises teachers elected by their colleagues as council members in order to enhance democracy in the school.

- Proposing a new salary scale for teachers whereby the teaching profession gains stature and the salaries of teachers are made equal to those of doctors and engineers, and promotions of teachers take place in accordance with their intellectual, professional and cultural growth and not their administrative designations.

- Sending senior masters on study courses to obtain master's degrees in their areas of specialization in order to develop their abilities in educational and academic leadership.

The Kingdom of Saudi Arabia

There is a ten-year plan (2004–2014) to develop education in the Kingdom of Saudi Arabia at a cost of 69 billion Saudi riyals. It consists of a stimulus program, which involves getting at least 40 percent of the children from age 4–6 absorbed in the kindergarten stage by the end of the plan period. This entails equipping government buildings for this purpose, implementing compulsory education from the primary to the intermediate stage, providing suitable buildings to accommodate the expected growth in students, and achieving international student standards in terms of academic attainment and performance.

This plan pays attention to talented students in the domains of science, art and literature. It is also concerned with upgrading educational systems, rehabilitating those with special needs and allowing horizontal expansion in *Ahli* (indigenous) education to a partnership level of 25 percent of the total number of students. Likewise, the plan will improve the teacher–student ratio to one teacher for every twenty students, as well as develop and apply periodically the competence test standards for teachers. In addition, teachers' licenses will be renewed every five years and will be subject to a system of monitoring, accountability and continuous assessment. The *Saudization* (or indigenization) of education will be 95 percent by the end of the plan.

A recent scientific report indicated that the most important pillars upon which the ten-year developmental plan rests include: Islamic religious principles, dealing with the quantitative and qualitative flood of information, consistency with the future requirements of the labor market, acquisition of necessary abilities by students to deal with the future economic trends, acquisition of knowledge and beneficial life skills by the students, and response to the social demands of education and reinforcing the spirit of informed citizenship.[13]

The KSA Ministry of Higher Education accords special importance to the quality of higher education. This has been reflected in establishing the National Department for Measurement and Assessment, the Higher Education Fund and the controlled expansion in scientific specialization by directing new departments and colleges to focus exclusively on the specializations needed by the country. More recently, the establishment of the Saudi National Commission for Academic Accreditation and Assessment has been approved and a strategic plan for higher education has been prepared.[14] The plan for developing education asserts the importance of students acquiring knowledge and beneficial life skills, responding to the social demands of education and reinforcing the spirit of conscious citizenship.[15]

The Sultanate of Oman

Oman has prepared an educational plan to develop all elements of education on the basis of the 2020 futuristic vision of its economy. The plan comprises several pillars, including lengthening the academic year, extending the learning day, developing the school curricula, apart from the a new system of primary education adopted since 1997. The development efforts exerted by the Ministry of Education included designing developed curricula to teach Science and Mathematics, according special attention to the English language and teaching it from Grade I, and reviewing the taught subjects in qualitative and quantitative terms. The plan includes the introduction of information and computer technologies, life education, economic and administrative sciences as subjects in the teaching plan. Moreover, the development plan included providing self-learning centers in the schools, appropriate laboratories, introducing the system of senior teacher and drawing up a training plan for the teachers, directors and instructors of self-learning centers. The Ministry aims to upgrade teacher qualifications for primary school teachers – from graduates of intermediate

[325]

colleges to the university level – in cooperation with the Ministry of Higher Education.

Ministry efforts also focused on the system of educational assessment and examinations, by establishing a specialized department to introduce techniques and systems to keep abreast of new trends in test setting, marking and benefiting from test results, including the approval of continuous assessment, making it an integral part of the processes of learning and teaching provided that a balance is maintained with regard to the individual needs of teachers.

In the context of partnership with society, Oman is witnessing a quantitative expansion in the number of *Ahli* and private colleges, while the Ministry of Higher Education is concerned with regulating such colleges through laws relating to their licensing, accreditation as well as funding and technical support. In the field of technical education and training, the Sultanate is a pioneer in introducing the General National Vocational Qualifications system and modifying it in accordance with the requirements of the Omani labor market and development goals.[16]

Oman's education strategy aims to achieve congruity between the policies of higher education and all the economic and social transformations that the Sultanate is currently experiencing in the course of its development. Its salient features are highlighted in an article by Suhail bin Salem Sa'ad al Kathiri, written at the beginning of 2006 proposing ways to developing this strategy.[17]

- According importance to measuring the quality of higher education output in the light of some important criteria which include the following:
  - The speed of the labor market's response in attracting graduates of higher education, which illustrates the level of suitability of the educational programs provided by the institutions of higher education to the requirements of the market.

[326]

- o The scale and the level of job-related perks obtained by the graduate at the workplace.
- o The percentage of graduates who enjoy job stability and the level of job turnover, which reflects the graduate's job satisfaction or lack of it, in relation to the work requirements and the incentives received.

- It is imperative that the anticipated development and modernization must cover education in general and higher education in particular as well as educational institutions in different parts of the education system, especially since it is evident that the previously proposed strategy for developing education has not achieved the desired goals.

- It is necessary to review some of the steps and procedures taken by the Ministry of Higher Education such as discarding a group of specializations offered by the College of Higher Education in the regions and converting them into University Colleges offering specializations that have not been based on a real study of the requirements of the labor market in these fields.

Al Kathiri maintains that if private higher education is given the responsibility for solving the output problems of higher education, it may be said that these problems are more cumbersome than the former's capacity to solve them in the absence of any clear vision and accurate analysis of the national economy requirements in terms of qualified personnel from these institutions. Moreover, the private universities' connections with different sectors of the national economy are weak and their plans and programs need to reflect the requirements of different economic sectors. These universities should not adopt plans and programs that fail to meet the needs of the labor market. In conclusion, the writer confirms the importance of relying on quality criteria in higher education and states that quality management should be based on three primary constituents in order to guarantee its success: partnership management, employing action teams and continuing improvement in processes, as well as other necessary things to upgrade the competence of higher education and connect it appropriately to the labor market in the Sultanate of Oman.[18]

The State of Qatar

The Ministry of Education carried out a process of universal development of curricula and text books. A document on developing the Arabic language curricula in all stages of education was prepared. The English language was introduced in the first grade since 1999. Geography and history were consolidated into one subject (social studies) and chemistry, physics and biology were consolidated in one subject (integrated sciences). New concepts and terms were introduced in the curricula such as voluntary work, peace, condemnation of violence, globalization and environmental education. Moreover, work on implementing the Developed Primary Schools project started in 2001. Two schools, each consisting of 11 classes, were chosen. Advanced curricula in the literary and scientific fields were prepared for the two schools and the project for Scientific Secondary Schools was implemented in 2000 in two schools (one for boys and the other for girls) in addition to two Developed Preparatory Schools under the Qatar Educational Project in 2002. The Ministry continues to cooperate with the College of Education at the University of Qatar, the Ministry of Civil Service and the training center to prepare teachers, in addition to holding several training sessions. The ministry founded a secondary school for industrial technology in 1999 and activated the administration's role in training and professional development by holding several training sessions. Studying started in the College of the North Atlantic College for and technical education training linked to the requirements of the market, especially the gas industry. A royal decree regarding the founding of the Qatar Technological College was issued in 1998 and the college awards a technological diploma in a number of modern specializations.[19]

Recently the State of Qatar has formulated a strategic education plan called "Education for a New Era." The plan aims to redesign and restructure the educational system. Seventeen billion dollars have been allocated for the plan and this amount will be spent on the infrastructure of general and higher education over a period of ten years. The implementation of the plan is supervised by the Higher Council for Education, which is chaired by H.H. the Emir of Qatar and administered by his wife Sheikha Mozah bint Nasser Al-Misnad. Several years ago the State of Qatar enlisted the help of the RAND Corporation to revise, assess and redesign the educational system on a modern basis.[20]

In addition, Qatar has started building a modern Education City that has attracted the five most famous universities in different specializations: medicine, engineering, administration, sciences and arts. A medical city of an international standard has been attached to the University City. A center for continuous education has been established that is modern in terms of curricula, output and links with society. Since 2004, Qatar has started re-engineering the government schools for general education. The administration of these schools has been entrusted to the private sector based on quality criteria and generous financial incentives. There are other initiatives and important developments intended to upgrade education.[21]

The Supreme Education Council held a preliminary meeting at the end of 2005 on the special criteria for the national curricula of Qatar. The meeting aimed to introduce participants to the new plans by which the state seeks to develop education.

At the meeting it was reasserted that the curriculum criteria constituted the cornerstone of the state's initiative to develop general education. These criteria covered four subjects: Arabic Language, English Language, Science and Mathematics, with a focus on content to train students to become participatory and productive citizens. In all stages of study the

[329]

emphasis would be on critical thinking, research, deduction and other intellectual skills in order to ensure the development of the student abilities in the realms of creative work, analytical thinking, problem-solving and other intellectual skills. This is essential because as the meeting showed, students who are able to absorb specific knowledge, concepts and skills, and also excel in annual national assessments based on these criteria can excel in international tests that qualify them to join the most outstanding international universities. The meeting concluded that the following aspects must be taken into consideration.[22]

- reviewing the national education criteria in other Arab countries, especially with regard to the Arabic language
- developing the curriculum criteria as a universal process aimed at assessing schools, students and teachers
- examining other educational aspects, such as helping guardians to choose schools suited to the needs of their children, and carrying out periodic, continuous, universal and critical assessment.

The State of Kuwait

There are a number of development documents in the field of education, including the final assessment report on the educational system, prepared in 1987 followed by determined efforts to develop education. Another document is the National Vision on Developing the Educational System by the First Quarter of the Twenty-first Century (prepared in 1999) and its recommendations on upgrading education. The Ministry of Education also drew up plans within the framework of the government's program for the years 1999, 2002 and 2003. Another document entitled: "A Primary Futuristic Strategy for Developing Education till 2025," was based upon the following: past educational experience, the trends referred to by assessment studies covering different stages, the consultations offered by international, Arab and regional organizations and experts on aspects of educational work in Kuwait, educational experiences in the contemporary world and their achievements, shortcomings and development goals. The strategy accords particular importance to the phase of the invasion of Kuwait and the consequent need to enhance national unity, expand the base of democracy and *shoura* ("consultation" within Islamic tenets) and develop voluntary work. The strategy was subject to wide scrutiny during the First National Conference on Education held during October 2001. It included a comprehensive review of the educational system and a number of development visions and proposals.

The special report issued by the Kuwaiti Ministry of Education (with technical support from the World Bank) on the country's education indicators reveals some important conclusions, which may be summarized as follows:

- According to 2003–2004 estimates, despite huge expenditure on education (6.3 percent of GDP), salaries accounted for 93 percent of the Ministry of Education budget.
- A high percentage (nearly one-fifth) of Kuwaiti students failed in the secondary stage in 2002–2003, with a higher percentage among males (22.4 percent) in comparison to females (17.2 percent).
- Low hours of actual teaching in the government schools compared to specified formal hours (because of absenteeism or other causes); the missed hours ranged between 112 hours in the primary stage and 235 hours in the intermediate stage.
- A clear reduction in scientific skills acquisition in Kuwait, especially in Mathematics and Science, and also in reading skills.
- The growing importance of private education, with the private schools constituting more than one third of all schools generally (37 percent) and nearly 42 percent of secondary schools.

The report summarizes education problems in Kuwait as follows: reduced knowledge, low level of skills, failure and dropping out, educational imbalances, lack of professional commitment by teachers, low investment spending on education compared to current expenditure, lack of measurement tools and periodic assessment of the performance of the educational system.

The report concludes by offering a number of recommendations, the most important of them being to encourage the private sector to enter the field of education; give financial incentives to guardians to enable them to choose appropriate schools; adopt the system of contract schools whereby the private sector is assigned the task of school management via a package of incentives, based on rules of quality management and justice—as Qatar has done recently by privatizing state schools and entrusting their management to the private sector.[23]

Reforming Education: Global and Arab Experiences

Education is the basic foundation for the advancement and development of thought. To the extent that education is developing and progressing in all spheres, thought advances and functions in a manner that deeply affects civilization structure, economic growth and social mobility. Education is the essential element in economic growth and the formation of human capital. Hence nations periodically review their position and correct their course with respect to achieving goals. This happens particularly in the advanced countries of the world. Several countries have remedied their level of education using methods such as school reform in Australia and New Zealand, state control, societal participation, partnership and networking in Bangladesh, curricula and educational leadership in Canada and the United States, continuity and quality education in France, as well as general reforms at the pre-school and primary education stages. Several studies on education, training and introducing a national teaching curriculum appeared in the United Kingdom in 1988. Also, a council to reform education was formed in

Japan, aimed at making education more responsive to serving economic and developmental goals.

The 1983 report entitled *A Nation at Risk* by the National Commission on Excellence in Education was the most important document on the status of education in America in the last few decades. It indicated that the country's problems stem mainly from the low academic levels of the student and the poor quality of education. The report also pointed an accusing finger at the teacher himself. The document was consistent with other reports in the sphere of Mathematics such as the *Curriculum and Evaluation Standards for School Mathematics: An Agenda for Action* and *Everybody Counts*: *A Report to the Nation on the Future of Mathematics Education* as well as criteria for the curriculum and evaluation of school mathematics. This last document had a great effect on developing the teaching of mathematics in public schools in the United States. The committee that had issued *A Nation at Risk* convened periodically till the end of the twentieth century. The report paved the way for the 1990 plan drawn up by President George Bush (Senior) entitled *America 2000*. This is an education strategy that encompassed many reform plans advocated by the 1983 report, which called for a developed and renewable educational system focused on innovation and pioneering achievements at school. The report notes that the failure to excel in Science and Mathematics may cause the United States to lose its global markets and its scientific and industrial supremacy.[24]

Many plans and strategies have appeared in Arab countries generally and the Gulf states in particular. Of these, the following are worth mentioning:

- Prevailing Trends in General Education and Professions in Arab Countries (1971)
- Strategy for Developing Arabic Education (1979)
- Ideal Planning for Education and Development (1986)

- A Futuristic Vision to Enhance the Social Status of the Teacher in the Arab World (1989)
- Educational Planning in Bahrain (1991)
- Educational Planning in the State of Qatar (1991)
- Educational Planning in Syria (1991)
- An Assessment of Education Planning in Egypt and the Plan for Reforming the Educational System (1992),
- The Realities of Development, Future Plans in the GCC States and the Role of Development in Satisfying their Needs (1995)
- The document issued by the Arab League Educational, Cultural and Scientific Organization (1995)
- The National Report on the Education Development in the State of Kuwait (1999)
- Present and Future General Trends in Educational Institutions up to the Secondary School Level in Kuwait (1999)
- The document on Envisaging Educational Action in the Member States of the Arab Bureau of Education for the GCC States (2000)
- Education Vision 2020: Plan for Developing Education in the UAE till 2020 (2002)
- Development of Universal Education in the GCC States: A Study on the Trends Mentioned in the Decision of the Supreme Council as Regards Education (2004).

However, it must be noted that all these studies, conferences, debates and strategic plans were insufficient to advance the educational process in the Arab world during the past decades, as I have pointed out in a previous study.[25] In that study I posed questions and offered answers on why many of these strategies and plans fail to achieve their goals. Among the reasons are the following: a lack of appropriate mechanisms of implementation, the frequent policy changes introduced by a succession of ministers and a shortage of resources. According to 1990–1995 statistics, the expenditure on funding research and development was only 0.2

percent of the GDP in the Arab countries, as mentioned in the Arab Human Development Report 2003. The corresponding expenditure was 3.1 percent of the GDP in the United States, Japan and Sweden and was 2.4 percent of the GDP in Germany, France, the United Kingdom, Italy, Canada and Australia.

In the aforementioned study, I observed that the educational systems were more candid in expressing our Arab realities and more capable of being positively influencing and deepening the sense of collective Arab identity. However, many Arab countries have recently distanced themselves from this collective Arab identity, and under the pretext of indigenization, have become more regional and local in outlook. Under the influence of globalization, Arabs are on the verge of losing their Arab cultural identity. Hence Arabic educational systems are locked in a struggle between two currents: the one seeking to confirm its narrow rationality and the other attempting to globalize education. The Arabic language faces grave challenges as it stands on the threshold of the knowledge society.[26]

An Arab education expert, Dr. Hamid 'Ammar, adds another dimension. He asserts that personality development through education is non-existent. Those entrusted with education reform have focused on the issue of knowledge, but this knowledge has parted company with human character formation. The process of acquiring knowledge and information is relatively cheap in terms of production whether in preparing books and study courses or setting tests. As for the general formation of the citizen, its cost is higher since work values include religious and human values, which are more difficult to inculcate. Regrettably, education in Arab countries has been linked to a certificate, which measures the amount of information one has acquired. Hence the certificate has become the frame of reference in granting a citizen a particular job. A certain amount of knowledge acquired by a human being qualifies him to take up a particular job. This ignores the fact that production requires values such as persistence, effort and sacrifice and all these values are not part of our educational curricula in the Arab world generally.[27]

As one Arab scholar has pointed out, the bitter fact is that education, which is supposed to eradicate unemployment and supply the Arab labor market with smart minds and trained hands, has added to further unemployment by supplying the labor market with individuals whose specializations are unnecessary. In many instances, educational plans have not taken into account the nature of development in general and the particular developments in the Arab labor market.[28]

It comes as a surprise to many scholars that the Gulf states have neglected to formulate curricula that consolidates aspects pertaining to petroleum—their main resource. In Egypt, agricultural studies are weak and this situation holds true for the Sultanate of Oman which is also dependent on agriculture. This specialization has not received sufficient support, although linked to national economy. Moreover, higher education in Arab countries is still traditional and stereotypical and has not included a great proportion of those in the higher education age bracket (24–28 years). This proportion is low in most Arab countries, at best not more than 13 percent, whereas the corresponding proportion is 65 percent in South Korea though the latter has started growing later than many Arab countries. Investment in scientific research in many Arab countries is merely 0.05 percent of the public budget and might reach 1 percent in countries like Egypt and Jordan. The achievement levels in scientific research, inventions and discoveries cannot be compared to those of any of the above mentioned countries despite the money spent on education.

There are many reasons why higher education has hesitated to support scientific research. The most important is the absence of a scientific research environment, the failure and the weakness of research techniques and the attitude of governments towards creating an appropriate research climate. This conclusion is confirmed by the fact that when students leave Arab countries to go to western communities, they participate effectively and employ their science and knowledge to develop the educational institutions they join and attain success in scientific achievement. This is so, particularly in the United States, where the scientific research environment is supported strongly and directly by political decision-makers.

Higher Education in the Arab World: Role of the University

The university is the institution entrusted with imparting intellectual, ethical and personal skills to individuals and producing specialized and trained graduates in different fields. It is the institution which seeks to provide the continuous education that has become necessary in the light of successive advances in different sciences and in the activities of daily life. Two of the most important basic principles on which university reform is built are independence and competition.[29]

The late Dr. Abdul Malik Al Hamar urged universities to be a tool for self-discovery in Gulf society. According to him, to define our position towards life as a whole we first ask ourselves: Who are we? What do we want? Where are we heading? How can we confront the challenges and problems of life? Consequently we announce our viewpoint or philosophy in the face of intellectual and societal currents in the world. We commit ourselves in terms of thought and in terms of what we say and do to what we announce and in this context we are identified with a cluster of civilizational values, which in turn, bring consistency and integration into our lives. Hence the role of the university, and consequently the development plan, is to break the shell of the surrounding civilizational mix—with its attendant subordination, contradiction, frustration and backwardness. Without this major role by the university, our society will not become part of the march of civilization and progress.

Dr. Al Hamar called upon universities to go beyond self-discovery and become a tool for liberating the Gulf individual from an illusory fear that is exerting a controlling power over the psyche—the fear of confronting a new civilization. He says, "In our society today the individual lives in fear of even the contemporary currents of modernity. Fear impedes thinking and buries conjecture. Fear mingled with hope generates foggy thinking, which does not help society to have a clear vision and thus cripples balanced planning for integrated development." To attain this liberation, Dr. Al Hamar emphasized the importance of "freedom" in creating an original Gulf culture because "original culture is not possible without freedom." [30]

The question of linking university education to meeting the requirements of development is the most difficult issue. It is more complex than it was twenty years ago because the world is moving away from the era of development (1970s, 1980s and 1990s) into the age of globalization where development has become a tale of the past and been replaced by the challenges of survival and its rapid repercussions. A student must acquire knowledge and beneficial life skills and must respond to the social demands made on education and reinforce the spirit of conscious citizenship.[31]

The university in its all inclusive concept is viewed as the primary institution concerned with seeking the truth, developing culture, and transferring knowledge and ideas to society through teaching, studies and research. It is a melting pot where the different attitudes of students, lecturers and concerned people come together and where ideas and related interests interact. Also, the nature of its work necessitates an appropriate scientific and regenerating atmosphere.

To carry out its mission effectively, the university must be granted sufficient guarantees of academic freedom and professional independence. These are concepts that can be absorbed and provided by societies that deal voluntarily with them—societies that guarantee freedoms to their citizens and are characterized by tolerance of different ways of thinking and co-existence with opposing viewpoints.

Professional independence means the right of the university to self-direction and the employment of its resources in a manner that serves institutional vision as well as free academic research and teaching, without unjust external restrictions that would paralyze its ability to act in the interest of the institution or constrain academic freedoms. Professional independence does not mean violating the law of the land or the absence of financial and administrative accountability. Rather, it is very close to the principle of accountability related to responsibility.

Despite these vital concepts, there is a lack of clear awareness and full understanding of their implications and limits not only among the public, which may be expected but also within the university community—at the level of the administration, the faculty and students. This absence of understanding and awareness is also true of the mission, principles and goals of the university and leads to increasing complications in the relationship between the university and society.[32]

Practical experience in Arab and Gulf universities demonstrates that their failure to fulfill their role stems from obstacles and practices within the institution, as well as the surrounding society. These obstacles and practices are outlined in the following points:

- *Lack of impact by Arab universities on the economic and social development of society:* The reason for this lies in the weakness of "need assessment research" into market requirements, as well as the failure to promote universities and market what they possess in terms of capabilities, experiences and human energies.

- *Absence of regulations or activities that study the causes for distinction and innovation among the faculty and find ways to discover, develop and invest in them.* The success and distinction gained by a university is based on the merit, diversity and the universality of the work done by staff members, as they are the most important input in institutions of higher education.

- *Lack of balance in dealing with university objectives:* Universities devote the greatest attention to teaching at the expense of scientific research. The needs of academic departments in terms of faculty members are estimated on the basis of dividing teaching hours by teaching load (9–12 hours) without taking into account that scientific research, community service and other tasks must be carried out by universities. On the other hand, the continuity of a staff member in his university job depends on his ability to teach even if he never conducts scientific research. A staff member might conduct two research studies in an academic year whereas another might not complete a research project started three years ago. A third researcher might never have conducted a research study since his appointment, despite being on the verge of retirement.

- *Universities fail to move beyond reconciliation and conservatism.* The Arab university tends to reconcile itself to the prevailing culture and customs in society. Such a role does not help to correct, develop or remedy what is existent. The university must lead society towards achieving the best, especially since it contains a great number of highly trained and competent personnel, who have received their education in established universities setting global scientific standards in very advanced countries. Thus they ought to serve as heralds of enlightenment, development, progress and innovation. However, in many cases, this effect has not been achieved.

- *Arab universities generally lack real financial or administrative independence:* Unless there is such independence, institutions of higher education will not prove to be pioneers in realizing the desired national goals.

- *Scarcity and lack of comprehensive data on research and development personnel in the Arab world:* This is referred to in the Arab Human Development Report, 2003.[33] What applies to Arab countries applies by necessity to the universities in the GCC states. There are no accurate statistics about the number of researchers, their specializations and geographical distribution, as well as the universities where they have done their postgraduate courses and their nationalities and gender, etc. The same thing applies to students of postgraduate courses in terms of their numbers and the rate of increase or reduction in these numbers over the years.

- *No accurate and updated statistics about research centers in the GCC states.* The absence of accurate statistics on research institutions is another obstacle in the way of progress.

- *Lack of statistics about research studies:* There are no accurate statistics about the number of research studies published by researchers in the universities of the GCC states in different specializations, or the number of books they write and publish every year.

- *Reduced funding for scientific research:* There is a clear drop in funding provided for scientific research on the part of the production and service sectors in Arab countries. Most of the government financing provided to educational institutions is expended on salaries in percentages that sometimes reach 89 percent.[34] Scientific research in the institutions of higher education and their affiliate centers is generally of an academic nature.

Proposals to Develop the Institutions of Higher Education

Ideas and proposals to develop the institutions of higher education are summarized below:

- The need to develop efforts aimed at spreading the culture of production and limiting the culture of consumption and import among those involved in higher education. This means encouraging innovation and initiatives among staff members through free and fair competition and prizes.

- The need for harmony and coordination between plans for developing higher education and general education so that each represents a link in the chain of overlapping and complementary activities.
- The need to improve the prevailing conditions in the environment of institutions of higher education. How can a scholar or faculty member achieve distinction by working at a foreign university for an academic year or a semester on sabbatical leave when no reader or scholar has heard of him despite spending more than a decade in his *alma mater*?
- Arab universities must enjoy full independence in introducing appropriate reforms consistent with market trends. Universities must have their own system of incentives while competing with other universities to guarantee improvement in educational quality and simultaneously obtain higher revenue. No doubt, creating a competitive environment will favor the quality of education and this is the aim of any reform.[35]
- Upgrading education requires the founding of independent institutions to evaluate the programs and institutions of higher education and accredit them to guarantee quality. Founding independent Arab institutions to guarantee the quality of education represents a qualitative shift in this field.[36]
- Paying attention to the process of establishing a knowledge society which is based on five pillars:
  o Allowing freedoms of public opinion, expression and assembly and guaranteeing them by good governance.
  o Spreading high quality education.
  o Indigenizing science and generalizing research and technological development in all societal activities to deal with the Information Age.
  o Making a determined shift to the pattern of producing knowledge and employing it competently in the Arab social and economic structure.

[342]

o   Establishing a general Arab paradigm of knowledge, which is open, enlightened and characterized by originality.[37]

- Concentrating as much as possible on an innovative style of teaching, which is "teaching via problem-solving." This is the one of the most important developments in medical education during the last twenty-five years. It is applied in three medical colleges that pioneered this scientific strategy. These colleges are affiliated to Al Gazira University in Wad Madani in Sudan, the Suez Canal University in Egypt and the Arabian Gulf University in the Kingdom of Bahrain. These three colleges, which were started during the period 1979–1982, preserve this educational philosophy today in addition to continuously developing the curricula.[38]

- It is important to build a system of "distance learning" to achieve the goal of expanding the education systems at all levels. Material, technical and human capabilities must be provided to meet the requirements such an expansion with concentration on preparing technical experts to manage distance learning. These include academics specialized in this field, specialists in designing, producing and using educational media, as well as specialists in distance learning programs and others.[39]

The Arabian Gulf University conducted a pioneer experiment in this field by founding a new educational program in the field of "distance learning." A number of qualified researchers have graduated from this program and are now training others in competencies within and outside this program.

Science, Education and Globalization

In the previous part of this study, the focus has been concentrated relatively on the academic performance of institutions of higher education. Naturally, it is not my intention to neglect the educational dimension because it is generally agreed that education is a process of continuous and universal change which moves the individual and society from their current reality to the ideal they want to become. To achieve this, many educational institutions complement one another: the family, the school, the mosque and others. These institutions become integrated with others, such as those related to information and culture, without impeding one another. Reducing the interaction between these institutions and leaving education to adjust itself in accordance with the market and the economy is a danger that cannot be overestimated.

Certainly, we need to renew education and the goals it seeks to achieve. These goals should lead to a clear improvement in the social and economic circumstances of people. This can be done by regaining confidence in the educational system as a major tool in effecting a social shift for individuals and groups and in establishing more rational attitudes towards life, work and social changes. As Muhammad Jawad Rida documents, the faculty members of Harvard University were asked an important question regarding the kind of education a student needs to be psychologically attuned to globalization. The answer highlighted three points:

First, we live in a world of rapid movement. This speed includes all basic aspects of life—traveling by jet planes, communicating via the Internet, and electronic trade. This world is characterized by a large overlap between networks of information and technology. These phenomena are proved by the need of the undergraduate to possess a "dynamic and resilient mind" that is aware of how to deal with an "alien culture" that may confront him with previously unknown situations.

Second, on the application side of "public education" it is expected to achieve two substantive changes in the mindset of the student:

- Understanding the relationship between the scientific and technological revolutions.

[344]

- Recognizing the importance of living and working as a "citizen in a global society." For such a transformation, the student must be given a basic education in the past achievements of humanity.

Third, the public education required for the mindset of the university student must include "training in making more accurate judgments about things, phenomena and different human situations and the imparting of ethical values."[40]

Conclusion

In the second half of the twentieth century, higher education has witnessed a quantitative and qualitative revolution. At the quantitative level, there has been a doubling of the number of universities and institutions of higher education. This development resulted from an increased awareness about the role of education at all levels of development. Most countries aimed at achieving the democratization of education and equal opportunity for qualified people in obtaining advanced education. At the same time, higher education as well as primary education in the Arab world is subject to a wave of frustrating criticism which is increasing from within and without. Officials responsible for education in Arab countries believe that education has not contributed sufficiently to universal and sustainable development when compared to education in India, South Korea and the countries of East Asia where growth is realizing record figures.

This chapter has reviewed the characteristic features of rapid quantitative and qualitative growth in all levels of education in the GCC states during the last three decades. Some strategies, programs and proposals to develop education at diverse levels in the six GCC states were presented. A critical view has been offered regarding the positive and negative aspects of past and present development strategies. Thereafter, part of this study has discussed the enlightening role of the university in society, presenting some achievements of the Gulf universities in recent years as well as their difficulties and obstacles. This study has employed an integrative perspective which links education to the other political, economic and cultural aspects of life. Links have also been highlighted between what is happening in the GCC states to what is happening in the Arab world and the world in general in the light of mechanisms of globalization, competition, the market economy, the knowledge explosion and other variables that can no longer be ignored, since they have arrived at the doorstep.

Lionel Jospin, the former Prime Minister of France, observed that the market is a means to an end, not an end in itself, and that the university is not just a place to impart knowledge and education, but also to teach democracy, qualify people and make individuals happy. In this sense, he maintains, we adhere to the role of the public sector in education and consequently to the basic responsibility of the state to achieve and guarantee equality of opportunity. Hence the rights to registration in universities must be revised on the basis of social justice and equal opportunities.[41]

In my view, much of what Jospin has said must be taken into consideration when drawing up plans and strategies to develop education in Arab countries as well as when implementing and following up these plans and strategies.

What is more, it was noted that in the report titled "A Nation at Risk," which revealed the low scientific standard of American students at that time, the most important reason for ascendancy was identified as perfecting the English language, followed by Mathematics and Physics and finally the computer. In the Arab world, the situation is reversed. There is official focus on the computer and foreign languages while the Arabic language is greatly neglected. Although foreign languages are certainly important, learning these languages should not be at the expense of the Arabic language. The national language is a tool of thought and

[346]

emotions whereas the foreign language is tool of communication and the difference between the two remains significant.

Concurrently, this study has reiterated the importance of ethical education, developing competitiveness and accepting the other, in addition to acquiring a sense of national identity, implanting original Arabic values in the souls of children and developing their cultural and aesthetic appreciation of Arabic and other living languages. We have to reject the baseless accusation that the Arabic curricula have led to the shaping of a mind that does not accept the other and to the creation of a human being who expresses differences through violence and inflexibility.

Losing Expertise to Other Countries: Halting the Arab "Brain Drain"

H.E. Dr. Ibrahim Guider

Migration is a demographic process whose numbers were and still are rising considerably in today's world as a result of several factors and circumstances which may vary from one society to another. In addition, a number of changes in the societal structure and composition can be attributed to this phenomenon. Therefore, the migration issue raises many questions and problems both at the level of the labor-exporting societies in particular, and at the pan-Arab level, in general.

Despite the increase in outward migration, particularly the movement of manpower between and among Arab countries, any study of this phenomenon and its social and economic consequences, whether positive or negative, will be hindered by a major constraint—the lack of pertinent information and statistics. This lack of information may be attributed to two main reasons:

First, some Arab countries have not yet conducted any census for their respective populations. Indeed, statistical programs already carried out in most Arab countries were impaired by many flaws and defects, notably the inconsistencies of definitions and connotations, categories and characteristics of expatriate labor.

Second, several Arab states refrain from publishing information relevant to their workforce, whether national or foreign, for security or political considerations, or delay releasing such data, thus making the information poorly-timed and outdated.

Realities of the Migration of Arab Brainpower

The migration of scientific and technical brainpower is one of the oldest issues that humanity has experienced, and this has led to creative interaction between civilizations since time immemorial. For instance, Chinese inventions were brought to the Arab world and later transferred to Europe after being improved and developed by Arab scholars and scientists.

However, the issue of the migration of scientists and technicians from the Arab world to developed countries cannot be gauged by the same criterion. It has proved to be one of the most serious challenges facing the Arab world, one that causes the slowdown of the processes of scientific, economic and social development and modernization. According to some researchers, it constitutes "an adverse transfer of technology." Greater numbers of Arab scholars and professionals are migrating from the Arab world after obtaining their postgraduate degrees, representing in a sense, the "surplus" output of the educational systems of their respective countries.

The imbalance and mismatch between the systems and methods of teaching and training, on the one hand, and the needs of local Arab labor markets, on the other, have led to surplus manpower. Therefore, individuals are compelled to seek job opportunities abroad. Living conditions are another factor that might force them to migrate. In addition, increasing numbers of students who migrate in order to complete their higher studies abroad prefer to stay in the destination countries.

In the course of this chapter, three different types of Arab brain drain may be identified:

- *External brain drain*: This is the most common type of brain drain, involving migration abroad.

- *Internal brain drain*: This type of brain drain is caused by the tendency of some Arab scientists to lead a marginal life in their own societies, focusing all their attention on acquiring knowledge purely for the sake of knowledge, as an end in itself, in anticipation of honorary awards and prizes.

- *Basic brain drain*: This type of brain drain results from the failure of some developing countries, including Arab countries, to enhance the intellectual potential of their population. It could be due to several factors, including political barriers, the malnutrition that affects mothers and children in Third World countries, and the lack of knowledge needed to create greater awareness of basic rights, which in turn can stimulate struggle for the consolidation of true democratic concepts and principles.

The phenomenon of skilled professionals and scientists migrating from the Arab countries is one of the most significant factors that affect the national economy, the population and manpower composition, and deprive these countries of their potential and capabilities, which could have been invested in socio-economic development projects. Several Arab countries, including Egypt, are in fact suffering from the effects of this phenomenon. According to its 2003 statistical data, Egypt's Central Agency for Public Mobilization and Statistics (CAPMAS) estimated the number of highly qualified Egyptian specialists who have migrated abroad at about 824,000 including some 2,500 scientists. (See Figure 15.1).

Figure 15.1
Number of Egyptian Scientists who have Migrated Abroad
(by end 2003)

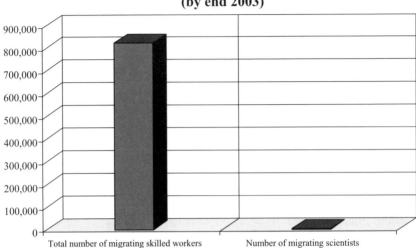

Source: Arab Labor Organization (ALO), Study on Employment Conditions in Arab Countries: The Case of Egypt (Cairo: ALO Publications, 2005).

Statistics also indicate that the shares of Egypt, Iraq, Lebanon, Syria, Jordan and Palestine of Arab scientists and engineers who have migrated to the United States were 60 percent, 10 percent, 10 percent, 5 percent, 5 percent, 5 percent, respectively (See Figure 15.2).

Statistics issued by the League of Arab States, the Arab Labor Organization (ALO) and other organizations concerned about this phenomenon have shown that the Arab world accounts for 31 percent of total "brain drain" emanating from developing states, that 54 percent of Arab students studying abroad do not return to their homelands, that three rich western countries – the United States, Canada and the United Kingdom – seek 75 percent of Arab experts, and that 50 percent of doctors, 23 percent of engineers and 15 percent of scientists migrate particularly to Europe, the United States and Canada. Arab doctors living in the United Kingdom represent approximately 34 percent of the total numbers of doctors working in this coumtry.[1]

[352]

Figure 15.2

**Percentage of Arab Scientists in the United States
by Nationality (2003)**

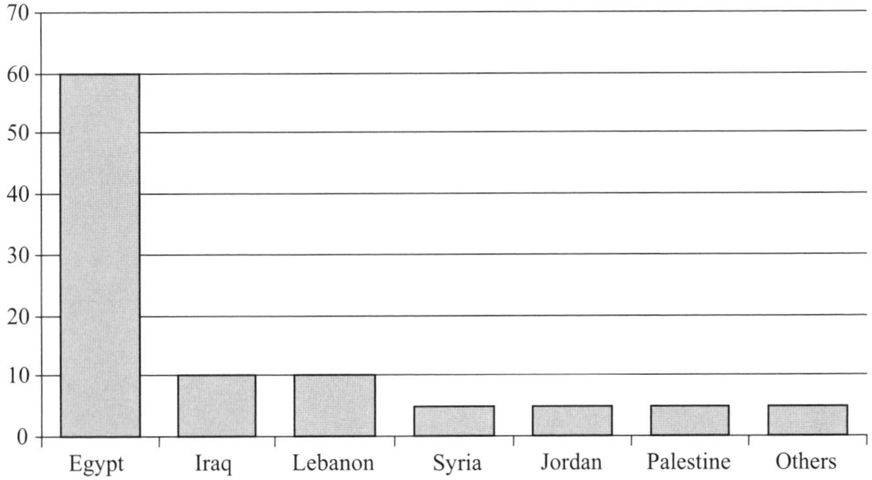

Source: Arab Labor Organization (ALO), Study on Employment Conditions in Arab Countries: The Case of Egypt
(Cairo: ALO Publications, 2005).

While Arab states, notably Egypt, are still suffering from huge losses
as a result of this brain drain, Israel is reaping considerable benefits,
thanks to the migration of highly qualified professionals from Russia and
other Eastern Europe and western states. Indeed, in terms of numbers,
Egypt is regarded as the "biggest loser" since the numbers of Egyptian
experts and specialists in vital, strategic disciplines working in the United
States, Canada, Australia, United Kingdom, France, Germany,
Switzerland, the Netherlands, Austria, Italy, Spain and Greece are
estimated at 318,000, 110,000, 70,000, 35,000, 36,000, 25,000, 14,000,
40,000, 14,000, 90,000, 12,000 and 60,000 respectively. The United
States hosts the lion's share at 38.6 percent, followed by Canada at 13.3
percent (See Figure 15.3).

Arab students who are sent abroad by their universities and research
centers to complete their higher education are considered the main source
of the Arab brain drain to western countries. For example, since early

[353]

1960s to 1975, the number of Egyptian students who decided not to return to Egypt after completing their studies (mainly in the United States, Canada, France and the United Kingdom) is estimated at 940 students (12 percent of the total number). During the period 1970–1980, 70 percent of Egyptian students sent to the United States preferred to stay there.[2]

Figure 15.3

Percentage Distribution of Egyptian Expertise in Receiving Foreign States (2003)

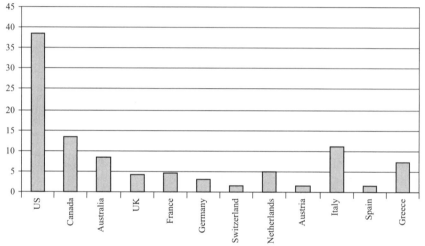

Source: Arab Labor Organization (ALO), Study on Employment Conditions in Arab Countries: The Case of Egypt (Cairo: ALO Publications, 2005).

Poverty is one of the important motivating factors behind the flood of migrants. In this context, this factor may be extended to include poor potential and facilities, shortage of basic services and deteriorating living standards. Also, it is linked to the insufficiency of job opportunities, exclusion, absence of social mobility as well as political instability and oppression, which includes arbitrary arrests, torture and physical liquidation for ideological, ethnic, cultural and religious reasons.

In addition to the psychological factors boosting the flow of the migrants and the financial attractions offered by these states, other reasons that are often cited are the availability of scientific research potential and the presence of the scientific community as catalysts for creativity and innovation in the receiving states.

According to the 2003 Human Poverty Index, Egypt falls within the "intermediate group" of states, where 3.10 percent of their populations are not expected to survive to the age of 40 years; 13 percent are deprived of safe water, 1 percent do not have health services, 12 percent have no access to sanitation facilities and 23.3 percent are living below the poverty line. During the five years from 1998 to 2003, per capita income averaged US$ 1015–1400.

Most talented individuals fall into the "fixed income" category. Hence, the steadily rising rates of unemployment and inflation pose additional pressures that lead them to migrate. Even for those who are fortunate to get high-income jobs, wages increased only by 1.1–2.1 percent, while the increase in prices averaged 2.8–22.3 percent.

Such factors would almost certainly oblige those highly qualified professionals either to migrate abroad or exploit their capabilities (by seeking additional part-time jobs) in order to secure additional income and improve their living standards.

Migration and Future Generations

The motivations behind the migration of both highly skilled professionals and ordinary workers may be similar, especially the economic ones. Hence, the decision to emigrate is fundamentally governed by the attracting factors, as is evident in the selective, predetermined policies designed by the industrialized world to attract experts and specialists from various countries.

The gravity of this phenomenon lies in its huge impact on the younger generations of qualified individuals in developing countries, particularly those belonging to social segments that are well-equipped and better positioned for migration.

In terms of social and financial dimensions, the gains achieved by the developed (receiving) states as a result of the brain drain are – conversely – equal to the losses incurred by the less developed (sending) states. In this respect, some studies have shown that the financial losses incurred by a country such as Egypt during the period from 1962–2000 in terms of its investment in the educational sector stood at 43–62 billion Egyptian pounds.[3]

Generally speaking, today it is estimated that Arab world loses up to US$2 billion annually as a result of the brain drain, and that Arab states had lost a total of US$11 billion in the 1970s alone.

In contrast, the migration of talented and highly educated Arabs is considered as a developmental gain to the states in which they opt to settle. At present, European countries and the United States host more than 450,000 Arab postgraduates, benefiting from their scientific and technological research. According to the UNESCO 1998 World Report on Science, 47.4 percent of 1995 world total technological patents were issued in Europe, while the shares of the United States and Japan (together with the newly industrialized countries) were 33.4 percent and 16.6 percent, respectively, compared to the Arab states' meager share of these patents.[4]

Any assessment of the role of social transformations in increasing (or decreasing) the migration rates of highly qualified professionals remains a controversial and debatable matter. Some analysts feel that patterns of societal change may bring about economic and social imbalances that could in turn lead to the absence of the desired social justice. This could explain why those talented people choose to migrate abroad to the more developed world.

Causes of the Arab "Brain Drain"

The Arab brain drain to foreign countries can be ascribed to economic, social, cultural and other causes, not to mention the allure of the scientific community in the receiving states and the tendency of most Arab students to settle in these states on account of the attractive facilities offered to them, especially when compared to the deteriorated economic, political and social conditions in many developing (sending) countries. Additionally, the influx of talented experts and specialists to the developed countries is regarded as one of the effects of the international division of labor and the inequitable world economic order.

All studies that have addressed the question of the brain drain from the Arab world have agreed upon a set of political, economic, social and personal factors that can be categorized into two types as follows:

1- Stimulating ("push") factors:

- The weakness or the inability of sending states to absorb experts and specialists in their own countries, rendering them either jobless or obliged to accept jobs incompatible with their original fields of specialization.
- Low incomes that they usually earn in their respective countries.
- The imbalance of the educational systems or the mismatch between these systems and development projects in most Arab countries.
- The political and social instability, which causes some highly educated individuals to suffer from estrangement in their own countries, and consequently resort to migration in search of greater freedoms and more stable conditions.
- Low expenditures allocated for scientific research projects in the Arab countries.
- The intensive reliance on western expertise at the expense of national talents.

[357]

In addition to the above-mentioned key factors, there may be other objective and subjective factors, including the nature of administrative bureaucracy and civil service systems, as well as other personal or family reasons.

2- Attracting ("pull") factors:

- The scientific and technological supremacy of the attracting states, and the atmosphere of stability and prosperity that these states normally enjoy.
- The availability of huge financial and material resources that enable these states to create distinctive, profitable job opportunities as strong lures to attract highly qualified migrants.
- The opportunities offered to scientists and technologists in the field of scientific research with a view to developing their skills and opening new, broader horizons for them.

The Negative Impacts of the Arab "Brain Drain"

The Arab brain-drain to Western countries has produced several adverse effects on both the present and future development processes in Arab countries. The main negative repercussions may be pinpointed as follows:

- The deprivation in terms of development processes and programmers designed to enhance the national economy and educational systems with scientific and productive capacities and energies, which are flowing instead into the veins of Western countries through migration, while Arab countries need their contribution in sectors such as economics, health, planning, scientific research and technology.
- The loss of massive Arab human and financial resources spent on educating and training competent and qualified young Arabs who are taken by the Western nations free of cost.

- The weakness and deterioration in scientific production and research in Arab countries, when compared to the scientific production of Arab migrants in the receiving states.

The stark irony here is the fact that the increase in the rates of brain drain from Arab states is associated with an increasing dependence of the latter on Western expertise in different fields at greater and sometimes exaggerated economic costs. This means that Arab states bear a two-fold loss because of this type of brain drain.

Any discussion on the issue of the Arab brain drain will have to address the following question: Why are all the efforts exerted by Arab countries to lure their talented migrants back home often doomed to failure whereas others have been successful in doing so?

The answer lies, at least partly, in the above-mentioned stimulating ("push") factors. However, other relevant aspects can be identified as follows:

- Most Arab states lack what may be described as a "balanced, comprehensive developmental strategy" whose important aim is the creation and advancement of intellectual, scientific and cultural environments that constitute the solid foundations of decent living standards, psychological stability and scientific production.
- The majority of projects in the Arab countries are often implemented by foreign companies with nominal participation by national firms, where the dominant contractual pattern is often one that does not entail technology transfer. Indeed, these projects are often set up on a "turnkey" basis, which allows fewer opportunities for Arab scientists and experts to assert their competence and gives them a sense of estrangement in their own countries. Moreover, this causes a huge waste in Arab resources by importing ready-made technology from the Western industrialized states, thus preventing the allocation of funding for research and development activities aimed at building an Arab technological base.

- The total absence of integration, or even coordination among Arab states to address the question of the Arab brain drain or of recruiting national highly skilled "human capital" (doctors, engineers, scientists, etc).

- Brain drain also results in widening the gap between the rich and poor countries since the migration of talented individuals to rich countries will yield considerable direct economic benefits for these countries, whereas it causes huge losses to the countries from which those individuals have migrated.

The United Nations Educational, Scientific and Cultural Organization (UNESCO) considers the brain drain an unusual form of scientific exchange among states because it is characterized by a unidirectional movement that inevitably flows into the developed countries, or by what is called the "adverse transfer of technology."[5]

Attempts by Arab States to lure back Arab Brainpower

Some Arab states have offered several enticements and incentives to encourage the return of highly qualified experts and specialists by enacting laws that offer the returnees certain advantages, notably Laws Nos. 154 (1974) and 189 (1980) issued by Iraq. These two laws allowed talented Iraqis and Arabs the right to obtain Iraqi nationality, reside and work in Iraq, as well as get financial grants, loans, land plots and customs exemptions.

To attract migrant Arab scientists to return, Kuwait and Libya have set up two research centers: the Kuwaiti Institute for Scientific Research, and the Arab Development Institute (established in Tripoli and Beirut), respectively.

In the first place, however, such efforts must focus on transforming and developing basic, ideological structures with a view to establishing a sound, favorable environment that will help to lure Arab intellectuals back home so as to benefit from their skills and qualifications.

Towards an Arab Strategy to End the "Brain Drain"

The dangerous negative impacts of the Arab brain drain on Arab developmental plans, in particular, call for solutions aimed at alleviating these effects and bringing the phenomenon to an end. It is believed that the ideal solution lies in shaping an integral and complementary Arab strategy to be drawn up jointly by the League of Arab States, the Arab Labor Organization, and the Arab League Economic and Social Council, in close cooperation with the UNESCO, the International Labor Organization (ILO) and other relevant non-governmental organizations in order to confront this problem.

The following proposals may also contribute to the achievement of this goal: [6]

- Conducting a comprehensive survey of highly skilled migrating Arab scientists in order to determine the number of migrants, their destinations, fields of activity and working conditions.

- Drawing up a centralized Arab strategy on a complementary basis to help Arab countries that face overwhelming manpower levels to get rid of their surpluses, and thereby enable those countries suffering from insufficiency to meet their manpower demands.

- Setting up research centers with scientific and developmental objectives and cooperating with concerned international and regional bodies to issue the necessary documents and rules needed to regulate the working conditions of migrating scientists and experts.

- Urging Arab governments to set up associations and leagues that absorb migrant expertise, eliminate all obstacles that might hinder their ties with their countries of origin, and facilitate their contributions to the processes of development and modernization of their homelands.

- Organizing periodical conferences for Arab migrants and soliciting their assistance and expertise regarding the transfer of technology and participation in the implementation of national development projects.
- Cooperating with the UNESCO in setting up scientific projects and institutions to train Arab cadres and attract migrant Arab professionals to run and contribute directly to the activities of such centers.

Recommendations on Migration

In conclusion, the following set of recommendations may collectively constitute a comprehensive strategy aimed at addressing the issue regarding the future of the Arab workforce under the challenges posed by the new world order:

- Reviewing the employment policies in Arab countries, supporting employment centers, and studying the trends and future needs of labor markets, giving priority to local citizens, followed by Arab nationals and foreign labor, in accordance with agreements concluded in this regard.
- Advancing the general development process by seeking proper internal solutions. These include making the optimum use of available resources and developing human resources in order to deal with future challenges such as population growth and unemployment.
- Drafting a comprehensive, long-term national master plan and sub-plans to determine the needs of the respective public sectors for qualified national manpower in the major spheres of development.
- Opening and revitalizing more national training institutions to ensure their involvement in different economic activities, as well as giving citizens the opportunity to join the training courses to be organized by these institutions.
- Focusing on the vital issue of productivity to highlight its importance in a manner that leads to increased growth rates in terms of gross national product and average per capita income.

- Raising the level of awareness regarding the importance of vocational training in qualifying the young generation to engage in productive activities, and implementing the principle of "youth social security" in the form of basic training or initial practical experience.
- Reviewing the educational and training systems and programs to ensure their consistency with the needs of the labor market for skills and professions.
- Supporting the participation by women in different sectors of the workforce in harmony with their abilities, qualifications and prevailing societal values and norms.
- Allowing citizens the opportunity to join higher education programs abroad, and taking all necessary measures that ensure their return to their homelands to contribute to the development of their respective societies.
- Examining the prevailing conditions in foreign labor markets to explore the volume and structure of external demand for Arab workers in order to enhance their skills and concentrate on the professions most needed by these markets. This also involves providing protection for Arab labor and managing the economic benefits derived from such labor policies.
- Solving all problems and obstacles facing Arab labor markets, including: the uneven geographical distribution of the workforce, imbalanced manpower allocation to different economic activities, shortcomings in the professional structure of the workforce, unemployment issues and the mismatch between education outputs and training systems on the one hand and the needs of local Arab markets on the other.
- Establishing a link between manpower needs and the basic requirements of the development process, by eliminating different forms of unemployment, boosting productivity rates, developing human resources, and increasing the output of the educational system.

[363]

WOMEN, POPULATION AND IMPACT ON DEVELOPMENT

Boosting the Role of Women in Development: A Case Study of Kuwaiti Women

H.E Dr. Massouma Al-Mubarak

The world today is witnessing rapid developments in different fields. It is undergoing major transformations because of the rapid technological advances in the fields of production, distribution, communication and information. These developments have given rise to the concept of the small global village. Arab countries no longer live in isolation from international events but form an integral part of this world. They have succeeded in handling some of these developments, but in other fields, especially the economic, social and institutional ones, they are still lagging behind.

Since 2002, several authorities, the foremost being the United Nations Development Program and the Arab Fund for Economic and Social Development, have prepared annual reports on human development in the Arab world. It is noteworthy that these reports have a common focus on empowering Arab women so as to reinforce their role in political, social and economic development and provide them with opportunities to build up their capabilities without gender discrimination. The Arab Human Development Report for 2002 has confirmed that one of the basic causes for unsatisfactory development in Arab countries is linked to inadequate empowerment of women. The empowerment of women via education, training, healthcare and provision of job opportunities will contribute towards boosting the standard of universal development. Hence one of the basic recommendations in the report urges Arab countries to adopt positive policies for the empowerment of women and what this entails in terms of building their capabilities, offering them employment and allowing them to be liberated.[1]

At the international level, the issue of women's empowerment has recently attracted great attention. This was attested by the participation of 189 states at the United Nations Millennium Summit convened at the UN headquarters in New York in 2000. The conference adopted the "millennium development goals." These objectives expressed the resolve of countries around the world to save mankind from extreme poverty and hunger and move it in the direction of real development. Eight millennium development goals were identified as follows:[2]

- Eradicate extreme poverty and hunger
- Achieve universal primary education
- Promote gender equality and empower women
- Reduce child mortality
- Improve maternal health
- Combat HIV and AIDS, malaria and other lethal diseases
- Ensure environmental sustainability
- Develop a global partnership for development

It is clear that the third objective relates directly to empowering women as part of the millennium development goals, which is supposed to be achieved by 2015. The performance of states with regard to achieving these goals is to be assessed every five years. The World Summit on Millennium Development Goals was held from September 14–16, 2005 and during this conference, follow up reports regarding the performance of individual states were presented.

The status of women has witnessed positive transformations in varying degrees during the past two decades. Women became heads of state in countries like Germany, Chile and Liberia. However, it must be emphasized that apart from the social violence practiced against women, 70 percent of the victims of violence emanating from civil or international wars are women and children. Global statistics confirm that more than 80 percent of social violence is perpetrated by relatives within the same family.

International covenants on human rights, including the Universal Declaration of Human Rights have devoted considerable segments to affirming the rights of women and protecting them in peace and war. Most countries, if not all, are parties to these covenants and most constitutions, if not all, confirm the principles of justice and equality before law and human rights. Yet has this created a better structure for women in the world and provided the necessary protection?

The Realities for Arab and Gulf Women

The Human Development Reports reveal that although some progress has been made, the current status of Arab women falls short of their aspirations. Arab women still face several obstacles that prevent them from playing an effective and real role in sustainable development. Social heritage still plays a role in marginalizing women in Arab societies in varying degrees. Although improvements have been recorded, the percentage of illiteracy among Arab women remains high at 60 percent. The percentage of those who use the Internet is very low, being not more than 5 percent. The percentage of female representation in parliaments is less than 4 percent. Moreover, the suffering endured by women through domestic violence is increasing in a tragic way. In short, women have a long way to go in their quest to achieve equality and efforts to empower them in public life are still unrealized.[3]

At the level of the GCC states, the positive changes in the role played by women in development may be more clearly recorded, either due to the economic factor, which has facilitated the policies of affluence that benefit both women and men and the surmounting of social obstacles (as

[369]

embodied in customs and traditions), or because of the policy of openness to more advanced societies. The participation of Gulf women in development has reached encouraging percentages, especially in the last fifteen years in the spheres of education, work and health and even their participation in the private sector as businesswomen. In the political sphere, the numbers of women in leading positions (ministers, under-secretaries and assistant under-secretaries) have increased. Women have gained the right to nominate themselves and vote. However, winning parliamentary seats is still affected by the novelty of the experience though this has been surpassed in the Sultanate of Oman where women won two seats in the *Shoura* (Consultative) Council in the 2003 elections.

Gulf women, who until very recently were viewed as marginalized and ineffective in the process of development, have now become effective participants in all spheres of life and society. Women have established an effective presence both at the Arab and international levels. Their experience in this regard has been successful and brilliant as represented by their participation in Arab and global forums and conferences. For instance, among the more than 60 country delegations that participated in the round table meeting of the World Summit on Millennium Development Goals referred to earlier, only five were chaired by women, three of whom were Arab delegates (representing Egypt, the UAE and Kuwait).

A long road lies ahead with regard to empowering women, eradicating all forms of discrimination against them, as well as ensuring their real and effective participation in development. While the authorities have a role in empowering women with regard to their rights, women have the responsibility of proving themselves and asserting their rights.

Reform and democracy are two important needs of Arab societies, which include women. These represent a challenge and not an option. Policies must be drawn up to implement them effectively so that this process is not just for form or cosmetic in character. The human rights record must be improved and the civil society organizations must be established. There must be a broader base for political participation and decision-making by empowering women and allowing them to enjoy their human, civil and political rights. Also, overall development must be realized in order to eradicate, or at least alleviate, the problems pertaining to poverty, education, heath and unemployment.

Role of Kuwaiti Women in Development: Present Realities and Future Horizons

The year 2005 was a turning point in the advancement of Kuwaiti women. In a session held on May 16, 2005, the National Assembly approved the amendment of Article 1 of the Elections Act No. 35 of 1962 granting Kuwaiti women their full political rights with regard to nomination and voting. This move marks the crowning achievement in a decades-long series of gains made by Kuwaiti women. The amendment was followed by the appointment of the first lady to the position of Minister in the State of Kuwait. In addition, two women were appointed to the Municipal Council, which consists of 16 members.

Although the approval for the political rights of Kuwaiti women was delayed, the state granted women several privileges that guarantee their social and economic rights and protect their role and status in society. These rights have been constitutionally and legislatively codified to guarantee that they are not compromised or violated.

On the other hand, Kuwaiti women have realized great achievements at the level of public work via women's civil societies, which are still undertaking important societal roles through several women's associations and other societal activities.

The advancement of Kuwaiti women still faces several challenges that require a creative vision and the exertion of more efforts in order to boost the role of women in the process of overall development—politically, socially and economically.

This study contributes to the dialogue on the futuristic vision of boosting opportunities for Kuwaiti women and expanding their role in development by discussing a cluster of fundamental issues.

Concern for Women in the State of Kuwait: A Profile

Since its independence in 1961, the State of Kuwait has shown concern for women and their rights. The most important landmarks in this process are the following:

The Constitution and Protection for Women's Status and Rights
The Kuwaiti constitution of 1962 provides for complete equality between all Kuwaiti citizens with respect to human dignity, rights and duties without any gender distinction (Articles 6, 7, 29, 30, 35, 36, 37, 40, 41, 42, 44, 45, 80). Article 41 of the constitution ensures the right to work for all Kuwaitis (both males and females) and the right to choose the type of work they prefer. The constitution gives women the freedom to practice commercial, professional and social activities without restriction via the procedures and acts that implement the constitution, such as the labor law pertaining to the private sector, the law regulating trade and the practice of commercial professions, the civil service regulations and the law on civil associations.

Privileges Given to Women by the Government
There are several privileges that are given to women by the government. Some of these are sanctioned by the above-mentioned Acts, which have been successively issued since the independence of the state in 1961. They include the following:[4]
* A woman who works in the government sector is given special maternity leave with full salary for two months for the delivery and four months of leave at half-pay following the maternity leave, in addition to child care leave at full salary to attend to her child in case of illness.

- A working woman is given special leave in two cases: the first is to take care of the family provided that the leave is not less than six months and not more than three years during the service; the second case is to accompany the husband if he goes abroad on an official mission.

- A woman working in the private sector is given special leave in case of childbirth for thirty days with full salary before delivery and forty days after delivery, as well as the right to have one hundred days without pay following this period.

- The state prohibits making women work at night in any institution except in healthcare institutions and bans the working of women in hazardous or health-threatening industries and professions.

- Providing several fields for vocational training in different spheres of work in addition to providing several specialized training sessions organized by the concerned governmental agencies such as the Kuwait University and the Public Authority for Applied Education and Training (PAAET).

- Establishing an Authority specialized in developing the local community: namely, the Administration for Community Development in the Ministry of Social Affairs and Labor. Ten centers have been opened with the aim of increasing the degree of coordination between the social services provided by different government authorities, employing and training women and helping capable women to work and take care of the family simultaneously, in addition to other programs and activities that serve women and the family generally within the scope of local communities in the state.

- Protecting women against poverty, particularly because they bear the greatest burden in case of the death of the husband, separation, or his failure to earn a living. The public aid legislations issued since 1962 in Kuwait have warded off the deterioration in the standard of living or the suffering of Kuwaiti women from poverty. These legislations stipulate the extending of aid and special care to certain groups, both men and women alike. These groups include divorcees, widows, elderly people, people unable to work, unmarried women, female students in different stages of education, pregnant women from the third month onwards, and mothers during the first year of the child's life in case the husband fails to provide support. The lowest level of aid to individuals is 137 Kuwaiti dinars per month while the highest level is 197 Kuwaiti dinars. Total aid to individuals and Kuwaiti families that support more than ten persons is 645 Kuwaiti dinars per month.[5]

These privileges, in addition to the laws pertaining to women's rights, have helped to provide an environment that supports Kuwaiti women in playing a substantial role in the economic and social spheres.

Participation in the Global Efforts to Combat Discrimination against Women
Kuwait has ratified the international Convention on the Elimination of all Forms of Discrimination Against Women (CEDAW), which was approved by the UN General Assembly on March 18, 1979 in a manner consistent with the rules of *Shari'a* [Islamic law]. The state has also ratified the Convention on the Rights of the Child of 1990 in addition to CEDAW. Moreover, the state has ratified the International Covenant on Civil and Political Rights of 1976 and the International Covenant on Economic, Social and Cultural Rights of 1976.

Basic Indicators of Current Realities for Kuwaiti Woman

The prevailing realities for Kuwaiti woman can be recorded by an overview of her economic, social and political role as follows:

Economic Role of the Kuwaiti Woman

GROWING PARTICIPATION OF WOMEN IN THE LABOR MARKET:

Kuwaiti women are contributing increasingly to the labor market (in the government and private sectors). This is evident when we compare the current percentages with those of past years. From 2.5 percent of the total

Kuwaiti labor force in 1965, the contribution by women rose to 3 percent in 1970, 9 percent in 1975, 25.7 percent in 1985 and 33 percent in 1999. It increased to 40.7 percent of the total national labor force in 2005. Moreover, the percentage of labor market participation for the total number of women in the state developed and increased from 0.7 percent in 1957 to 18 percent in 1998 and reached 41.8 percent in 2005.[6]

The increasing number of Kuwaiti women contributing to the labor market is obvious when we consider the percentage of working women compared to the total number of women of working age (age group of 15–55 years). In 1998, the percentage of participation in the labor market among those of working age reached 35 percent of the total number. In other words, there is one working woman for every three women of working age. This number rose to 45.5 percent in 2005—one of the highest participation percentages in the Arabian Gulf region.

As for the distribution between the public and private sectors, the percentage of Kuwaiti women working in the public sector reached 94.6 percent of the total Kuwaiti female labor force, numbering 52,027 in 1995. The number of Kuwaiti women working in the public sector was 108,251 in 2005 representing 85.1 percent of the total number of the Kuwaiti female labor force.[7]

The participation of women in the private and joint sectors is generally modest. The number of women in this sector was not more than 2,502 in 1995, which is 4.55 percent of the total labor force of Kuwaiti women. This percentage then rose to 8.84 percent (11,239) in 2005. Though the number of women in the private sector has increased fourfold in ten years, their percentage of the total Kuwaiti female labor force is still modest because the private sector primarily relies on the migrant labor force.[8]

WOMEN IN LEADING POSITIONS IN THE PUBLIC AND PRIVATE SECTORS

The contribution of women to the centers of decision-making has evolved. Women have occupied all positions up to that of ambassador in 1996. An

Undersecretary was appointed in both the Ministries of Higher Education and Planning. Moreover, many women have held positions as Assistant Undersecretaries in the Ministries of Education, Social Affairs and Labor, Housing and Public Works, and Information. A woman has been appointed Vice Chancellor of Kuwait University since 1994. Moreover, Kuwaiti women have chaired women's civil associations involved in community service. This development shows that the Kuwaiti community now gives women a special position in decision-making at all levels.

Statistics indicate that the number of women occupying higher administrative positions has increased from 704 in 2001, representing 11.3 percent of the total national labor force occupying higher administrative positions to 915 in 2005, representing 13 percent of the total.

It may be observed that women attain leadership positions in the private sector at a faster rate than in the government sector. Women in leadership positions in the private sector increased from 16.6 percent in 2001 to 19.3 percent in 2005 whereas the corresponding number in the government sector was 7.7 percent and 8.3 percent for 2001 and 2005, respectively. These indicators show the growing tendency to support the leadership of women in a developmental role along with their economic, social and educational roles.

Social Role of Kuwaiti Women

WOMEN'S EDUCATIONAL INTEREST AND LOW LEVEL OF ILLITERACY
Kuwait achieved the goal of equality between the sexes in education by 2000—fifteen years before the date specified in the millennium development goals.[9] Kuwaiti women have continued to receive education both inside and outside Kuwait since 1960, when six women obtained university degrees from Egypt. After the foundation of the University of Kuwait in 1966, women very clearly sought education and the number of female students grew from 38 in 1966 to 246 in 1970. In 1989, female students numbered more than half of all registered students. During the

period 1995–2004 the number of females in the university rose to 70 percent of the total number of registered students. The number of females with university degrees was estimated at 7.6 percent of all women in Kuwait, rising to 13 percent in 2004 and 13.1 percent the following year.[10]

On the other hand, Kuwaiti women achieved a great triumph in the sphere of eradicating illiteracy. The Ministry of Planning data shows that the percentage of illiteracy among women dropped from 16 percent in 1995 to 9.6 percent in 2005. In addition, the percentage of females (corresponding to males) who can read and write (age group 15–24) rose from 97.6 percent in 1993 to 99.2 percent in 2004.[11]

ROLE OF WOMEN IN CIVIL SOCIETY

Kuwaiti women made a distinguished contribution to social development within Kuwaiti society. They formed civil professional and cultural associations in addition to five specialized associations. The oldest is the Women's Cultural and Social Society (WCSS) which was formed in 1963. The Federation of Kuwaiti Women's Associations (FKWA) was given official recognition in 1994.[12]

The goal of these institutions is to develop awareness among Kuwaiti women of the issues affecting their society and reinforce their role in social and economic development. Moreover, Kuwaiti women had a great share in establishing a large number of community service societies numbering more than fifty. These societies include the Kuwait Society for Private Education, the Women's Biader Al-Salam Society, Kuwait Nursing Society, Kuwait Girl Guides Association, Islamic Welfare Society, Kuwait Girls Club and Kuwait Society for the Handicapped.

Moreover, women established several nurseries and developmental projects to protect mothers and children. This has been done as a contribution to providing appropriate opportunities for working mothers to bring up their children in a proper way. The total number of nurseries is 31.

In addition to all this, the openness of Kuwait as a state and the multi-cultural contacts maintained by its society through travel and trade, coupled with its economic openness and attraction of foreign labor had a great effect in making society in general and women in particular more flexible in emulating positive values in social behavior and lifestyle. Also, oil revenues and the fact that they have been used well by the government in the different aspects of social and economic development to provide basic services in the realms of health, education and housing have had a great effect in the development of Kuwaiti society in general and women in particular.

Political Role of Women

Kuwaiti women played a significant and vital role in resisting the Iraqi invasion of Kuwait in 1990 whether inside or outside their country. This resistance manifested itself in various forms, the most important of which saw Kuwaiti women gathering in the streets of Kuwait in demonstrations of protest against the Iraqi occupation in the early days of the invasion. Women organized a network of information and communication between the resistance and the government abroad. The network was used to convey secret information to the government on the resistance methods, to publish and distribute bulletins as well as to offer reassurance about those held in Iraqi detention camps and express sympathy to their relatives and the families of martyrs. The tasks also comprised giving first aid, preparing drugs, collecting them from hospitals and distributing them among the resistance and civilians in times of emergency.

Kuwaiti women abroad contributed to several media and academic conferences held in the United States, the United Kingdom and other European countries in addition to Arab countries like Egypt, Syria and all the other Gulf States. These conferences attempted to rally the support of Arab and global public opinion around the rights of the Kuwaiti people

[378]

and their legitimate government and condemn the practices of the former Iraqi regime inside Kuwait at that time.

As mentioned earlier, the Kuwaiti National Assembly approved the amendment of the Article 1 of the Elections Act on May 16, 2005 to grant women their full political rights with respect to voting and nomination. Following this amendment, the first lady minister in the history of Kuwait's political life was appointed in June of the same year and prior to this, two ladies were appointed members of the Municipal Council.

Kuwaiti women also participated in the municipal elections in the fifth constituency in which elections were held in April 2006. A female nominee reached the second position. Observers regarded this as an important qualitative development in Kuwaiti political life and practice.

Boosting Women's Role in Development: Strategic Departure Points

The status of Kuwaiti women in the future depends upon finding a universal action plan to develop their roles in different spheres and encourage them to participate fruitfully in economic and social development. Some of the most important proposals in this regard are as follows:

Formulating Stable Policies to Activate and Empower Kuwaiti Women

In this respect the Ministry of Planning has set itself the task of preparing "a national report on the status of Kuwaiti women" aimed at making a practical and comprehensive survey of the reality of Kuwaiti women and the challenges confronting them in order to find new policies and visions to deal with these challenges and seek ways to empower women in society so that they play an essential role in the process of development in the state.

[379]

Developing Legislation Pertaining to Women in all Spheres

- Pursuing the implementation of proposed legislation that encourages women to continue working without neglecting their family obligations. An instance is the proposal calling for the addition of an article to the Civil Service Act No.15 of 1979, which provides for special leave on half-pay to a wife who accompanies her husband abroad either when he is on an official study course, or on secondment for a duration over six months.

- Introducing more regulations pertaining to women working in the private sector that commit the latter to attracting Kuwaiti women labor as part of a program to replace migrant labor. Some believe that current laws do not satisfy the need for women to work in the private sector.

- Formulating new laws relating to women and the family, especially in the spheres of family and private custody and social care of the elderly.

- Developing existing legislation relating to women and the family in the fields of social insurance, public benefit societies, public aid, juveniles, combating drugs, work in the civil sector, civil service and the penal code.

- Expanding the role of women in education to support their developmental role.

- Endeavoring to develop educational policies and rewriting curricula to make them include the concepts and values that accord importance to the role of women in society and the vitality of their work, as well as implanting these concepts in the minds of the young.

- Researching the reasons behind the reluctance of women to enroll in certain specializations such as nursing and other medical specializations despite the real need of the health sector for the national labor force in these fields.

- Encouraging and motivating the economic role of women, especially outside the governmental sector.

- Expansion in supporting family projects that generate income in order to turn housewives into a productive force that contributes to the economic activity in the state. In this regard, the successful experiments in the state must be supported through "self-earning" projects directed at those who benefit from public aid to change them into a productive force in cooperation with the Ministry of Social Affairs and Labor and the General Secretariat of Endowments.

- Expanding the benefit for women, especially new graduates, from the umbrella of small projects in the state and directing concerned bodies – such as the program for restructuring the labor force in the executive branch of the state, the Kuwaiti Small Project Development Company (KSPDC), the Public Authority for Applied Education and Training – to give Kuwaiti women more opportunities to benefit from the small projects of these bodies and their relevant services as business incubators and others.

- Encouraging Kuwaiti girls and women who have dropped out of the education system and those who have not enrolled in higher education to join training programs to acquire appropriate skills in order to practice professions and jobs needed by the labor market and provided by certain authorities like the Public Authority for Applied Education and Training and the Kuwait University.

The five-year plan of the state (2006/2007–2010/2011) includes an integrated program to support and develop the initiatives of women in society and integrate them into the labor market by training 19,416 women during the plan period, as well as establishing 16 new model centers for the development of society with the target of supporting woman's participation in the labor market.

Developing the Umbrella of Social Insurance for Kuwaiti Women

Developing the umbrella of social insurance for Kuwaiti women is possible by affirming the role of the state in supporting working women and helping them to reconcile their professional obligations and family duties through a network of nurseries and day care centers located in different regions of the state and at the workplace as in European countries. This should be done in coordination with women's civil society organizations in order to develop the programs of children's clubs, training mothers and upgrading the competence of the staff employed in the children's clubs in the state.

Expanding the Role of Women's Civil Society in Kuwait

Women's civil society has important roles to play in the foreseeable future to support Kuwaiti women. The most important of these roles are:

- Confronting negative social phenomena and their implications for the Kuwaiti family such as the tendency towards excessive consumption, the alienation of youth, violence, fanaticism and all forms of extremism, as well as family problems.
- Implanting new types of consciousness and culture in the society such as political consciousness, the culture of elections, political participation of women, environmental consciousness of families, scientific culture and acquiring knowledge.

Encouraging and Training Kuwaiti Women to Practice Electoral Rights

The Ministry of Interior completed the registration of women in the electoral register in January 2006. The number of registered female voters was 194,614, which is more than the 139,179 male voters listed in the register. Thus initiatives to implant the culture of political participation and election rights for women have become active in Kuwait, where women are educated, aware of their political rights and know how to practice them.

The five-year development plan includes an integrated executive program whose aim is to boost the political rights of Kuwaiti women by training hundreds of female citizens in the skills needed to deal with all the stages of the election process—registration, voting, nomination and managing election campaigns.

On the other hand, the program includes raising the consciousness of voters with regard to their duties and rights generally, especially with reference to developing the skills of practicing political rights. The program is executed in cooperation with national civil society organizations as well as the UNDP, which provides technical support and expertise in the spheres of managing open dialogue, building political skills, follow-up and evaluation. Several Kuwaiti organizations of civil society are active in this respect such as the Women's Cultural and Social Society and the Federation of Kuwaiti Women Associations and other organizations that are preparing and implementing training programs on "Women and Political Work Skills."

Conclusion

Having completed this overview of the status of women's development in Kuwaiti society, it may be concluded as follows:

- There are several signs of concern being shown for women's issues in Kuwait as well as guarantees being provided for their social, economic and political rights. Such concern has been protected by the constitution since 1962. The constitution ensures complete equality in terms of human dignity, rights and duties between all Kuwaiti citizens without distinction.

- Kuwait participates positively in all regional and global efforts to assist women, support their causes and combat all forms of discrimination against them. This participation is embodied in the fact that Kuwait has signed all international conventions on eliminating discrimination against women and the International Covenant on Economic, Social and Cultural Rights for 1976.

- There are several aspects of development in the economic role of Kuwaiti women. Their contribution to the labor market has risen from 2.5 percent in 1965 to 40.7 percent in 2005. In addition, the number of women occupying higher administrative positions has increased from 11.3 percent of the total national labor force in the year 2001 to 13 percent in 2005.

- Kuwaiti women are heavily concentrated in the government sector with 85.1 percent in 2005, whereas their presence is very limited in the private sector and did not exceed 8.8 percent in the same year.

- Kuwaiti women have registered several positive indicators in the field of education and illiteracy. Kuwait achieved equality between the sexes in education by 2005 as one of the millennium development goals. The number of females registered in the university was 70 percent between 1995 and 2004. Illiteracy among women was reduced to 9.6 percent in 2005.

- Kuwaiti women contribute effectively to the efforts of social development, especially through their participation in civil society activities. There are five societies with women's interests. In addition women contribute to other public benefit societies.

- There are promising future prospects for the development of the political role of Kuwaiti women after the Kuwaiti National Assembly in May 2005 granted women their full political rights in voting and nomination.

To boost the role of Kuwaiti women in development, we recommend that attention be focused on the following:

- Recognizing the importance of formulating stable policies to empower Kuwaiti women and boost their role in society. This requires the preparation of a comprehensive national report on Kuwaiti women by the concerned parties under the sponsorship of the Ministry of Planning.

- Creating new legislation and developing existing laws pertaining to Kuwaiti women in all fields, especially proposed parliamentary legislation that will encourage working women to continue their work without violating their familial duties.

- Developing more special legislations and to help women working in the Kuwaiti private sector so as to open up new fields of employment outside the government sector.

- Encouraging Kuwaiti girls who have dropped out of the education system or have not enrolled in higher education to join suitable training programs to acquire skills that will qualify them to enter the labor market.

- Encouraging Kuwaiti women, especially new graduates, to benefit from the umbrella of small projects in the state.

- Expanding the role of women in education and developing education curricula in a manner that affirms and reinforces the role of women in society and simultaneously giving incentives to women to join professions such as nursing and other medical specializations.

- Developing the umbrella of social insurance so as to help women to reconcile their professional and familial obligations and support family projects that generate income aimed at turning housewives into a productive labor force playing an economic role in society.

Appendix

Table 16.1
Development of Kuwaiti Population and Society
by Gender (1995–2005)

Year	Males	Growth Rate	Females	Growth Rate	Total	Growth Rate
1995	344,800		350,276		695,076	
1996	357,163	3.59	362,576	3.51	719,739	3.55
1997	369,614	3.49	375,575	3.59	745,189	3.54
1998	382,058	3.37	390,200	3.89	772,258	3.63
1999	394,499	3.26	403,657	3.45	798,156	3.35
2000	407,871	3.39	418,212	3.61	826,083	3.50
2001	421,973	3.46	433,360	3.62	855,333	3.54
2002	435,852	3.29	448,698	3.54	884,550	3.42
2003	449,449	3.12	464,051	3.42	913,500	3.27
2004	463,399	3.10	479,493	3.33	942,892	3.22
2005	477,216	2.98	496,070	3.46	973,286	3.22
Average annual growth rate for the period (percent)		**3.30**		**3.54**		**3.10**

Source: Kuwait Ministry of Planning and Administrative Development Affairs, *Al Simaat al Asasiyya lil al Sukan wa al Qowa al 'Amila*, various publications.

Table 16.2
Development of the Kuwaiti Labor Force
by Gender (1995–2005)

Year	Males	Growth Rate	Females	Growth Rate	Total	Growth Rate
1995	117,409		549,976		172,385	
1996	119,258	1.57	57,071	3.81	176,329	2.29
1997	128,144	7.45	62,922	10.25	191,066	8.36
1998	136,450	6.48	69,740	10.84	206,190	7.92
1999	142,494	4.43	75,082	7.66	217,576	5.52
2000	147,976	3.85	79,554	5.96	227,530	4.57
2001	153,150	3.50	85,070	6.93	238,220	4.70
2002	162,032	5.80	96,508	13.45	258,540	8.53
2003	168,552	4.02	104,121	7.89	272,673	5.47
2004	176,369	4.64	114,377	9.85	290,746	6.63
2005	185,352	5.09	127,215	11.22	312,567	7.51
Average annual growth rate for the period (percent)		**4.67**		**8.75**		**6.13**

Source: Kuwait Ministry of Planning and Administrative Development Affairs, *Al Simaat al Asasiyya lil al Sukan wa al Qowa al 'Amila*, various publications.

[387]

Table 16.3
Rates of Contribution to Economic Activity
by Gender and Nationality (1995–2005)

Years	Kuwaitis			Non-Kuwaitis			Total		
	Males	*Females*	*Total*	*Males*	*Females*	*Total*	*Males*	*Females*	*Total*
1995	62.30	27.74	**44.59**	95.01	,61.86	**85.61**	88.11	47.70	**74.05**
1996	60.70	27.62	**43.74**	94.37	59.94	**84.21**	87.45	47.21	**73.19**
1997	63.05	29.35	**45.75**	94.11	60.57	**84.13**	87.97	48.71	**74.07**
1998	64.65	31.04	**47.32**	93.68	59.90	**83.69**	87.98	48.87	**74.16**
1999	64.92	32.01	**47.92**	93.33	58.90	**83.16**	87.62	48.39	**73.71**
2000	64.79	32.42	**48.02**	93.16	59.02	**83.13**	87.05	47.99	**73.06**
2001	64.31	33.16	**48.15**	92.96	60.01	**83.10**	86.53	48.68	**72.74**
2002	65.41	36.03	**50.14**	93.22	62.52	**83.85**	87.11	51.67	**74.10**
2003	65.42	37.23	**50.75**	93.43	63.31	**84.44**	87.47	52.66	**74.88**
2004	65.87	39.25	**52.00**	93.75	63.87	**85.02**	80.08	53.97	**75.98**
2005	66.72	41.82	**53.70**	94.00	62.97	**85.26**	88.84	54.62	**77.06**

Source: Kuwait Ministry of Planning and Administrative Development Affairs, *Al Simaat al Asasiyya lil al Sukan wa al Qowa al 'Amila*, various publications.

Table 16.4

Women Workers in Government Sector by Major Professional Groups and Nationality (2004)

Professional Groups	Kuwaitis	Percentage	Non-Kuwaitis	Percentage	Total	Percentage
Doctors & Science Graduates	1262	1.22	832	3.94	2094	1.68
Engineers	1584	1.53	138	0.65	1722	1.38
Economists & Legal Personnel	4333	4.20	354	1.68	4687	3.77
Teachers	30,698	29.73	6327	29.96	37,025	29.77
Directors & Supervisors	2533	2.45	77	0.36	2610	2.10
Literary Professions/Artists & Social Workers	6021	5.83	292	1.38	6313	5.08
Business/Saleswomen	85	0.08	3	0.01	88	0.07
Engineering Technicians	1258	1.22	16	0.08	1274	1.02
Medical & Scientific Technicians	4701	4.55	8754	41.46	13,455	10.82
Typists/Firewomen & Policewomen	46,124	44.67	3062	14.50	49,186	39.55
Craftswomen	380	0.37	33	0.16	413	0.33
Semi-skilled Workers	667	0.65	18	0.09	685	0.55
Workers in Services and Agriculture	834	0.81	175	0.83	1009	0.81
Ordinary Workers	1914	1.85	834	3.95	2748	2.21
Unspecified	864	0.84	200	0.95	1064	0.86
Total	**103,258**	**100**	**21,115**	**100**	**124,373**	**100**

Source: Kuwait Ministry of Planning and Administrative Development Affairs, *Al Simaat al Asasiyya lil al Sukan wa al Qowa al 'Amila*, various publications.

[389]

Table 16.5
Percentages of Kuwaiti Women in Leading Professions (2001–2005)

Years / Leading professions	2001 Government	2001 Public	2001 Joint	2001 Private	2002 Government	2002 Public	2002 Joint	2002 Private	2003 Government	2003 Public	2003 Joint	2003 Private	2004 Government	2004 Public	2004 Joint	2004 Private	2005 Government	2005 Public	2005 Joint	2005 Private
Administrative managers in the government	2.4	0	0	12.3	2.2	0	0	11.9	2.2	0	0	12.3	2.0	0	0	12.9	2.1	0	0	13.8
Chairmen of Board of Directors and general managers	3.9	0	0	5.7	3.9	0	0	6.2	4.1	0	0	6.3	3.9	0	0	6.5	4.1	0	0	6.2
Production managers (except agriculture)	4.8	0	0	0	4.5	0	0	0	6.4	0	0	0	6.3	0	0	0	6.4	0	0	0
Managers of financial establishments, banks and insurance companies	12.1	0	21.9	27.1	12.7	0	20.6	26.7	12.8	0	24.2	28.0	14.0	0	24.2	28.2	14.2	0	26.7	29.2
Managers of transport companies, transport and warehousing	1.2	0	0	0	1.1	0	0	0	1.2	0	0	0	1.2	0	0	0	1.2	0	0	0
Managers whose professions are unspecified	11.3	8.9	20.5	19.5	11.7	6.1	27.3	20.3	11.6	5.9	25.0	20.5	11.6	5.9	25.0	21.4	11.9	6.1	24.5	21.7

Source: Public Authority for Civil Information (data covering 2001–2005).

International Migration and the Demographic Structure of the GCC States

Dr. Mattar Ahmed Abdullah

Migration and mass movement from one place to another together constitute a natural phenomenon, which humankind has experienced through the course of history. Migration is divided into two types: internal migration within the borders of the same country, such as migration from rural to urban areas and vice versa, and international migration, which, in turn, is divided into several types. In this chapter, the focus is on what is known as "free migration," which is aimed at seeking work or stability. This has been the cause for the movement of whole communities from Europe and the ancient world to countries in the New World, such as the Americas and Australia. These migrations have resulted in creating regions that either expel or attract populations and countries that either export or import labor. Currently, these migrations are having both positive and negative effects on the countries of the world.

The Gulf has known migration since ancient times but international migration to the region has increased exponentially since the 1970s. This is mainly due to the growing oil revenues of the Gulf states and their escalating pace of development and modernization.

The increased rates of international migration to the region during the past century have various implications, the most significant of which is the massive demographic change. This change has created a new reality in terms of the population structure. The native citizens of the GCC states have become a small, marginalized minority. The focus of this chapter is on the problem of population structure, which is viewed as one of the outcomes of direct international migration on the Gulf states. The population structure has been chosen for discussion in this chapter because it poses great danger owing to its economic, social and security implications for the region and for Gulf communities.

To begin with, the scale of international migration and the countries hosting it will be reviewed. Thereafter, the discussion will shift to the impact of the influx of large numbers of migrants on the population structure of the GCC states and the consequent imbalance that has distorted this structure. Subsequently, an attempt will be made to sketch a future vision for rectifying the structural imbalance in the population of the GCC states and deal with some policies and strategies that I believe are important to stem the continuing exacerbation of the problem.

International Migration: Facts and Figures

One of the basic characteristics of populations is movement from one place to another. Freedom of movement has been globally recognized more than half a century ago by the approval of the United Nations Universal Declaration of Human Rights. Article 13 of the Declaration stipulates that "everyone has the right to freedom of movement and residence within the borders of each state" and that "everyone has the right to leave any country, including his own, and to return to his country."[1]

The International Conference on Population and Development (ICPD) held in Cairo in 1994, referred to the fact that organized international migration can have positive effects on the countries of origin and the countries of destination alike. For instance, migration can facilitate the transfer of skills and contribute to enriching cultures. Today, an unprecedented 175 million persons are resident outside the countries of their birth, which is more than double the number residing a generation ago. The vast majority of migrants contribute significantly to the host countries. At the same time, however, international migration entails the loss of human resources on the part of many originating countries and it may cause political, economic or social tensions in the countries that receive migrants.

The subject of international migration – along with its complex network of determinants and attendant demographic, social, economic and political consequences – has moved to the forefront of national and international concerns. Resident migrants have become a major issue over the few last years in an increasing number of countries. Quite recently, especially after the 9/11 attacks, some countries have tightened their policies with respect to migrants, refugees and political asylum seekers.

The United Nations is currently dealing with the various dimensions of international migration. For instance, the UN Secretariat has focused on collecting, analyzing and disseminating information on the magnitude of international migration, its trends and related policies. Other UN agencies are concerned with matters like human rights, internal displacement and reunion of families, undocumented migrants, trafficking in migrant persons, and the social and economic assimilation of migrants. In addition to this, specialized agencies concentrate on matters pertaining to their technical expertise and jurisdiction such as inflows of labor force, refugees, asylum seekers and money transfers.

However, there are few answers to the many questions arising from increasing concerns over international migration. To a great extent, this is linked to the lack of accurate and up-to-date information on international migration. The International Migration Report for 2002 attempts to answer some questions by providing a general profile of the scale of international migration, its trends and policies with regard to individual countries, regions and the entire world.

According to the above-mentioned report, round 175 million people currently live in countries in which they were not born. This figure represents 3 percent of the world population. Since 1970, the number of migrants has doubled and 60 percent of the world's migrants live in the most developed areas whereas 40 percent live in the least developed regions. Most of the world's migrants live in Europe (56 million), Asia (50 million) and North America (41 million). In the most developed regions, the ratio of migrants to the rest of the population is almost 1 to 10. As for developing countries, the ratio is approximately 1 to 70.[2]

Table 17.1 shows that the number of migrants in the world has increased during the last decade of the past century (1990–2000) by 21 million persons, or 14 percent. The total net growth of migrants took place in the more developed regions. Europe, North America, New Zealand and Japan together registered an increase in the number of migrants which reached 23 million, or 28 percent. During the same period, the number of migrants in North America rose by 13 million (48 percent) whereas this number rose by 8 million or 16 percent in Europe. In contrast, migrant populations in the less developed regions dropped by two million, and the number of resident migrants in Latin America and the Caribbean Sea dropped by one million or 15 percent.

In a period of only five years, from 1995 to 2000, the most developed regions of the world received 12 million migrants from the least developed regions, i.e. 2.3 million migrants every year. The largest annual increase was in North America, which absorbed 1.4 million migrants annually, followed by Europe with a net annual increase of 0.8 million, and Oceania with a more modest increase of 900,000 migrants annually (See Table 17.1).

Figure 17.1 shows the twenty countries with the largest number of international migrants. The United States comes in the first place with 35 million migrants, followed by Russia with 13 million, and Germany in the third place with 7 million. Figure 17.2 shows the twenty countries with the highest ratio of international migrants to the local population. These include four Gulf states: the UAE (72 percent), the State of Kuwait (58 percent), the Sultanate of Oman (27 percent) and the Kingdom of Saudi Arabia (26 percent).

Table 17.1

Number and Growth of Migrants by Major Regions (1990–2000)

Major Region / Years	1990 (in thousands)	2000 (in thousands)	Change 1990–2000	
			(in thousands)	(percent)
The world	153,956	174,781	2082	13.5
Most developed regions	81,424	104,119	2269	27.9
Least developed regions	72,531	70,662	-186	-2.6
Least developed countries	10,992	10,458	-53	-4.9
Africa	16,221	16,277	5	0.3
Asia	49,956	49,781	-17	-0.4
Europe	48,437	56,100	766	15.8
Latin America and Caribbean Region	6994	5944	-105	15.0
North America	27,597	40,844	1324	48.0
Oceania	4751	5835	108	22.8

Source: United Nations International Migration Report, 2002 (New York, NY: UN Publications, 2002) available at (www.un.org/esa/population/publications/ittmigrep2002/ittmigrep2002arab.doc)

Figure 17.1

Countries with the Largest Number of International Migrants (2000)

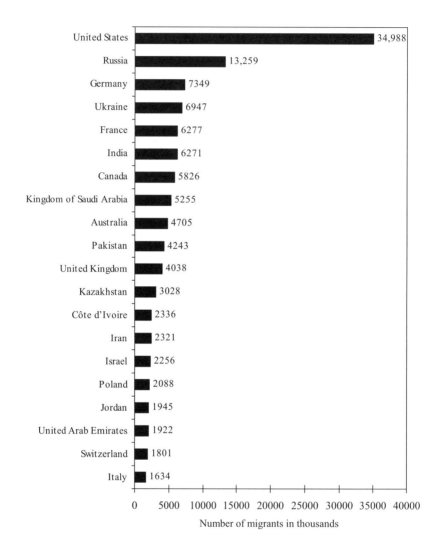

Number of migrants in thousands

Source: UN International Migration Report, 2002 (New York, NY: UN Publications, 2002) available at (www.un.org/esa/population/publications/ittmigrep2002/ittmigrep2002 arab.doc).

Figure 17.2
Countries with the Highest Percentage of International Migrants
(populations over one million)

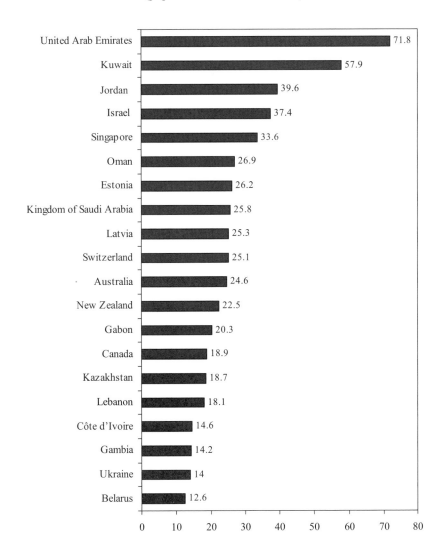

Note: Numbers indicate percentages of the total population

Source: UN International Migration Report, 2002 (New York, UN Publications, 2002) available at (www.un.org/esa/population/publications/ittmigrep2002/ittmigrep 2002arab. doc).

[397]

International Migration to the GCC States: Realities and Future

The Gulf region, especially Arab Gulf states, were well known for their commercial links with neighboring countries such as India, Pakistan and Iran. This was the case before oil became a fundamental factor in the economies of these states. Large numbers of inhabitants from neighboring countries were encouraged to migrate to the Gulf states to work as merchants and laborers, especially during the British colonial period.

The writings of scholars such as J. G. Lorimer and Sayid Nofal [3] have illustrated that the percentage of migrants from neighboring countries was generally low during that period. It did not pose any threat to the demographic situation of the region. However, this percentage started to rise after oil revenues were employed in the process of modernization and overall development, which began after the 1950s and is still ongoing. In particular, since the 1970s, the rates of international migration inflows to the Gulf Arab states, especially those coming from the Indian sub-continent and Asian countries like the Philippines, Indonesia and China, have witnessed an unprecedented, qualitative escalation.

It is worth mentioning that the phenomenon of migration between the regions of the Arabian Peninsula and the neighboring regions, such as Iraq, Oman, Yemen and the western coast of Iran is regarded as a natural historical phenomenon. The limited numbers of migrants from these regions to the Arabian Peninsula were easy to absorb and assimilate with the Gulf communities. Moreover, migrants had similar customs and cultures, which helped them to adapt to the host societies. Hence they were considered an addition to the national workforce, which used to play the major role in the different commercial and productive activities. The migrant workers of those times did not substitute the national workforce. In other words, the former did not marginalize the latter in the commercial, productive and administrative process as is the case today.

Perhaps the most significant consequence of the rising rates of international migration to the region in the past century is the great demographic change that the region is now witnessing. This has created new realities with regard to the population structure—the national populations in the GCC states have become a small, marginalized minority.

Imbalance in the Population Structure: A General Profile

There are several aspects to be considered with regard to the imbalance in the population structure. These include the imbalance in age-wise population distribution, whereby particular age groups dominate at the expense of others, thereby leading to an unnatural population growth. This is true of European societies, where the percentage of the elderly age group (60 plus) is high in comparison to the young age group. In the long run, such a situation will lead to the gradual disappearance of the populations in those countries.

Another aspect of the structural imbalance of the population is an abnormal increase in males or females owing to external factors like migration or wars. However, this chapter is concerned specifically with the structural imbalance in population that results from the influx of foreign labor into the Arab Gulf states on the basis of their desire to fill the gap in their labor force. Thus these external influxes have become the economic driving force of these states. The foreign labor force now constitutes the majority of the population while the local population has shrunk and become a minority in these states.

This inflow has led to an imbalance in the natural distribution of age groups in the Gulf societies. There are distortions in the population pyramid owing to the high number of foreign residents in the young age groups. In addition, the migrant labor force has brought with it different customs, traditions, cultures, languages and religions. These have been indigenized and become a part of the social reality of these societies.

The imbalance in the population structure has always been a cause for concern in several countries. In this respect, the most significant are the countries of Southeast Asia such as Malaysia where the British brought with them hundreds of thousands of Chinese and Indians during the colonial period. These migrants were naturalized and given Malaysian nationality at the time of independence. This move led to the eventual disintegration of Malaysia as a federation and the secession of Singapore due to the concentration of Chinese residents there, which turned the native Malays into an insignificant minority.

This superimposed population structure continues to have political and economic effects in Malaysia where the Chinese race controls the Malaysian economy. The Malaysian government enacted some laws to constrain the hegemony of the non-native race over the country by limiting government posts to native inhabitants only. As for Singapore, it is enjoying the zenith of economic prosperity although it is the smallest country in eastern Asia. However, the question to be asked here is: Where do the native inhabitants stand in relation to this economic prosperity? The original inhabitants of Singapore have become a minority since they represent only 14 percent of the total population while the Chinese represent 76.9 percent of the population of the country as in 2005.[4]

Migration is a thorny issue between advanced countries and developing ones because it is linked to several political, economic and social aspects. Worsening politico-economic conditions in developing countries force individuals to migrate to advanced nations. At the same time, advanced nations consider migrants a burden on their economies, especially unskilled labor. Hence many advanced nations have adopted policies aimed at reducing the influx of immigrants by providing aid to developing countries that export migrants or by signing investment and trade agreements with them.

The population structure of both advanced and developing countries is one of the reasons for migration. In the former countries, the rates of population growth are low, the elderly age group is rising and the numbers of the 15–25 age group need to expand. As for developing countries, they have a surplus of young people who are yearning to migrate and work abroad.

Fearing an imbalance in the population structure, the EU countries imposed constraints and obstacles to stem the inflow of migrants from developing countries. Although the percentage of migrants does not represent a danger to the original inhabitants since it represented only 12 percent of the total population in 2005, the EU is trying to reduce this percentage by imposing constraints on migration.[5] In addition, a spirit of hostility towards, and rioting against, migrants of different nationalities has started to surge, especially against Arabs and Muslims. In this respect, a former candidate for the position of the EU Commissioner for Justice and Internal Affairs observed: "Migration is a time bomb for the European Union. Member states must cooperate more closely so that the EU can control the flow of refugees."[6] Perhaps the events that occurred in France and some European countries during November 2005 indicate the danger represented by the migrant labor force to the receiving countries, whether advanced nations or developing ones such as the GCC states.

Advanced countries have been eager to benefit from international population conferences by steering the agendas towards serving their own interests. This was especially true during the International Conference on Population and Development (ICPD) convened in Cairo on September 5, 1994. They do so by pressurizing developing countries into adopting stricter population policies to constrain the population growth rates because they fear the flow of migrants towards the countries of the advanced North.

The Population Problem in the GCC States

Perhaps one of the most decisive contemporary issues confronted by the GCC states is the structural imbalance of the population, which has been exacerbated over more than a quarter century. Gulf officials are aware of the magnitude and implications of this problem, and though several research studies have been conducted and many solutions and recommendations have been proposed, the problem has been exacerbated to such an extent that it poses many dangers.

This problem is not limited to one state, but extends to most GCC states in differing degrees. In my view, the problem of the population structure must be tackled by the GCC states collectively, regardless of the percentage variations in the demographic imbalance in each individual state.

The imbalance in the population structure has reached a dangerous point since it has started to affect the identity and the socio-cultural character of the population, especially in the states where the nationals have become a minority, such as the UAE, Qatar and Kuwait. In addition, there are other serious implications. Foremost among these is the increase in the unemployment rate among GCC citizens in general, at all levels. It must be noted that 43 percent of GCC citizens are below 15 years of age. The number of secondary school graduates is expected to increase during the next five years at the rate of 8 percent annually. This means that GCC citizens will be entering the labor market in higher numbers and this will worsen the unemployment problem in the near future, especially among fresh young graduates.[7]

The continuing flow of foreign labor has created unemployment in the national labor force and the rate of unemployment has started to rise. This has created a new phenomenon in the Gulf societies, especially in the bigger states with high population density. This phenomenon exacerbates the situation of women's unemployment that the Gulf has always suffered from, owing to the prevailing customs and traditions of the community and the narrow spheres of work available to women. Unemployment is linked also to affluence and social factors. The limited availability of jobs and the low wages offered force the unemployed person, who perceives that the work is inappropriate for his social rank and his family's economic standard, to withdraw from the labor market rather than compete with expatriates for jobs that are not well-paid.

[402]

One of the GCC objectives is to increase cooperation and mutual assistance among its member states and thereby find appropriate solutions to the problems of Gulf societies. These solutions must be implemented so that the Gulf integration process continues. The demographic imbalance is one that calls for solidarity among the GCC states to find solutions and common means to tackle this problem. This is so because of the massive changes in the population structure caused by the Asian labor force during its stay. If these population imbalances are not handled quickly, they might lead in the future to economic, social and political risks that undermine the national identity or constitute a threat to regional security and stability. This explains the importance of shedding light on this decisive and urgent issue, which must be tackled by all GCC states collectively and with resolve.

Population Structure in the GCC States: Present Realities

The population of a country is one of the most important factors of production, which constitutes the capabilities of any state. This is so because it determines the state's ability to benefit from its population density by investing labor in its economic resources, channeling it into the development process and building up its capacities in all spheres including the military field.

The GCC states are collectively suffering from the disadvantages of having a low native population. On the contrary, they have the advantage of owning massive natural resources, predominantly oil. The GCC states are located close to countries characterized by high population that are in a position to export cheap labor. This situation has led to such large inflows of migrants coming from the neighboring countries to work in the GCC states that they now constitute the majority of the population.

Although the growth rate among the Gulf national labor force is high, so is the rate of unemployment. The replacement of foreign labor with national labor is still at a very low rate, and the process is not based on thoroughly studied plans and programs that seek to reduce future dependence on foreign labor. This portends an impending unemployment problem among the national labor force. Signs of this problem began to emerge late in the 20th century and high unemployment rates are continuing to rise.

Influx of Migrants and Demographic Change in the GCC States

Demographic change in the GCC states is generally linked to their economic transformation from traditional economies dependent on trade, hunting and basic agriculture to those dependent on oil revenues. This alteration in lifestyle has had a significant role in the population change, which is being experienced by the states of the region. This change has resulted in several problematic issues, the most hazardous being the issue the population structure.

The rise in oil revenues in the post-1973 period led to an increase in the number of migrants from all parts of the globe, including Iran and the Arab world—especially from the states of the Indian subcontinent, such as Pakistan, Bangladesh and India. All these migrants sought to benefit from the job opportunities created by the overall development in the GCC states. This influx led to a totally different and abnormal population structure.

Factors affecting population growth are restricted to births, deaths and migration. The difference between the number of births and deaths is defined as "natural increase," whereas migration helps to create an abnormal increase. The migration factor is responsible for the significant population increase being witnessed by the GCC states, with the exception of Bahrain and Oman. In 2002, the annual population increase in all the GCC states together was 942,977 persons.[8] Natural increase accounted for 66 percent to the annual population increase.

The modernization and development process in all the Gulf Arab states was forced to rely on migrant labor owing to the limited national labor force, which could not have met all the requirements for rapid progress and overall development. This was primarily due to the small indigenous population and the low level of economic activity among nationals, whose contribution to the labor force is 18–23 percent in most of the six GCC states. All this has resulted in a big population, with the number growing from 10 million in 1975 to 32.6 million in 2002. In 1975, migrants represented 26 percent of the total population in the six states while the labor force was 2.9 million. In the same year, the migrant labor force constituted 45 percent of the total labor force. In 1981, during the second oil boom, the population of the six GCC states stood at 12 million and the labor force numbered about 4 million. In the same year, the migrant labor force constituted more than half of the total labor force in all six GCC states.[9]

Table 17.2

Population Growth in the GCC States (1999–2002)

State	Population (1999–2002)				Growth Rate (2002)
	1999	*2000*	*2001*	*2002*	
UAE	3,033,000	3,247,000	3,488,000	3,754,000	6.5
Bahrain	620,989	637,582	654,619	672,124	3.6
Saudi Arabia*	20,335,864	20,846,884	21,381,638	22,007,753	3.2
Oman	2,325,438	2,401,256	2,477,687	2,537,742	2.5
Qatar	561,270	578,510	597,025	685,459	2.6
Kuwait	2,273,719	2,228,363	2,243,080	2,363,325	3.1
Total Population	**29,150,280**	**29,939,595**	**30,842,049**	**32,020,403**	**3.58****

*Estimated data.

** Average rate of population growth of the GCC states, 2002.

Source: GCC Secretariat General, Statistical Publication No. 13 (Riyadh: Information Center, Department of Statistics, 2004).

With the rise in population over the years, the demographic imbalance has also increased leading to a rapid deterioration. This situation has persisted despite the regional recession experienced during the 1980s on account of the drop in oil prices and revenues as well as shrinking development rates. The population in the six GCC states continued to grow rapidly till it reached 26.2 million in 1995 and 28 million in 1998. It continued to rise till the population of the GCC states reached more than 32 million in 2002 (See Table 17.2). This increase resulted from rising rates of imported migrant labor, which represented 35.4 percent of the total population in 2002 and 83 percent of the labor force in all the GCC states together. In my estimate, given this upward trend, the population is expected to reach 56 million in 2015 (See Table 17.3).

The population situation has worsened owing to the lack of a clear development vision and strategy that determines the optimal level of the population and the acceptable percentage of migrants in each GCC state. The irregular influx of migrants has exacerbated the problem. Legitimacy has been bestowed on this influx by the slogan of development, progress and economic openness. All this has had profound effects in the social, economic, political, cultural and security fields and continues to have dangerous implications for the Gulf communities.

Judging by the scant data available on the GCC states, official sources have tended to blur the realities of the demographic imbalance after failing to find a suitable solution. This situation is of particular concern to those states that have lost effective control over their population structure such as the UAE, Qatar and Kuwait.

Reference must be made here to the opportunity that became available to Kuwait in the early 1990s to reformulate its population policy. However, it did not take advantage of that opportunity and consequently, its present population structure is even worse than what it was prior to the Second Gulf War (1990–1991). The percentage of nationals was 37.4 percent of the total population in 2002 (See Figure 17.3).

Figure 17.3

Population Development in the GCC States (1975–2015)

(in millions)

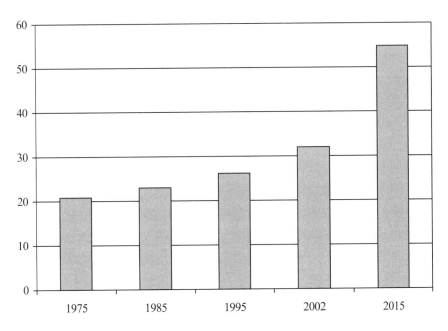

Source: GCC Secretariat General, Statistical Publication No. 13 (Riyadh: Information Center, Department of Statistics, 2004).

Based on the indicators given in Table 17.3, the GCC states, in accordance with the percentage of migrants in relation to the total population (as per 2002 statistics), may be divided into two groups: the first comprises Qatar, Kuwait and the UAE, where migrants constitute 72.4 percent of the total population of these states, and thus represents the majority in each state (73.0 percent, 62.6 percent and 78.5 percent, respectively). The second comprises Saudi Arabia, Bahrain and Oman. Migrants represent 27.6 percent (or nearly one third) of the total population in these states.

As a result of the huge and unlimited influx of migrant labor, the natural characteristics of the population composition in the GCC states have started to change. In 1995, the nationals constituted 66 percent of the total population in the GCC states. The percentage of nationals began to drop continuously till it reached 64.6 percent of the total population in 2002. According to my estimates, this percentage is expected to continue drop more sharply during the next eleven years to reach 60 percent of the total population in 2015. Out of the total GCC population, 68.7 percent is concentrated in Saudi Arabia, whereas 27.1 percent of the population is living in three states: the UAE, Oman and Kuwait. The remaining 4.2 percent are distributed between Bahrain and Qatar.

In the light of the foregoing discussion, it may be said that the core of the population problem in the GCC states stems from two significant facts. The first is that there is a drop in the percentage of nationals in relation to the total population and this decline is likely to continue in future if the influx of migrant labor remains at the current high level. Although some GCC states have taken positive steps to reduce the high influx of migrant labor, these steps are still modest and randomly executed. They represent only temporary remedies as they are not backed by a long-term policy conducive to a comprehensive solution.

The second fact is represented by the imbalance in the nationalities of the migrants. The Gulf landscape is currently witnessing the dominance of particular nationalities in the field of migration, especially from the countries located in the Indian subcontinent. Arab migration rates are generally low and this constitutes an anomaly that calls for immediate rectification because it entails considerable dangers for the Gulf communities in view of the international changes experienced by the region.

Here we must refer to the International Convention on the Protection of the Rights of All Migrant Workers and Members of their Families (referred to briefly as the Rights of Migrant Workers). This Convention has been in effect since 2003 when the required quorum of signatory states was achieved. The provisions of the Convention will be applied in accordance with the rules of the World Trade Organization (WTO) and the International Labor Organization (ILO) that ensure free movement of workers. It may be noted here that the GCC states are member states of the WTO, although they are not signatories to the Convention on the Rights of Migrant Workers.

Table 17.3

Population Distribution (Nationals and Non-Nationals) in the GCC States (2002)

State	Nationals			Non-Nationals			Total Population	Non-Nationals (percent)
	Males	*Females*	*Total*	*Males*	*Females*	*Total*		
UAE	404,443	402,667	807,110	2,151,230	795,660	2,946,890	3,754,000	78.5
Bahrain	210,814	207,126	417,940	175,407	78,777	254,184	672,124	37.8
Saudi Arabia	8,239,680	8,215,493	16,455,173	3,709,123	1,843,457	5,552,580	22,007,753	25.2
Oman	950,666	918,914	1,869,580	492,650	175,512	668,162	2,537,742	26.3
Qatar	92,721	92,353	185,074	345,266	155,120	500,386	685,460	73.0
Kuwait	435,852	448,698	884,550	989,189	489,586	1,478,775	2,363,325	62.6
Total Population	10,334,176	10,285,251	20,619,427	7,862,865	3,538,112	11,400,977	32,020,404	35.6

Source: GCC Secretariat General, Statistical Publication No. 13 (Riyadh: Information Center, Department of Statistics, 2004).

Factors Leading to Imbalance in the Population Structure

After achieving independence, the Arab Gulf states began to aspire for a qualitative shift by building advanced societies and modern cities with all services available for the citizens, and establishing a strong economy by relying on diverse sources of income. These aspirations were supported by the huge rise in oil revenues, which helped to accelerate socioeconomic development processes in all fields in a way that exceeded the expectations, plans and programs set by these states themselves. This led to a rise in the level of demand for labor, both local and foreign, and opened the floodgates for the influx of migrant labor force needed to implement those plans and programs.

Certain factors have helped to exacerbate the problem of the population structure in one way or another and allowed it to reach this level in the GCC states. Here an attempt will be made to summarize some of the causes of this problem:

Low National Population Levels

The low national population levels in the GCC states constitutes one of the most important factors that have given rise to the population problem. This factor impedes ambitious development projects—those that have already been implemented as well as those which are still being implemented. All these projects necessitate a huge labor force that the national population alone cannot satisfy.

Inadequacy of Regulations

Regulations being applied currently in the GCC states with respect to the migrant labor force were enacted in the 1970s or even earlier, at the start of the oil boom. Many economic regulations applied in the GCC states have been repeated or borrowed from the regulations of neighboring countries with economic systems that are different from those of the GCC states. These regulations have remained in force until today, with some official amendments. Hence it is imperative to formulate new regulations to cope collectively with the problem of the massive migrant labor force in the GCC states and to block all the inlets through which Gulf markets are still being flooded by migrant labor, which is injurious to the demographic structure.

Foreign Direct Investment

Many countries seek to lay down special laws for foreign direct investment since it is important for their economies. These laws help to attract foreign capital and hard currency as well as encourage modern methods of management and transfer of advanced technologies from abroad. All this serves to raise development levels and provides job opportunities for the nationals of these countries.

However, a wholly different situation prevails in the GCC states for several reasons. These include the absence of clear and specific investment laws in the Gulf states and the lack of data showing the extent of foreign investment in these states. This fact has enabled foreign investors to benefit from financing facilities and exploit opportunities in the local market by borrowing from local banks. Thus they have been transferring money within the country rather than bringing in fresh investment from outside. Also, foreign investors have depended on investment in projects that employ outdated or obsolete technologies that are labor-intensive, especially in terms of employing cheap and unskilled labor imported to the Gulf. Such projects have posed a big challenge to the national labor in the GCC states.

Hence the GCC states need to reformulate laws that govern foreign direct investment or review current laws to make them compatible with national interest, by invariably seeking out the investor who contributes to the transfer of advanced technology to the GCC states, employs national labor and as far as possible, avoids traditional investment avenues that are labor-intensive.

Engagement in Economic Activities

It is also important to review the laws concerning engagement in economic activities, which are regarded as one of the elements responsible for the exacerbation of the problem of the population structure in the GCC states. This is so because it has helped to spread practices such as visa trafficking, the setting up of front companies and institutions and the flooding of the labor market with marginal and cheap labor. Most laws and regulations were enacted at a time when the GCC states were encouraging the spread of different economic activities to meet the demands of an increasing population swelled by migrant labor. Such economic activities were not developed in a manner appropriate to the current situation.

Absence of Economic Development Plans

The development experience of the GCC states has been rich and distinctive, marked by great achievements over a short period of time. The GCC states have witnessed widespread activities and economic growth, which have spanned all sectors and helped to improve their economic indicators. Despite this growth, there are some criticisms raised against these economies. In terms of the labor market, these countries are suffering due to the inadequate management of matters relating to national and migrant labor forces alike, and the fact that the employment of migrant labor is not linked to real development requirements in the context of specific criteria and standardized specifications. With regard to the employment of migrant labor, the GCC states still work separately and allow the project owners to determine the kind of foreign labor that is required. In addition, they permit the employment of foreign labor without firm controls or restrictions. Thus the GCC states have reached a stage in which they can no longer maintain control over the labor market and the migrant labor force effectively competes with the national labor force and dominates the economy.

On the other hand, the GCC states fail to establish clear development concepts and conditions as well as lack the coordination needed to avoid the duplication of projects and industries. What is more, some states do not have a general development strategy with which to guide their economic plans. This has resulted in unplanned growth and distortion that is evident in the overall development structure. There are many contradictory and repetitive projects such as the spread of free zones which duplicate one another and do not serve economic purposes. Rather, they stimulate the employment of more migrant labor in the region. In addition, there are too many similar factories, which the region cannot accommodate because they are in excess of needs.

Inadequate Databases and Information on the Labor Force

Currently, information and databases have become the major support for countries in determining their strategies, formulating development plans and making economic decisions. In most countries, the ministries of planning and other similar institutions play the main role in constituting the information base of the country. This information base is relied upon in determining the country's developmental needs and path to progress. Based upon such information, economic projects and plans are prepared and recommendations are made as to the avenues for investment in material and human resources and the educational process that is best suited to meet the requirements of the labor market. In other words, such statistical planning helps to control the movement of labor and wards off the risks accompanying the influx of foreign labor.

In the GCC states, the role of these statistical planning institutions is quite weak. This has led to an obvious shortage in the availability of correct information on population and labor. The available data is contradictory and incomplete and drawn from a multiplicity of sources in the same state.

Weak Educational Standards and Training Outputs

During the last century, the GCC states focused on spreading education at all stages on a wide scale. However, educational outputs were not shaped in accordance with development requirements. Therefore, the GCC states found themselves facing a huge problem relating to the absorption of increasing numbers of national graduates during the last five years.

Although the numbers of graduates in the GCC states are high, these educated people have not been directed to take up specializations geared to the real needs of the labor market. Thus a huge gap has developed between development needs and graduate specializations and this has allowed migrant labor the opportunity to fill it. Therefore, the situation warrants the retraining of these graduates if the GCC states are to benefit from their capabilities and integrate them into the labor market.

In line with the current trend, it is expected that the number of graduates seeking jobs will rise to more than 7 million in the next ten years.[10] In contrast, the unemployment rates among Gulf nationals looking for jobs have risen in different degrees. The number of nationals seeking jobs in Saudi Arabia reached 300,000 in 2004. Whereas 163,817 Saudis enter the labor market annually, only 30,000 new jobs are being provided every year.[11] In the UAE, the number of job-seekers registered until 2005 with "Tanmia," the National Human Resource Development and Employment Authority reached 35,000 persons.[12]

The spread of education has contributed to higher human development indexes in the GCC states. According to the Human Development Index for 2005, the GCC states of Qatar, UAE, Bahrain and Kuwait occupy high ranks among the 57 states in the world that have achieved high levels of development. Qatar took the 40th rank globally and the first rank among Arab countries; the UAE claimed the 41st rank globally and the second among Arab countries, while Bahrain and Kuwait took the 43rd and 44th places respectively on the global scale. Oman and Saudi Arabia took the 71st and 77th ranks globally and were categorized as countries that have achieved average development rates according to the Human Development Report, 2005.[13]

Lack of a Clear Population Strategy

There was no clear and specific population strategy for the GCC states until 1998. In the last few years the GCC Secretariat General issued what is known as the General Framework of the Population Strategy for the

GCC Member States. This framework has given each state various options to achieve the goals laid down in the population strategy.

Prevalence of the Values of Dependence and Ostentation

With the growth of oil revenues in the 1970s, governments tried to gain the approval of their people by distributing the sudden wealth gained during that period to them in the form of gifts, aid and re-acquiring ownership over the houses allotted to nationals by paying them astronomical amounts under the guise of re-planning. This pattern has helped to increase the spirit of dependence by facilitating the use of migrant labor in the sphere of personal service, such as housemaids. Moreover, it has tended to encourage ostentation and the dominance of consumerism as a way of life. These changes have resulted from the failure to employ oil revenues in a proper way by building a more aware generation that is capable of contributing effectively towards managing the socioeconomic development gains achieved during the last century. Such changes have encouraged the continuation of total dependence on the migrant labor force in all spheres.

Private Sector Exempted from Social Cost

Reference must be made to the passivity of the private sector in employing national labor in the past. Its role was focused solely on achieving gains and profits. Hence, it totally depended on importing foreign labor without launching any initiative for employing, training and qualifying national labor. This situation has continued despite the repeated calls from Gulf governments for the private sector to employ nationals. This situation has lead to an increase in unemployment levels among national labor and the distortion of the population structure in the GCC states. This, in turn, requires a review of the private sector's part in developing Gulf communities and the formulation of a new strategy to enhance its role.

A Vision for Reducing Structural Imbalance in the Population

The population in the GCC states is currently passing through the second stage of what is known as "demographic transformation," characterized by high fertility and low mortality rates among citizens owing to advanced health services and high living standards.

Factors that are going to affect GCC population growth rates include the socio-cultural changes being witnessed by these states, the high unemployment rates among nationals including those who are well educated, and the entry of Gulf women into the labor market. This requires the formulation of appropriate population policies to deal with these changes based on specific objectives to be achieved under the unified population strategy.

The political will is needed to take high-level decisions on a population strategy that seeks to eradicate the existing imbalance in the demographic structure and to fix the criteria and set the procedures for importing migrant labor in accordance with actual needs. This must also take into consideration the prerequisites for the requirements of development, population harmony and the abrogation of the free market doctrine, which serves as a door through which unwanted labor enters the GCC states. The regulations governing the employment of domestic servants must also be reviewed in order to stipulate the numbers that individuals and families are legally permitted to bring into these states.

It is worth noting that there is no policy to determine the size of the migrant family in the six GCC states. It is well-known that the migrant labor in these states comes from the countries of the Indian subcontinent, characterized by high fertility rates. Hence some migrant families have an average of 7 members. This large family size exerts constant pressure on public services and utilities. Hence the GCC states must create awareness about controlling the size of migrant families, especially non-Arab families, so that their children do not exceed two in number. This would help to preserve the Arab-Islamic identity and culture of GCC societies and the good quality of services so that the Gulf nationals can gain optimum benefit from them.

Also, programs and plans must be set as part of a new policy on the role of the private sector in human development in order to make it attractive in the process of absorbing, training and employing the national labor. The percentage of national labor in the private sector does not exceed 8 percent in the GCC states together. The economic participation of male and female nationals must be increased and new spheres of work must be opened for Gulf women.

In order to work out strategies, plans and programs it is imperative to have a reliable and updated database of information on population and labor, developing and improving the management of statistics and methods of collecting and analyzing data on population and labor force in the GCC states, upgrading the level of accuracy and comprehensiveness of this data and updating it regularly, and having common definitions and concepts relating to population and the labor force.

An important goal for the GCC states is to achieve a balance between the nationalities in the labor force through a quota system so that no single nationality is predominant. Priority must be given to Arab and Muslim labor. The educational level of migrant workers must also be given due attention before permitting them to enter the GCC states. Their educational levels must be in harmonized with the work requirements in different economic sectors.

On the other hand, the six states also face the issue of disharmony between education outputs and development requirements. An ongoing review of educational systems is needed to ensure compliance with the requirements of the labor market. Technical education institutions and vocational training centers must be developed and nationals must be encouraged to enroll in them. This means providing for the material and human capabilities needed to develop such institutions. The civil service systems must also be improved to encourage Gulf women to work in manner that enables them to strike a balance between caring for their families and fulfilling work requirements.

Rectifying the population imbalance in each GCC state requires the implementation of a population policy with effective and strict strategies, programs, plans and procedures. These plans must be clear and time-bound, whether laying down long term or short term goals, and intended primarily to raise the proportion of nationals and turn them once again into the dominant society in the medium term (5–10 years). Second, nationals must form the majority and become the mainstream of the labor force. Third, the Arabic language must be made the language of official and commercial businesses. The percentage of migrant labor must be fixed at an acceptable level and should not exceed 10–15 percent of the total population and 25 percent of the total labor force in the long run (10–25 years).

It is worth noting that these proposals can either become the basis for strategies, plans and programs or they can be modified to suit the needs of individual states. These percentages might be considered excessive because no country in the world wishes to see such a high level of migrant labor. However, the situation is different in the GCC states in which migrant labor currently constitutes more than 39 percent of the total population. Hence providing a national labor force capable of replacing the migrant labor force cannot be achieved within a short period of time, but requires much longer. Therefore, these high levels have been proposed provided that they are reduced gradually till the desired percentages are reached at least within the next twenty-five years.

Reserving jobs for Gulf nationals may be a quick solution that can help to reduce dependence on migrant labor and absorb the annual increase in national labor in the GCC states. This will also help the free movement of Gulf labor between states suffering from high unemployment rates among their citizens and thus provide benefits from the residual energy and scientific capabilities of Gulf nationals. This will have many positive effects on the region and will reduce the negative effects of unemployment on the Gulf and improve the population structure in the six GCC states.

Moreover, reservation of jobs for Gulf nationals will have a positive effect on the economic situation of the GCC states. This will result from the reduction in foreign remittances by the migrant labor force, estimated at \$27 billion annually in 2004 (See Table 17.4). Estimates show that the remittances by the Arab labor force is only 5–15 percent of the worker's income and this is very low compared to that of the Asian labor force— amounting to 85 percent of the worker's income.

Reservation of jobs for Gulf nationals will allow the GCC states to derive maximum benefit from their educational output and their labor market. The surplus labor in some specializations will be employed in states suffering from shortages in these specialized fields. This can be achieved by unifying the civil service systems and labor laws so that Gulf citizens can move freely among the GCC states without losing privileges in their country of origin.

Job reservations for Gulf nationals is an acceptable solution to reduce the increasing rates of unemployment. It is also an important factor in limiting the influx of migrant labor seeking to benefit from job opportunities available in the GCC states. The continuous influx of migrant labor has exacerbated the imbalance in the general population structure. The implications of this problem are growing and they threaten the identity, culture and language of the Gulf communities. The late H.H. Sheikh Zayed bin Sultan Al Nahyan, the Founding Father of the UAE, in a speech delivered on December 2, 2003 on the occasion of the 32nd

National Day, warned against the danger of structural imbalance in the population:

> The most dangerous phenomenon to the future of our country and our national identity is the imbalance in the population structure...This imbalance threatens the stability of our society and the destiny of our generations...This imbalance must be rectified and corrected.[14]

Table 17.4
Scale of Remittances by Migrant Labor from the GCC States and their Growth Rates (1975–2004)

Year	Transfers from the GCC States (billion $)	Period	Growth Rate (percent)
1975	1.6	1975–1980	331.0
1980	6.9	1980–1985	43.5
1985	9.9	1985–1990	41.0
1990	16.7	1990–1995	46.0
1995	24.3	1995–2000	1.2
2000	24.6	2000–2004	10.6
2004	27.2		

Source: Abu Dhabi Chamber of Commerce and Industry, report on "Migrant Money and its Impact on the National Economy" (Abu Dhabi: ADCCI Information Center, February, 2005).

Proposed Policies and Strategies

To rectify the imbalance in the population structure of the GCC states, I would like to propose the following policies and strategies:

- Adopting a new employment policy to benefit from the total national labor force and directing them as far as possible towards productive jobs, thus avoiding a situation of hidden unemployment and the crowding of nationals in government offices.

[420]

- Replacing migrant labor by nationals by activating policies approved by some GCC states and substituting the quantitative and illiterate labor force by a qualitative, professional, technical and educated labor force.
- Reducing the needs of the GCC states for migrant labor force by giving priority to productive jobs in economically and socially feasible sectors, and gradually giving the employer the responsibility to meet the indirect cost of the migrant labor force, including health insurance and a minimum wage.
- Putting in place a strategy to develop and boost the capabilities of national human resources and link the needs of the labor market to different educational programs and curricula in public and private educational institutions, whether at the vocational or university level; retraining the national labor force seeking employment in a manner consistent with market requirements and establishing specialized centers within the GCC states in order to share their cost and guarantee their financial and academic support.
- Reviewing the conditions for engaging in commercial and professional activities and stipulating new conditions to limit the demands for commercial licenses. This can be done by introducing commercial insurance for such licenses and abolishing the system of sponsorship for commercial licenses that is currently operative in the GCC states.

Finally, I must emphasize the important role played by international migration in building the economy of the GCC states. However, this economic development must take place through an integrated population strategy comprising different stages. The first goal is to control the influx of migrant labor to the GCC states during the next ten to twenty five years. Its second goal is to reduce the percentages of migrant population to acceptable levels so that they do not exceed 20 to 25 percent of the total national population. Additionally, it must restore harmony to the population structure, reinstate the Arabic language and limit the rising unemployment rates among the national labor force.

CONTRIBUTORS

H.E. ABDULRAHMAN BIN HAMAD AL-ATTIYAH is currently Minister of State for the State of Qatar and has been the Secretary-General of the Gulf Cooperation Council (GCC) since 2002. He has held several positions in the State of Qatar, including Undersecretary of the Foreign Affairs Ministry (1998–2002), Ambassador Extraordinary (non-resident) of Qatar to Greece (1986–1992), Ambassador Extraordinary of Qatar (non-resident) to Italy (1985–1991), and Qatar Alternate Governor to the International Fund for Agricultural Development (IFAD) (1985–1992). He was the General Coordinator of the 9th Islamic Summit Conference held in November 2000 in Doha. He is also the Deputy Chairman of the Permanent Qatari-Palestinian Committee to Support Jerusalem, a Member of the Arab Thought Forum (Amman) and an Associate Member of the Strategic Studies Center in Khartoum.

H.E. Abdulrahman Al-Attiyah has participated in several regional and international meetings and conferences, including the 17th Arab Summit (Algeria, March 2005), the Arab–South American Summit (Brazil, May 2005), the World Economic Forum ("Davos Forum") Extraordinary Annual Meeting (Amman, June 2003), and the US–Arab Economic Forum (Detroit, 2003). He also headed the delegation of the GCC General Secretariat that attended the UN General Assembly sessions convened during the period 2002–2005. H.E. Abdulrahman Al-Attiyah has received a number of honors, including Commander of the Legion of Honor (Ordre Royale de la Légion d'Honneur), the premier order of the French Republic (1985); the Order of Merit (as Grand Officer) of the Italian Republic (1992); the Commander of the National Cedar Order of the Republic of Lebanon (2004), and the Order of Independence–First Class of the United Arab Emirates (2005). He received a BA in Political Science and Geography from Miami University, Florida, in 1972.

DR. BOURHAN GHALIOUN is Professor of Political Sociology and Director of the Centre d'Etudes sur l'Orient Contemporain (CEOC) [Center for

Contemporary Oriental Studies] at the Sorbonne University in Paris since 1990. He worked in several international research centers before attaining his present position. He is a member of several international societies and editorial boards of academic journals. In addition to his academic activities, Dr. Ghalioun has participated regularly in the ongoing theoretical and political discussion in the Arab world for many years. Since 1975, he has played a prominent role in reviving and spreading the idea of democracy, and initiating discussion on the subject in Arabic literature.

In addition to hundreds of articles and research studies published in the Arab and international press, Dr. Ghalioun has published tens of books including *al Arab wa 'Alam ma ba'ad September 11* (*Arabs and the Post-September 11 World),* (Damascus: Dar al Fikr, 2005), *al Arab wa tahawolat al 'Alam* (*Arabs and World Transformations*) (Beirut and Casablanca: al Markaz al Thaghafi al Arabi, 2004) and *al Mihna al Arabia: al Dawla didd al Umma* (*The Arab Predicament: The State Versus the People*) (Beirut: Markaz Dirasat al Wihda al Arabia, 1992). Dr. Ghalioun studied Philosophy and Social Science at Damascus University and pursued his postgraduate studies in France, where he obtained a doctorate in Political Sociology from the University of Paris-VIII in 1974. He also obtained the State Doctorate in Humanities from the Sorbonne in 1982.

H.E. YASSER ABED RABBO has been a member of the Palestine Liberation Organization (PLO) Executive Committee since 1971. He has also acted as head of the PLO Department of Culture and Information since 1974. He currently heads the Palestinian Peace Coalition (PPC) which he helped to found in 2001. He became Minister of Culture and Information in the first Palestine National Authority (PNA) government in 1994. In 2003 he became the Minister of Cabinet Affairs in the first government of Mahmoud Abbas (Abu Mazen). Mr. Abed Rabbo holds a BA in Economics and Political Science from the American University in Cairo and is due to receive an honorary Ph.D from Paris University.

H.E. Abed Rabbo is a prominent figure in Palestinian politics. He participated in the establishment of the Democratic Front for the Liberation of Palestine (DFLP) in 1969. Since 1974 he has participated in

[424]

the drafting of the political agenda of the PLO, including the Declaration of Independence and the Palestinian Peace Initiative (1988), which called for a two-state solution and accepted UN resolution 242 as a basis for ending the conflict with Israel. During 1990–2000, he led the Palestinian Democratic Union (FIDA), which broke away from the DFLP. He led informal negotiations with an Israeli group headed by Yossi Beilin, which resulted in launching the Geneva Initiative of October 2003. He also headed the first delegation to the dialogue between the United States and the PLO, which was launched in Tunis (1988); led the Palestinian delegation to the Permanent Status negotiations (1999–2000); and participated in the negotiations at Wye River in 1998, Camp David in 2000 and Taba in 2001. He was part of the team which secretly negotiated the Oslo Accords in 1993, and has participated in all negotiations to implement the Accords since 1994.

DR. ADNAN PACHACHI is a Member of the Iraqi parliament and Chairman of the Coalition of Independent Iraqis. He became a member of the Iraqi Interim Governing Council, which was formed after the fall of the former Iraqi regime in April 2003 and also chaired the Council on a rotation basis. Dr. Pachachi completed his undergraduate studies at the American University of Beirut in 1943, majoring in Political Science and obtained his doctorate in Political Science from Georgetown University, USA in 1949. Dr. Adnan Pachachi's long career in the Iraqi Foreign Service began in 1944 when he joined the Iraqi Diplomatic Corps. His first overseas assignment was as an Attaché to the Iraqi Embassy in Washington (1945–1949). After serving for a year as the Iraqi Consul in Alexandria, Egypt, Dr. Pachachi became Assistant Director of the Political Department for United Nations and International Conference Affairs in the Iraqi Ministry of Foreign Affairs, a position he held until 1953. He was posted back to the Iraqi Embassy in Washington in 1953 and returned to the Iraqi Ministry of Foreign Affairs in 1957 as Head of International Affairs and later as Iraq's Permanent Representative at the United Nations. In 1965, Dr. Pachachi was appointed as the Minister of Foreign Affairs and held this position until 1967. During his tenure he participated in a number of committees and councils both in the United Nations and in the Iraqi Foreign Ministry on legal and security issues ranging from the Congo and Yemen to the Non-Aligned Movement.

After his resignation from the Iraqi Diplomatic Corps in 1969, Dr. Pachachi moved to the United Arab Emirates. He was honored with a Ministerial title and appointed as a Member of the Abu Dhabi Executive Council, holding this position until 1991. Between 1974 and 1993 he was the Personal Representative of the late H.H. Sheikh Zayed bin Sultan Al Nahyan, the Founding Father of the UAE and accompanied him on a number of official state visits. He served on the Board of Directors of the Abu Dhabi National Oil Company (ADNOC) and Abu Dhabi Investment Authority (ADIA). Dr. Pachachi also represented the UAE at the Non-Aligned Movement's Conference in 1973, the Arab Summit of 1974 and the OPEC Conference of 1975. Whilst in the UAE, Dr. Pachachi helped to draft the country's constitution.

DR. ATIF KUBURSI is Professor of Economics at McMaster University in Canada, having joined the University in 1969 as Assistant Professor. He taught economics at Purdue University, was Senior Visiting Scholar at Cambridge University (UK), and lectured and consulted at Harvard University. In 1972, Dr. Kubursi formed Econometric Research Limited and has served continuously as its President. In 1982, he joined the United Nations Industrial Development Organization (UNIDO) as Senior Development Officer. Since then, he worked as a team leader of several UNIDO missions to Indonesia, Thailand, Saudi Arabia, Kuwait, Sudan and Egypt.

Dr. Kubursi is Associate Editor of the *Canadian Journal of Development Studies* and serves on the Editorial Board of the *Arab Studies Quarterly*. He has authored seven books in the field of economics and has written over two hundred articles and reports. In his consulting activities, he has specialized in the areas of economic development strategies, impact analysis and regional planning with special emphasis on the environment, tourism and industrial development. Dr. Kubursi has frequently lectured on globalization issues, economic development, oil and industrialization, impact of tourism on provincial and local economies, political economy of development, Arab affairs and on environment-economy linkages. He is also a frequent TV and radio commentator on economics and Middle Eastern affairs.

DR. AMR HAMZAWY is a Senior Associate at the Carnegie Endowment for International Peace (CEIP) in Washington, DC. He is a noted Egyptian political scientist and has taught at Cairo University and the Free University of Berlin. Dr. Hamzawy has extensive knowledge of Middle East politics, with specific expertise on European efforts toward political reform in the region. His research interests include the changing dynamics of political participation in the Arab world and the role of Islamist opposition groups, especially in Egypt and the Gulf countries.

Dr. Hamzawy's studies at Cairo University focused on political reform and democratization in the Arab world, civil society, Islamism, and the cultural impacts of globalization processes. He received his Ph.D from the Free University of Berlin, where he worked at the Center for Middle Eastern Studies. He has published several books in English and German including: *Zeitgenössisches politisches Denken in der arabischen Welt. Kontinuität und Wandel (Orient-Institut, 2005), Civil Society in the Middle East (Verlag Hans Schiler, 2003); Religion, Staat und Politik im Vorderen Orient (LIT Verlag, 2003).*

H.E. DR. MOHAMMED BIN ALI KOUMAN has been the Secretary-General of the Arab Interior Ministers Council since 2001. He has held several academic posts, the last of which was as Dean of the Faculty of Law, at the College of Economics and Administrative Sciences at King Saud University (1993–2001). Dr. Kouman obtained a BA degree in Law from King Saud University in 1982 and a Master's degree from the Université de Poitiers (France). In 1992, he received his Ph.D. in Criminal Law and Sciences from the same university.

Dr. Kouman has published several books and studies, including *Al Waseet fi Dirasat al Andhima; Jara'im al Taqleed wa al Tazweer fi al A'lamat al Tijariyah;* and *Butlan al Khibra fi al Mawad al Jina'iyah.* He

[427]

has also written a number of articles and research studies in some specialized areas. An active practitioner in the fields of law and arbitration, he took part in several committees in the Kingdom of Saudi Arabia as well as in many conferences and academic symposiums.

DR. AHMED JAMEEL AZM is a researcher at the Emirates Center for Strategic Studies and Research (ECSSR). He studied at Edinburgh University where he obtained a doctoral degree in Political Science.

Dr. Ahmed Jameel writes regularly in a number of Arab newspapers, including the London-based *Al Hayat*, the Jordanian *Ad-Dastur* and *Al Ghad*, and the Emirati *Al-Ittihad*. His published research studies include "Al Mujta'a Al Ordoni fi al Dirasat al Gharbiya (Jordanian Society in Western Studies) in *Tariykh Al Ordon al Ijtima'ai* (*The Social History of Jordan*) (Amman: Markaz al Ordon al Jadeed, 2004), and another study entitled "The Reconceptualisation of Conflict Management," *Conflict and Development: An Interdisciplinary Journal*, Issue 7 (July 2005).

DR. METIN HEPER is Chairperson of the Department of Political Science, Director of the Centre of Turkish Politics and History and Dean of the Faculty of Economics, Administrative and Social Sciences at Bilkent University, Ankara. He is also the Founder and Council Member of the Turkish Academy of Sciences, and a Board Member of the Scientific and Technological Research Council of Turkey. Professor Heper previously taught at the Middle East Technical University, Boğaziçi University and Koç University in Turkey and served as Associate Rector at the Middle East Technical University and as Dean at Bilkent and Koç Universities.

During his long career, Professor Heper has held many scholarly positions: Research Fellow at Harvard University, Lester Martin Fellow at the Hebrew University of Jerusalem, Fulbright Scholar and Visiting Professor at the University of Connecticut, Simon Senior Research Fellow at the University of Manchester, England, Research Fellow and Visiting Professor at Princeton University, and Madeleine Haas Russell Visiting Professor of Non-Western and Comparative Studies at Brandeis University. Professor Heper gained his BA degree from Istanbul

University, Turkey in 1963. He went on to complete his Master of Public Administration (MPA) program in 1968, followed by his Ph.D in 1971, both at Syracuse University, USA.

DR. GARY HART has been extensively involved in international law and business since his retirement from the US Senate. A strategic advisor to major US corporations, he has also worked as a teacher, author and lecturer. He is currently Wirth Chair Professor at the University of Colorado and Distinguished Fellow at the New America Foundation. For 15 years, Senator Hart was Senior Counsel to Coudert Brothers, a multinational law firm. He was Co-Chair of the US Commission on National Security for the 21st Century and was also Co-Chair of the task force of the Council on Foreign Relations that produced the report: "America Unprepared—America Still at Risk," in October 2002. He was President of Global Green, the US affiliate of Green Cross International. He is a founding member of the Board of Directors of the US–Russia Investment Fund; a former member of the Defense Policy Board; and a member of the Council on Foreign Relations. Senator Hart is currently a member of the National Academy of Sciences task force on Science and Security. He represented the State of Colorado in the Senate from 1975 to 1987. In 1984 and 1988, he was a candidate for his party's nomination for President. As a Senator, he served in the Armed Services Committee and was an original founder of the Military Reform Caucus. He was also a member of the Senate Environment Committee, Budget Committee and Intelligence Oversight Committee.

Dr. Gary Hart has been Visiting Fellow at All Souls College, a Chatham Lecturer, and a McCallum Memorial Lecturer at Oxford University. He has also been a Global Fund Lecturer at Yale University, a Regents Lecturer at the University of California and a visiting lecturer at the Yale Law School. Dr. Hart has authored fourteen books, the more recent being: *The Shield and the Cloak: The Security of the Commons* (Oxford University Press, 2006); *God and Caesar in America: An Essay on Religion and Politics* (Fulcrum Books, 2005); *The Presidency of James Monroe*, in the American Presidency series edited by Arthur Schlesinger,

Jr. (Time Books/Henry Holt, 2005); *The Fourth Power: A New Grand Strategy for the United States in the 21st Century* (Oxford University Press, July, 2004); and *Restoration of the Republic: The Jeffersonian Ideal in 21st Century America* (2002). He has earned a Doctor of Philosophy degree from Oxford University and graduate law and divinity degrees from Yale University.

DR. AMITAV ACHARYA is Deputy Director and Head of Research at the Institute of Defense and Strategic Studies, Nanyang Technological University, Singapore. Prior to this appointment, he was a Fellow of the John F. Kennedy School of Government at Harvard University and a Professor of Political Science at York University, Toronto. Professor Acharya's areas of specialization include Asian security, regionalism and multilateralism, and international relations theory. He is a founding co-president of the Asian Political and International Studies Association (APISA), and a member of the editorial board of *Pacific Review, Pacific Affairs, European Journal of International Relations* and *Global Governance*. He is a regular writer and commentator on international public affairs.

Among Dr. Acharya's publications are 12 books (including five self-authored and seven edited or co-edited), an *Adelphi Paper* for the International Institute for Strategic Studies, and a number of other monographs, book chapters and articles in various journals. His academic books include: *Constructing a Security Community in Southeast Asia: ASEAN and the Problem of Regional Order* (Routledge, 2001, Chinese translation, Shanghai People's Press, 2004), and *Regionalism and Multilateralism: Essays on Cooperative Security in the Asia Pacific,* 2nd edition (Eastern Universities Press, 2003). His earlier book was *The Quest for Identity: International Relations of Southeast Asia,* (Oxford, 2000) He has co-edited the book *Reassessing Security Cooperation in the Asia Pacific* (MIT Press, 2005). He is also the author of *The Age of Fear: Power Versus Principle in the War on Terror* (Rupa and Co and Marshall Cavendish, 2004).

DR. MARINA S. OTTAWAY specializes in democracy and post-conflict reconstruction issues. Her diverse interests cover civil society, democracy, rule of law reform, political reform, non-governmental actors, foreign and humanitarian aid, human rights, Islam, the Middle East, Iraq, Africa, Afghanistan and the Balkans. She is a Senior Associate and Director of the Middle East Program in the Democracy and Rule of Law Project at the Carnegie Endowment for International Peace. The Project is a research endeavor that analyzes the state of democracy around the world and the efforts by the United States and other countries to promote democracy. Her current work focuses on political transformation in the Middle East and the reconstruction efforts in Iraq and Afghanistan.

Dr. Ottaway has carried out research in Africa and the Middle East and has taught at the University of Addis Ababa, the University of Zambia, The American University in Cairo and the University of the Witwatersrand in South Africa. She has published a number of articles and books over the years, the most recent of which is *Uncharted Journey: Democracy Promotion in the Middle East* (co-edited with Thomas Carothers).

THE HONORABLE WILLIAM S. COHEN, former US Secretary of Defense is the Chairman and CEO of the Cohen Group, a strategic business consulting firm in Washington, DC. Secretary Cohen currently serves on the corporate boards of Viacom, AIG, and Head Sports, and the advisory boards of Intel Corporation, Barrick Gold International and Harmony Airways. Secretary Cohen is a Senior Counselor at the Center for Strategic and International Studies. He is the World Affairs Contributor for CNN and appears weekly on CNN programs. He has written or co-authored ten books—four non-fiction works, four novels and two poetry books. Born in Bangor, Maine, he received a BA in Latin from Bowdoin College (1962), and a law degree from Boston University Law School (1965).

William S. Cohen served as the 20th US Secretary of Defense (January 1997 to January 2001) His appointment marked the first time in modern US history that a President chose an elected official from the other party to be a member of his cabinet. A three-term United States

Senator (1979 to 1997), he also served in the US House of Representatives for three terms (1973 to 1979), and as Mayor of Bangor, Maine (1971 to 1972). While in Congress, he served on the House Judiciary Committee during the impeachment proceedings in 1974 and the Iran-Contra Committee in 1987.

H.E. SHEIKH NAHYAN MABARAK AL NAHYAN is the UAE Minister of Higher Education and Scientific Research since February 2006, after holding earlier positions as the UAE Minister of Education (2004–2006) and the Minister of Higher Education and Scientific Research (1990–2004). He is also the Chancellor of the UAE University (since 1983), Chancellor of the Higher Colleges of Technology (since 1988), and Chancellor of Zayed University (since 1998). H.E. Sheikh Nahyan has thus played a leading and distinguished role in the educational advancements made by the United Arab Emirates. Additionally, H.E. Sheikh Nahyan is very active in the field of industry and is ranked as a successful businessman, both at the UAE and international levels. H.E. Sheikh Nahyan chairs a dynamic international investment group covering banks, construction firms, petrochemical companies, hotels and real estate. He heads or serves as a member of the board of directors of many establishments and corporations.

H.E. Sheikh Nahyan also sponsors and chairs or actively participates in many conferences pertaining to different spheres of life in the UAE and the Gulf region. He also supports several charitable institutions and as the Honorary President of Abu Dhabi's Future Center, devotes special attention to students with special needs. H.E. Sheikh Nahyan has received many honors, awards and medals at the local, regional and international levels, including the Global Advocacy Recognition Award of the Global Association of Teachers of English for Speakers of Other Languages (TESOL); the Sheikh Hamdan bin Rashid Al Maktoum Award for Distinguished Academic Performance (Educational Personality of the Year, 2003); the Civil Order of Oman; and the Crescent of Pakistan Medal. H.E. Sheikh Nahyan completed his high school studies at the Millfield School, UK and thereafter attended Magdalen College, Oxford.

[432]

H.E. DR. FAISAL AL-RUFOUH is Deputy Dean of the Faculty of Humanities and Social Sciences and Chairman of the Political Science Department at the University of Jordan in Amman. Previously, he served as a researcher with the Center for Strategic Studies at the University of Jordan (1986–1990), before becoming a full-time lecturer and Assistant Professor and then an Associate Professor in the Political Science Department of the University. He was granted a professorship in 2003. Dr. Al-Rufouh has also served as Visiting Professor at the Brigham Young University in the United States and as a lecturer at the Royal Jordanian National Defense College. He became Minister of Social Development, then Minister of Administrative Development, and later Minister of Culture in the first government formed during the rule of His Majesty King Abdullah II bin Al Hussein.

Dr. Al-Rufouh has published nine books, in Arabic and English, as well as 40 papers which have appeared in various international journals. Dr. Faisal Al-Rufouh received a Ph.D in International Relations in 1986 from Jawaharlal Nehru University, New Delhi, India, and an M.Phil in International Politics from the School of International Studies in the same university in 1983. He also holds a degree in Political Science from the College of Law and Politics, Baghdad University, awarded in 1979.

DR. RAFIA OBAID GHUBASH has been President of the Arabian Gulf University (AGU) in Manama, Kingdom of Bahrain since April 2001. Previously, she served as Dean of the Faculty of Medicine and Health Sciences (FMHS) at the United Arab Emirates University in Al Ain, UAE from the year 2000. Dr. Ghubash is an active member of several international and Arab Gulf professional societies and academic institutions, including the Emirates Medical Association (UAE) and the Advisory Committee of the Arab Thought Foundation. She is also Deputy Secretary General of the Sheikh Hamdan Bin Rashid Al Maktoum Award in Medical Sciences (UAE). Dr. Ghubash received a Ph.D in social and psychiatric epidemiology from the University of London in 1992.

Dr. Ghubash has published more than 35 scientific papers in leading international journals. Her most significant scientific contributions include participating in the Advisory Committee of the United Nations Development Program for the second Arab Human Development Report (2003) and writing a background paper for the third report (2004). She has also submitted a number of working papers which she has presented at regional and international conferences, the most important of which were delivered at the conferences of the Arab Thought Foundation and other institutions concerned with the reform of higher education.

H.E. DR. IBRAHIM GUIDER has been the Director General of the Cairo-based Arab Labor Organization since 1999. In Libya, he served as the Secretary General (Minister) of the Workforce, Training and Employment (1993–1999), Secretary General of Public Security (1984–1990) and Secretary General of Youth and Sports (1979–1984). He also held a number of posts at the local, Arab and international levels including: Head of Libya's Social Specialists League; Chairman of the Founding Committee of the Arab Specialists Association (1979); Chairman of the Arab Group for Social Security at the International Social Security Association and member of the latter's board of directors (8 years); and member of the International Labor Organization's Governing Body (Geneva) for two terms.

Dr. Ibrahim Guider has published a number of research studies including: "Arab Manpower and Challenges of the Era"; "Human Development: Methods and Programs," "Arab Women and the Process of Production, and "Social Protection for Workers and Productivity Enhancement." Some of his other works include: *The Arab Islamic Revolution; Benefits of Social Security*; *The Development of Human Resources and Policies for Creating New Job Opportunities; The Crises of Culture and Arab Intellectuals;* and *Arab Society and the Challenges of the Era.* In February 2002, Dr. Guider received the Order of Commander of the National Cedar, an honor conferred by the Republic of Lebanon. He holds a Master's degree in the Social Organization of Management and Political Sociology and a Ph.D degree in the Development of Human Resources and Social Economy.

H.E. DR. MASSOUMA AL-MUBARAK has been the Minister of Transport in the State of Kuwait since July 2006. Previously, she was the Minister of Planning and the Minister of State for Administrative Development Affairs since June 2005. The first woman to hold a ministerial post in the history of Kuwait, she is also the first female representative in the Kuwaiti Parliament by virtue of being a minister, in accordance with the Kuwaiti constitution. Dr. Al-Mubarak has held several academic posts, the most recent as the Head of the Political Science Faculty at the University of Kuwait (2001–2002). She was also a Visiting Professor at the Universities of Bahrain (1991) and Denver (Colorado, USA) (1986–1988). She is member of several committees and associations, including the Book Assessment Committee at the Ministry of Information and the National Council for Culture, Arts and Letters (1996–2002); Kuwait University's Faculty Association; as well as a number of public benefit associations such as the Graduates Society; Economists Society; Journalists Society; Kuwaiti Women's Cultural Society; the Human Rights Society of Kuwait; the Kuwaiti Human Rights Committee and the Kuwaiti Women's Issues Committee and the Committee for Review of Women's Affairs.

Dr. Massouma Al-Mubarak's areas of specialization include international relations, international law, international organizations and diplomacy; foreign policies and political development in the Third World; as well as human rights and women's causes. She is a regular writer for a number of daily newspapers including: *As-Siyassah* and *Al Qabas* (Kuwait); *Al Watan* (Saudi Arabia); and *Akhbar Al Khaleej* (Bahrain). Dr. Massouma Al-Mubarak earned a Bachelor's degree in Political Science from Kuwait University (1971), a Diploma in Planning from the Arab Planning Institute, Kuwait (1973), and a Master's degree in Political Science from the Northern Texas University (1976). She received a Ph.D degree in International Relations from the University of Denver (Colorado, USA) in 1982 and also took her Master's degree in International Relations from the same university.

DR. MATTAR AHMED ABDULLAH is Plans and Programs Advisor for the United Nations Development Program in the UAE, a post he has held since 2001. He has sought to establish dialogue between official agencies and various civil society organizations to facilitate the transfer of technical expertise from UN organizations to support development in the UAE. Previously, Dr. Mattar Abdullah was Director of the Census Section of the Abu Dhabi Planning Department, where he supervised the creation of a census database and conducted several field surveys and research projects in Abu Dhabi. He also contributed to business development by issuing various census bulletins, including the *Standard Prices Bulletin, Annual Census Book* and *Abu Dhabi: Facts and Figures* and other publications covering social and economic aspects of the emirate. Before joining the Planning Department, he served in the Ministry of Public Works and Housing as Supervisor of the Surveying and Planning Section, where he helped to prepare the first set of multidimensional topographic maps produced for the country after the establishment of the UAE Federation.

Dr. Mattar Abdullah has made several contributions to issues affecting Emarati society, especially with regard to the population structure, labor force, development and emiratization. He published a book entitled *Khalal al Tarkiyba as Sukaniya wa Toruq I'lajihi* and another entitled *al Tanmia al Rifiya fi Dawlat al Imarat al 'Arabia al Mutahida*. In addition to several articles in local newspapers, he has also published a study titled "Waq'i al Tarkiyba al Sukaniya wa Mostaqbalah fi Dawlat al Imarat al 'Arabia al Mutahida" in the ECSSR *Emirates Lecture Series*. Dr. Mattar obtained a BA in Geography from the University of Cairo in 1976 and a Master's degree from Eastern Michigan University, USA in 1985. He also obtained a Diploma in Demographic Studies from the UN Demographic Institute in Cairo. Dr. Mattar received a Ph.D in Urban Development from the University of Wales, UK, in 1996.

Introduction

1. In terms of numbers, the *Arab Manual on Human Rights and Development*, published by the UNDP and the Arab Organization for Human Rights, counted at least 150 Arab non-governmental organizations working in the field of human rights, either generally or as specialist organizations. This is in addition to eight national human rights societies and four parliamentary human rights committees. See Mohsin Awad (ed.), *Al Dalil al 'Arabi: Hiqoq al Insan wa al Tanmia* (www.arabhumanrights.org/dalil/ch_8.htm).

2. One of these petitions entitled "Shurakaa fi al Watan" (Partners in the Homeland) was submitted to Prince Abdullah bin Abdul Aziz (prior to his accession) by the Shiites on April 30, 2003 and included demands for achieving full equality in citizenship (www.aljazeera.net/NR/exeres/D06168A6-DA8B-4339-9FB7-82A66AE12A3C.htm)

3. The full text of the project was published first in the London-based *Al Hayat* newspaper on February 13, 2004. It may be recalled that the project is an extension of the Middle East Partnership Initiative proposed by the US Department of State on December 12, 2002.

4. For details on all internal and external reform initiatives in the Arab world, see *Arab Human Development Report 2004*, "Towards Freedom in the Arab World" (New York, NY: UNDP Publications, 2005), 25–29.

5. For an in-depth study on political generations in the Arab world, see Volker Perthes, *Arab Elites: Negotiating the Politics of Change* (Boulder, CO and London: Lynne Rienner Publishers, 2004).

6. See Nadir Farjani, "Ihtimalat al Nahda fi al Watan al 'Arabi bain Taqrir al Tanmia al Insaniya al 'Arabia wa Mashrou'i al Sharq al Awsat al Kabir" [The Potential for Renaissance in the Arab World between the Arab Human Development Report and the Broader Middle East Project], *Emirates Lecture Series* no. 88 (Abu Dhabi: Emirates Center for Strategic Studies and Research, 2004), 48.

7. See Haitham Man'aa, "Al Munazamat al 'Arabia Ghair al Hikomiya: Asas al Binaa al Demoqrati wa al Madani" [Arab Non-Governmental Organizations: The Foundation for Democratic and Civil Building], a lecture delivered in 1999 (www.achr.nu/stu5.htm).

Chapter 2

1. United Nations Development Program (UNDP), *Arab Human Development Report 2002* "Creating Opportunities for Future Generations" (New York, NY: UNDP, 2002), 2, 3, 40, 76.

2. The London-based *Al Hayat* published the complete version of the Greater Middle East Initiative on February 13, 2004. Washington presented a scaled down version to the G-8 summit held in Sea Island, Georgia in June 2004. The summit adopted the project under the title: "Partnership for Progress and a Common Future with the Region of the Broader Middle East and North Africa."

3. To view the text of the Pledge of Solidarity and Cohesion see the website of the Palestinian Ministry of Information (www.minfo.gov. ps/documents/arabic/24-05-04.htm).

4. To view the text of "Towards an Initiative for Political Reform in Arab Countries," see the website of the Arabic Network for Human Rights Information (www.hrinfo.net/egypt/cihrs/pr040329.shtml).

5. To view the text of the Alexandria Statement see the website of the Arab Reform Forum (www.arabreformforum.org/ar/document.html).

6. See the text of the "Amman Declaration for Political and Electoral Reform," issued on October 9, 2004, on the Carnegie Endowment for International Peace website (www.carnegieendowment.org/pdf/Amman_Declaration.pdf).

7. To view the complete and final version of the "Roadmap," see the UN website (daccessdds.un.org/doc/UDOC/GEN/N0334877.pdf?Open Element).

8. See the statement issued by the National Campaign for Election Reform on May, 2005 (www.pngo.net/elections/PR_elections_10_05 .htm).

Chapter 4

1. United Nations Development Program, *Arab Human Development Report 2003: Building a Knowledge Society* (New York, NY: UNDP, 2003).

2. World Bank, World Development Reports, various issues.

3. See Antoine B. Zahlan, "Globalization and Science and Technology Policy," *Forum* vol. 4, no. 3, December, 1997–January 1998.

4. UNIDO, Global Industry Reports, various issues.

5. World Bank, op. cit.

6. UNIDO, op. cit.

7. Ibid.

8. World Bank, op. cit.

9. Ibid.

10. UNDP, Arab Human Development Report, 2002.

11. Zahlan, op. cit., 13.

12. Ibid.

13. Ibid.

14. UNDP, Arab Human Development Report, 2003, 73.

15. World Bank op. cit and "The Determinants of FDI in Developing Countries," UNCTAD, 2002.

16. Ibid.

17. Ibid.

18. UNDP, Arab Human Development Report, 2003.

19. World Bank, op. cit.

20. UNDP, Arab Human Development Report, 2002.

21. Ibid.

Chapter 6

1. *The Arab Convention for the Suppression of Terrorism* adopted by the Arab Interior Ministers Council and the Council of Arab Ministers of Justice, Cairo, April 1998, 2.

2. See decisions of the Islamic Jurisprudence Council published on the website of the Muslim World League (http://www.themwl.org/publications)

3. *Arab Convention for the Suppression of Terrorism*, op. cit, 3.

4. Al-Anfâl chapter, verse 60.

5. Al-Ma'ida chapter, verse 33.

6. Quoted from Brigadier Dr. Ali bin Faiz al-Juhni, *Al Fahm al Marfood lil il Irhab al Mafrood* (Riyadh: Naif Arab Academy for Security Sciences, 2001), 186.

7. General Dr. Muhammad Fathi Eid, *Waq'i al Irhab fi al Watan Al 'Arabi* (Riyadh: Naif Arab Academy for Security Sciences, 1999), 137.

8. Ahmed al Hiwaiti et al, *'Alaqat al Jariyma wa al Inhraf fi al Watan Al 'Arabi* (Riyadh: Naif Arab Academy for Security Sciences, 1998), 233.

9. In addition to the previous reference, one can review, 'Atif Abdul Fatah, 'Ajwa, al *Bitala fi al 'Alam Al 'Arabi wa 'Alaqataha bi Al Jariyma* (Riyadh: Arab Center for Security Studies and Training, 1406 Hijri).

10. Khalid al Zawawi, *Al Bitala fi al 'Alam Al 'Arabi al Mushkila wa al Hal* (Cairo: The Nile Arab Group, 2004), 28.

11. Samir Na'eem Ahmed, *Al Muhadidat al Iqtisadiya wa Ijtima'iya lil al Tataruf al Dini fi al Mujtam' al 'Arabi* (Beirut: Pan Arab Studies Center, 1990), 226.

12. Samir Na'eem Ahmed, op. cit., 227.

13. Muhammad Rifqi Isa, "Masadir al Tataruf kama Udrikha al Shabab fi Misr wa al Kuwait, Dirasa Muqarana," *Majalat al Bihooth al Tarbawia*, University of Qatar, Year 7, no. 13 (January 1998), 77–130.

14. Sheikh Muhammad Hayat Al Sindi, *Sharh al Arba'in al Nawawia al Musama Tuhfat al Muhibeen fi Sharh al Arba'in*, commentary by Muhammad Shaib Sharif (Beirut: Dar Ibn Hazm, 2005), 45.

15. Apart from the fact that drug addiction makes the addict vulnerable to criminal gangs, indications are that a bond grows between terrorist

groups and drug-trafficking gangs. By virtue of this connection, each benefits from the capabilities of the other.

Chapter 7

1. See Francis Fukuyama, *The End of History and the Last Man* (London: Penguin Books, 1992), 15.

2. See Al-Arabiya Net, October 11, 2005 (www.alarabiya.net/ Articles/ 2005/10/11/1760.htm).

3. See Al-Arabiya Net September 24, 2005 (www.alarabiya.net/ Articlep. aspx=17075).

4. See "Can Anyone Stop the Rise of Gulf Airlines?" *MEED*, May 6, 2006.

5. Quoted from the website of "Hai'at al-Takhasiyya" in Jordan (www.epc.gov.jo).

6. Quoted from Amal Al Mihairi, "Mohammed bin Zayed: Khaskhasat al Sharikat tastahdif Twa'z'i al Thawara," *Al Ittihad* newspaper, Abu Dhabi, May 1, 2006.

7. Quoted from Reem al-Mahmoud, "Hussain al Nowais: Abu Dhabi lan Tastaqeel min Dawraha tijah al Emarate al Ukhra," *Ash Sharq al Awsat*, London, July 8, 2006.

8. See Mohammad Ezz Al Deen, "World Bank Changes its Policy in the GCC," *Gulf News*, Dubai, February 14, 2006.

9. See Manuel Castells, *The Power of Identity* (Oxford: Blackwell Publishing, 2004), 22.

10. Castells, op. cit., 7-9.

11. Alain Gresh, "Saudi Arabia: Reality Check," *Le Monde Diplomatique*, February 2006 (http://www.mondediplo.com/2006 /02/02saudi).

12. An interview with Al Sheikh Abdul Mohsin al 'Abaikan, *Ash Sharq al Awsat*, London, May 15, 2005.

13. See Nathan J. Brown, Amr Hamzawy, and Marina Ottaway, "Islamist Movements and the Democratic Process in the Arab World: Exploring Gray Zones" *Carnegie Paper no. 67* (Washington, DC: Carnegie Endowment for International Peace, March 2006), 10–11.

14. See Jihad al-Mansi, "Tawqiyf arb'a Nowab Islamiyyn 'ala Khalfiyat al T'aziya fi al-Zaraawi wa Wasf Ahadhom laho bil al Shaheed," *Al Ghad*, Amman, June 12, 2006.

15. See "Panorama: Tafjiyrat Amman wa Dahayaha," Al-Arabiya Net, June 14, 2006 (www.alarabiya.net/Articlep.aspx?p=24709)

16. See Turki Ali al-Rab'ih, "Al Watinya al Mazmoma fi al Khitab al Islami," *Al Hayat*, London, February 4, 2006.

17. See Bruce Rutherford, "The Ballot Box Can Moderate Islamists," *Christian Science Monitor*, February 9, 2006.

18. See "Jabha Mutahida lil al Mu'aradah lil Itaha bi al Nizam al Suri, *Al-Ittihad*, Abu Dhabi, March 18, 2006.

19. See *Le Monde Diplomatique*, op. cit.

20. Quoted from Turki Ali al-Rab'ih, op. cit.

21. On this review and the understanding of Sayid Qutb, Mohammad Qutb and Rachid Ghannouchi of the terms "democracy," "secularism" and "nationalism" see Turki Ali al-Rab'ih, op. cit.

22. Ahmed Kamal Abu Al Majed, "Awlad Haratna li Nageeb Mahfouz Tanal Bra'atha al Islamiya," *Al Hayat*, December 30, 2005.

23. Walid 'Awad, "Hamas sa Tadman al Musa'dat al Kharijiya wa 'Adam Ijbaar al Nisaa ala Irtidaa al Hijab," *Al Quds Al 'Arabi*, London, February 9, 2006.

24. See Ibrahim Gharaiba, "Al Haraka al Islamiya: Hal Takon al Shariyyk al Asasi fi al Tahwlat al Jariya," *Al Hayat*, January 7, 2006.

25. Ibrahim Gharaiba, "Al Ikhwan wa Jabhat al 'Amal," *Al Ghad*, Amman, June 24, 2006.

26. See Castells, op. cit, 1.

27. Castells, op.cit., 19

28. "The World through their Eyes," *The Economist*, February 26 to March 4, 2005, 21.

29. See Samah al Jawhari, "Itlaq akthar min 15 qanat fadaiya Arabiya fi 'Am 2004...wa qanwat al musiqa al akthar intsharan wa Mushada taliyha al Monaw'at," *Ash-Sharaq al-Awsat*, London, December 31, 2004.

30. See *Le Monde Diplomatique*, op. cit.

31. On the dynamics of transferring ethnic conflict from one state to another see David A. Lake and Donald Rothschild (eds), *The International Spread of Ethnic Conflict: Fear, Diffusion, and Escalation* (Princeton, NJ: Princeton University Press), 256.

32. See *Al Siyassah*, Kuwait, May 14, 2004. See also "Al-Kuwait tatahim Iran bi Tajawoz al Hidood al Diplomasiya," *Ash-Sharaq al-Awsat*, London, May 13, 2004.

33. See "Al-Kuwait Takhsha Taqseem al Iraq wa Tohazir min Tafashi al Taifiya fi Dowal al Jiwar," *Ash Sharq al-Awsat*, London, April 12, 2004.

34. See Kuwait News Agency (KUNA), May 12, 2004.

35. For instance, Salah al Fadli wrote in the Kuwaiti *Al Rai al-'Am* on April 13, 2005 commenting on the demand for an interpellation of Ahmed al-Jarallah, the Minister of Health that this revealed that

"under the pretext of equality in citizenship, the simple expressions of courtesy have failed the test." Here the writer points out that some representatives refused the interpellation because it was presented by Shiites and the tribes of al 'Awazim.

36. The Kuwaiti *Al Watan* on April 17, 2004 pointed to the fact that Shiite political functionaries, businessmen and former ministers held meetings intending to form a political bloc named the "National Shiite Bloc." On October 24, 2005 *Al Hayat* published that five Shiite political groups agreed on establishing a Shiite coalition named "Coalition of National Alliances." An official in this coalition announced that they "will work via the constitution and laws but we have issues relating to sectarian discrimination in positions and places of worship."

37. See Hassan M. Fattah, "An Island Kingdom Feels the Ripples from Iraq and Iran," *The New York Times*, April 16, 2006.

38. "Al Islamiyya" Contests the Answer of the Government relating to 'Naturalization' in the Next Session" *Al Wasat*, Bahrain, August 16, 2005, and "Bahraini Societies Demand that the Government Adhere to the Naturalization Act," Al Qanat website, July 2003 (www.alqanat. com/news/shownes.asp?id=14970); and "Bahrain: A Well-attended Debate Demands an Investigation of the Naturalization Process for Gulf and Arab nationals and Withdrawal of Nationality from Undeserving Persons," *Ash Sharq al-Awsat*, London, July 18, 2003.

39. See *Le Monde Diplomatique*, op. cit.

Chapter 8

1. Halil İnalcık, *The Ottoman Empire: The Classical* Age, *1300–1600*, translated by Norman Itzkowitz and Colin Imber (New York, NY:

Praeger, 1973). See also Bernard Lewis, *The Emergence of Modern Turkey* (London: Oxford University Press, 1961).

2. Avigdor Levy, "The Military Policy of Sultan Mahmud II," *International Journal of Middle Eastern Studies* 2 (1971): 21–39.

3. Nur Yalman, "Islamic Reform and Mystic Tradition in Eastern Turkey," *Archives Européenne des Sociologies* 10 (1969): 41–60. See also Niyazi Berkes, *The Development of Secularism in Turkey* (Montreal: McGill University Press, 1964).

4. Carter V. Findley, *Bureaucratic Reform in the Ottoman Empire: The Sublime Porte, 1789–1922* (Princeton, NJ: Princeton University Press, 1980).

5. Şerif Mardin, *The Genesis of Young Ottoman Thought: A Study in the Modernization of Turkish Political Ideas* (Princeton, NJ: Princeton University Press, 1958).

6. Roderic Davison, *Reform in the Ottoman Empire, 1856–1876* (Princeton, NJ: Princeton University Press, 1963).

7. Stanford J. Shaw and Ezel Kural Shaw, *History of the Ottoman Empire and Modern Turkey, Vol. II. Reform, Revolution, and Republic: The Rise of Modern Turkey, 1808–1975* (New York, NY: Cambridge University Press, 1977), 259–60.

8. Shaw and Shaw, op. cit., 249–50.

9. On the late nineteenth-century and early twentieth-century Ottoman period, see Kemal H. Karpat, "The Transformation of the Ottoman Empire, 1789–1908," *International Journal of Middle East Studies* 3 (1972): 243–81; Selim Deringil, *The Well-Protected Domains: Ideology and the Legitimation of Power in the Ottoman Empire, 1876–1909* (London: I.B. Tauris, 1999); and Feroz Ahmad, *The*

Young Turks: The Committee of Union and Progress in Turkish Politics 1904–1914 (Oxford: Clarendon Press, 1969).

10. Uriel Heyd, *Foundations of Turkish Nationalism: The Life and Teachings of Ziya Gökalp* (London: Harvill Press, 1950), 63–8.

11. The Turks began to take surnames in 1934.

12. Dankwart A. Rustow, *Turkey: America's Forgotten Ally* (New York, NY: Council on Foreign Relations, 1987), 13.

13. Dankwart A. Rustow, "Turkey's Liberal Revolution," *Middle East Review* 12 (1985), 5.

14. Kemal H. Karpat, *Turkey's Politics: The Transition to Multi-Party System* (Princeton, NJ: Princeton University Press, 1959), 54.

15. On Atatürk, see Lord Kinross, *Atatürk: A Bibliography of Mustafa Kemal, Father of Modern Turkey* (New York, NY: William Murrow, 1978, 1994), See also Andrew Mango, *Atatürk* (London: John Murray, 1999).

16. On İsmet İnönü, see Metin Heper, *İsmet İnönü: The Making of a Turkish Statesman* (Leiden: Brill, 1998).

17. Halil İnalcık, "The Ottoman Methods of Conquest," *Studia Islamica* vol. 2 (1954): 204–29; idem, "Suleiman the Lawgiver and Ottoman Law" *Archivum Ottomanicum* 1 (1969): 105–38.

18. For an elaboration of this point, see Metin Heper, "Turkey between the East and West," in Emmanuel Adler, Beverly Crawford, Federica Bichi, and Raffaella Del Sarto (eds) *Convergence of Civilizations: Constructing a Mediterranean Region* (Toronto: University of Toronto Press, 2006).

19. David Barchard, *Turkey and the West* (London: Routledge, 1985). See also Metin Heper, Heinz Kramer, and Ayşe Öncü (eds) *Turkey and the West: Changing Political and Cultural Identities* (London: I.B. Tauris, 1993).

20. Dankwart A. Rustow, "Atatürk as Founder of a State," *Daedalus* 98 (1968): 793–823.

21. Heper, *İsmet İnönü*, op. cit., Chapter Six.

22. Şerif Mardin, *Din ve İdeoloji* (Religion and Ideology) (Ankara: Sevinç Matbaası, 1969), 137.

23. Reported in *Milliyet*, Istanbul, February 2, 1994.

24. Peter Suzuki, "Encounters with Istanbul: Urban Peasants and Village Peasants," *International Journal of Comparative Sociology* vol. 5, no. 2 (1964), 213.

25. Ned Levine, "Value Orientations among Migrants in Ankara, Turkey," *Asian and African Studies* vol. 8, nos. 1–2 (1973), 58.

26. The author had earlier reported these findings on the identity transformation and cognitive secularization of Turks as well as the related references in his study, "Islam and Democracy in Turkey: Toward a Reconciliation?" *The Middle East Journal* vol. 51, no. 1 (Winter 1997): 34–5.

27. *Milliyet*, April 9, 1993. The 1993 survey was carried by Professor Binnaz Toprak of Boğaziçi University and Professor Ali Çarkoğlu of Sabancı University. Both universities are in Istanbul.

28. For the revival of Islam in Turkey, too, see Jeremy Salt, "Nationalism and the Rise of Muslim Sentiment in Turkey," *Middle Eastern Studies* vol. 31, no. 1 (1995): 12–27.

29. To give just one example, while in the 1973 national elections, the National Salvation Party (NSP) had garnered 11.8 percent of the votes, in the 1977 national elections its vote dropped to 8.3 per cent. In both 1973 and 1977, the NSP was the only religiously-oriented party that competed in the elections.

30. This is what the author's colleague used to say when both were serving as part-time faculty members at the Turkish Naval Academy in Istanbul in the early 1980s. The military in Turkey has always been a staunchly secularist institution and those teaching them have always been carefully picked from among faculty members presumed to have a similar inclination.

31. Reported in Heper, *İsmet İnönü*, op. cit., 131.

32. Heper, *İsmet İnönü*, op. cit., 188.

33. Heper, *İsmet İnönü*, op. cit., 187.

34. Metin Heper, "A Weltanschauung-Turned-Partial Ideology and Normative Ethics: 'Atatürkism' in Turkey" *Orient* 25, no. 1 (1984), 88.

35. Heper, *İsmet İnönü*, op. cit., 43.

36. Giovanni Sartori, *The Theory of Democracy Revisited. Part One: The Contemporary Debate* (Chatham, NJ: Chatham House Publishers, 1987), 51–5. See also Sartori, *The Theory of Democracy Revisited. Part Two: The Classical Issues* (Chatham, NJ: Chatham House Publishers, 1987), 269.

37. In the civics books during the Atatürk period, one did not come across "Atatürkism" with the suffix "ism." See Türker Alkan, "Turkey: Rise and Decline of Legitimacy in a Revolutionary Regime," *Journal of South Asian and Middle Eastern Studies* 4 (1980), 37–48. The term "Atatürkism" was coined in the post-Atatürk period.

38. These developments are discussed at length in Metin Heper, *The State Tradition in Turkey* (Walkington, UK: The Eothen Press, 1985), Chapter Four.

39. The author has first developed this argument in his study "The 'Strong State' and Democracy: The Turkish Case in Comparative and Historical Perspective," in S. N. Eisenstadt (ed) *Democracy and Modernity* (Leiden: E. J. Brill, 1992).

40. Kemal. H. Karpat, "Turkish Democracy at Impasse: Ideology, Party Politics and the Third Military Intervention," *International Journal of Turkish Studies* 2 (1981): 1–43; Ergun Özbudun, "Turkish Party System: Institutionalization, Polarization and Fragmentation," *Middle Eastern Studies* 17 (1981): 228–40; and Metin Heper and Filiz Başkan, "The Politics of Coalition Government in Turkey, 1961–1999," *International Journal of Turkish Studies* 7 (Summer 2001): 68–89.

41. Heper, *The State Tradition in Turkey*, op. cit., Chapter Six.

42. Metin Heper and Menderes Çınar, "Parliamentary Government with a Strong President: The Post–1989 Turkish Experience," *Political Science Quarterly* vol.111, no. 3 (Fall 1996): 493.

43. Metin Heper, "The Justice and Development Party Government and the Military in Turkey," *Turkish Studies* vol. 6, no. 2 (2005): 215–31.

44. Halil İnalcık, "[Turkey:] The Nature of Traditional Society," in Robert E. Ward and Dankwart A Rustow (eds) *Political Modernization in Japan and Turkey* (Princeton, NJ: Princeton University Press, 1964), 44.

45. M. N. Turfan, *Rise of the Young Turks: Politics, Military and the Ottoman Collapse* (London: I. B. Tauris, 1998).

46. William Hale, *Turkish Politics and the Military* (London: Routledge, 1994), 91–2.

47. Metin Heper, 'The European Union, the Turkish Military, and Democracy," *South European Society and Politics* vol. 10, no. 1 (April 2005): 33–44.

48. The military gave briefings on the "threat" to members of the judiciary, universities and the media. The public at large joined the bandwagon, by turning their lights on and off at 9.00 p.m. every evening so as to register their protest against the government. In the event, Prime Minister Erbakan and his cabinet felt obliged to resign. For the full story, see Metin Heper, "Civil–Military Relations, Political Islam and Security: The Turkish Case," in Constantine P. Danopoulos, Dhirendra Vajpey, and Amir Bar-or (eds) *Civil–Military Relations, Nation-Building, and National Identity: Comparative Perspectives* (Westport, CT and London: Praeger, 2004), 191.

49. In the event, the author and his colleague chose not to respond to this question and quickly changed the subject! On the military and politics in Turkey, see inter alia, Kemal H. Karpat, "Military Interventions: Army–Civilian Relations in Turkey Before and After 1980," in Metin Heper and Ahmet Evin (eds) *State, Democracy and the Military: Turkey in the 1980s* (Berlin and New York, NY: Walter de Gruyter, 1988); George Harris, "The Role of the Military in Turkey: Guardians or Decision-Makers?" in Heper and Evin, op. cit.; Hale, *Turkish Politics and the Military*, op. cit., and Metin Heper and Aylin Güney, "The Military and the Consolidation of Democracy: The Recent Turkish Experience," *Armed Forces and Society* vol. 26, no 4 (Summer 2000): 635–57.

50. Reported in Heper, "The European Union, the Turkish Military and Democracy," op. cit., 41.

51. The Sheikh was Mehmet Esat Coşan, and his order was the Nakshibendi Order.

52. On the NSP, see Jacob M. Landau, "The National Salvation Party in Turkey," *Asian and African Studies* 11 (1976): 1–57 and Türker Alkan, "The National Salvation Party in Turkey" in Metin Heper and Raphael Israel (eds) *Islam and Politics in the Modern Middle East* (Beckenham, UK: Croom Helm, 1984).

53. Jenny White, "Pragmatist or Ideologues: Turkey's Welfare Party in Power," *Current History* vol. 94, no. 588 (1995): 7–12; M. Kamrava, "Pseudo-Democratic Politics: The Rise and Demise of Turkey's Refah Party," *British Journal of Middle Eastern Studies* vol. 25, no. 2 (1998): 275–302; Haldun Gülalp, "Political Islam in Turkey: The Rise and the Fall of the Refah Party," *The Muslim World* vol. 89, no. 1 (1999): 22–44. See also Gülalp, "Globalization and Political Islam: The Social Base of Turkey's Welfare Party," *International Journal of Middle East Studies* 33 (2001): 507–59.

54. The secular Republic had converted Haghia Sofia into a museum.

55. On "National View," see Ahmet Yıldız, "Politico-Religious Discourse of Political Islam in Turkey: The Parties of National Outlook," *The Muslim World* vol. 93, no. 2 (April 2003): 187–209 and Fulya Atacan, "Explaining Religious Politics at the Crossroad: AKP–SP," *Turkish Studies* vol. 6, no. 2 (June 2005): 187–99.

56. Binnaz Toprak, "Islam and Democracy in Turkey," *Turkish Studies* vol. 6, no. 2, (June 2005): 167–86.

57. On the Virtue Party, see Gérard Groc, "The Virtue Party: An Experiment in Democratic Transition," in Stefanos Yerasimos, Günter Seufert and Karin Vorhoff (eds) *Civil Society in the Grip of Nationalism: Studies on Political Culture in Contemporary Turkey* (Istanbul: Orient Institut-Institutes Français d'Études Anatoliennes,

2000) and Birol Yeşilada, "The Virtue Party," in Barry Rubin and Metin Heper (eds) *Political Parties in Turkey* (London: Frank Cass, 2002).

58. On the JDP, see Metin Heper, "The Victory of the Justice and Development Party in Turkey," *Mediterranean Politics* vol. 8, no. 1 (Spring 2003): 127–34. See also Heper, "A Democratic-Conservative Government by Pious People: The Justice and Development Party in Turkey" in Ibrahim M. Abu-Rabi (ed.) *Blackwell Companion to Contemporary Islamic Thought* (New York, NY: Blackwell, 2005); and Erhan Doğan, "The Historical and Discursive Roots of the Justice and Development Party's EU Stance," *Turkish Studies* vol. 6, no. 3 (September 2005), 421–37. On Recep Tayyip Erdoğan, see Metin Heper and Şule Toktaş, "Islam, Modernity and Democracy in Contemporary Turkey: The Case of Recep Tayyip Erdoğan" *The Muslim World* vol. 93, no. 2 (April 2003): 157–85.

Chapter 10

1. Shaun Breslin, Richard Higgott and Ben Rosamond, "Regions in Comparative Perspective," in Shaun Breslin et al, *New Regionalisms in the Global Political Economy* (London: Routledge, 2002),13.

2. For two important views on this, see Alan S. Milward, *The European Rescue of the Nation-State* (London and New York, NY: Routledge, 2000); Robert Jackson, "Sovereignty in World Politics: A Glance at the Conceptual and Historical Landscape," in Jackson (ed.) *Sovereignty at the Millennium* (Oxford: Blackwell, 1999), 31.

3. *The Responsibility to Protect: Report of the International Commission on Intervention and State Sovereignty* (Ottawa: International Development Research Centre, December 2001).

4. This section is based on Amitav Acharya, "So Similar, Yet So Different," *Straits Times,* Singapore, January 4, 2006.

5. For an extended discussion of the similarities and differences in the origins of ASEAN and GCC, see Amitav Acharya, "Regionalism and Regime Security in the Third World: Comparing the Origins of the ASEAN and the GCC" in Brian L. Job (ed.) *The (In)security Dilemma: National Security of Third World States* (Boulder, CO: Lynne Rienner, 1991), 143–164.

6. Amitav Acharya, "Regional Military-Security Cooperation in the Third World: A Conceptual Analysis of the Association of Southeast Asian Nations," *Journal of Peace Research*, vol. 29, no. 1 (January 1992): 7–21.

7. On the evolution of the GCC member's relations with the United States, see Amitav Acharya, *US Military Strategy in the Gulf: Origins and Evolution under the Carter and Reagan Administrations* (London and New York: Routledge, 1989).

8. Amitav Acharya, "Politics, Security and Regionalism in the Gulf: A Review Article," *Gulf Report*, no. 22 (June 1989), 28–33.

9. Amitav Acharya, "Association of Southeast Asian Nations: Security Community or Defence Community?" *Pacific Affairs*, vol. 64, no. 2 (Summer 1991): 159–178.

10. For an extensive review of security cooperation in the GCC, see Amitav Acharya, *The Gulf Cooperation Council and Security: Dilemmas of Dependence 1981–88* (London: Gulf Centre for Strategic Studies, 1989); see also Acharya, "Gulf States' Efforts to Ensure Collective Security," *Pacific Defence Reporter*, vol.12, no.10 (July 1986), 11–13.

11. Amitav Acharya, *The Quest for Identity: International Relations of Southeast Asia* (Singapore: Oxford University Press, 2000).

12. Ghanim Alnajjar, The GCC and Iraq," *Middle East Policy*, vol. vi, no. 4, October 1, 2000.

13. For an earlier overview of the complexities in the US–GCC relationship, see John Duke Anthony, "The US–GCC Relationship: A Glass Half-Empty or Half-Full? *Middle East Policy*, May 1, 1997; F. Gregory Gause III, "The Approaching Turning Point: The Future of US Relations with the Gulf States," Saudi-American Forum, May 20, 2003 (http://www.Saudi-American-Forum.org.)

14. See for example, two reports issued by the Stanley Foundation: "The Future of Persian Gulf Security: Alternatives for the 21st Century," September 3–5, 2005, and "The United States, Iran, and Saudi Arabia: Necessary Steps Toward a New Gulf Security Order," *Policy Dialogue Brief*, October 20–22, 2005 (Warrenton, VA: The Stanley Foundation).

15. Andrew Rathmell, Theodore Karasik and David Gompert, *A New Persian Gulf Security System*, Issue Paper (Santa Monica, CA: RAND Corporation, 2003).

16. A concert is a group of great powers that assume the primary responsibility for managing regional or international security affairs. The relevant model is the European Concert, which assumed responsibility for managing European security order following the defeat of Napoleon and the Congress of Vienna. In Asia, a Concert model for managing the Korean Peninsula conflict has received much attention, and the ongoing Six-Party Talks can be seen as the kernel of a limited Concert approach to Northeast Asian security. See Amitav Acharya, "A Concert of Asia?" *Survival*, vol. 41, no. 3 (Autumn 1999), 84–101.

17. Rathmell, Karasik and Gompert, op. cit., 9.

18. Joseph McMillan, Richard Sokolsky and Andrew C. Winner, "Toward a New Regional Security Architecture," *Washington Quarterly,* vol. 26, no. 3 (Summer 2003):161–175.

19. *The Future of Persian Gulf Security: Alternatives for the 21ˢᵗ Century*, op. cit., 2.

20. Amitav Acharya, "East Asian Integration is Test for Big Powers," *Financial Times*, December 14, 2005.

21. David Priess, "The Gulf Cooperation Council: Prospects for Expansion," *Middle East Policy*, January 1, 1998.

22. On the concept of security community, see Emanuel Adler and Michael Barnett, *Security Communities* (Cambridge: Cambridge University Press, 1998). The specific application of the concept to Southeast Asia can be found in Amitav Acharya, *Constructing a Security Community in Southeast Asia: ASEAN and the Problem of Regional Order* (London and New York, NY: Routledge, 2001).

Chapter 11

1. Sheri Berman, "Civil Society and the Collapse of the Weimar Republic," *World Politics*, vol. 49, no. 3, April 1997.

2. Motoko Mekata, "Building Partnership Toward a Common Goal: Experiences of the International Campaign to Ban Landmines" in Ann M. Florini (ed.) *The Third Force* (Washington, DC: Carnegie Endowment for International Peace, 2000), 143-176.

3. Marina Ottaway and Thomas Carothers, *Funding Virtue: Civil Society Aid and Democracy Promotion* (Carnegie Endowment for International Peace, 2000).

4. Eva Bellin, *Stalled Democracy: Capital, Labor and the Paradox of State-sponsored Development* (Ithaca, NY: Cornell University Press, 2002).

5. Samuel Huntington, *Political Order in Changing Societies* (New Haven, CT: Yale University Press, 1968).

Chapter 13

1. See Immanuel Kant, Appendix to "Observations on the Feeling of the Beautiful and Sublime," in *Kant's Works*, vol. 2 (New York, NY: Mysl Publishers, 1964) 206.

2. See Plato, "Gorgiy II," *Collected Works*, vol. 1 (New York: NY: Mysl Publishers, 1990), 524.

3. Ibid, 524–6.

4. Ibid.

5. For further details, see W. F. Ogburn, *Social Change* (London: Routledge and Kegan Paul, 1922).

6. For further details, see Anthony Smith, *Social Change* (New York, NY: Alfred Knopf, 1976).

7. For further details, see UNDP, *Human Development Report 1990* (New York, NY: Oxford University Press, 1990).

8. *Al-Hayat* daily, February 13, 2004.

9. Ibid.

10. See Nader Fergany, "Higher Education in Arab Countries: Human Development and Labour Market Requirements," (Cairo: Almishkat Centre for Research, 2001), available online (www. almishkat.org).

11. Ibid.

12. For further details, see S. Qasem, "The Arab States," in *UNESCO World Science Report* (London: Oxford University Press, 1998), 151–165.

13. See M. Sid-Ahmed, "Review of Antoine Zahlan's work, "The Challenges of Science and Technology: Progress without Change," in "Technological Challenge," *Al-Ahram Weekly*, October 14–20, 1999.

14. Ibid.

15. See M. El-Sayed Said, "In Search of Researchers," *Al-Ahram Weekly*, November 4–10, 1999.

16. See UNDP, *Arab Human Development Report 2003* (New York, NY: Oxford University Press, 2003), particularly Tables A-2, A-3, A-4.

17. These remarks are put together from the Keynote Address of Mervat Tallawy (Secretary General, United Nations Economic and Social Commission for Western Asia), to the Second Annual Conference of the Arab International Women's Forum (AIWF) "Women in the Arab World: Windows of Opportunity Opening Wider in Business and Public Life," London, October 23, 2003, ESCWA, Press Release, October 27, 2003.

18. See Human Rights Watch, "The Internet in the Mideast and North Africa: Free Expression and Censorship," May 1999. Available at Human Rights Watch website (http://www.hrw.org/hrw/advocacy/ internet/ mena/int-mena.htm).

19. See: J. Lincoln, *Middle East Governments on the World Wide Web,* Working Paper, no. 6, Washington Institute for Near East Policy Research, February 1999, 1.

20. See Ithiel da Sola Pool, *Technologies without Boundaries* (Cambridge, MA: Harvard University Press, 1990), 8. For a learned discussion of Da Sola Pool, in the context of the Middle East, see Jon W. Anderson, *Arabizing the Internet, The Emirates Occasional Papers*, no. 30 (Abu Dhabi: ECSSR, 1998).

21. See C. Bryant, "Civic Nation, Civil Society, Civil Religion," in J.A. Hall (ed.) *Civil Society: Theory, History, Comparison* (Cambridge, MA: Polity Press, 1995), 136–157.

22. For further details, see Paul Wapner, "Politics Beyond the State: Environmental Activism and World Civic Politics," *World Politics*, vol. 47 (April 1995): 311–340.

23. For further details, see J. Cohen and A. Arato, *Civil Society and Political Theory* (Cambridge, MA: MIT, 1992).

24. Ibid.19.

25. See Alejandro Portes and A. Douglas Kincaid, "The Crisis of Authoritarianism: State and Civil Society in Argentina, Chile and Uruguay," *Research in Political Sociology*, vol.1 (1985): 54.

26. See G. Ekiert, "Democratization Processes in Eastern Central Europe: A Theoretical Reconsideration," *British Journal of Political Science*, vol. 21 (1991): 26–55.

27. The Amman Declaration, April 1999, is the founding document of the Middle East Virtual Community (MEVC), which is a regional endeavor to establish a network of individuals in the Middle East through the use of ICT. For further details on MEVC, refer to Michael Hudson, "Information Technology, International Politics and Political Change in the Arab World," available online (http://nmit.georgetown. edu/index/workingpapers.html).

Chapter 14

1. Muhammad Dikare, "Higher Education in the Twenty-first Century: A Vision and Action" (in Arabic), paper presented at UNESCO's Global Conference on Global Education, Paris, October 5–9, 1998.

2. Hamad Ali al Sulaiti and Ahmed Ali al Sidawi, "The Project of Envisaging Educational Work in the Arabian Gulf" (in Arabic) (Riyadh: Arab Education Bureau for the GCC States, 1998).

3. Hamid Ammar, "Education Concerns in the Arab World" (in Arabic), an interview, *Al Ma'rifa* magazine, no. 41, December 1998 (www.bab.com/articles/full_article.cfm?id=2571).

4. Salem Mubarak al Falaq, "A Nation at Risk: An Approach to Education Curricula in the Arab World," (in Arabic) November 1, 2005 (www.saaid.net/manahej/45.htm).

5. Final Report of the Ninth Conference of Ministers of Higher Education and Scientific Research in the Arab World, Arab League Educational, Cultural and Scientific Organization, Damascus, December 5–18, 2003.

6. Abdul Razaq Faris al Faris, "The Project of Envisaging Educational Work in the Arab World," (in Arabic). See website of the Arab Education Bureau for the GCC States, 1998.

7. Hamid Ammar, op. cit.

8. Sa'eed Abdullah Harib, "A Forward Vision" (in Arabic), Human Development Debate to honor Dr. Osama al Kholi, Arabian Gulf University, the Kingdom of Bahrain, 2003.

9. Report on the Development of Universal Education in the GCC States, Riyadh, Secretariat General of the GCC States, 2004.

10. The Minister of Education announces the aims and plans for developing education by 2020 based on the foundations of modernity and increasing fusion with society to serve universal development, UAE-based *Al Bayan*, September 1, 1999.

11. In this section on the Kingdom of Bahrain, I have relied on the interview with Dr. Ali Fakhro, the former Minister of Education and Health, Bahrain-based *Al Wasat*, December 2, 2005.

12. Ibid.

13. The Final Report of the Program of Strategic Planning in the Field of Education, organized by the Arab Center for Educational Training for the GCC States, Doha, Qatar, January 11–14, 2004.

14. Ibid.

15. GCC Secretariat General, "Development of Universal Education in the GCC States," January 2004, a report based on the directives mentioned in the decision of the Supreme Council, Session 23, Doha, December 2002.

16. Report on "Development of Universal Education in the GCC States," op cit.

17. Suhail bin Salem al Kathiri, "The Strategy of Developing Higher Education in the Sultanate" (in Arabic), *Oman* newspaper, January 1, 2006.

18. Ibid.

19. "The Higher Council for Education Develops the Criteria for the National Curricula of the State of Qatar" (in Arabic), *Al Watan* newspaper, December 1, 2005.

20. Ibid.

21. Ahmed Bishara, "The Silent Crisis in Education" (in Arabic), the Kuwait-based *Al Qabas* newspaper, April 11, 2005.

22. Ibid.

23. Ibid.

24. Salem Mubarak Al Falaq, "A Nation at Risk," op. cit.

25. Rafia Obaid Gubash, "Arab Education: Reality and Methods of Development," a study presented to the Arab Forum on Education, Beirut, Lebanon, February 7–20, 2004.

26. Ali al Hawat, Remarks on Chapter Four: "Building Human Capabilities and Education" in Arab Human Development Report, 2002, prepared by the UNDP and Arab Fund for Economic and Social Development.

27. Hamed Ammar, op. cit.

28. Muhammad Dikare, op. cit.

29. Sidqi 'Abdean, "Reforming Universities: A Korean Vision" (in Arabic), *Al Khaleej* newspaper, February 7, 2006.

30. Muhammad Jawad Rida, "The Driving Forces and Inertia in the Universities and Institutions of Higher Education: Harmonizing Output with the Requirements of Development in the GCC States," Bahrain, December 28–29, 2004.

31. Ibid.

32. Abdullah Yusuf Al-Ghanim, "Universities and Institutions" (in Arabic), in the book entitled *The University Debate Today and Future Horizons* (in Arabic), University of Kuwait, November 25–27, 1996.

33. Arab Human Development Report, 2003, 72.

34. Arab Human Development Report, 2003, 273.

35. Sidqi 'Abdean, op. cit.

36. op.cit.

37. The *Arab Human Development Report 2003: Towards Founding a Knowledge-based Society, UNDP.*

38. Ibid.

39. Ibid.

40. Muhammad Jawad Rida, op. cit.

41. Mahmoud Dikare, op. cit.

Chapter 15

1. See Salim Al Abdali, "Economic Concerns: Arab Brain Drain," Part 2, *Al Watan* daily, Oman (www.alwatan.com/graphics/2005/02feb/6.2/dailyhtml/opinion.html).

2. *Al-Balagh* online newspaper. "Two Billion Dollars in Losses due to Arab Brain Drain" (www.balagh.com/thagafa/zp04kv5x.htm).

3. Ibid.

4. See United Nations Educational Scientific and Cultural Organization, *World Science Report* (Paris: UNESCO, 1998).

5. *Al-Balagh* online newspaper "Halting the Brain Drain?" (www.balagh. com/thagafa/shopdnp.htm).

6. See General Secretariat, Arab Inter-Parliamentary Union, "Memo by the General Secretariat on Arab Brain Drain: Drawing up Clear Policies to Absorb Talented Arabs and Curb their Migration Abroad," *Al Barlaman Al Arabi Journal*, Year 22, no. 82 (Damascus: AIPU, December 2001).

Chapter 16

1. See United Nations Development Program, *Arab Human Development Report 2002: Creating Opportunities for Future Generations* (New York, NY: UNDP, 2002)

2. UN General Assembly, "A Detailed Guide for Implementing the UN Declaration about the Millennium: The Report of the Secretary General."

3. See *Arab Human Development Report 2002*, op. cit.

4. Kuwait Ministry of Planning and Administrative Development Affairs, "Country Profile" (State of Kuwait), report submitted to the Economic and Social Commission for Western Asia (ESCWA).

5. Ministry of Social Affairs and Labor of Kuwait, "Annual Report," 2004.

6. Kuwait Ministry of Planning and Administrative Development Affairs, *Al Majmo'ua al Ihsaiyya*, various publications.

7. Kuwait Ministry of Planning and Administrative Development Affairs, *Al Simaat al Asasiyya lil al Sukan wa al Qowa al 'Amila*, various publications.

8. Ibid.

9. Kuwait Ministry of Planning and Administrative Development Affairs, "The Report of the State of Kuwait on the Millennium Development Goals: Achievements and Challenges," April 2003.

10. See Kuwait University, database of registered students and graduates.

11. *Al Simaat al Asasiyya lil al Sukan wa al Qowa al 'Amila*, op. cit.

12. See the Economic and Social Commission for Western Asia, Report of the Arab Women's Center, 2003 (New York, NY: ESCWA, 2003).

Chapter 17

1. See United Nations, *International Migration Report 2002* (New York, NY: United Nations Publications, 2002). Available online (www.un.org/esa/population/publications/ittmig2002/ittmigrep2002arab.doc). Data and statistics given in this part of the chapter have been taken primarily from this source.

2. Ibid.

3. See John Gordon Lorimer, *Dalil al Khaleej al-'Arabi*, translated by the office of the H.H. the Emir of Qatar, Department of History, C1–6, Department of Geography C1–7 (Doha: 1984).

4. See Singapore Department of Statistics, *Statistics Singapore 2006*.

5. See United Nations, *World Population Policies 2005* (New York, NY: UN Publications, 2006.

6. "Europe fears consequences of the migration time bomb," *Al Yaum Al Electroni*, August 25, 2004 (www.alyaum.com/issue/page.php?IN=11394&p=15)

7. "The Labor Force File in the Gulf" "Bil Mirsad" program, Al Arabiya satellite channel, Dubai, April 22, 2004 (www.alarabiya.net/article.aspx?v=5276)

8. GCC Secretariat General, *Statistics Publication*, no 13 (Riyadh: Information Center, Department of Statistics, 2004).

9. Ibid.

10. *Al Bayan* newspaper, Dubai, February 13, 2006, 8.

11. An interview with Dr. Gazi al-Qusaibi, "Ida'aat" program, Al Arabiya satellite channel, Dubai, June 1, 2004.

12. UAE *Human Resource Report 2005* (Dubai: The National Human Resource Development and Employment Authority, 2005).

13. United Nations Development Program. *Human Development Report 2005: International Cooperation at a Crossroads: Aid, Trade and Security in an Unequal World* (New York, NY: UNDP, 2005). Available online (www.un.org/arabic/esa/hdr/2005/pdf/hdr05_ar_complete.pdf).

14. "Zayed warns against the imbalance of the population structure in the UAE," Al-Jazeera Net, December 2, 2003 (www.aljazeera.net/News/archive/archive?Archive=65710).

BIBLIOGRAPHY

'Ajwa, 'Atif Abdul Fatah. Al *Bitala fi al 'Alam Al 'Arabi wa 'Alaqataha bi Al Jariyma* (Riyadh: Arab Center for Security Studies and Training, 1406 Hijri).

Abu Al Majed, Ahmed Kamal. "Awlad Haratna li Nageeb Mahfouz Tanal Bra'atha al Islamiya." *Al Hayat,* December 30, 2005.

Acharya, Amitav. "Gulf States' Efforts to Ensure Collective Security." *Pacific Defence Reporter*, vol.12, no.10 (July 1986).

Acharya, Amitav. "A Concert of Asia?" *Survival*, vol. 41, no. 3 (Autumn 1999).

Acharya, Amitav. "Association of Southeast Asian Nations: Security Community or Defence Community?" *Pacific Affairs*, vol. 64, no. 2 (Summer 1991).

Acharya, Amitav. "East Asian Integration is Test for Big Powers." *Financial Times*, December 14, 2005.

Acharya, Amitav. "Politics, Security and Regionalism in the Gulf: A Review Article." *Gulf Report*, No. 22 (June 1989).

Acharya, Amitav. "Regional Military-Security Cooperation in the Third World: A Conceptual Analysis of the Association of Southeast Asian Nations." *Journal of Peace Research*, vol. 29, no. 1 (January 1992): 7–21.

Acharya, Amitav. "Regionalism and Regime Security in the Third World: Comparing the Origins of the ASEAN and the GCC" in Brian L. Job (ed.) *The (In)security Dilemma: National Security of Third World States* (Boulder, CO: Lynne Rienner, 1991).

[467]

Acharya, Amitav. "So Similar, Yet So Different," *Straits Times,* Singapore, January 4, 2006.

Acharya, Amitav. *Constructing a Security Community in Southeast Asia: ASEAN and the Problem of Regional Order* (London and New York, NY: Routledge, 2001).

Acharya, Amitav. *The Gulf Cooperation Council and Security: Dilemmas of Dependence 1981–88* (London: Gulf Centre for Strategic Studies, 1989).

Acharya, Amitav. *The Quest for Identity: International Relations of Southeast Asia* (Singapore: Oxford University Press, 2000).

Acharya, Amitav. *US Military Strategy in the Gulf: Origins and Evolution under the Carter and Reagan Administrations* (London and New York, NY: Routledge, 1989).

Adler, Emanuel and Michael Barnett. *Security Communities* (Cambridge: Cambridge University Press, 1998).

Ahmad, Feroz. *The Young Turks: The Committee of Union and Progress in Turkish Politics 1904–1914* (Oxford: Clarendon Press, 1969).

Ahmed, Samir Na'eem. *Al Muhadidat al Iqtisadiya wa Ijtima'iya lil al Tataruf al Dini fi al Mujtam' al 'Arabi* (Beirut: Pan Arab Studies Center, 1990).

Al Abdali, Salim. "Economic Concerns: Arab Brain Drain," Part 2, *Al Watan,* Oman (www.alwatan.com/graphics/2005/02feb/6.2/dailyhtml/ opinion. html).

Al Arabiya. "The Labor Force File in the Gulf." *Bil Mirsad* program, Dubai, April 22, 2004 (www.alarabiya.net/article. aspx?v=5276)

Al Arabiya. An interview with Dr. Gazi al-Qusaibi, *Ida'aat* program, Dubai, June 1, 2004.

Al Bayan. UAE, February 13, 2006.

Al Bayan. UAE, September 1, 1999.

Al Fadli, Salah. *Al Rai al'Am.* Kuwait, April 13, 2005.

Al Faris, Abdul Razaq Faris. "The Project of Envisaging Educational Work in the Arab World" (in Arabic). Website of the Arab Education Bureau for the GCC States, Riyadh, 1998.

Al Faris, Sa'eed Abdullah Harib. "A Forward Vision" (in Arabic). Human Development Debate to honor Dr. Osama al Kholi, Arabian Gulf University, Kingdom of Bahrain, 2003).

Al Hawat, Ali. Remarks on Chapter Four: "Building Human Capabilities and Education" in Arab Human Development Report, 2002. UNDP and Arab Fund for Economic and Social Development.

Al Hayat, London, October 24, 2005.

Al Hiwaiti, Ahmed et al. *'Alaqat al Jariyma wa al Inhraf fi al Watan Al 'Arabi* (Riyadh: Naif Arab Academy for Security Sciences, 1998).

Al Jawhari, Samah. "Itlaq akthar min 15 qanat fadaiya Arabiya fi 'Am 2004…wa qanwat al musiqa al akthar intsharan wa Mushada taliyha al Monaw'at." *Ash Sharaq al-Awsat*, London, December 31, 2004.

Al Kathiri, Suhail bin Salem. "The Strategy of Developing Higher Education in the Sultanate" (in Arabic). *Oman,* January 1, 2006.

Al Khaleej. 'Abdean, Sidqi. "Reforming Universities: A Korean Vision" (in Arabic), February 7, 2006.

Al Mihairi, Amal. "Mohammed bin Zayed: Khaskhasat al Sharikat tastahdif Twa'z'i al Thawara." *Al Ittihad*, Abu Dhabi, May 1, 2006.

Al Qanat. "Bahraini Societies Demand that the Government Adhere to the Naturalization Act." July 2003 (www.alqanat.com/news/shownes. asp?id=14970);

Al Sindi, Sheikh Muhammad Hayat. *Sharh al Arba'in al Nawawia al Musama Tuhfat al Muhibeen fi Sharh al Arba'in*, commentary by Muhammad Shaib Sharif (Beirut: Dar Ibn Hazm, 2005).

Al Siyassah. Kuwait, May 14, 2004.

Al Sulaiti, Hamad Ali and Ahmed Ali al Sidawi. "The Project of Envisaging Educational Work in the Arabian Gulf" (in Arabic). Website of the Arab Education Bureau for the GCC States, Riyadh, 1998.

Al Wasat. "Al-Islamiyya Contests the Answer of the Government relating to 'Naturalization' in the Next Session." Bahrain, August 16, 2005.

Al Watan. Kuwait, April 17, 2004.

Al Watan. "The Higher Council for Education Develops the Criteria for the National Curricula of the State of Qatar" (in Arabic). Kuwait, December 1, 2005.

Al Yaum Al Electroni. "Europe Fears Consequences of the Migration 'Time Bomb.'" August 25, 2004 (www.alyaum.com/issue/page.php?IN= 11394&p=15).

Al Zawawi, Khalid. *Al Bitala fi al 'Alam Al 'Arabi al Mushkila wa al Hal* (Cairo: The Nile Arab Group, 2004).

Al-Arabiya Net. "Panorama: Tafjiyrat Amman wa Dahayaha." June 14, 2006 (www.alarabiya.net/Articlep.aspx?p=24709)

Al-Arabiya Net. October 11, 2005 (www.alarabiya.net/ Articles/2005/10/ 11/1760.htm).

Al-Arabiya Net. September 24, 2005 (www.alarabiya.net/ Articlep.aspx =17075).

Al-Balagh. "Halting Brain Drain?" (www.balagh.com/thagafa/shopdnp. htm).

Al-Balagh. "Two Billion Dollars in Losses due to Arab Brain Drain" (www. balagh.com/thagafa/zp04kv5x.htm).

Al-Ghanim, Abdullah Yusuf. "Universities and Institutions" in *The University Debate Today and Future Horizons* (in Arabic). University of Kuwait, November 25–27, 1996.

Al-Hayat. February 13, 2004.

Al-Ittihad. "Jabha Mutahida lil al Mu'aradah lil Itaha bi al Nizam al Suri." Abu Dhabi, March 18, 2006.

Al-Jazeera Net. "Zayed Warns against Imbalance in the UAE Population Structure," December 2, 2003 (www.aljazeera.net/News/archive/archive?Archive=65710).

Al-Juhni, Brigadier Dr. Ali bin Faiz. *Al Fahm al Marfood lil il Irhab al Mafrood* (Riyadh: Naif Arab Academy for Security Sciences, 2001).

Alkan, Türker. "The National Salvation Party in Turkey" in Metin Heper and Raphael Israel (eds) *Islam and Politics in the Modern Middle East* (Beckenham, UK: Croom Helm, 1984).

Alkan, Türker. "Turkey: Rise and Decline of Legitimacy in a Revolutionary Regime." *Journal of South Asian and Middle Eastern Studies* vol. 4 (1980).

Al-Mahmoud, Reem. "Hussain al-Nowais: Abu Dhabi lan Tastaqeel min Dawraha tijah al Emarate al Ukhra." *Ash Sharq al-Awsat*, London, July 8, 2006.

Al-Mansi, Jihad. "Tawqiyf arb'a Nowab Islamiyyn 'ala Khalfiyat al T'aziya fi al-Zaraawi wa Wasf Ahadhom laho bil al Shaheed." *Al Ghad*, Amman, June 12, 2006.

Alnajjar, Ghanim. "The GCC and Iraq." *Middle East Policy*, January 10, 2000.

Al-Rab'ih, Turki Ali. "Al Watinya al Mazmoma fi al Khitab al Islami." *Al Hayat*, London, February 4, 2006.

Ammar, Hamid. "Education Concerns in the Arab World" (in Arabic). An interview in *Al Ma'rifa*, no. 41, December 1998 (www.bab.com/articles/full_article.cfm?id=2571).

Anderson, Jon W. "Arabizing the Internet." *The Emirates Occasional Papers* no. 30 (Abu Dhabi: ECSSR, 1998).

Anthony, John Duke. "The US–GCC Relationship: A Glass Half-Empty or Half-Full? *Middle East Policy*, January 5, 1997.

Arab Center for Educational Training for the GCC States. "The Final Report: Program of Strategic Planning in the Field of Education." Doha, Qatar, January 11–14, 2004.

Arab Inter-Parliamentary Union. "Memo by the General Secretariat on Arab Brain-Drain: Drawing up Clear Policies to Absorb Talented Arabs and Curb their Migration Abroad," *Al Barlaman Al Arabi Journal*, Year 22, no. 82 (Damascus: AIPU, December 2001).

Arab Manual on Human Rights and Development (UNDP/Arab Organization for Human Rights).

Arab Reform Forum. "The Alexandria Declaration" (www.arabreformforum. org/ar/document.html).

Arabic Network for Human Rights Information. "Towards an Initiative for Political Reform in Arab Countries" (www.hrinfo.net/egypt/cihrs/ pr040329.shtml).

Ash Sharaq al-Awsat. "Al-Kuwait tatahim Iran bi Tajawoz al Hidood al Diplomasiya." London, May 13, 2004.

Ash Sharq al-Awsat. "Al-Kuwait Takhsha Taqseem al Iraq wa Tohazir min Tafashi al Taifiya fi Dowal al Jiwar." London, April 12, 2004.

Ash Sharq al-Awsat. "Bahrain: A Well-attended Debate Demands an Investigation of the Naturalization Process for Gulf and Arab nationals and Withdrawal of Nationality from Undeserving Persons." London, July 18, 2003.

Ash Sharq al-Awsat. Interview with Al-Sheikh Abdul Mohsin al-'Abaikan. London, May 15, 2005.

Atacan, Fulya. "Explaining Religious Politics at the Crossroad: AKP–SP." *Turkish Studies* vol. 6, no. 2 (June 2005).

Awad, Mohsin (ed.). *Al Dalil al 'Arabi: Hiqoq al Insan wa al Tanmia* (www.arabhumanrights.org/dalil/ch_8.htm).

Awad, Walid. "'Hamas sa Tadman al Musa'dat al Kharijiya wa 'Adam Ijbaar al Nisaa ala Irtidaa al Hijab." *Al Quds Al 'Arabi*, London, February 9, 2006.

Barchard, David. *Turkey and the West* (London: Routledge, 1985).

Bellin, Eva. *Stalled Democracy: Capital, Labor and the Paradox of State-Sponsored Development* (Ithaca, NY: Cornell University Press, 2002).

Berkes, Niyazi. *The Development of Secularism in Turkey* (Montreal: McGill University Press, 1964).

Berman, Sheri. "Civil Society and the Collapse of the Weimar Republic." *World Politics*, vol. 49, no.3, April 1997.

Bishara, Ahmed. "The Silent Crisis in Education" (in Arabic). *Al Qabas,* Kuwait, April 11, 2005.

Breslin, Shaun, Richard Higgott and Ben Rosamond. "Regions in Comparative Perspective," in Shaun Breslin et al, *New Regionalisms in the Global Political Economy* (London: Routledge, 2002).

Brown, Nathan J., Amr Hamzawy and Marina Ottaway. "Islamist Movements and the Democratic Process in the Arab World: Exploring Gray Zones" *Carnegie Paper* no. 67 (Washington, DC: Carnegie Endowment for International Peace, March 2006).

C. Bryant. "Civic Nation, Civil Society, Civil Religion," in J.A. Hall (ed.), *Civil Society: Theory, History, Comparison* (Cambridge, MA: Polity Press, 1995).

Carnegie Endowment for International Peace. "Amman Declaration for Political and Electoral Reform." October 9, 2004 (www.carnegie endowment. org/pdf/Amman_Declaration.pdf).

Castells, Manuel. *The Power of Identity* (Oxford: Blackwell Publishing, 2004).

Cohen J. and A. Arato. *Civil Society and Political Theory* (Cambridge, MA: MIT, 1992).

Da Sola Pool, Ithiel. *Technologies without Boundaries* (Cambridge, MA: Harvard University Press, 1990).

Davison, Roderic. *Reform in the Ottoman Empire, 1856–1876* (Princeton, NJ: Princeton University Press, 1963).

Deringil, Selim. *The Well-Protected Domains: Ideology and the Legitimation of Power in the Ottoman Empire, 1876–1909* (London: I.B. Tauris, 1999).

Dikare, Muhammad. "Higher Education in the Twenty-first Century: A Vision and Action" (in Arabic). Paper presented at UNESCO's Global Conference on Global Education, Paris, October 5–9, 1998.

Doğan, Erhan. "The Historical and Discursive Roots of the Justice and Development Party's EU Stance." *Turkish Studies* vol. 6, no. 3 (September 2005).

Economic and Social Commission for Western Asia. Report of the Arab Women's Center, 2003 (New York, NY: ESCWA, 2003).

Eid, General Dr. Muhammad Fathi. *Waq'i al Irhab fi al Watan Al 'Arabi* (Riyadh: Naif Arab Academy for Security Sciences, 1999).

Ekiert, G. "Democratization Processes in Eastern Central Europe: A Theoretical Reconsideration." *British Journal of Political Science*, vol. 21 (1991).

Ergun, Özbudun. "Turkish Party System: Institutionalization, Polarization and Fragmentation." *Middle Eastern Studies* vol. 17 (1981).

Ezz Al Deen, Mohammad. "World Bank Changes its Policy in the GCC." *Gulf News*, UAE, February 14, 2006.

Fakhro, Dr. Ali. Former Minister of Education and Health, interview in *Al Wasat*, Bahrain, December 2, 2005.

Farjani, Nadir. "Ihtimalat al Nahda fi al Watan al 'Arabi bain Taqrir al Tanmia al Insaniya al 'Arabia wa Mashrou'i al Sharq al Awsat al Kabir" [The Potential for Renaissance in the Arab World between the Arab Human Development Report and the Broader Middle East Project], *Emirates Lecture Series* no. 88 (Abu Dhabi: Emirates Center for Strategic Studies and Research, 2004), 48.

Fattah, Hassan M. "An Island Kingdom Feels the Ripples from Iraq and Iran." *The New York Times*, April 16, 2006.

Fergany, Nader. "Higher Education in Arab Countries: Human Development and Labour Market Requirements" (Cairo: Almishkat Centre for Research, 2001), available online (www. almishkat.org).

Findley, Carter V. *Bureaucratic Reform in the Ottoman Empire: The Sublime Porte, 1789–1922* (Princeton, NJ: Princeton University Press, 1980).

Fukuyama, Francis. *The End of History and the Last Man* (London: Penguin Books, 1992), 15.

Gause III, F. Gregory. "The Approaching Turning Point: The Future of US Relations with the Gulf States." Saudi-American Forum, May 20, 2003 (http://www.Saudi-American-Forum.org.).

GCC Secretariat General. "Development of Universal Education in the GCC States," January 2004. Based on directives of the Supreme Council, Session 23, Doha, December 2002.

GCC Secretariat General. *Statistics Publication* no. 13 (Riyadh: Information Center, Department of Statistics, 2004).

Gharaiba, Ibrahim. "Al Haraka al Islamiya: Hal Takon al Shariyyk al Asasi fi al Tahwlat al Jariya." *Al Hayat*, January 7, 2006.

[475]

Gharaiba, Ibrahim. "Al Ikhwan wa Jabhat al 'Amal." *Al Ghad*, Amman, June 24, 2006.

Ghubash, Rafia Obaid. "Arab Education: Reality and Methods of Development." A study presented to the Arab Forum on Education, Beirut, Lebanon, February 7–20, 2004.

Groc, Gérard. "The Virtue Party: An Experiment in Democratic Transition," in Stefanos Yerasimos, Günter Seufert and Karin Vorhoff (eds) *Civil Society in the Grip of Nationalism: Studies on Political Culture in Contemporary Turkey* (Istanbul: Orient Institut-Institutes Français d'Études Anatoliennes, 2000).

Gülalp, Haldun. "Globalization and Political Islam: The Social Base of Turkey's Welfare Party." *International Journal of Middle East Studies* vol. 33 (2001).

Gülalp, Haldun. "Political Islam in Turkey: The Rise and the Fall of the Refah Party." *The Muslim World* vol. 89, no. 1 (1999).

Hale, William. *Turkish Politics and the Military* (London: Routledge, 1994).

Harris, George. "The Role of the Military in Turkey: Guardians or Decision-Makers?" in Metin Heper and Ahmet Evin (eds) *State, Democracy and the Military: Turkey in the 1980s* (Berlin and New York, NY: Walter de Gruyter, 1988).

Heper, Metin. "The Justice and Development Party Government and the Military in Turkey." *Turkish Studies* vol. 6, no. 2 (2005).

Heper, Metin and Aylin Güney. "The Military and the Consolidation of Democracy: The Recent Turkish Experience." *Armed Forces and Society* vol. 26, no 4 (Summer 2000).

Heper, Metin and Filiz Başkan. "The Politics of Coalition Government in Turkey, 1961–1999." *International Journal of Turkish Studies* vol. 7 (Summer 2001).

Heper, Metin and Menderes Çınar. "Parliamentary Government with a Strong President: The Post–1989 Turkish Experience." *Political Science Quarterly* vol. 111, no. 3 (Fall 1996).

Heper, Metin and Şule Toktaş. "Islam, Modernity and Democracy in Contemporary Turkey: The Case of Recep Tayyip Erdoğan." *The Muslim World* vol. 93, no. 2 (April 2003).

Heper, Metin, Heinz Kramer and Ayşe Öncü (eds) *Turkey and the West: Changing Political and Cultural Identities* (London: I.B. Tauris, 1993).

Heper, Metin. 'The European Union, the Turkish Military and Democracy." *South European Society and Politics* vol.10, no. 1 (April 2005).

Heper, Metin. "A Democratic-Conservative Government by Pious People: The Justice and Development Party in Turkey" in Ibrahim M. Abu-Rabi (ed.) *Blackwell Companion to Contemporary Islamic Thought* (New York, NY: Blackwell, 2005).

Heper, Metin. "A Weltanschauung-Turned-Partial Ideology and Normative Ethics: 'Atatürkism' in Turkey." *Orient* vol. 25, no. 1 (1984).

Heper, Metin. "Center and Periphery in the Ottoman Empire with Special Reference to the Nineteenth Century." *International Political Science Review* 1 (1980).

Heper, Metin. "Civil–Military Relations, Political Islam and Security: The Turkish Case," in Constantine P. Danopoulos, Dhirendra Vajpey and Amir Bar-or (eds), *Civil-Military Relations, Nation-Building, and National Identity: Comparative Perspectives* (Westport, CT and London: Praeger, 2004).

Heper, Metin. "Islam and Democracy in Turkey: Toward a Reconciliation?" *The Middle East Journal* vol. 51, no. 1 (Winter 1997).

Heper, Metin. "The 'Strong State' and Democracy: The Turkish Case in Comparative and Historical Perspective," in S. N. Eisenstadt (ed) *Democracy and Modernity* (Leiden: E. J. Brill, 1992).

Heper, Metin. "The Victory of the Justice and Development Party in Turkey." *Mediterranean Politics* vol. 8, no. 1 (Spring 2003).

Heper, Metin. "Turkey between the East and West," in Emmanuel Adler, Beverly Crawford, Federica Bichi, and Raffaella Del Sarto (eds) *Convergence of Civilizations: Constructing a Mediterranean Region* (Toronto: University of Toronto Press, 2006).

Heper, Metin. *İsmet İnönü: The Making of a Turkish Statesman* (Leiden: E.J. Brill, 1998).

Heper, Metin. *The State Tradition in Turkey* (Walkington, UK: The Eothen Press, 1985).

Heyd, Uriel. *Foundations of Turkish Nationalism: The Life and Teachings of Ziya Gökalp* (London: Harvill Press, 1950).

Hudson, Michael. "Information Technology, International Politics and Political Change in the Arab World" (http://nmit.georgetown.edu/ index/workingpapers.html).

Human Rights Watch. "The Internet in the Mideast and North Africa: Free Expression and Censorship," May 1999. Available online (http://www. hrw.org/hrw/advocacy/internet/ mena/int-mena.htm).

Huntington, Samuel. *Political Order in Changing Societies* (New Haven, CT: Yale University Press, 1968).

İnalcık, Halil. "Suleiman the Lawgiver and Ottoman Law." *Archivum Ottomanicum* 1 (1969).

İnalcık, Halil. "[Turkey:] The Nature of Traditional Society," in Robert E. Ward and Dankwart A Rustow (eds) *Political Modernization in Japan and Turkey* (Princeton, NJ: Princeton University Press, 1964).

İnalcık, Halil. "The Ottoman Methods of Conquest," *Studia Islamica* 2 (1954).

İnalcık, Halil. *The Ottoman Empire: The Classical* Age, *1300–1600.* Translated by Norman Itzkowitz and Colin Imber (New York, NY: Praeger, 1973).

International Development Research Centre. *The Responsibility to Protect: Report of the International Commission on Intervention and State Sovereignty* (Ottawa: International Development Research Centre, December 2001).

Isa, Muhammad Rifqi. "Masadir al Tataruf kama Udrikha al Shabab fi Misr wa al Kuwait, Dirasa Muqarana," *Majalat al Bihooth al Tarbawia*, University of Qatar, Year 7, no. 13 (January 1998).

Islamic Jurisprudence Council. Decisions published on the website of the Muslim World League (http://www.themwl.org/publications).

Jackson, Robert. "Sovereignty in World Politics: A Glance at the Conceptual and Historical Landscape," in Jackson (ed.) *Sovereignty at the Millennium* (Oxford: Blackwell, 1999).

Kamrava, M. "Pseudo-Democratic Politics: The Rise and Demise of Turkey's Refah Party." *British Journal of Middle Eastern Studies* vol. 25, no. 2 (1998).

Kant, Immanuel. Appendix to "Observations on the Feeling of the Beautiful and Sublime" *Kant's Works*, vol. 2 (New York, NY: Mysl Publishers, 1964).

Karpat, Kemal H. "Military Interventions: Army–Civilian Relations in Turkey Before and After 1980," in Metin Heper and Ahmet Evin (eds)

State, Democracy and the Military: Turkey in the 1980s (Berlin and New York, NY: Walter de Gruyter, 1988).

Karpat, Kemal H. "The Transformation of the Ottoman Empire, 1789–1908." *International Journal of Middle East Studies* 3 (1972).

Karpat, Kemal H. *Turkey's Politics: The Transition to Multi-Party System* (Princeton, NJ: Princeton University Press, 1959).

Karpat, Kemal. H. "Turkish Democracy at Impasse: Ideology, Party Politics and the Third Military Intervention." *International Journal of Turkish Studies* vol. 2 (1981).

Kinross, Lord. *Atatürk: A Bibliography of Mustafa Kemal, Father of Modern Turkey* (New York, NY: William Murrow, 1978 and 1994),

Kuwait Ministry of Planning and Administrative Development Affairs. "Country Profile" (State of Kuwait), report submitted to the Economic and Social Commission for Western Asia (ESCWA).

Kuwait Ministry of Planning and Administrative Development Affairs. *Al Majmo'ua al Ihsaiyya*, various publications.

Kuwait Ministry of Planning and Administrative Development Affairs. *Al Simaat al Asasiyya lil al Sukan wa al Qowa al 'Amila*, various publications.

Kuwait Ministry of Planning and Administrative Development Affairs. "The Report of the State of Kuwait on the Millennium Development Goals: Achievements and Challenges," April 2003.

Kuwait Ministry of Social Affairs and Labor. "Annual Report," 2004.

Kuwait News Agency (KUNA), May 12, 2004.

Kuwait University. Database of registered students and graduates.

Lake, David A. and Donald Rothchild (eds). *The International Spread of Conflict, Fear, Diffusion, and Escalation* (Princeton, NJ: Princeton University Press).

Landau, Jacob M. "The National Salvation Party in Turkey." *Asian and African Studies* vol. 11, no. 1, (1976).

Le Monde Diplomatique, February 2006.

Levine, Ned. "Value Orientations among Migrants in Ankara, Turkey." *Asian and African Studies* vol. 8, nos. 1–2 (1973).

Levy, Avigdor. "The Military Policy of Sultan Mahmud II." *International Journal of Middle Eastern Studies* 2 (1971).

Lewis, Bernard. *The Emergence of Modern Turkey* (London: Oxford University Press, 1961).

Lincoln, J. "Middle East Governments on the World Wide Web," Working Paper, no. 6, Washington Institute for Near East Policy Research, February 1999.

Lorimer, John Gordon. *Dalil al Khaleej al-'Arabi*. Translated by the office of the H.H. the Emir of Qatar, Department of History, C1-6, Department of Geography C1-7 (Qatar: 1984).

Man'aa, Haitham. "al Munazamat al 'Arabia Ghair al Hikomiya: Asas al Binaa al Demoqrati wa al Madani" [Arab Non-Governmental Organizations: The Foundation for Democratic and Civil Building], 1999 lecture (www.achr.nu/stu5.htm).

Mango, Andrew. *Atatürk* (London: John Murray, 1999).

Mardin, Şerif. "Center and Periphery: A Key to Turkish Politics?" *Daedalus* 102 (1973).

Mardin, Şerif. "Power, Civil Society and Culture in the Ottoman Empire." *Comparative Studies in Society and History* 11 (1969).

Mardin, Şerif. *Din ve İdeoloji* [Religion and Ideology] (Ankara: Sevinç Matbaası, 1969).

Mardin, Şerif. *The Genesis of Young Ottoman Thought: A Study in the Modernization of Turkish Political Ideas* (Princeton, NJ: Princeton University Press, 1958).

McMillan, Joseph, Richard Sokolsky and Andrew C. Winner. "Toward a New Regional Security Architecture." *Washington Quarterly,* vol. 26, no. 3 (Summer 2003).

Mekata, Motoko. "Building Partnership Toward a Common Goal: Experiences of the International Campaign to Ban Landmines" in Ann M. Florini (ed.) *The Third Force* (Washington, DC: Carnegie Endowment for International Peace, 2000).

Middle East Economic Digest. May 6, 2006.

Milliyet. Istanbul, April 9, 1993.

Milliyet. Istanbul, February 2, 1994.

Milward, Alan S. *The European Rescue of the Nation-State* (London and New York, NY: Routledge, 2000)

National Campaign for Election Reform. Statement, May 2005 (www.pngo. net/elections/PR_elections_10_05.htm).

New York Times, January 16, 1996.

Ogburn, W. F. *Social Change* (London: Routledge and Kegan Paul, 1922).

Ottaway, Marina and Thomas Carothers. *Funding Virtue: Civil Society Aid and Democracy Promotion* (Washington, DC: Carnegie Endowment for International Peace, 2000).

Palestinian Ministry of Information. "Pledge of Solidarity and Cohesion" (www.minfo.gov.ps/documents/arabic/24-05-04.htm).

Perthes, Volker. *Arab Elites: Negotiating the Politics of Change* (Boulder, CO and London: Lynne Rienner Publishers, 2004).

Plato. "Gorgiy II," *Collected Works*, vol. 1 (New York: NY: Mysl Publishers, 1990).

Portes, Alejandro and A. Douglas Kincaid, "The Crisis of Authoritarianism: State and Civil Society in Argentina, Chile and Uruguay." *Research in Political Sociology*, vol.1 (1985).

Priess, David. "The Gulf Cooperation Council: Prospects for Expansion." *Middle East Policy*; January 1, 1998.

Qasem, S. "The Arab States," in *UNESCO World Science Report* (London: Oxford University Press, 1998).

Rathmell, Andrew, Theodore Karasik and David Gompert. *A New Persian Gulf Security System*, Issue Paper (Santa Monica, CA: RAND Corporation, 2003).

Rida, Muhammad Jawad. "The Driving Forces and Inertia in the Universities and Institutions of Higher Education: Harmonizing Output with the Requirements of Development in the GCC States." Bahrain, December 28–29, 2004.

Rustow, Dankwart A. "Atatürk as Founder of a State," *Daedalus* 98 (1968).

Rustow, Dankwart A. "Turkey's Liberal Revolution." *Middle East Review* 12 (1985).

Rustow, Dankwart A. *Turkey: America's Forgotten Ally* (New York, NY: Council on Foreign Relations, 1987).

Rutherford, Bruce. "The Ballot Box can Moderate Islamists." *Christian Science Monitor*, February 9, 2006.

Said, M. El-Sayed. "In Search of Researchers." *Al-Ahram Weekly*, November 4–10, 1999.

Salem Mubarak al Falaq, "A Nation at Risk": An Approach to Education Curricula in the Arab World (in Arabic). November 1, 2005 (www. saaid.net/manahej/45.htm).

Salt, Jeremy. "Nationalism and the Rise of Muslim Sentiment in Turkey." *Middle Eastern Studies* vol. 31, no. 1 (1995).

Sartori, Giovanni. *The Theory of Democracy Revisited. Part One: The Contemporary Debate* (Chatham, NJ: Chatham House Publishers, 1987).

Sartori, Giovanni. *The Theory of Democracy Revisited. Part Two: The Classical Issues* (Chatham, NJ: Chatham House Publishers, 1987).

Secretariat General of the GCC States. "Report on the Development of Universal Education in the GCC States." Riyadh, 2004.

Shaw, Stanford J. and Ezel Kural Shaw, *History of the Ottoman Empire and Modern Turkey, Vol. II. Reform Revolution, and Republic: The Rise of Modern Turkey, 1808–1975* (New York, NY: Cambridge University Press, 1977).

Sid-Ahmed, M. "Review of Antoine Zahlan's work, 'The Challenges of Science and Technology: Progress without Change,'" in "Technological Challenge." *Al-Ahram Weekly*, October 14–20, 1999.

Singapore Department of Statistics. *Statistics Singapore 2006.*

Smith, Anthony. *Social Change* (New York, NY: Alfred Knopf, 1976).

Suzuki, Peter. "Encounters with Istanbul: Urban Peasants and Village Peasants." *International Journal of Comparative Sociology* vol. 5, no. 2 (1964).

Tallawy, Mervat. Secretary General, United Nations Economic and Social Commission for Western Asia, Keynote Address to the Second Annual Conference of the Arab International Women's Forum

(AIWF). "Windows of Opportunity in Business and Public Life," London, October 23, 2003, ESCWA, Press Release, October 27, 2003.

The Roadmap to Peace. UN website (daccessdds.un.org/doc/UDOC/GEN/N 0334877.pdf?OpenElement)

The Arab Convention for the Suppression of Terrorism. Arab Interior Ministers Council and the Council of Arab Ministers of Justice, Cairo, April 1998.

The Broader Middle East Initiative. "Partnership for Progress and a Common Future with the Region of Broader Middle East and North Africa." *Al Hayat,* February 13, 2004.

The Economist. "The World through their Eyes." February 26 to March 4, 2005.

The Ninth Conference of Ministers of Higher Education and Scientific Research in the Arab World. "The Final Report." Arab League Educational, Cultural and Scientific Organization, Damascus, December 5–18, 2003.

The Stanley Foundation. "The Future of Persian Gulf Security: Alternatives for the 21st Century," September 3–5, 2005 (Warrenton, VA: The Stanley Foundation, 2005).

The Stanley Foundation. "The United States, Iran, and Saudi Arabia: Necessary Steps Toward a New Gulf Security Order." *Policy Dialogue Brief,* October 20–22, 2005 (Warrenton, VA: The Stanley Foundation, 2005).

Toprak, Binnaz. "Islam and Democracy in Turkey." *Turkish Studies* vol. 6, no. 2, June (2005).

Turfan, M. N. *Rise of the Young Turks: Politics, Military and the Ottoman Collapse* (London: I. B. Tauris, 1998).

[485]

UAE Human Resource Report 2005 (Dubai: National Human Resource Development and Employment Authority, 2005).

UNCTAD. "The Determinants of FDI in Developing Countries," 2002.

UNIDO, Global Industry Reports, various issues.

United Nations Development Program (UNDP). *Arab Human Development Report 2002: Creating Opportunities for Future Generations* (New York, NY: UNDP, 2002).

United Nations Development Program. *Arab Human Development Report 2004: Towards Freedom in the Arab World* (New York, NY: UNDP, 2005), 25–29.

United Nations Development Program. *Arab Human Development Report 2003: Building a Knowledge Society* (New York, NY: UNDP, 2003).

United Nations Development Program. *Human Development Report 1990* (New York, NY: Oxford University Press, 1990).

United Nations Development Program. *Human Development Report 2005: International Cooperation at a Crossroads: Aid, Trade and Security in an Unequal World* (New York, NY: UNDP, 2005).

United Nations Educational Scientific and Cultural Organization, *World Science Report* (Paris: UNESCO, 1998).

United Nations General Assembly. "A Detailed Guide for Implementing the UN Declaration about the Millennium: The Report of the Secretary General."

United Nations. *International Migration Report 2002* (New York, NY: United Nations Publications, 2002). Available online (www.un.org/esa/population/publications/ittmig2002/ittmigrep 2002arab.doc).

United Nations. *World Population Policies 2005* (New York, NY: UN Publications, 2006.

Wapner, Paul. "Politics Beyond the State: Environmental Activism and World Civic Politics." *World Politics*, vol. 47 (April 1995).

White, Jenny. "Pragmatist or Ideologues: Turkey's Welfare Party in Power." *Current History* vol. 94, no. 588 (1995).

World Bank, World Development Reports, various issues.

Yalman, Nur. "Islamic Reform and Mystic Tradition in Eastern Turkey." *Archives Européenne des Sociologies* 10 (1969).

Yeşilada, Birol. "The Virtue Party," in Barry Rubin and Metin Heper (eds) *Political Parties in Turkey* (London: Frank Cass, 2002).

Yıldız, Ahmet. "Politico-Religious Discourse of Political Islam in Turkey: The Parties of National Outlook." *The Muslim World* vol. 93, no. 2 (April 2003).

Zahlan, Antoine B. "Globalization and Science and Technology Policy," *Forum* vol. 4, no. 3, December, 1997–January 1998.

INDEX

A

Abbas, Mahmoud 47, 50–1
Abdülhamit II, Sultan 174
Abdullah, King of Saudi Arabia 152
Abu Dhabi 147–8
advocacy NGOs 258, 259–64
Afghan-Arabs 124
Afghanistan 43, 124, 211, 214, 244
Africa 231
African Union 232
agriculture 76, 336
Akef, Muhammad Mahdi 94
Alabbar, Mohammad Ali 146
Al Ahmed, Sheikh Sabah 166
Al-Arabiya 144, 306
Alexandria Library 45, 47
Al Farhan, Ishaq 157–8
Al-Futuh, 'Abd al-Min'am Abu 115
Al Gazira University 343
Algeria 83
   civil war 95
   education 304
   Internet 85
   and Islamism 116, 154
   science studies 86
Algerian Armed Jammaa Islamiyya 94
Al Hamar, Abdul Malik 337–8
Al Hassan, Mohammad Abu 166
Al Hayat 156
Al Hayat Kalima 152
Al-Hunaidi, 'Azzam 153
Ali, Ben 99
Al-Irian, Issam 109, 154–5
Al-Jama'a Al-Islamiyya 107
Al-Jazeera 144, 306
Al-Jazzaf, Mahdi 148
Al-Jihad 107
Al Kathiri, Suhail bin Salem Sa'ad 326–8
Al Majed, Kamal Abu 157

Al Maktoum, H.H. Sheikh Mohammed bin Rashid 289
Al-Maqdisi, Abu Muhammad 152
Al-Misnad, Sheikha Mozah bint Nasser 329
Al Nahda Party 94, 156
Al Nahyan, H.H. General Sheikh Mohammed bin Zayed 147, 289
Al Nahyan, H.H. Sheikh Khalifa bin Zayed 288
Al Nahyan, H.H. Sheikh Zayed bin Sultan 294, 419–20
Al Nowais, Hussain 147–8
Al-'Obeikan, Sheikh Abdul Mohsin 152
Al 'Ouda, Sheikh Salman 152
Al Qaeda 27, 150, 152, 205–6
Al-Rab'iu, Turki Ali 156
Al-Sadat, Anwar 101, 104, 106
Al Safar, Hassan 167
Al Sanea, Rajaa: *Banat al Riyadh* 163
Al Sharhan, Ali Abdul Aziz 320
Alternative List 52, 53
Al-Thani, Sheikh Hamad bin Khalifa 329
Al Turabi, Hassan 160
Al Uthmani, Saad Eddin 94
Al Zalzala, Yusuf 166
Al-Zarqawi, Abu Musab 153
APEC 249
Arab Development Institute 360
Arab Fund for Economic and Social Development 367
Arabian Peninsula 398
Arab Interior Ministers Council 131–4
Arab–Israeli conflict 15, 44, 168
   fundamentalism cause 160, 161
   and Palestine 57
   terrorism cause 123–4
Arab Labor Organization 361

Arab League 140, 149, 237, 238, 241, 252
Arab League Economic and Social Council 361
Arab Nasserist Party 106
Arab States Broadcasting Union 140
Arab Summit, Tunis 44, 45
Arafat, Yasser 48
ARF (ASEAN Regional Forum) 247–52
ASEAN 235
  and ARF 250
  compared with GCC 238–41
  emergence of 234, 238
  as Gulf security model 248–52
  regional security community 251–2
ASEAN Charter 252
ASEAN Plus Three 241
ASEAN Way 237–8
Asia
  democracy in 243, 245
  diversity of 233, 251
  financial crisis 242–3, 245
  long-term conflicts 248–9
  migrant numbers 394, 395
  recent dangers 242–3
  regionalism
    economic interdependence 251
    sovereignty challenges 241–7
    vs Arab World 233–47
  regional security
    as Arab model 247–50
    and conflict control 242
    security community 251–2
  US approach in 246
Asian Pacific Economic Corporation 241
Asian Relations Conference 234
Atatürk (Mustafa Kemal) 175, 178, 182–3, 188
Australia 332, 335
"axis of evil" 220, 244

B
Baghdad Pact 235
Bahçeli, Devlet 187
Bahrain
  education 304, 321–3
  inwards migration 407
  sectarianism 165, 166–7
Bandung Conference 231, 235–7
Bangladesh 332
Bargouthi, Mustafa Al 52
Bayanoni, Ali Sadreddin el 155
Bayar, Celal 182
Beirut Summit 44–5, 57
Berlin Wall 281, 299
Bin Laden, Osama 152
Bolivar, Simon 231
Bosnia 181, 211, 274
"brain drain"
  and Arab World 350–5
  causes of 350, 355, 357–8
  negative aspects 358–60
  non-returning students 350, 353–4
  prevention strategy 361–3
  return enticements 360–1
  types of 351
Brazil 82
bread revolutions 21–2, 30
Broader Middle East 25
Broader Middle East Initiative 28, 42–4
Bush Doctrine 244
Bush, George (Senior) 333
Bush, George W. 211
Business Council, Arab 45
businesses
  educational support 292
  student training 291
  and women 304–5, 370
business organizations 258, 262, 264–6

C
Cairo Declaration 50
Caliphate 150, 176, 245
Cambodia 237, 240
Canada 332, 335, 352
Caribbean Region 394, 395

Carter administration 239
Castells, Manuel: *The Power of Identity* 150
CEDAW 45, 304, 374
Child, Convention on the Rights of 374
Chile 77, 84
China 67
  and ASEAN/ARF 241, 250
  civil society role 253
  economic reform 69
  education in 75
  and Taiwan 249
Çiller, Tansu 189
civil conflict 21–2, 30
Civil and Political Rights, International Covenant on (1966) 53, 374
civil society
  definition debate 255–6
  growing influence 22
  relationship with state 150–1
  role of women 377–9, 382
  see also Islamic movements; non-state actors
civil society organizations
  Amman Declaration for Reform 46–7
  Arab suspicion of 55
  definitions of 255, 256–7
  and economic reform 15, 253
  and governments 277–8
  and ICT 307
  limited role of 32, 56, 309
  persecution by regimes 29, 55
  and political reform 44–7, 253
  and social change 22, 253, 308–9
  types of 255
  vs political parties 271, 274
  see also advocacy NGOs; business organizations; labor unions
Clinton, Bill 283
Cold War 237, 238, 270
  and communism 213
  and containment 219
  US *realpolitik* 216–17
colleges *see* universities/colleges

Colombia 214
colonial period 55, 230, 398
Committee of Union and Progress 188
communism 213, 214, 238–9
community-based organizations 257–8
competition 280, 287
computer ownership 85–6, 87, 321
constitutional institutions 16–17
consumption 71–2, 316, 415
Coptic Christians 115, 117, 118, 154
Criminal Police, Arab Bureau of 132, 135–6
criticism, social 284
Croatia 273
CSCE 249
Cuba 253
culture, Arab
  and education 297–8, 347
  and globalization 335
  and the media 310
  and migration 399, 417
  projection to West 141–2
  vs economic reform 70

D
Dae-jung, Kim 279–80
Dana Gas Company 145
democracy 13, 15, 168–9
  Arab world vs West 41
  as hegemony camouflage 31
  and Islamic movements 95–6
  and NGOs 270
  and political parties 270–1, 272
  principles of 59–60
  as reform slogan 23
  US aims for Arab World 25, 42–4, 245–6
  vs terrorism 141
  world movement 24
Democratic Party (DP) 182, 187, 189
development and modernization
  challenges to 14–15
  early Turkish experience 173–4
  and inward migration 404–5
  and political reform 24

distance learning 343
domestic servants 415, 416
Dubai Media City 161
Dumlupinar, Battle of 178

E
East Asia ("Asian tigers") 78–9,
312, 313
East Asian Summit 241, 249
Eastern Europe 24, 260, 299
Ecevit, Bülent 187
economic dependence 415
economic growth 23, 301
economic reform
    as terrorism weapon 142
    critical actions 68–9
    diagnosing problems 69
    failure in 1970s/1980s 160
    learning from others 69–70
    reforms needed 88–90
    structural challenges 71–87
    transformations 143, 144–9
    vision for change 67–9
Economic Research Forum 45
economic self-sufficiency 13
Economic, Social and Cultural Rights,
    International Covenant on 374, 384
economy
    export orientation 80
    external borrowing 80–1
    oil
        market fluctuation exposure 72
        oil dependence 65, 68, 71, 72
        "old" industries bias 75–6
        vs Western countries 41
    see also economic reform;
        individual countries
education
    Arabization of 320, 324
    co-education 158
    and cultural values 335
    distance learning 343
    and ethical values 296–7
    and labor market 14, 311–14
    low expenditure on 86, 316

low standards 14, 23, 75, 86, 301,
    312–17
    math/science shortfall 86, 313–14,
        317, 336
    quality of 288–90
    reform overview 332–7
    and social change 290, 295–8,
        300–3
    strategies 317–32, 333–4
    and terrorism 129
    what is needed 287–9
    women 302, 303, 304, 310,
        376–7, 384
    see also schools;
        universities/colleges; individual
        countries
Egypt 21, 82, 83, 86
    attitude to democracy 107–8
    borrowing 80
    "brain drain" 351–2, 353, 354, 356
    education 336, 376
    elections
        MB success 42, 101, 103, 111–13,
            154–5
        parliamentary 42, 102–3, 109–10,
            113, 154–5
        presidential 29, 42, 101–2, 108
    exports 79
    and Islamism 94, 95, 99, 100,
        101–4, 107, 109–14, 154
    manufacturing 77
    migration conditions 355
    Nasser regime 232
    NDP
        dealing with the MB 116–19
        and "democracy" 105–6, 108–9
        dominance measures 103–4, 106,
            108, 113
        economic policies 104–5
        loss of seats 102–3, 112
        opposition parties 109–14, 272,
            273
        professional syndicates 265
        and reform 46, 47
        sectarianism in 165

Egyptian Center Party (Al Wasat)
95, 107
Egyptian Jihad 93
Egyptian Movement for Change
(Kifaya) 102
Emaar 146
EMP (Euro-Mediterranean
Partnership) 25, 26
environmental groups 259, 262–3
equal rights 15, 45, 304, 345
Erbakan, Necmettin 189
Erdoğan, Recep Tayyip 187, 193
Ergüder, Üstün 190
ethical values 296–7
Ethiopia 235
Europe
democracy in 183–4
population imbalance 399
as US reform partner 25
European Coal and Steel Community
229, 234–5
European Union
and migrants 394, 395, 401
regional trading blocs 66
Turkey's membership hopes 189,
193, 196
vs loss of sovereignty 229–30
Evren, General Kenen 187
exports
decline in 80
high-tech deficiency 79
primary products reliance 72, 77
year 2000 breakdowns 79

F
family 128, 129, 291
Faris, Mohammad Abu 153
Fatah movement 52, 53
Fayad, Salam 52
federalism 61–2
Felicity Party (FP) 192–3
financial markets 66
First World War 178
Former Soviet Union 24
France 82, 332, 335

Franklin, Benjamin 212
freedom 199–200
Friedman, Thomas L.: *The World is
Flat* 280, 281
FSU (former Soviet Union) 260
Fukuyama, Francis 144
functionalism 229

G
GATT 66
Gaza Strip 49
GCC 16, 76, 238, 250
compared with ASEAN 238–41
conflict control 242, 252
economy
1980s recession 406
2025 forecast 146
free trade efforts 251
lack of development plans
412–13
oil dependence 71
education 315–32, 413–14, 417–18
foreign investment 411
formation of 238
labor market
percentage of migrants 405, 406
preferring nationals 418–19
migrants
family size 416–17
foreign remittances 419, 420
and GCC population 399, 405,
406, 407
inadequate regulations 410
migration
history of 398–9
and native population 408
and population growth 404–6
and unemployment 402
mobile phones 83
population
demographic transformation 416
distribution (2002) 409
lack of strategy 414–15
low native population 399, 403,
404–5, 408, 410

[493]

population growth 404–6
  1975–2015 407
  1999–2002 405
population imbalance
  factors leading to 399, 406,
    409–16
  overview 399, 401–3
  policies/strategies 416–21
  private sector
    and social unity 148–9
    use of foreign labor 415, 417
  unemployment 402, 403–44,
    416, 419
  women's role 369–70, 416, 418
Germany 335
Ghad (Tomorrow) Party 101, 112, 113
Ghana 232, 235
Ghannouchi, Sheikh Rachid 156
Gharaiba, Ibrahim 158–9
globalization 22, 65–7, 214, 215, 305
  and Arab culture 335
  education for 344–5
  and media 161
  and social change 308
  and telecommunications 280
  vs development 338
GNGOs 8
Gökalp, Ziya 174–5
Gomaa, Noman 101
governments
  bloated bureacracies 72
  change of role 169
  and ICT 306
  and the media 162–4, 268–70
  and non-state actors 253–4,
    260–70, 275, 276–8
  and privatization 147, 148
  qualities needed 276–7
  secularism moves 155–6
  transparency/accountability 16,
    33–4
  see also ruling elites
Greece
  invasion of Anatolia 178
  Turkish population exchange 180–1

Grenada 232
Gresh, Alain 163
Gulf War (1990–91) 241

H
Habib, Muhammad 115
Hamas 52, 53, 155, 158, 247
Hamilton, Alexander 206
health care 13, 416
Hegel, G.W.F. 255–6
Henry, Patrick 207
higher education see
  universities/colleges
Holy Quran 124–5
human development
  empowerment of women 367–8
  GCC achievements 414
  Human Development Index 414
  measures needed 88–90
Human Development Report, Arab 23,
  27, 41, 301, 335, 340, 369
humanitarian intervention 232–3, 242,
  244–5
Human Poverty Index 105, 355
human resources 65, 300
human rights 13, 15, 44–5, 244
  organizations 259, 262, 263
  protection of women 368
Human Rights, Arab Organization
  for 45
Human Rights, Universal Declaration
  of (1948) 53, 254–5, 369, 392
Huntington, Samuel 276
Hussein, Saddam 240–1, 277

I
ICBL 260
ICT 66, 75
  and social change 306–8, 310
  see also Internet
illiteracy 14, 74, 301, 302, 304, 310,
  312, 369, 377, 384
ILO 361, 409
IMF 245
Independent Palestine 52, 53

India 234, 241, 249, 250
  as migrant source 408, 416–17
individualism 146, 148, 169
Indochina 238
Indonesia 84
  as ASEAN threat 239
  Conference on 234
  democracy in 245, 246
  fall of Suharto 243
Industrial Revolution 266
industry
  factor productivity fall 81
  fragmented structures 73
  inefficient practices 74
  larger firms shortage 73–4
  resource-based bias 77
  stagnant manufacturing 76–7
Information Revolution 143, 202,
  214–15, 269, 306
İnönü, İsmet 175, 178, 182–3
inter-governmentalism 229
international community
  Arab legitimacy needed 15
  empowerment of women 368
  population imbalance 399–401
  projecting Arab-Islamic world to
    141–2
  as terrorism cause 124
  see also Western countries;
    individual countries
Internet
  as media form 161, 269
  penetration of 84–5, 307
  relative freedom 307–8
  and women 307, 369
  worldwide learning 281, 291
investment
  from foreign lands
    and economic change 144
    telecommunications 83
    World Bank loans 148
  public participation 145–6, 168, 169
  and regional unity 148–9
Iran 165–6, 235
  GCC approach 240

Islamic Revolution 239
  migrants 398
  nuclear crisis 247
  and regional security 250
Iraq 15, 83, 168, 235, 244
  borrowing 80–1
  "brain drain" 352, 353
  Constitution 61–2
  as democracy model 59–63
  elections in 29, 42, 61
  GCC relationship 240–1
  media freedom 60
  migration 398
  political instability 15, 28, 60–1
  and sectarianism 164, 166, 167
  suggested US action 222–3
  US occupation of 27, 28, 43, 55,
    211, 221, 245, 277
Iraqi Council of Representatives 59,
  61, 62
Iraqi Islamic Party 159
Iraq–Iran War 24, 240
Islam
  confronting terrorism 140–1
  interpretation clashes 126–7
  peace and tolerance 291
  terrorism condemned by 125–6
  terrorism and Jihad 124–5, 151
  Turkish approach 175–6, 179–80,
    181, 190–3, 194, 196–7
  see also Shari‘a
Islamic Action Front (IAF) 95, 98, 153
Islamic liberalism 155–9
Islamic Liberation Party 150
Islamic movements 22, 25–6, 143
  characteristics 93
  moderate groups
    illiberality of 96
    "legitimacy-building" of 149–50,
      151, 169
    openness to West 96, 97–8
    political reform 97–116
    religion vs democracy 94–7,
      114–15
  political groups 150–1, 154–5

distinction between 159–61
liberalism of 155–9
rejection of violence 151–4
popularity of 98
regime clashes 30, 94, 98
violent groups 93–4, 107, 149,
    151–4
Islamic Salvation Front 116
Islamist Awakening Party (Al Nahda)
    99
Israel
    as Arab threat 234, 237
    education 312
    high-tech exports 79
    and Palestinian elections 51, 57
    and regional security 249, 250
    skilled emigrants 353
    Western support for 30, 37
Issues of Arab Reform: Vision and
    Implementation 45–6
Italy 335

J
Jamaat al-Islamiyya 129
Japan 66, 83, 333, 335, 394
Jefferson, Thomas 207–8
Jemma Islamiah group 244
Jerusalem 49, 51
Jihad 124–5, 151, 205
Jordan 21, 76, 82, 83, 85, 86
    borrowing 80
    "brain drain" 352, 353
    democracy moves 42
    education 302, 304
    export breakdown 79
    and Islamism 94, 98, 99, 117, 153,
        154, 157–9
    liberalization trend 147
    literacy 74
    manufacturing 77
Jospin, Lionel 346
justice 282
Justice and Development Party (JDP)
    (Turkey) 187–8, 192–3

Justice and Development Party (PJD)
    (Morocco) 94, 98

K
Kemal, Mustafa (Atatürk) 175, 178,
    182–3, 188
Kennedy, John F. 282
Khuwailid, Khadijah bint 305
Kifaya 109, 110
knowledge
    Arab "knowledge gap" 301
    Arab translation levels 41
    and education 296
knowledge society 342–3
Komensky, Jan Amos 298
Korea 76, 86
Kosovo 232
Kurds 61, 222
Kuwait 83, 86
    borrowing 80
    and "brain drain" 360
    constitution 372, 383
    education 304, 330–2
    exports 79
    gender equality
        economic activity 388
        labor force 387
        population/society 386
    Internet 85
    Iraqi invasion 24, 241, 378
    and Islamism 99, 154
    manufacturing 77
    migrants 395, 402, 406, 407
    sectarianism in 165–6, 167
    women
        and civil society 377–9, 384
        and education 376–7
        empowerment of 41–2, 158, 371,
            379–85
        government privileges 372–4
        in government sector 389
        in labor market 374–5, 384
        as leaders 375–6, 384
        in leading professions 390
        political role 378–9, 384

Kuwaiti Institute for Scientific
  Research 360

L
labor market
    databases on 413
    and education 14, 74, 311–14, 317,
      336, 417–18
    foreign labor 399, 402, 403–21
    graduate job seekers 413–14
    role of women 14, 374–5, 416, 418
    surplus manpower 87, 301, 350
    and technology 267
    training students for 291
labor unions 264–7
language
    Arabic 335, 346–7, 418
    English 317, 325, 328, 346
Latin America 74, 85–6, 230, 231,
  394, 395
Lausanne Peace Treaty 181
laws
    and economic activities 411
    foreign investment 410–11
    and NGOs 260–2
    terrorism laws 133
    women's rights 380–1
leadership 283, 291
    "generation of sons" 5
League of Arab States 231, 234, 236,
  238, 361
Lebanon 82, 83, 85, 86, 235
    "brain drain" 352, 353
    education 302, 304
    elections 42
    and Islamism 100, 154
    literacy 74
    sectarianism 165
Liberia 211
Libya 307, 360
life expectancy 74–5
lobbies 259

M
Madison, James 207

Maghreb region 82
Mahfouz, Nagib: *Children of Gebelawi*
  157
Malaysia 77, 399–400
Mandela, Nelson 39
Marx, Karl 299
media
    and Arab unity 162, 305
    and globalization 161
    and governments 162–4, 268–70
    Iraqi freedom of 60
    private sector in 162–4, 168
    and social change 161–4, 268–70,
      305–6
    and terrorism 130, 138–40, 142
    see also radio stations; TV satellite
      channels
medical education 343
Mexico 86
Middle East
    US hegemony 25, 27
    US post-9/11 agenda 25, 42
    and WMD 15, 46
    see also individual countries;
      regions
Migrant Workers, Rights of 408–9
migration
    Arab overview 349–50
    "brain drain"
    international
      by country 396
      by major region 395
      overview 391–6
    reduction strategies 362–3
    see also individual countries
Migration Report, International 393–4
Mitchell, George 279
modernization *see* development and
  modernization
Monnet, Jean 235
Morocco 21, 80, 85
    foreign investment in 83
    and Islamism 94, 98, 99, 100
Motherland Party 186–7
Mubarak, Gamal 108

Mubarak, Hosni 99, 101–2, 104, 108, 119
Muhammad VI, King of Morocco 98
Muskie, Edmund S. 279
Muslim Brotherhood 42, 153
  Guidance Bureau 156–7
  and political reform 101–16
  reasons for success 111–14
  reform plan 99
  religion vs democracy 114–16
  repression of 94, 99, 104, 109, 154, 265
Myanmar regime 244, 245

N
Naif University for Security Sciences 132, 136–7
NAM (Non-Aligned Movement) 235–6
Nasser, Gamel Abdul 231, 235, 236
National Democratic Party (NDP) 102–3
National Front for Change and Reform 110, 113
Nationalist Action Party 187
National Order Party (NOP) 191, 192
National Progressive Unionist (Tajammu) Party 112
National Salvation Party (NSP) 191
National Security Council (NSC) 184, 186
nation-states 160, 169
  and developing countries 230, 236
  erosion of authority 215
NATO 216, 222, 232
Nehru, Jawaharlal 235, 236, 238
neo-functionalism 229
New Wafd Party (NWP) 101, 106, 112
New Zealand 332, 394
NGOs see individual organizations
Nigeria 273–4
9/11 events 95, 281
  and migration 393
  and reform drive 25, 42, 55
  and US interventions 27, 214
  US security rethink 206, 208

Nkrumah, Kwame 231, 235
non-state actors
  positive/negative roles 275
  transformational role 253–78
  see also civil society organizations
Noor, Ayman 101
North America 394, 395
North Korea 244, 248, 249, 250, 253
Novel Crimes, Commission on 134

O
OAS 232, 238
Oceania 394, 395
OECS 232
Ogburn, W.F. 299
Oklahoma City bombing 281
Olmert, Ehud 57
Oman 86
  education 325–8, 336
  migrants 395, 398, 407
  women in politics 370
Organization of African Unity 238
OSCE 248, 249, 250
Ottoman Empire 173–4, 176–8, 188, 194
Özal, Turgut 187
Özkök, General 187, 190

P
Pakistan 245, 249, 250
Palestine
  "brain drain" 352, 353
  coalition government need 57
  elections
    Legislative Elections, 2006 49–54, 155
    number of voters 51, 52
    overall incidence of 42
  Intifada of 2000 3
  as key to Arab reform 43–4, 45
  liberal Islam 158
  reform initiatives 47–9, 155
pan-Africanism 231
pan-Americanism 231
pan-Arabism 231, 236, 237, 241

pan-nationalism 231–2
Peninsula Shield 240
philosophy, Western 297
PLO 57
pluralism 156–7
Police and Security Commanders,
    Arab 134
political movements 270
political parties 270–4
political reform
    1970s abortion of 21, 30
    Arab demands 22–4
    Arab opposition to 27–8
    moderate Islamists 97–100
    and Muslim Brotherhood 101–16
    progress/development link 24
    Western role
        Arab suspicion 30–1, 54–5
        BME initiative 28, 42–4
        calls for reform 22, 24–8, 30–1,
            54–6
        withdrawal of pressure 28–9
political society organizations 270–8
politics
    and terrorism 123–4
    and women 42, 49, 50, 52, 158,
        368, 369, 370, 371, 378–9, 382–3
Popular Front for the Liberation of
    Palestine 52
PNC 160
population
    2050 forecast
    nationals in minority 399–400, 402
    youth bias 290
    see also migration; individual
        countries
Population and Development,
    International Conference on (ICPD)
    392–3, 401
Posse Comitatus Act 208–9
poverty 23, 41, 105, 127–8, 283, 354
private sector 105, 144
    and the media 162–4, 168
    and national labor 415, 417
    regional benefits 147–9

and universities 302, 303
professional syndicates 265–6
Progressive National Unionist Party
    106
property ownership 144

Q
Qatar 145, 302, 304
    education strategy 328–30
    migrants 402, 406, 407

R
R & D (Research & Development) 73,
    83, 334–5
radio stations 60
reform
    1970s beginnings 21
    Arab cooperation need 38
    conditions for 36–9, 56–7
    new wave of 22–7
    reasons for failure 30–6
    West
        abortion of reform 27–30
        early opposition 22, 24
        eventual support 22
        see also economic reform; political
            reform
regionalism
    Asian vs Arab: background 233–8
    and conflict-control 230–1, 241–2
    developing countries 230
    and economic reform 67–8
    European vs developing world 228
    and humanitarian intervention
        232–3
    vs sovereignty 228–33
regional security
    Asia as model 247–52
    conflict control 241–2
    GCC vs ASEAN 240–1
    inclusion of Iran 250, 252
    inclusion of Israel 249, 250, 252
    multilateral approaches 246–7
        Arab security community 252
        concert model 247

cooperative security 247–50
trans-national dangers 245
regional trading blocs 66–7
religious fundamentalism 160–1
rentier economies 36, 146
Republican People's Party 175, 180–1, 182, 189
research centers 302
"Roadmap" plan 48
Romania 181
Roosevelt Administration 231
Rousseau, Jean-Jacques 298
ruling elites
    control of security forces 34
    inability to change 32–6
    loss of legitimacy 23, 24, 26
    opposition to reform 27–8, 29, 31–2, 55, 97, 169
    Western support 22, 25–7, 37
Russia 250
Russian Revolution 271

S
Salih, Maryam 158
Sana'a Declaration 47
Sartori, Giovanni 183
Saudi Arabia 83, 86, 145
    education 304, 324–5
    elections in 29, 42
    and the GCC 239
    industrial cities 71, 73
    Internet/computers 84, 85, 86, 307
    "Islamic liberalism" in 155
    job-seekers 414
    manufacturing 77
    media openness 163
    migrants 395, 396, 407
    sectarianism in 165
schools 75, 78–9, 312
Schuman, Robert 235
science & technology
    Arab World vs S. Korea 76
    deficient performance 24, 72, 81, 303, 312, 336
    inadequate publications 82

knowledge transfer 72
patent numbers 83, 313, 356
R & D deficiency 73, 83, 334–5
research shortcomings 302, 336
as terrorism cause 281
SEATO 240
Second World War 182
sectarianism 143, 164–8
secularism
    and Islam 155–6
    in Turkey 176–7, 179, 181, 194–5
security services
    control by elites 34
    private militias 60–1
    terrorism training 136–7
September 11 events *see* 9/11 events
Serbia 273
service industries 76
Sezer, Ahmet Necdet 187–8
Shari'a
    definition of terrorism 122
    as terrorism cause 124–5, 126
Shiite Arabs 165, 166, 167, 222
Singapore 67, 400
Smith, Margaret Chase 279
social change
    and education 295–8, 300–3
    fear of 337–8
    and ICT 306–8
    and the media 161–4
    overview 298–300
    role of women 303–5
    vs social order 299–300
social insurance 382
social services 15
Somalia 214
South America 231
Southeast Asia 74–6, 85, 86, 237, 240
South Korea 67, 80, 249, 250
    education 313, 336
    high-tech exports 79
    scholarly output 82
sovereignty
    Asian regionalism 228–33, 241–7, 249

developing countries 230
nation-states 215
US "limit to sovereignty" 244
Soviet Union 241
collapse of 213, 311
economic reform 69–70
Sudan 80, 159–60
Suez Canal University 343
Suharto, Thojib N. J. 239, 243
Sukarno, Ahmed 239
Sunni Arabs 166, 167, 222
supra-nationalism 229
Sweden 83, 335
Switzerland 82
Syria 74, 77, 80, 82
"brain drain" 352, 353
education 304
Internet/computers 84, 85, 86
Islamic moderation 155

T
Taiwan 67, 249, 250
technology *see* science & technology
telecommunications
and global competition 280
high mobile phone cost 83–4
number of phone lines 83, 84
terrorism
9/11 effect 27, 42, 55
Arab strategies
Arab cooperation 131–7
prevention strategies 137–42
in Asia 243, 244
Caliphate notion 150, 245
causes
economic 127–8, 129, 283
political 123–4
religious 124–7
civilizational causes 127
definitions of 121–2
Islamic focus 122–3
non-security confrontation 140–2
plans for dealing with 133–4
as reform driver 24–5
research studies/publications 134–5

socio-psychological causes 128–30
and technology 281
vs resistance 122
Terrorism, Arab Convention for the
Suppression of 121–2, 132–3
Third Way 52, 53
Toffler, Alvin: *Future Shock* 279–80
Tolstoy, Leo 298
tourism sector 128
training 74
trans-border issues 149
transitional economies
and non-state actors 259, 275,
277–8
and political parties 272–4
True Path Party 189
Tunisia 77, 79, 84, 85, 86
education 304
foreign investment in 83
and Islamism 99, 156
private sector 266
Turkey 84, 154, 155, 157, 235
1961 Constitution 184–6
democracy 181, 195–6
and Islam 190–3
and the military 184, 186–90
rational democracy 183, 184
economic revolution 197
and Islam 175–6, 179–81, 190–3,
194, 196–7
military interventions 183–4,
186–7, 189–90, 196
revolutions 178–80, 182, 183
secularization 176–7, 179, 181,
194–5, 197
Westernization 173–5, 177–8,
182–4, 188, 193–4
Turkish Republic 174, 176, 179, 185,
188, 194, 195
Turkish War of Independence 181
"turnkey" projects 72, 359
TV satellite channels 60, 161
and Arab unity 162, 305
political issues 161–2

U

UAE 83, 85, 86
    education in 288–94, 302, 304
        strategies 319–21
    job-seekers 414
    liberalization trends 147
    migrants 395, 396, 402, 406, 407
    public share offering 145
UNDP 23, 41, 42
unemployment 74, 336, 416
    and economic growth 23
    forecast 41
    and foreign labor 402, 403–4
    numbers 87, 128, 301
    and population growth 14
    and terrorism 127–8
UNESCO 360, 361, 362
United Arab Republic 236
United Kingdom 332, 335, 352
United Nations
    Declaration on the Right to
        Development 9–10
    failure of 124
    humanitarian intervention 233, 242
    migration 393
    Millennium Summit 368
United Nations Charter 230–1
United Nations Development Program
    367
United States
    Arab democracy aims 25, 42–4,
        245–6
    Arab migrants in 352, 353, 354
    Arab opposition to 28, 55
    and ARF 250
    business organizations 266
    Constitution of 200–1, 206–7, 210,
        212
    education 86, 313, 332
        A Nation at Risk 333, 346
    and GCC/ASEAN security 239
    grand strategy
        formulation of 212–20
        principle-based 220–3
    huge trade deficit 216

import dependence 216
principles of democracy 199–205,
    216–17
    application abroad 201–5
    equality 282, 283
    vs interests 204–5
R & D spending 83, 335
regional trading blocs 66
security
    approaches to 218–20, 244
    separation of military 206–12
terrorism
    containment of 219
    homeland security debate 208–12
    response to 205–12
    unpreparedness 205–6, 211
    "war on terror" 27, 124, 214,
        218, 244
universities/colleges
    deficiencies 301–2, 313
        reasons for 339–41
    development proposals 341–3
    female students 302, 304, 376–7,
        384
    global increase 311, 345
    graduate numbers 312, 377, 413
    low enrolment figures 314–15
    low scholarly output 81–2
    major tasks 292–3
    private sector 302, 327
    research output 82
    role of 337–9, 346
    science
        shortfall 86, 336
        students (Arabs vs S. Koreans) 76

V

Vietnam 237, 238–9, 240, 250
Virtue Party 192

W

"war on terror" 27, 44, 124, 214, 218,
    244, 282–3
Washington, George 272
water supply 41, 68, 283

Weber, Alfred 299
Welfare Party (WP) 189, 191, 192
West Bank 49
Western countries
  Arab marginalization 37–8, 127
  Arab policies vs reform 36–7
  Arab resentment of 38
  credibility gap 30–1, 54–5
  reform drive 22, 24–8, 30–1, 54–6
  as terrorism cause 127
Westphalian sovereignty 230, 231,
  236, 241, 244
women
  and education 302, 303, 304, 310,
    376–7, 384
  empowerment of 367–8, 370–1
  equal rights 45, 304
  and ICT 307, 369
  illiteracy of 301, 304, 310, 369,
    377, 384
  and labor market 14, 374–5, 402,
    416, 418
  participation vs West 41
  and politics 42, 49, 50, 52, 158,
    368, 369, 370, 371, 378–9, 382–3

and social change 303–5, 310,
  367–8
violence towards 369
wearing of *hijab* 158
women's movements 305
Women's Organization, Arab 45
women's rights organizations 259
World Bank 148, 300
WTO 66, 408–9

Y
Yemen 47, 83, 99, 302, 304, 398
Yemeni Reformist Union 95
Yilmaz, Mesut 187
youth
  media effect 310
  and terrorism 128–30
Yugoslavia 213, 273

Z
Zarqa Private University 158
Zhou En-lai 235
ZOPFAN 239